C2 Advanced Vocabulary
Volume II

Version 3.0

Noelle Cline

Published by Reetiforp, LLC Publishing, a division of Reetiforp, LLC

Reetiforp Publishing books are available at special quantity discounts to use for sales promotions, employee premiums, or educational purposes. Please email our Marketing Department to order or for more information at workbooks@c2educate.com. Please report any errors or corrections to edward.kim@c2educate.com.

To Students and Parents:

The C2 Advanced Vocabulary curriculum is designed to help students build a large usable vocabulary in a short amount of time. By using this book alongside the instruction of a tutor at a C2 Education Center, a student will learn hundreds of words and greatly improve his or her performance on the verbal portions of standardized tests like the SAT and ACT.

This book contains a wide variety of exercises designed to guide the student through the process of learning a new word in an incremental manner. Students will use context clues to develop an initial impression of a word. This impression will be refined through subsequent exercises. Finally, the student will be able to use the word with confidence and understand its meaning in complex sentences.

Thank you for participating in the C2 Advanced Vocabulary program. We hope that you enjoy your time learning with us!

—The C2 Education Curriculum Department

C2 Advanced Vocabulary 1

First Impressions:

Using the example sentences below, write your own definition of each boldfaced word. Then write the letter of the definition from the box that best matches your definition.

A adjective: magnificent; dignified; royal	**C** adjective: insightful; aware; wise
B verb: to consider; to think over	**D** noun: a falling into an inferior condition; moral decay

1. ___A___ She may seem **regal**, but the aging actress is quite rude and vulgar in private.

REGAL means: _____wonderful_____

2. ___D___ The politician bemoaned the **decadence** of modern society, claiming that the country needed to return to traditional values.

DECADENCE means: _____defeat_____

3. ___B___ Because of the overwhelming evidence, the jury didn't take long to **deliberate** over the man's guilt.

DELIBERATE means: _____to think maybe_____

4. ___C___ Only the most **perceptive** patrons of the theater noticed the small mistake in the third act.

PERCEPTIVE means: _____aware_____

A noun: a disease; an agent that causes widespread harm	**C** noun: a member of a powerful, wealthy ruling class
B noun: the favoring of friends and relatives in business and politics	**D** adjective: lacking power or liveliness

5. ___A___ Ireland's Great Famine was caused by a **blight** that destroyed many of the potatoes that the poor relied upon as their main source of nourishment.

BLIGHT means: _____disease_____

6. ___B___ Your promotion of your incompetent cousin over our best team member is bald-faced **nepotism**.

NEPOTISM means: _____having friends_____

7. ___C___ The Prince and the Pauper is a classic tale that describes the interactions between a beggar and an **aristocrat**.

ARISTOCRAT means: _____wealth_____

8. ___D___ Faced with the sheer overwhelming force of the enemy's onslaught, the commander felt **impotent** to stop the advance.

IMPOTENT means: _____less power_____

Divide and Conquer:

Choose the correct word to complete each of the following sentences.

9. In a blatant show of (**nepotism** / aristocracy), Sidney promoted her son to vice president, even though her son had done no work over the previous month.

10. As he stepped down from the carriage in his frock coat and top hat, the (perception / **aristocrat**) tossed a coin to the beggar.

11. The principal declared that the new rash of cheating on standardized tests was a (deliberation / **blight**) that threatened the integrity of the entire educational process.

12. If you are (**perceptive** / regal) when viewing your opponent, you will notice bad habits that make her defeatable.

13. The series of paintings showed a civilization growing from a fledgling city, reaching its cultural peak, falling into (**decadence** / deliberation), and finally returning to nature.

14. The student council (**deliberated** / absolved) for weeks before choosing a location for the prom.

15. Harold's purebred hound has a (**regal** / decadent) air that is the result of years of training and competition at dog shows.

16. The invaders forced the nation to give up its heavy weapons, rendering the military practically (**impotent** / regal).

Hot and Cold:

Write the word from the lesson that is most nearly the *OPPOSITE* of the boldfaced word or words in each sentence below.

17. The Roman Empire was known at various times for both its **refinement** and its _decadence_.

18. It is unusual that one who normally is so _perceptive_ should be **oblivious** to such an obvious clue.

19. Those of _regal_ backgrounds often refuse to marry those of **undignified** birth.

20. Living with many children has been a(n) _blight_ to my health since they bring so much illness home with them, but it has been a **blessing** for my happiness.

21. The CEO was accused of _nepotism_ when his son was promoted before a more senior employee, angering those who expected more **impartiality**.

22. Feeling _impotent_ after being fired from her job, Sara was eager to return home where she felt **powerful** once more.

23. While some prefer to _deliberate_ before taking action, others prefer to act **impulsively**.

24. Coming as he was from a rather wealthy family, Chris felt himself quite the _aristocrat_ and disdained to interact with any person whom he considered a **commoner**.

Applying Yourself:

Choose the best word to complete each of the following sentences.

25. Sherlock Holmes was always _____ of his surroundings, taking in every detail and drawing advanced conclusions from what he saw.
    (A) impotent
    (B) perceptive
    (C) deliberate
    (D) regal
    (E) aristocratic

26. Oftentimes, people who rush into things without _____ over the consequences end up regretting their actions.
    (A) dispelling
    (B) professing
    (C) deliberating
    (D) relegating
    (E) disparaging

27. Before going out to meet the commoners, the King garbed himself in _____ purple robes and a crown.
    (A) regal
    (B) decadent
    (C) aristocratic
    (D) perceptive
    (E) impotent

28. We felt the church had descended into _____ and resolved to repair its moral fiber.
    (A) deliberation
    (B) aristocracy
    (C) blight
    (D) perception
    (E) decadence

29. Nowadays, _____ are represented by powerful corporate persons in addition to elected officials.
    (A) aristocrats
    (B) atonements
    (C) skirmishes
    (D) manifestos
    (E) deliberations

30. Grasshoppers can be a(n) _____ upon crops; they can destroy acres in a matter of days.
    (A) impotence
    (B) nepotism
    (C) aristocrat
    (D) perception
    (E) blight

31. I felt utterly _____ when confronted by the tears of my teammate's widow, unable to console her and drained of joy as I was.
    (A) perceptive
    (B) deliberate
    (C) aristocratic
    (D) regal
    (E) impotent

32. Too often, our organization engages in _____ rather than hiring unknown, but eminently qualified, applicants.
    (A) impotence
    (B) blight
    (C) perception
    (D) nepotism
    (E) deliberation

On Your Own:

Write one sentence using each word below to demonstrate your understanding of the word's meaning.

33. **nepotism** hiring my daughter wasn't nepotism but good business

34. **aristocrat** the trout is the aristocrat of freshwater fish.

35. **regal** His regal forehears

36. **impotent** He was seized with an impotent anger

37. **decadence** He denounced Western decadence

38. **perceptive** An extraordinarily perceptive account of their relationship.

39. **deliberate** A deliberate attempt to provoke conflict

40. **blight** the vines suffered blight and disease.

C2 Advanced Vocabulary 2

First Impressions:

Using the example sentences below, write your own definition of each boldfaced word. Then write the letter of the definition from the box that best matches your definition.

A	verb: to provide written evidence; to record in detail	**C**	verb: to censure; to rebuke
B	adjective: grinding down; irritating in manner	**D**	adjective: having a harsh sound; having an irritating quality

1. ___B___ The announcement that there would be extra homework was met with **strident** protests from the students.

STRIDENT means: _grinding_

2. ___A___ The proud parents **documented** on film every step of their child's development.

DOCUMENT means: _proof_

3. ___D___ Azalea's **abrasive** manner made it difficult for her to keep friends, since few could handle her loud, confrontational style of conversation.

ABRASIVE means: _bad sound_

4. ___C___ Since Tomi failed to consistently **reprove** her dog Sniffles when he tore apart neighbors' gardens as a puppy, Sniffles continued to destroy the plants until the neighborhood forced Tomi to retrain her dog.

REPROVE means: _scold_

A	adjective: requiring immediate attention	**C**	adjective: related to difficult or obscure subject matter
B	noun: lack of morals; depravity	**D**	verb: to list; to mention one by one

5. ___D___ Aileen **enumerated** the groceries her mother would need to get when she went shopping.

ENUMERATE means: _list out_

6. ___B___ Mrs. Kim felt that the moral influence of our teachers was the only force preventing society from falling into complete **turpitude**.

TURPITUDE means: _no morals_

7. ___C___ Nick was surprised to find that a course that at first had dealt only with basic information began to delve into highly **recondite** subject matter.

RECONDITE means: _difficult subject_

8. ___A___ **Exigent** circumstances demanded a sudden change of plans.

EXIGENT means: _needing now_

Divide and Conquer:

Choose the correct word to complete each of the following sentences.

9. Dracula descended into **(enumeration / turpitude)** as he attacked people to serve his ghoulish needs.

10. The matter is not **(exigent / strident)**; we can review it in the morning after we have rested.

11. We entered the library looking for a simple book on optics but left with a pile of texts on **(abrasive / recondite)** subjects, including quantum mechanics.

12. The Duke **(enumerated / reproved)** the Capulets and the Montagues for their violent skirmishes and threatened that further violence would be met with banishment.

13. Ellison's new book **(enumerated / documented)** Murdoch's single-minded pursuit of the Wall Street Journal in 2007.

14. His comments were not without the trademark barbs that have made the at times **(abrasive / strident)** chairman a legend on Capitol Hill.

15. There is also a column to **(enumerate / reprove)** clearly how much money must be paid each and every month to have that particular credit card paid off in three years.

16. The teacher uses her long nails to scratch the blackboard in a(n) **(strident / exigent)** display of classroom control.

Hot and Cold:

Write the word from the lesson that is most nearly the *OPPOSITE* of the boldfaced word or words in each sentence below.

17. I had a **soothing** cup of tea to calm me after receiving a rather _abrasive_ talking-to from my temperamental manager.

18. Why write a paper about the _reprove_ mazes of the Bible's many moral codes when you could choose a more **accessible** topic like symbolism in the Old Testament?

19. The _exigent_ needs of the fast-paced restaurant business are much more difficult to meet than those of a **slow-paced** antique shop dealing in low-pressure transactions.

20. Though she had been known for her _turpitude_ in her youth, living as she was as a small-time thief and con artist, her later **uprightness** was a welcome surprise.

21. We were sent to the war zone to _document_ the daily lives of those struggling in war-torn areas, but we did **not record** anything gruesome enough to please the drama-hungry press.

22. The committee _strident_ the young senator's idea for a bold new tax program but **applauded** her willingness to take a risk in presenting it to them.

23. The _abrasive_ shrieking of parrots in the forest pierces the **soft hum** of insects and the wind through the great canopy leaves.

Applying Yourself:

Choose the best word to complete each of the following sentences.

24. The _____ bungle at home forced us to abandon our vacation plans and attend to the problem.
    (A) exigent
    (B) abrasive
    (C) reproved
    (D) enumerated
    (E) documented

25. Bernice attempted to defend herself against the allegations, but I had _____ her irresponsible behavior over the previous few months and had hard evidence of everything I said.
    (A) incensed
    (B) reproved
    (C) documented
    (D) enumerated
    (E) polarized

26. A(n) _____ attitude will earn you enmity, not camaraderie.
    (A) abrasive
    (B) reproved
    (C) enumerated
    (D) exigent
    (E) recondite

27. When smoke alarms begin to lose battery life, they issue a(n) _____ beeping designed to irritate homeowners into swiftly removing the offending parts.
    (A) strident
    (B) recondite
    (C) enumerated
    (D) documented
    (E) reproved

28. During the unpopular Vietnam War, legions of college students took to the streets to _____ the government.
    (A) polarize
    (B) incense
    (C) enumerate
    (D) document
    (E) reprove

29. Alas, we must all enroll in physical chemistry; I cannot imagine a more _____, time-consuming course.
    (A) reproved
    (B) enumerated
    (C) strident
    (D) exigent
    (E) recondite

30. Step up to the microphone and _____ the list of fallen heroes in alphabetical order, so that we might all hear their names.
    (A) polarize
    (B) document
    (C) reprove
    (D) incense
    (E) enumerate

31. The raiding parties contained men of _____ who would pillage without reservation.
    (A) stridency
    (B) turpitude
    (C) documentation
    (D) exigency
    (E) abrasion

On Your Own:

Write one sentence using each word below to demonstrate your understanding of the word's meaning.

32. **exigent** The exigent demands of the more took a toll on her voice.

33. **turpitude** acts of moral turpitude

34. **strident** His voice had become increasingly sharp, almost strident.

35. **enumerate** There isn't space to enumerate all his works.

36. **document** The photographer spent years documenting the lives of miners.

37. **abrasive** Her abrasive & arrogant personal style won her few friends.

38. **recondite** The book is full of recondite information.

39. **reprove** He was reproved for obscenity.

C2 Advanced Vocabulary 3

First Impressions:
Using the example sentences below, write your own definition of each boldfaced word. Then write the letter of the definition from the box that best matches your definition.

A	adjective: unpleasant because of excess; excessively sweet	**C**	adjective: not able to exist in harmony
B	adjective: easily approachable; friendly; pleasant	**D**	adjective: favoring or exercising total control; not democratic

1. ____C____ My American electronics were **incompatible** with Australian power outlets, so I had to purchase an adapter.
INCOMPATIBLE means: _no harmony_

2. ____D____ Leila resisted her mother's **authoritarian** attitude towards punishments: failing one history test did not warrant two weeks of grounding.
AUTHORITARIAN means: _favored_

3. ____A____ Though Marissa enjoyed the first of her Halloween candies, the twentieth proved to be rather **cloying**.
CLOYING means: _unpleasant cause excess_

4. ____B____ Because she had been expecting her new teacher to be more strict, Rachael was surprised at how **affable** the man really was.
AFFABLE means: _nice_

A	adjective: not having serious purpose or value; carefree and not serious	**C**	verb: admit that something is true after first denying it; admit (defeat) in a contest
B	verb: to soothe, to calm; to bring peace to	**D**	verb: impose an unwelcome or unnecessary person or thing on

5. ____C____ Even when we lose a battle we should not **concede** defeat in the war.
CONCEDE means: _admiting the truth_

6. ____D____ My father **foisted** a load of laundry into my arms and told me to wash it.
FOIST means: _unwelcome_

7. ____A____ The judge threw the **frivolous** lawsuit out of the court to make time for more serious cases.
FRIVOLOUS means: _no seriousness_

8. ____B____ Roxanne hoped to **pacify** the screaming baby with his favorite toy.
PACIFY means: _relaxed_

Divide and Conquer:
Choose the correct word to complete each of the following sentences.

9. When she learned that her electronics were (**incompatible** / **affable**) with the local power outlets Bridgitte was forced to buy an adapter.

10. While Joanne loved the optimism of mid-20th century musicals, Denise found their consistently positive message to be (**cloying** / **frivolous**).

11. The girl's (**affable** / **frivolous**) nature made it easy for her to charm her schoolmates.

12. There would be no (**foisting** / **pacifying**) such a power-hungry dictator with mere concessions.

13. Harold felt that Congress wasted time on (**frivolous** / **affable**) and implausible legislation while failing to enforce important existing laws.

14. The professor's (**frivolous** / **authoritarian**) presence and voice caused all of the students to take their seats silently at once..

15. Their arguments never seemed to end, because neither was willing to (**foist** / **concede**) victory to the other.

16. My groupmates (**foisted** / **conceded**) the majority of the work onto me.

Hot and Cold:
Write the word from the lesson that is most nearly the *OPPOSITE* of the boldfaced word or words in each sentence below.

17. I gave the newcomer to the party a(n) _affable_ smile, hoping to make her feel more comfortable, but was rebuked with an **unfriendly** scoff.

18. The _authoritarian_ government seemed to have a stranglehold over its people, who would have much preferred a more **democratic** government with less control over their daily lives.

19. Usually music _pacifies_ the baby when she's crabby, but today the melodies seemed to further **enrage** her.

20. The judge resented having to deal with _frivolous_ law suits over things like ruined jackets and broken fences and preferred to spend his time on more **serious** claims.

21. I dislike the _cloying_ scent of strong floral perfumes and prefer the more **mild** smell of a person's natural body.

22. The attorney _conceded_ that his client had been present at the time the crime was committed, but **denied** that the client had anything to do with what happened.

23. As part of the peace agreement, the dominant country had to stop _foist_ their laws on surrounding nations and **concede** an ocean port to the nearest small country.

24. The two may seem like a(n) _incompatible_ pair—one being cheerful and extroverted, the other being glum and shy—but in fact, the two are **well-suited** friends who get along perfectly.

Applying Yourself:
Choose the best word to complete each of the following sentences.

25. *Kramer vs. Kramer* is a film about a divorce between two _____ people who decide they'd be better off apart.
    (A) foisted
    (B) cloying
    (C) incompatible
    (D) conceded
    (E) pacified

26. Our team chose to _____ rather than continue in a game in which we were losing by 15 runs.
    (A) endorse
    (B) condone
    (C) concede
    (D) foist
    (E) pacify

27. She has a(n) _____ manner that instantly puts interviewers at ease, making them feel as though they're talking to an old friend.
    (A) frivolous
    (B) cloying
    (C) affable ← circled
    (D) authoritarian
    (E) foisted

28. I prefer only a few semi-sweet chocolate chips in my cookies; otherwise, I risk making a(n) _____ dessert.
    (A) authoritarian
    (B) foisted
    (C) frivolous
    (D) affable
    (E) cloying ← circled

29. Don't try to _____ your responsibilities onto me; do your own job!
    (A) foist ← circled
    (B) condone
    (C) pacify
    (D) concede
    (E) endorse

30. Only with assertive movements can you _____ the angry dog; it needs to be reassured by a leader in the pack.
    (A) endorse
    (B) concede
    (C) foist
    (D) condone
    (E) pacify ← circled

31. The serious-minded girl thought _____ debates were a waste of time.
    (A) incompatible
    (B) authoritarian
    (C) pacified
    (D) frivolous ← circled
    (E) foist

32. Some believe that China's _____ system of capitalism allows for markets to flourish under tight controls.
    (A) authoritarian ← circled
    (B) incompatible
    (C) foisted
    (D) frivolous
    (E) affable

On Your Own:

Write one sentence using each word below to demonstrate your understanding of the word's meaning.

33. **cloying** _A romantic, rather cloying story_

34. **foist** _Don't let anyone foist inferior goods on you._

35. **concede** _I had to concede that I'd overreacted_

36. **incompatible** _Cleverness & feminity were seen as incompatible_

37. **frivolous** _Rules to stop frivolous lawsuits_

38. **pacify** _He had to pacify angry spectators._

39. **affable** _An affable and agreeable companion_

40. **authoritarian** _the transition from an authoritarian to a democratic regime_

C2 Advanced Vocabulary 4

First Impressions:
Using the example sentences below, write your own definition of each boldfaced word. Then write the letter of the definition from the box that best matches your definition.

A adjective: complete; certain; pure; perfect; ultimate	**C** adjective: undeveloped; unable to succeed
B verb: to urge; to start; to provoke	**D** adjective: inclined to believe with little evidence

1. ___D___ Jane instinctively distrusted any new idea that she heard, but she was frustratingly **credulous** of any information that supported what she already believed.
CREDULOUS means: _believe with little to no evidence_

2. ___B___ The professor carefully chose questions that would **instigate** thought-provoking discussion among the students.
INSTIGATE means: _restart_

3. ___A___ We have **absolute** knowledge that that Earth is a sphere because we have pictures of it.
ABSOLUTE means: _complete_

4. ___C___ After two **abortive** attempts to organize his office, Brian called in the help of a professional.
ABORTIVE means: _incomplete_

A noun: an infection; the process of being infected	**C** adjective: filled with plenty; abundant
B noun: the humorous confusion of one word for another that is very similar in sound	**D** noun: a tightrope walker

5. ___D___ The **funambulist** entertained and frightened the audience by dancing across a thirty-foot cable without using a net.
FUNAMBULIST means: _a rope walker_

6. ___C___ The **bountiful** harvest could be shared by the entire town.
BOUNTIFUL means: _filled_

7. ___B___ The university president apologized for uttering the **malapropism**, "We are proud of our perverse faculty."
MALAPROPISM means: _confusion_

8. ___A___ Although Jung-Su loved his sister, he kept away from her to prevent **contagion** of her chicken pox.
CONTAGION means: _infection_

Divide and Conquer:
Choose the correct word to complete each of the following sentences.

9. Vaccines are useful tools for preventing (**contagion** / **malapropisms**).

10. Sabrina always remembered her wedding as the (**abortive** / **absolute**) happiest day of her life.

11. The farmers were grateful for the plentiful rain and warm sun that granted them a(n) (**bountiful** / **absolute**) harvest in the fall.

12. The (**instigator** / **funambulist**) amazed the audience by balancing on a rope while juggling balls.

13. Jen had a hard time getting along with large groups of people because she often (**instigates** / **aborts**) heated debates over controversial subjects.

14. The animated character Wile E. Coyote is remembered for his (**abortive** / **absolute**) (and often disastrous) attempts to catch the Road Runner.

15. (**Instigated** / **Credulous**) persons were surprised when there was no disaster at the end of the Mayan Long Count Calendar.

16. The mayor of Boston uttered an unfortunate (**malapropism** / **contagion**) when, describing his predecessor, he said, "He was a man of great statue."

Hot and Cold:
Write the word from the lesson that is most nearly the *OPPOSITE* of the boldfaced word or words in each sentence below.

17. _Credulous_ as a child, Pat managed to ask such sincere questions that the **skeptical** con man thought perhaps it was Pat who was fooling him.

18. Never able to fully express himself, Greg made several _abortive_ attempts to explain his feelings before he felt that his efforts had been even remotely **successful**.

19. With my father, who often changed his mind, I was never sure whether a "no" was _absolute_ or whether it might be **uncertain** enough to lead to a "yes" if I pushed the issue.

20. After a **spare** winter harvest, the spring harvest was thankfully _bountiful_.

21. Every child is set to receive an **inoculation** to keep him or her from being affected by the dangerous _contagion_ prevalent this time of year.

22. When one member of the crowd tried to _instigate_ violence, the woman at the podium knew she had to act fast if she wanted to **prevent** a riot from forming.

Applying Yourself:
Choose the best word to complete each of the following sentences.

23. We couldn't stop laughing when our host uttered the following _____: "He is a man of great statue."
    (A) instigation
    (B) malapropism
    (C) contagion
    (D) credulity
    (E) funambulist

24. These sheep need to be more skeptical and less _____ of their newly appointed leader.
    (A) credulous
    (B) contagious
    (C) bountiful
    (D) instigated
    (E) abortive

25. The _____ harvest will be enough to feed the country for years to come.
    (A) abortive
    (B) bountiful
    (C) credulous
    (D) absolute
    (E) instigated

26. The plague was a very powerful _____, spreading rapidly throughout Europe during the Dark Ages and killing nearly 25% of the world's population.
    (A) funambulist
    (B) malapropism
    (C) instigation
    (D) contagion
    (E) bounty

27. The effect of the cold was _____; I felt the chill to my bones.
    (A) absolute
    (B) instigated
    (C) bountiful
    (D) abortive
    (E) credulous

28. Ringling Brothers circus employs lion tamers, clowns, expert riders, and above them all, _____.
    (A) funambulists
    (B) instigations
    (C) contagions
    (D) bounties
    (E) malapropisms

29. They managed to incite a riot by _____ a few of the most frustrated activists to turn to violence.
    (A) aborting
    (B) polarizing
    (C) inaugurating
    (D) instigating
    (E) atoning

30. Our _____ attempt to wrest control of the government ended when the scandal broke.
    (A) abortive
    (B) absolute
    (C) contagious
    (D) bountiful
    (E) credulous

On Your Own:

Write one sentence using each word below to demonstrate your understanding of the word's meaning.

31. **credulous** He sold miracle cures to desperab? credulous clients.

32. **funambulist** the funambulist fell off the rope.

33. **malapropism** she's famous for her hilarious malapropism

34. **bountiful** the ocean provided a bountiful supply of fresh seafood.

35. **contagion** the rooms held no risk of contagion

36. **absolute** Absolute secrecy.

37. **instigate** they instigated a reign of terror

38. **abortive** an abortive attempt to overthrow the gov.

C2 Advanced Vocabulary 5

First Impressions:

Using the example sentences below, write your own definition of each boldfaced word. Then write the letter of the definition from the box that best matches your definition.

A	adjective: having leaves that fall off annually; not permanent	C	adjective: based on facts
B	adjective: required for a purpose	D	verb: to overlook; to forgive; to imply approval

1. ___B___ A wide variety of interpersonal skills are **requisite** to the job of a tutor.

REQUISITE means: ___has a purpose___

2. ___C___ They collected plenty of **empirical** data from their experiments.

EMPIRICAL means: ___has facts___

3. ___D___ The teacher's reluctance to punish the girls suggested that he might **condone** their

behavior.

CONDONE means: ___to overlook___

4. ___A___ **Deciduous** trees help to regulate a house's energy costs by blocking the sun's heat in the

summer and allowing sunlight to warm the house in the winter.

DECIDUOUS means: ___falling leaves___

A	verb: to approve; to support	C	adjective: in an early stage
B	noun: a person who studies a subject, especially art, merely for personal amusement	D	adjective: without money

5. ___C___ The United Nations sent soldiers to maintain the safety of the revolutionary leaders of the

incipient democracy.

INCIPIENT means: ___early___

6. ___B___ A true **dilettante**, Roberto dabbled in musicianship but never practiced with enough

seriousness to become a performer.

DILETTANTE means: ___a studier of a subject___

7. ___D___ Many American families were **impecunious** during the Great Depression, when many

people lost their jobs and savings.

IMPECUNIOUS means: ___no money___

8. ___A___ Zara **endorsed** her friend's campaign for Student Council President by handing out

buttons with his name on it.

ENDORSE means: ___approval___

Divide and Conquer:
Choose the correct word to complete each of the following sentences.

9. David had never harbored dreams of becoming a concert pianist; he was satisfied to remain a mere (requisite / **dilettante**).

10. The (**impecunious** / incipient) students were unable to buy food until their loans were granted.

11. The teacher was strict about the completion of assignments, but (**condoned** / polarized) minor offenses like speaking out of turn.

12. The bare branches of the (**deciduous** / condoned) trees reached up into the winter sky like hands.

13. Though the changes were as yet (**incipient** / empirical), the tension in the air was a clear sign of the massive turmoil to come.

14. The board (**endorsed** / polarized) the view and published a memo encouraging the executives to adjust their policies accordingly.

15. I don't have the (empirical / **requisite**) cash to purchase the car, so I must save for several months before I can own it.

16. Joanne was disappointed by the lack of suggestions for raising children based on (**empirical** / endorse) evidence rather than folk wisdom.

Hot and Cold:
Write the word from the lesson that is most nearly the *OPPOSITE* of the boldfaced word or words in each sentence below.

17. The mayor _endorsed_ Sally Write for city council because the two shared similar political beliefs and **opposed** Mike Frohely, who he viewed as an untrustworthy wild card.

18. Anita's _incipient_ interest in art, instigated by her art professor, would grow into its **developed** form as a true passion for the subject.

19. We have many **hypothetical** explanations for the event, but nothing _empirical_.

20. While walking with my little cousin, I pointed out that _deciduous_ trees were often leafless during the winter, while **unchanging** trees kept their shapes and colors all year long.

21. I do not _condone_ **violent** behavior and cannot stand those who do not **reject** harming others outright.

22. The American Dream tells that even the most _impecunious_ dreamer can, with enough hard work, become **rich**.

23. The school counselor tried to ensure each student had his or her _requisite_ classes so that no one would be unable to graduate or get bogged down taking **unnecessary** courses.

24. I have always been a _dilettante_ in matters of poetry, enjoying but never excelling in the art, but lately I've had an itch to become a **professional**.

Applying Yourself:
Choose the best word to complete each of the following sentences.

25. After a stressful week, I _____ the plan to release tension by playing basketball.
    (A) condone
    (B) eulogize
    (C) pantomime
    (D) admonish
    (E) patronize

26. While he never told us "no," his stern look suggested that he did not _____ our behavior.
    (A) engender
    (B) reproach
    (C) condone
    (D) inaugurate
    (E) eulogize

27. Sheila could not abide the _____ in her academy; while she studied the Impressionist masters diligently, many others took only a casual interest.
    (A) incipience
    (B) endorsement
    (C) empiricism
    (D) dilettantes
    (E) requisitions

28. The lab's _____ experiments were inconclusive; wait until a more refined process is established.
    (A) incipient
    (B) deciduous
    (C) empirical
    (D) impecunious
    (E) requisite

29. The _____ duties of a telemarketer include asking awkward questions, disturbing people during dinner, and maintaining a thick skin.
    (A) impecunious
    (B) condoned
    (C) incipient
    (D) empirical
    (E) requisite

30. She had just as many _____ relatives as she had wealthy ones.
    (A) requisite
    (B) endorsed
    (C) empirical
    (D) deciduous
    (E) impecunious

31. Although we have no _____ evidence, our instincts are telling us this is a terrible idea.
    (A) incipient
    (B) requisite
    (C) deciduous
    (D) empirical
    (E) impecunious

32. Johnny cursed his grandfather for having planted _____ trees, as it meant that huge piles of leaves had to be raked every autumn.
    (A) impecunious
    (B) incipient
    (C) requisite
    (D) deciduous
    (E) condoned

On Your Own:

Write one sentence using each word below to demonstrate your understanding of the word's meaning.

33. **impecunious** A titled but impecunious family.

34. **endorse** The report was endorsed by the college.

35. **deciduous** Small, thin deciduous scales equally cover nearly the entire body.

36. **dilettante** A the dilettante approach to science

37. **empirical** They provided considerable empirical evidence to support their argument.

38. **condone** The college can't condone any bad behavior.

39. **requisite** The application will not be processed until the requisite fee is paid.

40. **incipient** He could feel incipient anger building up.

C2 Advanced Vocabulary 6

First Impressions:

Using the example sentences below, write your own definition of each boldfaced word. Then write the letter of the definition from the box that best matches your definition.

A	adjective: corresponding to something else in amount	**C**	adjective: having a strong opinion for one side of an issue
B	noun: destruction by chemical action, such as rust	**D**	adjective: prone to noticing small defects; difficult to please

1. _____ Citizens will not be chosen to be part of a jury if it is shown that they have **biased** opinions of the defendant..

BIASED means: _____

2. _____ In today's science class, students will observe the **corrosion** of a penny in hydrochloric acid.

CORROSION means: _____

3. _____ The baker worked hard to create a product so perfect that it would satisfy even the most **captious** customers.

CAPTIOUS means: _____

4. _____ Rather than responding with a **proportionate** punishment, my parents grounded me for a month for forgetting to put my dish in the dishwasher.

PROPORTIONATE means: _____

A	adjective: causing sleep; sleepy or drowsy	**C**	verb: to lessen; to weaken
B	verb: to release from guilt; to declare someone free from blame	**D**	noun: attacker

5. _____ The priest will **absolve** me of my sins after I confess them to him, meaning that I'll no longer be held accountable for the bad things I've done.

ABSOLVE means: _____

6. _____ The plaintiff began to tell the story of his assault, carefully avoiding the eyes of the **aggressor** in the defendant's box.

AGGRESSOR means: _____

7. _____ No bad teacher or experience could **diminish** my love for reading.

DIMINISH means: _____

8. _____ Because Annabel was having so much difficulty sleeping, her doctor prescribed her a remedy guaranteed to make her more **soporific**.

SOPORIFIC means: _____

Divide and Conquer:
Choose the correct word to complete each of the following sentences.

9. Many citizens did not approve of the new chief justice because they believed that he was highly **(biased / diminished)** in many areas which demand neutrality in a public figure.

10. The Cold War was a period of mutual distrust and fear, but neither the United States nor the Soviet Union openly acted as a(n) **(aggressor / corrosion)** to the other.

11. We expect that punishments will be **(proportionate / soporific)** to crimes.

12. Fred and Gina refused to let the bad weather **(absolve / diminish)** their enjoyment of their vacation.

13. Giovanna's **(soporific / captious)** nature was a bother to her friends, but it was essential for her job as a news editor.

14. Alexander's victory was enthralling, but your dull account of it borders on **(soporific / captious)**.

15. Over time, the salt used to melt snow on northern roads causes patches of **(corrosion / aggressors)** to develop on many vehicles.

16. Though Adam had broken the dishwasher, his mother **(diminished / absolved)** him saying that it was a poor-quality piece of equipment and was bound to break anyway.

Hot and Cold:
Write the word from the lesson that is most nearly the *OPPOSITE* of the boldfaced word or words in each sentence below.

17. Usually, when my alarm goes off I slap at it with a(n) _____ bat of the hand, unwilling to get out of bed, but today I awoke feeling **alert** and eager to start the day.

18. Despite her attempts to be **dispassionate** in regards to the trial, Judge Winslow found herself _____ against violent criminals, so she recused herself in order to maintain judicial fairness.

19. Claire's body is _____, but Luis' arms are **incongruent** with his short stature.

20. Rachel blames the _____ of the garage door on the rain and has bought a serum said to help with the **fortification** of metal against water.

21. In the dark, misty alleyway it was difficult to tell which of the pair was the **defender** and which the _____.

22. This particular church tends not to **condemn** people for their sins and instead focuses on ways to _____ them.

23. Tanya's math skills seem to be _____ at the same rate that her reading skills are **strengthening**.

24. Mr. Sanders is a rather strict and _____ boss who will notice if even a feather is out of place at his store, but he is most **forgiving** of his children and fails to notice even their most major flaws.

Applying Yourself:
Choose the best word to complete each of the following sentences.

25. Thanks to her generous efforts for charity, she was _____ from the crimes she had committed earlier in her life.
    (A) ruminated
    (B) rebuked
    (C) diminished
    (D) corroded
    (E) absolved

26. The dictator became more desperate as his power began to _____.
    (A) diminish
    (B) transmute
    (C) belie
    (D) supplant
    (E) absolve

27. The _____ of his bicycle was due to the fact that he had left it in the rain all weekend long.
    (A) aggressor
    (B) absolution
    (C) proportion
    (D) bias
    (E) corrosion

28. Judges are to refrain from being _____; they must hear all evidence before rendering an objective opinion.
    (A) biased
    (B) soporific
    (C) aggressive
    (D) proportionate
    (E) absolved

29. The _____ assailed the other with crude insults and mockery.
    (A) aggressor
    (B) absolution
    (C) bias
    (D) corrosion
    (E) proportion

30. The retiring cartoonist's _____ attitude reached its zenith when he criticized his successor for using a slightly different shade of orange.
    (A) absolved
    (B) biased
    (C) captious
    (D) soporific
    (E) corrosive

31. We can't invite the old professor to the symposium; his lectures are not just _____ —they're coma-inducing.
    (A) aggressive
    (B) diminished
    (C) absolved
    (D) corrosive
    (E) soporific

32. Each of the dogs received a different amount of food _____ to its size.
    (A) corrosive
    (B) proportionate
    (C) absolved
    (D) diminished
    (E) biased

On Your Own:

Write one sentence using each word below to demonstrate your understanding of the word's meaning.

33. **diminish** _____

34. **captious** _____

35. **proportionate** _____

36. **absolve** _____

37. **aggressor** _____

38. **corrosion** _____

39. **biased** _____

40. **soporific** _____

C2 Advanced Vocabulary 7

First Impressions:

Using the example sentences below, write your own definition of each boldfaced word. Then write the letter of the definition from the box that best matches your definition.

A	adjective: showing a clear bias or purpose	**C**	noun: an order of a judge requiring a change in action
B	noun: a short, witty saying	**D**	noun: good judgment; skill

1. _____ Oscar Wilde was a master of the **epigram**; his sharp wit and clear insight shone clearly through many of his popular quotations.

EPIGRAM means: _____

2. _____ The **injunction** required the landlord to replace his leaking septic system or pay a hefty fine.

INJUNCTION means: _____

3. _____ Greg's **acumen** in social matters makes him the perfect person to help us resolve this sensitive issue.

ACUMEN means: _____

4. _____ Though the news network claims to be fair in its reporting, its stories are clearly **tendentious**.

TENDENTIOUS means: _____

A	noun: empty and excessive boasting	**C**	noun: a dishonest cheat, trickster, or thief; a rebel
B	noun: a hermit; a loner	**D**	adjective: tentative; temporary

5. _____ The new government was merely **provisional**—a temporary body to rule the land until a more stable system could be implemented.

PROVISIONAL means: _____

6. _____ Said by neighbors to have been a **recluse**, the man lived alone in the house.

RECLUSE means: _____

7. _____ Mr. Smith denounced his rival as a **rogue**, scallywag, braggart, and criminal.

ROGUE means: _____

8. _____ Annoyed by the **braggadocio** of his brother, Mark would do almost anything to prove that Kevin's pride was baseless and excessive.

BRAGGADOCIO means: _____

Divide and Conquer:
Choose the correct word to complete each of the following sentences.

9. An **(injunction / epigram)** written to commemorate the Spartan soldiers buried at Thermopylae reads, "Stranger, announce to the Spartans that here we lie, having fulfilled their orders."

10. *Apocalypse Now* is about an army officer's task to apprehend a **(tendentious / rogue)** colonel who once had been a model soldier.

11. Brandon's **(acumen / injunction)** in algebra makes him a great tutor for his brother.

12. Kamir's boasting seemed like mere **(braggadocio / epigram)** until I saw his impressive performance in the dojo.

13. Science has no room for those who are **(provisional / tendentious)**; scientists must be able to evaluate information from a neutral standpoint.

14. The **(rogue / provisional)** workers were hired to assist regular staffers during the summer rush the business experienced.

15. The **(injunction / epigram)** forbade the overzealous photographer to come within 1000 feet of the actor's home.

16. The woman who was mugged continues to take her daily walks in the park, not willing to allow the ordeal to turn her into a(n) **(recluse / acumen)**.

Hot and Cold:
Write the word from the lesson that is most nearly the *OPPOSITE* of the boldfaced word or words in each sentence below.

17. Margene made up for **her lack of skill** in the kitchen with her construction and gardening _____.

18. Initially the movement's most pious **angel**, Klaus turned into a(n) _____ when he began to see the negative effects the political shift was having.

19. The _____ governor is set to maintain power only as long as he can prove his worth; if he can't, another, more **permanent** candidate will take his place.

20. Yolanda's gentle **humility** softened the effects of her partner's obnoxious _____ as he tried to show off in front of the potential clients.

21. Half the jury was _____ in its eagerness to convict the accused, while the other was **ambivalent** and showed no indication of making up its mind one way or another.

22. Because she had been a(n) _____ for most of her life, preferring to spend time alone with her books and paintings than with others, Tanya's parents were surprised when she became a popular **social butterfly** in college.

23. At times, a well-written _____ can have an even greater impact on public opinion than the most comprehensive **tome**.

Applying Yourself:
Choose the best word to complete each of the following sentences.

24. Football players display _____ prior to games, and their bragging often contributes to team rivalries.
    (A) reclusiveness
    (B) epigrams
    (C) braggadocio
    (D) injunctions
    (E) acumen

25. In *The Sting*, Robert Redford and Paul Newman play _____ who try to cheat an old adversary out of money.
    (A) epigrams
    (B) recluses
    (C) acumens
    (D) rogues
    (E) injunctions

26. It became clear that his housing arrangements were not permanent but _____.
   (A) provisional
   (B) reclusive
   (C) discursive
   (D) tendentious
   (E) rogue

27. Stacy thinks that _____ cable news networks have a negative effect on the objectivity of civil political discourse.
   (A) discursive
   (B) rogue
   (C) tendentious
   (D) reclusive
   (E) provisional

28. Tombstones, while usually having trite sayings, occasional have _____ such as, "She dealt in the currency of dignity".
   (A) rogues
   (B) recluses
   (C) acumens
   (D) injunctions
   (E) epigrams

29. The teachers remained on strike until the court's _____ against them.
   (A) acumen
   (B) injunction
   (C) recluse
   (D) epigram
   (E) rogue

30. As a(n) _____, he lives outside of the town and doesn't seem to enjoy talking to others when at work or shopping for groceries.
   (A) recluse
   (B) epigram
   (C) acumen
   (D) injunction
   (E) rogue

31. His business _____ was superb: By age thirty, he had already made millions of dollars.
   (A) acumen
   (B) rogue
   (C) reclusiveness
   (D) epigram
   (E) injunction

On Your Own:
Write one sentence using each word below to demonstrate your understanding of the word's meaning.

32. **braggadocio** _____

33. **epigram** _____

34. **tendentious** _____

35. **injunction** _____

36. **recluse** _____

37. **provisional** _____

38. **acumen** _____

39. **rogue** _____

C2 Advanced Vocabulary 8

First Impressions:

Using the example sentences below, write your own definition of each boldfaced word. Then write the letter of the definition from the box that best matches your definition.

A	verb: to banish to an inferior position; to delegate; to assign	**C**	verb: to declare openly
B	adjective: related to an uncle; having the qualities of an uncle	**D**	adjective: not restrained by morals

1. _____ The pastor loudly condemned the **licentious** behavior of the wicked world.

LICENTIOUS means: _____

2. _____ Eunice finally **professed** her love for Harold in the touching finale of the series.

PROFESS means: _____

3. _____ Mr. Thomas treated his students with such **avuncular** goodwill that he seemed almost like a family member.

AVUNCULAR means: _____

4. _____ The athletes were **relegated** to the bench after they were found guilty of truly terrible sportsmanship.

RELEGATE means: _____

A	adjective: sweet and charming	**C**	verb: to put into effect; to supply with tools
B	adjective: false; misleading	**D**	verb: to belittle

5. _____ It's important not to **disparage** or discount the idea of changing the world one brick at a time.

DISPARAGE means: _____

6. _____ He also pledged to **implement** quickly criteria set as conditions for visa-free travel, allowing greater freedom of movement within the continent.

IMPLEMENT means: _____

7. _____ Although the information must have been accurate in the 1950's, it is now considered **fallacious**.

FALLACIOUS means: _____

8. _____ The **winsome** host delighted the guests with her amusing stories.

WINSOME means: _____

Divide and Conquer:
Choose the correct word to complete each of the following sentences.

9. At first the argument sounded valid, but in truth every fact presented was **(fallacious / implemented)**.

10. The **(winsome / licentious)** boy offered the widow a bouquet picked from his backyard.

11. Our team's best player has been **(relegated / disparaged)** to a backup role because of injuries.

12. Mayor Johnson **(professed / implemented)** his support for the candidate, even going so far as to shout admiring messages from the rooftops.

13. Michelle scolded her brother for his **(professed / licentious)** ways.

14. Though Edward has no children of his own, he has certainly fulfilled his **(relegated / avuncular)** duties with each of his nieces and nephews.

15. The school board **(implemented / professed)** a new policy intended to increase the number of books read in the curriculum.

16. Cruel people **(relegate / disparage)** themselves as much as they demean the supposed targets of their ire.

Hot and Cold:
Write the word from the lesson that is most nearly the *OPPOSITE* of the boldfaced word or words in each sentence below.

17. No matter how much the rest of the world may _____ you and make you feel small, your family will always be here to **praise** your accomplishments.

18. Though he was usually a rather **moral** man, Rodrigo would take vacations to far-off countries, during which he would often get into fights or trouble with the law for his _____ behavior.

19. Lydia quickly learned the advantage of adopting a sweeter, more _____ manner of speaking to people after her usual **abrasive** style proved itself off-putting.

20. Frank had no trouble _____ his love for his favorite hockey team, but thought it better to **hide** his utter disdain for his father-in-law's home team.

21. Because the customers before them had **upgraded** to the most comfortable rental car available, the Johnsons were _____ to an ancient model without air conditioning or properly padded seats.

22. The argument appeared at first to be **sound**, but upon further reflection turned out in fact to be _____.

23. The City of Camden has agreed to fund and _____ a composting program under the conditions that the county will **prevent** neighboring cities from dumping more waste on Camden's grounds.

Applying Yourself:
Choose the best word to complete each of the following sentences.

24. Because I had exposed corruption within the agency, my superiors _____ me to a boring post in the back office.
    - (A) disparaged
    - (B) relegated
    - (C) implemented
    - (D) embellished
    - (E) professed

25. I could turn to my _____ older colleague as if he were actually a trusted family member.
    - (A) avuncular
    - (B) disparaged
    - (C) fallacious
    - (D) relegated
    - (E) licentious

26. Because our _____ colleague sweet-talked the agent, we were able to secure back-stage passes to the concert.
(A) relegated
(B) licentious
(C) winsome
(D) professed
(E) fallacious

27. You should be aware that your behavior will not bring us praise; it will _____ the whole family.
(A) relegate
(B) profess
(C) implement
(D) embellish
(E) disparage

28. Machiavelli recommended that rulers be _____ and act in the best interest of themselves and their nations rather than let themselves be guided by "right" and "wrong".
(A) licentious
(B) relegated
(C) implemented
(D) professed
(E) disparaged

29. I _____ my love for that woman to whomever will listen to my words..
(A) embellish
(B) profess
(C) disparage
(D) implement
(E) relegate

30. The election season spawns _____ commercials meant to hide the real issues.
(A) fallacious
(B) winsome
(C) avuncular
(D) relegated
(E) professed

31. Allow me to _____ the proposed changes to our policy, and I will show you the true meaning of efficiency.
(A) implement
(B) profess
(C) relegate
(D) disparage
(E) embellish

On Your Own:
Write one sentence using each word below to demonstrate your understanding of the word's meaning.

32. **licentious** _____

33. **disparage** _____

34. **relegate** _____

35. **avuncular** _____

36. **fallacious** _____

37. **profess** _____

38. **implement** _____

39. **winsome** _____

C2 Advanced Vocabulary 9

First Impressions:

Using the example sentences below, write your own definition of each boldfaced word. Then write the letter of the definition from the box that best matches your definition.

A	noun: an opponent or adversary	**C**	adjective: sharp; harsh; having a particularly bad taste or smell
B	adjective: rushing and wild with excitement	**D**	verb: to expose false claims and ideas

1. _____ The morality of the film is murky at best; many viewers find that they sympathize with the **antagonist** rather than the traditional hero.

ANTAGONIST means: _____

2. _____ While many teenagers are convinced that the web encyclopedia is a respectable source of information, several studies have **debunked** its reliability.

DEBUNK means: _____

3. _____ The **frenetic** pace of the stock market floor contrasted sharply with the quiet and calm of Jiyoung's yoga studio.

FRENETIC means: _____

4. _____ Acrid odors filled the air after the jug of vinegar smashed open on the tile floor.

ACRID means: _____

A	adjective: sweet; excessively sentimental	**C**	verb: to portray; to describe
B	adjective: favorable to health	**D**	adjective: excessively careful; painstaking; scrupulous

5. _____ Minh **depicted** the Vietnamese landscape so well that Kanal could actually imagine the scene in front of him when he closed his eyes.

DEPICT means: _____

6. _____ The sentimental story of the lost dog following its owners to their new home seemed excessively **saccharine** after the grim war piece.

SACCHARINE means: _____

7. _____ The **meticulous** Anna caught every error when she examined mock-up of the week's magazine but sometimes exasperated other editors when she insisted on proofreading for the fourth time.

METICULOUS means: _____

8. _____ Dr. Colson advised her patient to make many **salutary** changes to his lifestyle in order to ward off heart disease.

SALUTARY means: _____

Divide and Conquer:
Choose the correct word to complete each of the following sentences.

9. The painting **(depicts / debunks)** a young man gazing out across a field of freshly cut hay.

10. It takes a(n) **(meticulous / antagonistic)** eye and trained hands to create such photorealistic portraits.

11. The critic was typically **(acrid / salutary)** in his review of the film; he was well-known for his frank and even cruel writing.

12. The popular television show features two engineers who use science to **(depict / debunk)** popular ideas that are mistaken.

13. The **(acrid / frenetic)** energy of the party kept everyone dancing well into the early hours of the morning.

14. Jason's stoic nature clashed strongly with his girlfriend's **(saccharine / frenetic)** musings.

15. The **(depiction / antagonist)** promised to heap destruction upon the hero's household.

16. **(Frenetic / Salutary)** habits, such as exercising and eating vegetables, can extend a person's life by years.

Hot and Cold:
Write the word from the lesson that is most nearly the *OPPOSITE* of the boldfaced word or words in each sentence below.

17. The host's _____ toast about how utterly valuable we all were to him and how he would die if anything ever happened to any of us was met with a **bitter** "yeah, right" by one the grumpier attendees.

18. Some parties worked as hard to _____ the theory as others tried to **reinforce** it.

19. The _____ stench of the crematorium was one of the worst parts of the downtown area; not even the local candle shop could infuse the air with enough **soothing** scents of chamomile or lavender to overcome the smell.

20. The _____ river seemed to be rushing in every direction as it flowed downstream, in stark contrast to the perfectly **still** lake that stood nearby.

21. Ivana, a(n) _____ painter who insisted that each detail of her work be perfect, couldn't understand more **careless** styles of art that seemed to hold no regard for accuracy.

22. In our family, the oldest and youngest siblings are usually the _____ who begin fights with each other, and the rest of us must choose which we'll select as our **ally**.

23. A(n) _____ glass of red wine with dinner improves blood circulation and heart health; a case of beer before bed, however, is quite **sickening**.

Applying Yourself:
Choose the best word to complete each of the following sentences.

24. The coach's _____ criticisms, more personal than professional, made losing the game even more painful.
   (A) salutary
   (B) debunked
   (C) acrid
   (D) frenetic
   (E) saccharine

25. During overtime, the _____ pace of the early game took its toll on the exhausted players.
   (A) depicted
   (B) meticulous
   (C) acrid
   (D) debunked
   (E) frenetic

26. I'd rather stay home than pay to see another _____ romantic comedy that shows none of the emotional complexities of real life.
    (A) salutary
    (B) acrid
    (C) frenetic
    (D) saccharine
    (E) antagonistic

27. The film *Schindler's List* _____ the violence of the Holocaust in brutal detail.
    (A) inaugurates
    (B) jeopardizes
    (C) debunks
    (D) depicts
    (E) antagonizes

28. Though he tried for hours to _____ the theory, in the end he was forced to admit that it must be true.
    (A) antagonize
    (B) depict
    (C) debunk
    (D) inaugurate
    (E) jeopardize

29. Although you might feel that work gives your life purpose and vigor, a more _____ lifestyle of calm and self-care leads to lower blood pressure, less stress, and more time for your family.
    (A) debunked
    (B) salutary
    (C) saccharine
    (D) depicted
    (E) acrid

30. Sherlock Holmes' _____ is Professor Moriarty, who attempts to foil Holmes' powers of deduction at every opportunity.
    (A) depiction
    (B) nepotism
    (C) renaissance
    (D) antagonist
    (E) recluse

31. The staff writer's careless attitude towards grammar irritated the _____ copy editor, who, despite being on a tight deadline, spent a significant amount of time correcting each mistake.
    (A) debunked
    (B) frenetic
    (C) acrid
    (D) meticulous
    (E) antagonistic

On Your Own:
Write one sentence using each word below to demonstrate your understanding of the word's meaning.

32. **meticulous** _____

33. **antagonist** _____

34. **acrid** _____

35. **depict** _____

36. **salutary** _____

37. **debunk** _____

38. **saccharine** _____

39. **frenetic** _____

C2 Advanced Vocabulary 10

First Impressions:

Using the example sentences below, write your own definition of each boldfaced word. Then write the letter of the definition from the box that best matches your definition.

A	noun: a person who cheats others out of money or other assets; a person who obtains things by fraud or deceit	**C**	noun: uprightness; wholeness; tendency to act ethically
B	adjective: without feeling; imperturbable; stoical	**D**	adjective: sudden and blunt

1. _____ Akira couldn't understand how Matthew could be so **impassive** about the topic, showing no emotion despite his personal involvement in it.

IMPASSIVE means: _____

2. _____ Martin's **integrity** led him to donate all of his allowance to a local charity.

INTEGRITY means: _____

3. _____ Prosecutors called him a master **swindler** who pocketed millions while claiming personal bankruptcy.

SWINDLER means: _____

4. _____ Mr. Atkins strove for efficiency in his meetings, and his **brusque** responses to questions often intimidated or offended his clients.

BRUSQUE means: _____

A	noun: refusal of any compromise; stubbornness	**C**	adjective: showing proper behavior or manners
B	adjective: happening at the same time or at the same rate	**D**	noun: a wearing down or reduction over time

5. _____ It is unusual to find a waiter at a fine restaurant who does not behave in a **decorous** manner.

DECOROUS means: _____

6. _____ An accurate clock is a carefully engineered device with countless parts moving in a precise, **synchronous** manner.

SYNCHRONOUS means: _____

7. _____ Though some valued Miguel's firmness in his opinions, others condemned it as immature **intransigence**.

INTRANSIGENCE means: _____

8. _____ Though the military could not hope to win through a direct assault, they planned to reduce the opposing force's numbers over time through a war of **attrition**.

ATTRITION means: _____

Divide and Conquer:
Choose the correct word to complete each of the following sentences.

9. The harmony parts at the beginning of the song are **(integral / synchronous)**, but the solos at the end are sung separately.

10. Kansas City police said they are thanking a bank clerk for his quick thinking in helping to stop a **(swindler / attrition)** in action.

11. The countess was highly **(decorous / impassive)**, having entertained ambassadors and diplomats from an early age.

12. The organization suffered a(n) **(attrition / swindler)** in membership over the years until it finally was forced to close.

13. Harold apologized for his **(brusque / impassive)** reply, explaining that he was in a rush to get to his club's meeting.

14. Because Susan recognized Marco's **(integrity / intransigence)**, she had no trouble trusting him to act as treasurer for the club.

15. The continued **(intransigence / attrition)** of the other party has prevented any semblance of a compromise.

16. Hilary's **(brusque / impassive)** gaze as she witnessed a bully knock her little brother to the ground caused her parents to worry over her lack of emotion..

Hot and Cold:
Write the word from the lesson that is most nearly the *OPPOSITE* of the boldfaced word or words in each sentence below.

17. Six-year-old Leroy's _____ contrasted sharply with the **compliance** of his elder sister, Tish; while Leroy refused to do anything he was asked, Tish would happily agree to any requests.

18. She appears _____, seemingly unaffected by the story, but I know that these types of films make my mother very **emotional** and that she'll probably think about it for a long time.

19. With a(n) _____ bow, Sir William exited the conversation with the insultingly **rude** stranger while keeping his sense of chivalry intact.

20. The _____ of your bones can be attributed to old age, but if you begin to exercise and eat plenty of calcium and vitamin D, your skeleton should experience some **fortification**.

21. The judge's _____ was called into question when a young lawyer accused him of **dishonesty** in his rulings.

22. While customers often approached her as though she were a(n) _____ trying to trick them out of their hard-earned cash, Camile was an **honest person** who only wanted to set people up in cars they could afford.

23. Don't mistake Joanne's _____ manner for rudeness; she's quite **warm and kind** once you get past her initial demeanor..

Applying Yourself:
Choose the best word to complete each of the following sentences.

24. Be careful when you walk to the bazaar, as _____ await to relieve the unwary of their possessions.
    - (A) travails
    - (B) theologies
    - (C) swindlers
    - (D) proletariats
    - (E) zephyrs

25. Although all the other jurors eventually gave in and agreed on the verdict of "guilty," Ms. Craigg remained _____ in her defense of the defendant.
    - (A) impassive
    - (B) intransigent
    - (C) integral
    - (D) decorous
    - (E) brusque

26. The _____ piano teacher didn't waste time soothing her student; instead, she just said, "Wrong; play it right this time."
   (A) decorous
   (B) brusque
   (C) intransigent
   (D) synchronous
   (E) integral

27. Yolanda was _____ when she heard that she had been found guilty, making people believe that she was a cold-hearted person.
   (A) decorous
   (B) synchronous
   (C) brusque
   (D) integral
   (E) impassive

28. Make sure to know which utensil is used for which course at the black-tie dinner if you want to display _____ behavior.
   (A) unremitting
   (B) decorous
   (C) synchronous
   (D) brusque
   (E) integral

29. _____ without replenishment had rendered our once-mighty sales force inadequate to the task at hand.
   (A) Theology
   (B) Attrition
   (C) Exasperation
   (D) Swindler
   (E) Extrovert

30. Susan was the only one with enough _____ to withstand the temptations to sell our mother's farm.
   (A) attrition
   (B) integrity
   (C) fabrication
   (D) intransigence
   (E) brusqueness

31. The ball's landing was _____ with the player's, and the violent collision could be heard from across the stadium.
   (A) decorous
   (B) impassive
   (C) brusque
   (D) integral
   (E) synchronous

On Your Own:
Write one sentence using each word below to demonstrate your understanding of the word's meaning.

32. **attrition** _____

33. **impassive** _____

34. **Intransigence** _____

35. **brusque** _____

36. **decorous** _____

37. **synchronous** _____

38. **swindler** _____

39. **integrity** _____

C2 Advanced Vocabulary 11

First Impressions:

Using the example sentences below, write your own definition of each boldfaced word. Then write the letter of the definition from the box that best matches your definition.

A	adjective: sincerely remorseful or repentant	C	noun: opponent; enemy
B	adjective: unwilling to accept refusal	D	adjective: very impressive

1. _____ Despite the customer's **peremptory** tone, the waiter calmly attempted to explain that fulfilling the request would simply be impossible.

PEREMPTORY means: _____

2. _____ The **contrite** child apologized for her mistake with tears in her eyes.

CONTRITE means: _____

3. _____ The **stupendous** engineering feats achieved by the ancient Romans are praised even today.

STUPENDOUS means: _____

4. _____ My **adversary** raised her sword in defense but couldn't manage to completely block the blow.

ADVERSARY means: _____

A	adjective: blameless; impeccable	C	adjective: firm in support of a cause or idea
B	adjective: extremely poor	D	noun: a strong inclination; a liking

5. _____ The police were pretty sure the wife was the culprit, but without any evidence, she was **irreproachable**.

IRREPROACHABLE means: _____

6. _____ I am known to frequent the library, as I have always had a **penchant** for reading.

PENCHANT means: _____

7. _____ Kyle was such a **staunch** supporter of the president that he donated to his reelection campaign.

STAUNCH means: _____

8. _____ The members of the **penurious** family were dependent on the support of their church while the parents looked for jobs.

PENURIOUS means: _____

Divide and Conquer:

Choose the correct word to complete each of the following sentences.

9. In another blow to our **(penurious / adversarial)** families, the city is closing yet another homeless shelter.

10. Kareem finally eased his conscience by finding his old friend and expressing a(n) **(contrite / adversarial)** apology.

11. When I said that I love the outdoors, I meant that I have a **(penchant / staunchness)** for picnicking.

12. Senator Wallace marshaled her **(peremptory / staunch)** allies to defeat the dangerous but tempting bill.

13. Hannah resented the fact that her parents viewed her brother, Simon, in such a(n) **(staunch / irreproachable)** light while punishing her for minor offenses.

14. I was so stunned by his **(irreproachable / peremptory)** manner that I fulfilled his request even though it violated company guidelines..

15. Bill Gates is a person with **(irreproachable / stupendous)** wealth.

16. In chess, one player moves the black pieces while his or her **(contrition / adversary)** moves the white.

Hot and Cold:

Write the word from the lesson that is most nearly the *OPPOSITE* of the boldfaced word or words in each sentence below.

17. Always a risk-taker, Deborah had a(n) _____ for extreme sports and a **disinclination** for sitting still.

18. In life, your _____ will try to compete with and overcome you while your **allies** will try to help you along the way.

19. Since I grew up in a(n) _____ area of town with broken-down houses and a blighted population, I wasn't sure what to make of the manicured lawns and spacious homes in the **wealthy** neighborhood uptown.

20. Jenny's _____ apology for breaking the window moved me, while her brother's **remorseless** smirk made me want to ground him for a year.

21. The boss' _____ demands won her far less compliance than a more **accommodating** tone would have.

22. I am a(n) _____ supporter of women's rights, but I feel a little **ambivalent** about the topic of abortion.

23. He thought that his grades were _____, especially as they had been **unimpressive** the year before.

24. I am hardly _____ in the disintegration of my marriage; for the past 5 years, I have been **guilty** of prioritizing work and play over family.

Applying Yourself:

Choose the best word to complete each of the following sentences.

25. The _____ head coach forced his players to stay an hour after practice, silencing all protestations with a stubborn stare.
    (A) peremptory
    (B) contrite
    (C) stupendous
    (D) penurious
    (E) staunch

26. I wonder if there is a connection between her _____ for blurring the line between church and state and her tendency to treat myth as history.
    (A) contrition
    (B) staunchness
    (C) penchant
    (D) irreproachability
    (E) adversary

27. _____ criminals typically receive more lenient sentences than obstinate ones.
    (A) Adversarial
    (B) Staunch
    (C) Contrite
    (D) Stupendous
    (E) Penurious

28. Don't worry about Jason's loyalty; he's been a _____ supporter of our cause from the beginning.
    (A) penurious
    (B) stupendous
    (C) irreproachable
    (D) staunch
    (E) peremptory

29. It seems as though he has taken his role as the _____ too seriously — many of his co-stars have been disturbed by his new, villainous attitude off-set.
    (A) staunchness
    (B) penchant
    (C) contrition
    (D) adversary
    (E) irreproachability

30. The first time I flew in an airplane, I was in awe of the _____ feats of humankind.
    (A) contrite
    (B) peremptory
    (C) irreproachable
    (D) staunch
    (E) stupendous

31. Although the detective had a strong hunch that Mr. Carmine was guilty, he knew that legally she was _____.
    (A) stupendous
    (B) contrite
    (C) irreproachable
    (D) peremptory
    (E) staunch

32. "Banana Republic" is a term used to describe a country with vast inequalities between the mega-rich and the _____ lower class.
    (A) peremptory
    (B) penurious
    (C) staunch
    (D) contrite
    (E) irreproachable

On Your Own:
Write one sentence using each word below to demonstrate your understanding of the word's meaning.

33. **peremptory** _____

34. **stupendous** _____

35. **penurious** _____

36. **irreproachable** _____

37. **contrite** _____

38. **staunch** _____

39. **adversary** _____

40. **penchant** _____

C2 Advanced Vocabulary 12

First Impressions:

Using the example sentences below, write your own definition of each boldfaced word. Then write the letter of the definition from the box that best matches your definition.

A	noun: an item of food that is rare but desirable	**C**	verb: to dance and celebrate in an excited fashion
B	verb: to consist of; to be made up of	**D**	noun: an attempt to give a false impression

1. _____ Fine caviar is widely considered a **delicacy** and people are willing to pay huge sums to enjoy it at home.

DELICACY means: _____

2. _____ Since Mark only spent six months living in Mexico, it is likely that his new accent is merely an **affectation**.

AFFECTATION means: _____

3. _____ The King James Bible **comprises** 80 books--the 39 of the Old Testament, the 27 of the New Testament, and the 14 of the Apocrypha.

COMPRISE means: _____

4. _____ During the school dance, the students **cavorted** and enjoyed each other's company.

CAVORT means: _____

A	noun: a state of high annoyance or impatience	**C**	adjective: impartial or neutral
B	adjective: irritable; easily angered	**D**	noun: a very slight offense or sin

5. _____ There were many things to hold against him: he was personally **irascible** and difficult to be around.

IRASCIBLE means: _____

6. _____ The children's ceaseless demands left the babysitter in a state of total **exasperation** by the end of the night.

EXASPERATION means: _____

7. _____ Colleen controlled her strong feelings in an attempt to give **dispassionate** advice.

DISPASSIONATE means: _____

8. _____ Margaret was surprised to be punished so harshly for a mere **peccadillo**.

PECCADILLO means: _____

Divide and Conquer:
Choose the correct word to complete each of the following sentences.

9. The babysitter's **(exasperation / delicacy)** was understandable, as the triplets had been up to nothing but mischief all night.

10. Mitchell was usually **(comprised / irascible)** after a long, stressful day, so his sister knew to leave him alone.

11. The team's strategy for the season **(cavorted / comprised)** three main parts: consistent daily practice of skills, plenty of rest, and a weekly review of performance in past games.

12. Good cheese is a **(peccadillo / delicacy)** that should be enjoyed with other fine foods.

13. Because Arzael's many neuroscience textbooks are gathering dust, it is likely that they are simply part of an **(exasperation / affectation)** of a scholarly disposition.

14. The judge tried to take a **(comprised / dispassionate)** approach to his work, deciding cases solely by the law rather than by his personal opinions.

15. Tania **(exasperated / cavorted)** with her friends all night in celebration of her birthday.

16. What you might see as a mere **(exasperation / peccadillo)** can be seen as a horrible offense by someone from another culture.

Hot and Cold:
Write the word from the lesson that is most nearly the *OPPOSITE* of the boldfaced word or words in each sentence below.

17. While all around her _____ with gay abandon, Judith **sat quietly** and pondered her mortality.

18. French fries, a **common food**, have been transformed into a(n) _____ at the new gourmet restaurant.

19. The traveler wanted to find some aspect of **authenticity** within the city, apart from the _____ of the tourist center that tried to appeal to visitors' knowledge of the city's illustrious, but ancient, past.

20. You forgot to hand out your business card, but that's a(n) _____ rather than an **insult** and no one will hold it against you.

21. I tried to hide my _____ with the child's bad behavior, as a nanny should have nothing if not **patience**.

22. In his old age, Grandpa has grown from a **tender and gentle man** into a(n) _____ curmudgeon who seems constantly annoyed with the rest of us.

23. I don't care if I'm accused of being **biased** in favor of the underdog; as the principal of this school, I simply cannot remain _____ in such an obvious case of cruel and prolonged bullying.

24. Mozart's body of work is _____ of a large number of pieces for many different instruments but does **not include** a single piece for an electric bass, which had not been invented during his lifetime.

Applying Yourself:
Choose the best word to complete each of the following sentences.

25. In certain countries, snails are considered a(n) _____ and are served at the most sought-after restaurants.
    (A) affectation
    (B) peccadillo
    (C) exasperation
    (D) dispassion
    (E) delicacy

26. Smoking a pipe and wearing a tweed jacket are _____ meant to portray a scholarly vibe.
    (A) affectations
    (B) delicacies
    (C) exasperations
    (D) peccadilloes
    (E) implements

27. Benji's mistakes left his boss in a consistent state of _____, wondering when Benji would ever learn the job.
    (A) delicacy
    (B) exasperation
    (C) dispassion
    (D) irascibility
    (E) antagonist

28. Walk softly next to Al's office during tax season; the unending questions that he must answer make him a(n) _____ accountant.
    (A) saccharine
    (B) comprised
    (C) salutary
    (D) irascible
    (E) cavorting

29. Don't worry about your gaffe; it was only a(n) _____, at worst.
    (A) antagonist
    (B) exasperation
    (C) peccadillo
    (D) affectation
    (E) delicacy

30. They spent all night _____ at the wedding reception, dancing, laughing, and singing together.
    (A) debunking
    (B) antagonizing
    (C) cavorting
    (D) exasperating
    (E) comprising

31. The Challenger's engine is _____ of modernized versions of classic muscle-car parts.
    (A) cavorted
    (B) depicted
    (C) comprised
    (D) converged
    (E) exasperated

32. Approach the decision with a(n) _____ rather than an emotional approach..
    (A) exasperated
    (B) irascible
    (C) comprised
    (D) partisan
    (E) dispassionate

On Your Own:
Write one sentence using each word below to demonstrate your understanding of the word's meaning.

33. **cavort** _____

34. **affectation** _____

35. **exasperation** _____

36. **irascible** _____

37. **peccadillo** _____

38. **dispassionate** _____

39. **comprise** _____

40. **delicacy** _____

C2 Advanced Vocabulary 13

First Impressions:

Using the example sentences below, write your own definition of each boldfaced word. Then write the letter of the definition from the box that best matches your definition.

A	adjective: unprejudiced; impartial; neutral	**C**	adjective: one-sided; prejudiced; committed to a party
B	noun: a formal system that separates people by race or other criteria	**D**	noun: the coming together of multiple items at one point

1. _____ Under **apartheid** in South Africa, ethnic Africans were denied the right to elect the leaders of their government.

APARTHEID means: _____

2. _____ The author was clearly **partisan** when it came to economics: the book was littered with capitalist comments, even in subplots that didn't involve the subject.

PARTISAN means: _____

3. _____ The two debating students asked the **disinterested** teacher to act as a mediator between them.

DISINTERESTED means: _____

4. _____ The **convergence** of research in interface design, high-speed wireless networks, and miniaturization led to the widespread adoption of the smart phone in the 2000s.

CONVERGENCE means: _____

A	verb: to slow up; to loosen	**C**	adjective: puzzled; lost in thought
B	verb: to do extremely well	**D**	adjective: said or done in jest; joking

5. _____ Filipe was **bemused** by the unexpected changes to his web browser; it took him several moments to understand the new interface.

BEMUSED means: _____

6. _____ I was trying to be **jocular**, but apparently they took me seriously.

JOCULAR means: _____

7. _____ Managers of food banks and pantries never see the demand **slacken**, but they do see their food supplies dwindle.

SLACKEN means: _____

8. _____ Natalie **excels** in algebra but has a hard time with history.

EXCEL means: _____

Divide and Conquer:
Choose the correct word to complete each of the following sentences.

9. We **(slackened / converged)** our pace in order to more fully appreciate the amazing sunset.

10. Michael's acquaintances admired his **(disinterested / slackened)** stance on politics, for he never took sides before carefully evaluating each party's ideas.

11. Jim sat with a **(jocular / bemused)** expression on his face as he pondered how best to proceed with the project.

12. The speaker broke the ice by beginning his speech with a few **(jocular / excellent)** remarks.

13. The legislator argued that the denial of marriage rights based on these criteria was, in effect, a new **(convergence / apartheid)**.

14. The company oddly brags of being a source of **(disinterested / partisan)**, one-sided reporting from Washington D.C.

15. Some brilliant comedians and artists have **(excelled / converged)** in adapting to the demands of digital media.

16. The location of the city at the **(convergence / jocularity)** of three major rivers led it to become very important in the shipping industry.

Hot and Cold:
Write the word from the lesson that is most nearly the *OPPOSITE* of the boldfaced word or words in each sentence below.

17. We must come to a point of mutual **agreement** before _____ interests divide us all.

18. Half the class seemed _____ by the puzzle, staring into space as they tried to make sense of it, while the other half was **alert** and rapidly writing down the solution into their notebooks.

19. The judge's _____ ruling surprised the court, since he was known to be **biased** in matters of marriage law, ruling in favor of the mother regardless of the circumstances.

20. After witnessing the terrible effects of _____ on local race relations, Gina became even more convinced that **desegregation**, and the resultant intermingling of the races, was the only answer.

21. The chef **failed** at most baking projects but _____ in grilling.

22. The _____ air in the room as the associates laughed and teased each other ended abruptly when the **stern** CEO walked into the meeting room.

23. The _____ of the two rivers into a single stream at Arrow Point also marked the **divergence** the hiking trail into 3 separate paths.

24. The rower _____ the resistance of the left oar and **tightened** his grip on the right in order to turn the canoe to the left.

Applying Yourself:
Choose the best word to complete each of the following sentences.

25. Her face looked _____ when I asked her about the day, and I knew that her mind had been somewhere else.
    (A) disinterested
    (B) partisan
    (C) slackened
    (D) jocular
    (E) bemused

26. While trying to _____ his belt, Jerry accidentally tightened it.
    (A) enfranchise
    (B) slacken
    (C) covet
    (D) vitalize
    (E) converge

27. If members of the jury are not _____ in the case, there is a risk that the trial will be unfair.
    (A) bemused
    (B) excellent
    (C) slackened
    (D) partisan
    (E) disinterested

28. He _____ at his chosen job, and was praised by everyone he worked for.
    (A) converged
    (B) confronted
    (C) excelled
    (D) slackened
    (E) enfranchised

29. _____ politics in the senate is paralyzing our country; we need to learn to compromise.
    (A) Bemused
    (B) Disinterested
    (C) Jocular
    (D) Excellent
    (E) Partisan

30. Due to Kyle's _____ tone, Stan felt insulted by his friend's comment about the bad grade Stan received on the chemistry test.
    (A) disinterested
    (B) converged
    (C) slackened
    (D) jocular
    (E) excellent

31. That day in July marks the _____ of many interstellar phenomena, so make sure to pack your telescope.
    (A) convergence
    (B) apartheid
    (C) jocularity
    (D) excellence
    (E) slackening

32. Nelson Mandela, the first democratically elected president of South Africa, endured years of imprisonment under the regime that used _____ to separate the races.
    (A) disinterest
    (B) apartheid
    (C) convergence
    (D) jocularity
    (E) slackening

On Your Own:

Write one sentence using each word below to demonstrate your understanding of the word's meaning.

33. **disinterested** _____

34. **convergence** _____

35. **jocular** _____

36. **bemused** _____

37. **excel** _____

38. **slacken** _____

39. **apartheid** _____

40. **partisan** _____

C2 Advanced Vocabulary 14

First Impressions:

Using the example sentences below, write your own definition of each boldfaced word. Then write the letter of the definition from the box that best matches your definition.

A	noun: a person known for having wisdom	**C**	adjective: extremely tidy; excessively formal and proper
B	noun: an argument involving great amounts of discussion	**D**	noun: the state of being first in order, rank, or importance

1. _____ The controversial presidential election of 2000 provoked a storm of **logomachy** that has not yet subsided today.

LOGOMACHY means: _____

2. _____ For 40 years, the **primacy** of Hank Aaron's home run record went unchallenged.

PRIMACY means: _____

3. _____ The **prim** hostess insisted that none of her female guests be left alone with only men for company, claiming that improper scenarios might occur.

PRIM means: _____

4. _____ He is a **sage**, a combination professor, historian, and politician whose words are fuel for the intellect.

SAGE means: _____

A	adjective: divine and supernatural	**C**	adjective: sharp and incisive
B	adjective: lacking a sense of right and wrong	**D**	adjective: fertile or productive

5. _____ Though many people disagree about what is right or wrong, very few healthy individuals can be said to be truly **amoral**.

AMORAL means: _____

6. _____ The pioneers were overjoyed to find a new home full of fresh water and **fecund** land for farming.

FECUND means: _____

7. _____ Several **numinous** experiences inspired Joan of Arc to lead French soldiers in a divinely-appointed uprising against their invaders.

NUMINOUS means: _____

8. _____ The comedian sharply criticized several celebrities with his **trenchant** wit.

TRENCHANT means: _____

Divide and Conquer:
Choose the correct word to complete each of the following sentences.

9. The **(sage / logomachy)** lived in the remote mountains, but we needed his counsel so badly that we made the trip.

10. The hostess was so **(prim / numinous)** as to make us conscious of even small breaks of etiquette.

11. While some found the pundit's commentary **(amoral / trenchant)** and witty, others found it merely belligerent and oafish.

12. The speaker argued that science need not be **(amoral / fecund)**; in fact, he believed that many ethical questions can be answered through the scientific method.

13. The lighting formed a **(numinous / fecund)** glow around her head, as if she had descended from heaven.

14. The issue being debated was so controversial that intense **(primacy / logomachy)** extended well into the evening.

15. The land was highly **(fecund / trenchant)**, yielding a large quantity of nutritious crops with a minimum of effort on the farmers' part.

16. President Truman appreciated the **(primacy / logomachy)** of developing nuclear weapons, and allocated many resources to meeting that goal.

Hot and Cold:
Write the word from the lesson that is most nearly the *OPPOSITE* of the boldfaced word or words in each sentence below.

17. The once-_____ valley, which had provided food for a large population, has been turned **barren** due to overworking of the soil.

18. You kids require such _____ to solve your problems; back in my day, a single nod, containing a thousand **tacit words**, was enough to convey our entire meaning.

19. The _____ waits and listens before speaking; the **fool** charges into any discussion assuming he or she already knows best.

20. My **messy** room, which I haven't properly tidied in months, will probably disgust my _____ sister when she comes to visit.

21. One symptom of psychopathy is a(n) _____ state—it's not that psychopaths refuse to be **scrupulous**; it's that they simply lack a moral code.

22. The _____ of the presidency has been challenged by the rebellion; revolutionaries would like to see the **subordination** of the president to a parliament.

23. Rhonda proposed a(n) _____ attack against those causing destruction in the neighborhood and said in no **vague** terms that the vandals ought to pay a serious price for their deeds.

24. The little girl, dressed in her angel's costume for the pageant, seemed to have a _____ glow as she sang; in those moments, she was more than a mere **earthly** being.

Applying Yourself:
Choose the best word to complete each of the following sentences.

25. _____ demands that we afford the general the utmost obedience.
    (A) Fecundity
    (B) Amorality
    (C) Primacy
    (D) Primness
    (E) Logomachy

26. After all the petty bickering, Lindsay's _____ argument settled the issue in one fell swoop.
    (A) amoral
    (B) sage
    (C) trenchant
    (D) numinous
    (E) fecund

27. Children are born _____ into the world; parents should work to instill a sense of right and wrong in them.
(A) fecund
(B) sage
(C) amoral
(D) prim
(E) numinous

28. In the sheer number of hours spent, no _____ has surpassed the debates over last year's budget.
(A) travail
(B) logomachy
(C) erudition
(D) fecundity
(E) primacy

29. For eons, the Nile River valley became more _____ when the river flooded and deposited nutrient-rich silt on the farmland.
(A) sage
(B) numinous
(C) prim
(D) fecund
(E) trenchant

30. Victorian England, with its _____ ladies focused on Queen and country, gave way to a more liberal era.
(A) prim
(B) numinous
(C) amoral
(D) trenchant
(E) sage

31. Only one person could solve our dilemma: a _____, weathered by time and heavy with the wisdom of years.
(A) primacy
(B) logomachy
(C) travail
(D) sage
(E) vitality

32. _____ experiences can drive the faithful to spread their spiritual beliefs.
(A) Prim
(B) Numinous
(C) Amoral
(D) Primal
(E) Trenchant

On Your Own:
Write one sentence using each word below to demonstrate your understanding of the word's meaning.

33. **primacy** _____

34. **fecund** _____

35. **sage** _____

36. **numinous** _____

37. **prim** _____

38. **amoral** _____

39. **logomachy** _____

40. **trenchant** _____

C2 Advanced Vocabulary 15

First Impressions:

Using the example sentences below, write your own definition of each boldfaced word. Then write the letter of the definition from the box that best matches your definition.

A	adjective: curious	**C**	noun: an additional passage added onto the end of an existing work
B	adjective: indispensable; relating to life; required for living	**D**	adjective: not fully developed

1. _____ Miss Lynde is an **inquisitive** woman who will ask a million questions until she's satisfied with the information.

INQUISITIVE means: _____

2. _____ The **coda** at the end of the symphonic piece is the most complicated part, having been added years later when the composer was more advanced in talent.

CODA means: _____

3. _____ The teacher recommended that I develop my **inchoate** notions into a clearer thesis.

INCHOATE means: _____

4. _____ Renee played a **vital** role in her team's victory, scoring both goals and making several other key plays.

VITAL means: _____

A	adjective: innocent; peaceful	**C**	adjective: not direct
B	adjective: scholarly or learned, especially from books	**D**	noun: a difficult, laborious, or painful effort

5. _____ It seems odd that someone as **erudite**, articulate, and suave as she should get entangled in one controversy after another.

ERUDITE means: _____

6. _____ Wishing to delay the end of his journey as long as possible, Mathieu took a **circuitous** route back to his apartment.

CIRCUITOUS means: _____

7. _____ I have written a novel about the **travails** of a good-hearted but unfortunate young woman named Anne.

TRAVAIL means: _____

8. _____ The **dovish** nation avoided any major conflicts with other nations for a period of two hundred years.

DOVISH means: _____

Divide and Conquer:
Choose the correct word to complete each of the following sentences.

9. The **(dovish / inquisitive)** child's favorite word was "why".

10. European Jews, gypsies, homosexuals, and disabled people faced tremendous **(erudition / travails)** and persecution during World War II.

11. Some versions of the book include a **(coda / travail)** with additional information.

12. The psychologists maintains that emotional health is as **(vital / erudite)** to a person's wellbeing as food and water.

13. She wrote a thoughtful, informed, and **(erudite / inchoate)** letter to the president.

14. The current draft of your essay is rather **(inchoate / circuitous)**; a more direct approach would likely be more effective.

15. The **(inchoate / erudite)** notion swam in the back of Suelgi's thoughts for days before it finally grew into a full-fledged plan.

16. Compared to her rambunctious and argumentative brother, Susan is refreshingly **(vital / dovish)**.

Hot and Cold:
Write the word from the lesson that is most nearly the *OPPOSITE* of the boldfaced word or words in each sentence below.

17. The _____ Democrats wanted to avoid war at all costs, while the more **hawkish** Republicans advocated using the country's military might.

18. Frankie insisted to his employees that while their performance was important, it was **peripheral** to the _____ importance of their reliability and honesty.

19. Tanya tends to argue in a(n) _____ manner that makes it hard to see her point; I prefer more **direct** styles of communication.

20. After seeing my numerous _____, my boss told me to take the afternoon off and experience **relaxation**.

21. The **completed** report had no room for Liz's _____ ideas about where the project could possibly end up in 20 years' time.

22. The professor, by far the most _____ person in the room of **unlearned** undergraduates, took pleasure in granting his knowledge to the uneducated mass.

23. One of the puppies was _____ about the vacuum, but the other was **uninterested**.

Applying Yourself:
Choose the best word to complete each of the following sentences.

24. A(n) _____ added to the end of the book detailed the later lives of the main characters.
    (A) travail
    (B) coda
    (C) erudition
    (D) asylum
    (E) vitality

25. The debate club tried to make sense of Lisa's _____ argument and then realized that she could have made the point in one, concise sentence.
    (A) circuitous
    (B) inquisitive
    (C) erudite
    (D) dovish
    (E) vital

26. The _____ of her peers did not worry the pitiless woman.
    (A) vitality
    (B) asylum
    (C) eruditition
    (D) travails
    (E) confrontation

27. In such _____ company, those who have not completed the assigned reading look quite silly.
    (A) dovish
    (B) vital
    (C) inchoate
    (D) erudite
    (E) circuitous

28. Idris was always _____, constantly asking about how things worked.
    (A) circuitous
    (B) vital
    (C) dovish
    (D) erudite
    (E) inquisitive

29. Chamberlain's _____ response was inadequate to the threat posed by Hitler.
    (A) circuitous
    (B) vital
    (C) dovish
    (D) inchoate
    (E) inquisitive

30. When stranded on a desert island, first secure _____ items such as food, water, and shelter.
    (A) inchoate
    (B) inquisitive
    (C) dovish
    (D) erudite
    (E) vital

31. Kristin argued that kids should not play football too early, as their _____ bodies cannot handle the punishment.
    (A) inquisitive
    (B) inchoate
    (C) vital
    (D) circuitous
    (E) erudite

On Your Own:

Write one sentence using each word below to demonstrate your understanding of the word's meaning.

32. **circuitous** _____

33. **vital** _____

34. **inchoate** _____

35. **dovish** _____

36. **coda** _____

37. **erudite** _____

38. **inquisitive** _____

39. **travail** _____

C2 Advanced Vocabulary 16

First Impressions:

Using the example sentences below, write your own definition of each boldfaced word. Then write the letter of the definition from the box that best matches your definition.

A	noun: a place of safety and protection; a hospital for the mentally ill	**C**	adjective: dissipated; wasteful; wildly immoral
B	adjective: indisputable; not open to question	**D**	verb: to desire something that belongs to another

1. _____ Naveena's mother was concerned that her daughter's new **profligate** friend could introduce Naveena to drug abuse.

PROFLIGATE means: _____

2. _____ Lizl found that she was more satisfied with her own possessions after she learned not to **covet** the possessions of others.

COVET means: _____

3. _____ The refugees fleeing their warring homeland sought **asylum** in sympathetic nations.

ASYLUM means: _____

4. _____ Although Wikipedia is a popular quick research source, the fact that anyone in the world can edit the encyclopedia prevents its information from being at all **incontrovertible**.

INCONTROVERTIBLE means: _____

A	verb: to challenge; to oppose; to stand or meet face-to-face	**C**	verb: to grant the rights of citizenship, especially the right to vote
B	adjective: quiet, peaceful, or calm; unaffected by emotions	**D**	adjective: eager to help; careful; concerned

5. _____ Brant's celebration of success was short-lived once he remembered all of the other obstacles that **confronted** him.

CONFRONT means: _____

6. _____ The Nineteenth Amendment to the United States Constitution officially **enfranchised** women, who until that time were denied the right to vote in many parts of the country.

ENFRANCHISE means: _____

7. _____ I was pleased to find that the customer service representative whom I had expected to be rude and unhelpful turned out to be surprisingly **solicitous**.

SOLICITOUS means: _____

8. _____ The Japanese garden was a **tranquil** place—perfect for quiet contemplation or meditation.

TRANQUIL means: _____

Divide and Conquer:
Choose the correct word to complete each of the following sentences.

9. The foreign spy was given **(confrontation / asylum)** in the home of a member of the resistance movement.

10. Some cities have Red Light Districts, in which **(enfranchised / profligate)** activities are tolerated in otherwise moral or even conservative societies.

11. Little Hanseul surprised everyone when he single-handedly **(confronted / coveted)** the schoolyard bully.

12. The groundbreaking bill **(enfranchised / confronted)** an entire class of people who had existed as a subclass of the population for centuries.

13. Though Miguel tried very hard to be satisfied with his own possessions, he found it difficult not to **(covet / confront)** his sister's birthday presents.

14. Through meditation and discipline, Paul reached a **(confrontational / tranquil)** state that even raucous children could not disrupt.

15. Because of the increasing ease of use of photographic manipulation software, photographs are no longer **(incontrovertible / profligate)** evidence in a courtroom.

16. Toby's was frustrated with his attempt to navigate the cavernous library, but fortunately, a **(profligate / solicitous)** librarian helped him find his book.

Hot and Cold:
Write the word from the lesson that is most nearly the *OPPOSITE* of the boldfaced word or words in each sentence below.

17. The monk looked **disturbed** for only a moment after hearing the sad news; his face quickly melted into its usual _____ state and he continued meditating.

18. While women had long been _____ in Ireland, women in the United States were still **disenfranchised**, and the right to choose leaders fell upon American men.

19. Scientists have provided _____ evidence that the earth is becoming warmer, but disbelievers in global warming still consider these studies **disputable**.

20. Grandpa Walt was grateful for the _____ young woman, as he was had expected his new neighbors to be **unhelpful**.

21. This _____ lifestyle you lead among gamblers and the young, wasteful rich will burn every last penny from your pocket; I urge you to take a more **prudent** approach to your affairs.

22. Compared to the peaceful _____ of the resort, the poor area around the beach seems a real **war zone** of drug traffickers and beggars.

23. When Sheryl began to _____ her brother's new car, she knew she should clear her mind and learn to become **indifferent** toward the possessions of others.

24. Unwilling to _____ the dragon, the knight instead **cowered** behind his horse while covering his eyes.

Applying Yourself:
Choose the best word to complete each of the following sentences.

25. Although the skeptics tried to disprove it, the professor's evidence for his work was _____.
    (A) confronted
    (B) enfranchised
    (C) solicitous
    (D) incontrovertible
    (E) tranquil

26. After all the evidence was gathered, after all other possibilities were eliminated, we _____ Brandon about stealing merchandise.
    (A) crystallized
    (B) confronted
    (C) exacerbated
    (D) coveted
    (E) enfranchised

27. The changing of the feudal system meant that the poor classes were finally _____ after years of being disallowed from participating in elections.
(A) confronted
(B) exacerbated
(C) crystallized
(D) enfranchised
(E) coveted

28. How can we be _____ to the stranded driver when we don't know what harm he could pose us?
(A) covetous
(B) solicitous
(C) tranquil
(D) incontrovertible
(E) enfranchising

29. Don't _____ what other people have; some people will always have more than you, and some will always have less.
(A) exacerbate
(B) covet
(C) enfranchise
(D) crystallize
(E) confront

30. Allowing the convicted embezzler to run the treasury was like letting the inmates run the _____.
(A) asylum
(B) confluence
(C) enfranchisement
(D) confrontation
(E) tranquility

31. Meditation can lower blood pressure and induce a(n) _____ state in the mind.
(A) tranquil
(B) enfranchised
(C) covetous
(D) profligate
(E) solicitous

32. The stereotypical fraternity party isn't complete without plenty of wildly _____ activities.
(A) covetous
(B) confronted
(C) profligate
(D) incontrovertible
(E) solicitous

On Your Own:

Write one sentence using each word below to demonstrate your understanding of the word's meaning.

33. **solicitous** _____

34. **asylum** _____

35. **covet** _____

36. **enfranchise** _____

37. **profligate** _____

38. **tranquil** _____

39. **incontrovertible** _____

40. **confront** _____

C2 Advanced Vocabulary 17

First Impressions:
Using the example sentences below, write your own definition of each boldfaced word. Then write the letter of the definition from the box that best matches your definition.

A	verb: to erode to the point of being unrecognizable; to cause to disappear	**C**	verb: to defy openly
B	adjective: concerned with equality and fairness	**D**	verb: to represent in a picture; to portray in words; to describe or outline with precision; to describe or depict in words or gestures

1. _____ As punishment for their crimes, the juveniles were required to spend fourteen hours **effacing** graffiti from walls in the city.

EFFACE means: _____

2. _____ At the heart of most democracies is an **egalitarian** belief that each citizen should have an equal voice in changing the government.

EGALITARIAN means: _____

3. _____ Oksana quickly began to describe the plan, using the mud at her feet to **delineate** the layout of the fort so that she could point out where everyone would take their positions.

DELINEATE means: _____

4. _____ We must be harsh in our punishment of those who openly **flout** the rules.

FLOUT means: _____

A	verb: to revere	**C**	adjective: strong; powerful; formidable
B	verb: to take a winding course; to wander; to ramble	**D**	adjective: firmly established by nature or habit; intrinsic

5. _____ Currently, trucks **meander** through downtown streets to get to the port from Interstate 395.

MEANDER means: _____

6. _____ Generally, an employee cannot sue for injuries caused by conditions **inherent** in the work he or she is tasked to perform, since the employee knew the conditions of the job prior to taking it.

INHERENT means: _____

7. _____ Though his opponent was **redoubtable**, the young wrestler did not lose hope that he could win.

REDOUBTABLE means: _____

8. _____ The young priest-in-training was instructed to **venerate** the image by kissing its feet three times.

VENERATE means: _____

Divide and Conquer:
Choose the correct word to complete each of the following sentences.

9. Centuries of rain and wind have **(effaced / delineated)** the names inscribed on these old gravestones.

10. The stream **(meandered / flouted)** for miles around trees and rocks before finally emptying into the pool.

11. One of the **(flouted / inherent)** difficulties of any new business venture lies in obtaining sufficient funds to launch the business before there is a steady profit flow.

12. Jeannie saw her mother as a most **(redoubtable / effaced)** figure in her life, and one she hoped to emulate.

13. Many who look at the ancient Athenian democracy as an example of **(egalitarian / effaced)** government fail to realize that slavery was commonplace in the city-state.

14. Society tends to **(venerate / flout)** sports stars and celebrities while ignoring the hardworking plumbers, mailmen, and farmers who form the infrastructure of society.

15. The police commissioner vowed to track down and punish those who would **(flout / meander)** the laws of the land.

16. The new treaty **(delineated / flouted)** the regions that each nation would control during the peace.

Hot and Cold:
Write the word from the lesson that is most nearly the *OPPOSITE* of the boldfaced word or words in each sentence below.

17. I find it incredibly difficult to _____ these complicated feelings; any attempt I make is **obfuscated** by my inability to explain how I feel.

18. Most people _____ the excessively strict laws, knowing the police would never have time to arrest all of them, but a few insisted on **obeying** every rule to the letter.

19. I preferred to _____ through the park and take in the sites at a leisurely pace, while Manuel wanted to **take a direct course** to get to where he was going.

20. Fulvia maintains that her love for the piano is _____; she was drawn to the instrument even as a child, before she had **acquired** any ability to play it.

21. Vandals _____ the inscription from the statue so that the words could no longer be seen, but a committee was formed to raise funds to **inscribe** the words once more.

22. While the figurehead has a small minority of devoted followers who _____ him, most people in the country **revile** his corruptness and look forward to the end of his term.

23. I grew up viewing my father as a(n) _____ parental figure and my mother as the more **comforting** one.

24. While there is much talk of ancient _____ societies, no evidence exists to suggest that any society was ever less **authoritarian** than those that exist today.

Applying Yourself:
Choose the best word to complete each of the following sentences.

25. General Stuart _____ the enemy's location so that Lee was able to flank the Union army without having seen its position himself.
    (A) effaced
    (B) delineated
    (C) venerated
    (D) meandered
    (E) flouted

26. She _____ Senator Snow's poise, eloquence, and moral views, viewing her as something of a hero.
    (A) flouted
    (B) venerated
    (C) meandered
    (D) delineated
    (E) effaced

27. The fact that the other party can legally cancel the deal at any time is a flaw _____ to the contract.
    (A) malleable
    (B) egalitarian
    (C) flippant
    (D) redoubtable
    (E) inherent

28. We were hoping to see intricate detail, but centuries of sandstorms had _____ the exterior of Egypt's Sphinx.
    (A) flouted
    (B) meandered
    (C) effaced
    (D) venerated
    (E) delineated

29. The stream _____ back and forth through the valley.
    (A) effaced
    (B) meandered
    (C) venerated
    (D) delineated
    (E) flouted

30. Finland runs the world's most _____ educational system; each student receives the same amount of attention and resources.
    (A) egalitarian
    (B) redoubtable
    (C) effaced
    (D) delineated
    (E) flouted

31. Those climbing Everest will frequently _____ the mandatory turnaround time in a fit of summit fever.
    (A) meander
    (B) flout
    (C) delineate
    (D) efface
    (E) venerate

32. Hercules was a(n) _____ fighter, able to take on ten times his number of enemies and still win.
    (A) inherent
    (B) venerated
    (C) egalitarian
    (D) redoubtable
    (E) meandering

On Your Own:
Write one sentence using each word below to demonstrate your understanding of the word's meaning.

33. **egalitarian** _____

34. **efface** _____

35. **delineate** _____

36. **inherent** _____

37. **venerate** _____

38. **meander** _____

39. **flout** _____

40. **redoubtable** _____

C2 Advanced Vocabulary 18

First Impressions:

Using the example sentences below, write your own definition of each boldfaced word. Then write the letter of the definition from the box that best matches your definition.

A	adjective: generous; charitable; not intended for profit; expressing goodwill	**C**	noun: change or movement in the course of development
B	noun: an appropriate return for something	**D**	noun: a conference between opposing sides, often to negotiate a truce

1. _____ The insurance company offered products and services to protect customers from nearly all of life's financial **vicissitudes**.

VICISSITUDE means: _____

2. _____ Because the two countries seemed on the verge of war, an outside power came in to hold a **parley** between them and resolve the issue.

PARLEY means: _____

3. _____ Despite her assurance that the money was a gift, Ted wondered whether she was being truly **benevolent** or if she would really make him pay her back.

BENEVOLENT means: _____

4. _____ My **requital** for Jenna's generosity was a lovingly prepared home-cooked meal.

REQUITAL means: _____

A	noun: an obstacle; something blocking one's way	**C**	verb: to praise, to glorify
B	verb: to put in danger	**D**	adjective: twisted out of shape; incorrect

5. _____ The disaster victims **extolled** the governor for her quick response in their time of need.

EXTOL means: _____

6. _____ I'd hate to **jeopardize** my job by showing up late too many times.

JEOPARDIZE means: _____

7. _____ Rhonda faced many **impediments** on her road to a college degree, like a lack of funds and a family who wanted her to stay at home.

IMPEDIMENT means: _____

8. _____ Bianca considered each and every detail of her plans carefully to prevent any part from going **awry**.

AWRY means: _____

Divide and Conquer:

Choose the correct word to complete each of the following sentences.

9. A(n) **(requited / benevolent)** man might use his money to fund libraries, charities, and schools.

10. Instead of rigidly adhering to the plan, we will rely on our ability to react to the **(vicissitudes / parley)** that will follow.

11. Marcus planned his project so carefully that no obstacle could set things **(awry / requited)**.

12. Her short stature was a(n) **(impediment / jeopardy)** to her riding on rollercoasters.

13. My brother held a **(vicissitude / parley)** to try to solve the differences between our sister and me.

14. The religion strictly forbids its followers from **(parleying / extolling)** other idols or gods.

15. The judge ordered that I pay a **(vicissitude / requital)** of $400 for the damage I caused to my roommate's property.

16. I fear that the babysitter **(jeopardizes / impedes)** our children's safety when she smokes around them.

Hot and Cold:

Write the word from the lesson that is most nearly the *OPPOSITE* of the boldfaced word or words in each sentence below.

17. The _____ of life may take us across the planet and bring us to many new beliefs and ideas, but my intention to remain your friend is a **constant**.

18. Dad was right in the middle of _____ the virtues of my coffee cake when Jake popped in to **denigrate** my baking skills, just to be rude.

19. Flynn's mistake might _____ our mission, but now he's willing to do anything to **protect** it.

20. The pirate asked the opposing captain to _____, but that captain only wanted to continue **fighting**.

21. I knew Rhonda well and knew that her comment was intended to be _____, and the seemingly **unkind** look on her face betrayed her good intentions.

22. I can provide you **assistance** by removing any _____ to your success.

23. Something seems horribly _____ when the head nurse, usually responsible for keeping the ward operating in an **orderly** fashion, is out for the week.

24. Though gambling often requires players to endure a monetary **loss**, most view the thrill of playing as a form of _____.

Applying Yourself:

Choose the best word to complete each of the following sentences.

25. The robber requested a(n) _____ with his enemies so that they could discuss issues without fighting.
    (A) benevolence
    (B) jeopardy
    (C) parley
    (D) requital
    (E) impediment

26. The fight between the Montagues and Capulets was a series of back-and-forth _____ for wrongs done in the past.
    (A) requitals
    (B) benevolence
    (C) parleys
    (D) impediments
    (E) jeopardy

27. The best of plans can go _____ if even one person doesn't do his or her job.
    (A) awry
    (B) benevolent
    (C) requited
    (D) extolled
    (E) jeopardized

28. Designers must be flexible to keep up with the _____ of the fashion world.
    (A) requitals
    (B) impediments
    (C) vicissitudes
    (D) parleys
    (E) jeopardy

29. We fear that if we cut our spending, we may _____ the growth of the company.
    (A) jeopardize
    (B) impede
    (C) litigate
    (D) parley
    (E) extol

30. The supposedly _____ nonprofit was actually a front for a money laundering ring.
    (A) awry
    (B) requited
    (C) extolled
    (D) benevolent
    (E) jeopardized

31. My lack of a driver's license was a(n) _____ to getting to where I needed to go.
    (A) jeopardy
    (B) requital
    (C) impediment
    (D) vicissitude
    (E) parley

32. After 9/11, New Yorkers _____ Mayor Rudy Giuliani's decisive response.
    (A) impeded
    (B) parleyed
    (C) jeopardized
    (D) extolled
    (E) requited

On Your Own:

Write one sentence using each word below to demonstrate your understanding of the word's meaning.

33. **jeopardize** _____

34. **benevolent** _____

35. **awry** _____

36. **requital** _____

37. **extol** _____

38. **impediment** _____

39. **parley** _____

40. **vicissitude** _____

C2 Advanced Vocabulary 19

First Impressions:
Using the example sentences below, write your own definition of each boldfaced word. Then write the letter of the definition from the box that best matches your definition.

A	adjective: cunning or skillful	**C**	verb: to present as a basis for argument
B	verb: to be enough; to be adequate or sufficient	**D**	noun: the total range of a thing

1. _____ It does not **suffice** to merely apologize; you have to mean what you say, too.

SUFFICE means: _____

2. _____ In my paper, I **posit** that Greece was a less important world power in the ancient world

than it is made out to be.

POSIT means: _____

3. _____ The magician amazed the audience with his **artful** sleight of hand.

ARTFUL means: _____

4. _____ The restaurant serves the **gamut** of American food, from hot dogs to grits.

GAMUT means: _____

A	noun: a small exclusive group	**C**	adjective: placed in or belonging in a lower rank or order; of less importance; subject to or under the authority of a superior
B	noun: a rant; a long, angry speech about a specific topic	**D**	noun: the length of time for which something lasts

5. _____ Because he was not accepted by any of the **cliques**, the first months at the new school

were very lonely for Martin.

CLIQUE means: _____

6. _____ Each **subordinate** commander is held responsible for the actions of his unit and must

report to his higher-ups.

SUBORDINATE means: _____

7. _____ Frieda shortened the **duration** of her cold by drinking lots of water.

DURATION means: _____

8. _____ I found the professor's book to be less of an objective resource and more of a **polemic**.

POLEMIC means: _____

Divide and Conquer:
Choose the correct word to complete each of the following sentences.

9. I slept through the entire **(duration / clique)** of the train ride.

10. Several faculty members formed an intellectual **(clique / gamut)**, harshly criticizing any viewpoints that they felt challenged their own.

11. Looking at my newly-born son, I felt the **(duration / gamut)** of emotions from fear to joy.

12. My father **(suffices / posits)** that if I were nicer, I'd get along better with my mom.

13. Frank Martin wrote a strongly-worded **(gamut / polemic)** against political oppression.

14. New recruits are **(subordinate / artful)** to the lieutenant, who has power over nearly every aspect of their lives.

15. A character in Oliver Twist is known as the **(Artful / Subordinate)** Dodger due to his skill as a pickpocket.

16. No account **(suffices / posits)** to fully explain what happened in Roswell, New Mexico.

Hot and Cold:
Write the word from the lesson that is most nearly the *OPPOSITE* of the boldfaced word or words in each sentence below.

17. He answered the _____ about the coming election with a **non-combative response**.

18. The general growled that _____ soldiers should not interrupt their **superior** officers.

19. One high school had a problem with _____ that would exclude specific students and isolate them socially; the other had no such problems—its students formed an **inclusive society**.

20. There was no reason for the police officer to _____ who had burned down the house, as he **deduced** who had done it.

21. The camp guards told me that the rice they had given me would _____, but I knew that it **wouldn't be enough**.

22. Sally has only learned a **portion** of hairstyling and has yet to practice the _____ of styles.

23. After Cindy's _____ explanation of what had happened, which seemingly covered every detail perfectly, I felt like a **bumbling** fool trying to clumsily explain my side of the story.

Applying Yourself:
Choose the best word to complete each of the following sentences.

24. _____ negotiation calls for diplomacy, prodding, and occasionally, a stern tone.
    (A) Subordinate
    (B) Miniscule
    (C) Artful
    (D) Posited
    (E) Sufficient

25. There have been many recent _____ published arguing both for and against the current president.
    (A) pinnacles
    (B) husks
    (C) polemics
    (D) durations
    (E) cliques

26. A simple meal of soup will _____, thank you.
    (A) matriculate
    (B) duration
    (C) suffice
    (D) dissipate
    (E) posit

27. I _____ that there is a connection between the number of birds in the area and the weather.
    (A) matriculate
    (B) suffice
    (C) polemic
    (D) posit
    (E) dissipate

28. David broke his toe during the first dance sequence and limped for the _____ of the show.
    (A) clique
    (B) gamut
    (C) duration
    (D) polemic
    (E) subordination

29. When our competitor assumed control of our department, John, the former director, was made _____ to Tim, his new boss.
    (A) artful
    (B) miniscule
    (C) sufficient
    (D) subordinate
    (E) posited

30. It seemed as though the _____ only felt secure in its uniform and exclusionary tactics.
    (A) gamut
    (B) polemic
    (C) duration
    (D) subordination
    (E) clique

31. The store held a _____ of books on every topic from fiction to math.
    (A) subordination
    (B) clique
    (C) duration
    (D) polemic
    (E) gamut

On Your Own:
Write one sentence using each word below to demonstrate your understanding of the word's meaning.

32. **gamut** _____

33. **posit** _____

34. **duration** _____

35. **polemic** _____

36. **clique** _____

37. **artful** _____

38. **suffice** _____

39. **subordinate** _____

C2 Advanced Vocabulary 20

First Impressions:

Using the example sentences below, write your own definition of each boldfaced word. Then write the letter of the definition from the box that best matches your definition.

A	verb: to impress at the first glance	**C**	noun: a special feature that adds value or comfort
B	noun: extra payment granted above what is typical; gratuity or tip	**D**	adjective: green; full of growing plants

1. _____ The landscapers were given a **perquisite** for their unusually excellent work on the garden.

PERQUISITE means: _____

2. _____ Community members contributed to turn the ugly, brown, empty lot into a **verdant** garden.

VERDANT means: _____

3. _____ The apartment complex offered several **amenities**, including a workout room and a swimming pool.

AMENITY means: _____

4. _____ Kaelyn's impressive resume would **prepossess** potential employers before she set foot in an office for an interview.

PREPOSSESS means: _____

A	adjective: showing gentleness or kindness; not harmful	**C**	noun: something unusual or out of the ordinary
B	noun: a lack of something	**D**	noun: style of speaking or writing; word choice; enunciation

5. _____ Clear **diction** is essential in professional writing, as improper word usage will create a poor impression of the author.

DICTION means: _____

6. _____ A **dearth** of available capital greatly slowed the growth of the economy.

DEARTH means: _____

7. _____ The doctors were worried about an **anomaly** they found on my x-ray, saying that such an unusual mass might indicate cancer.

ANOMALY means: _____

8. _____ Aaron nearly passed out in relief when the tests proved that his tumor was **benign**.

BENIGN means: _____

Divide and Conquer:

Choose the correct word to complete each of the following sentences.

9. One of the **(amenities / anomalies)** of the job was a period of three weeks of paid vacation.

10. If new waiters work hard, their incomes will balloon with the **(perquisites / dearth)** granted for outstanding service.

11. With her confident stride and immaculate dress, Stacy **(prepossessed / rebuked)** her prospective employers, who offered her a job.

12. Our unit parachuted into an isolated clearing of the **(benign / verdant)** forest, trees and thick vegetation obscuring our view to only ten meters in.

13. Because Jack was the last in his class to choose a subject for the project, there was a(n) **(dearth / amenity)** of interesting topics available.

14. Not only does the dog play harmlessly with Maria's children—it is **(anomalous / benign)** to complete strangers as well.

15. A(n) **(anomaly / diction)** in Cindy's behavior indicated that she was feeling off-the-mark.

16. The overall effect of the speech was highly effective, though a few quirks in **(diction / amenity)** made individual sentences confusing.

Hot and Cold:

Write the word from the lesson that is most nearly the *OPPOSITE* of the boldfaced word or words in each sentence below.

17. One of the **disadvantages** of this car, which I believe is larger than any of its exciting _____, is that we can't even afford it.

18. I was _____ by the woman's confident air and generous smile, but **unimpressed** by her extremely expensive shoes.

19. This **barren and lifeless** landscape will be a(n) _____, beautiful riot of color and life come springtime.

20. Dressed as an old beggar, the **malignant** queen put on a falsely _____ countenance to trick Snow White into taking a poisoned apple.

21. Last year, while business was good, we received a substantial _____ at the end of our year, just in time to pay for Christmas gifts; this year, we received a **deduction** instead, supposedly due to "significant company burden".

22. The **typical** winter weather was marked by a(n) _____ of a sunny day.

23. We hoped that the **excess** of delicious food at the party would make up for the _____ of dessert; we simply couldn't find a cake-maker who was available to provide sweets in time.

Applying Yourself:

Choose the best word to complete each of the following sentences.

24. A blizzard in June would be something of a(n) _____.
    - (A) anomaly
    - (B) dearth
    - (C) amenity
    - (D) perquisite
    - (E) diction

25. Visitors to the U.S. often consider the hefty 20% tip at restaurants to be an obnoxious _____.
    - (A) perquisite
    - (B) anomaly
    - (C) amenity
    - (D) dearth
    - (E) diction

26. The rain forest, with its enormous trees, flowering plants, and vibrant colors was the essence of _____ terrain.
    (A) agnostic
    (B) prepossessed
    (C) benign
    (D) anomalous
    (E) verdant

27. A(n) _____ of collected taxes has caused the Greek economy to spiral into recession.
    (A) diction
    (B) anomaly
    (C) perquisite
    (D) dearth
    (E) amenity

28. The cysts require no treatment and are entirely _____ in nature.
    (A) anomalous
    (B) prepossessed
    (C) benign
    (D) verdant
    (E) agnostic

29. The writer's _____ doesn't reflect the vocabulary of people in the time or place of his story.
    (A) perquisite
    (B) dearth
    (C) diction
    (D) amenity
    (E) anomaly

30. The hotel was replete with _____, including a pool, a spa, and free breakfast.
    (A) anomaly
    (B) diction
    (C) amenities
    (D) dearth
    (E) perquisites

31. Hashim _____ his interviewer with his sharp suit and knowledge about the company.
    (A) prepossessed
    (B) sequestered
    (C) precluded
    (D) collaborated
    (E) litigated

On Your Own:

Write one sentence using each word below to demonstrate your understanding of the word's meaning.

32. **perquisite** _____

33. **dearth** _____

34. **diction** _____

35. **amenity** _____

36. **anomaly** _____

37. **verdant** _____

38. **prepossess** _____

39. **benign** _____

C2 Advanced Vocabulary 21

First Impressions:

Using the example sentences below, write your own definition of each boldfaced word. Then write the letter of the definition from the box that best matches your definition.

A	noun: a preoccupation with physical comforts and things	**C**	noun: seriousness
B	adjective: excited; moving quickly	**D**	noun: a person who spends extravagantly or wastefully

1. _____ You should spend more time considering your options; the **gravity** of the situation cannot be overestimated.

GRAVITY means: _____

2. _____ The religious Amish are most well-known for their rejection of technology and other common luxuries that might promote **materialism**.

MATERIALISM means: _____

3. _____ Mikhail was an utter **spendthrift**; it seemed that any money that entered his hands slipped back out a few moments later.

SPENDTHRIFT means: _____

4. _____ The old dog grew **animated** and seemed five years younger when we introduced a new puppy into the house.

ANIMATED means: _____

A	adjective: having an offensive odor; stinking	**C**	adjective: not skilled; incompetent
B	adjective: bulky; large	**D**	verb: to begin; to originate; to receive into a group

5. _____ After it had lain hidden behind the radiator for three weeks, the missing Easter egg emitted an odor that could only be described as **fetid**.

FETID means: _____

6. _____ Lucas is an **inept** carpenter whose creations always fall apart.

INEPT means: _____

7. _____ Michelle's puffy winter coat was so **voluminous** that she almost feared becoming lost inside of it.

VOLUMINOUS means: _____

8. _____ To break the awkward silence, Aman tried to **initiate** a conversation.

INITIATE means: _____

Divide and Conquer:

Choose the correct word to complete each of the following sentences.

9. Jimmy had been a(n) **(inept / voluminous)** dancer, but, after years of practice, he became quite competent.

10. Dana's **(ineptitude / materialism)** led to an overstuffed closet and a depleted bank account.

11. **(Voluminous / Inept)** railcars dotted the shipping yard, waiting to be loaded with the relief supplies for an entire nation.

12. Dasiah leapt back with an **(initiated / animated)** wiggle when her friends jumped out and yelled "Surprise!"

13. The team decided to **(initiate / animate)** a new tradition of weekly meetings to discuss any problems or concerns.

14. A(n) **(fetid / animated)** smell drifted from the open door of the refrigerator that had been shut off for three weeks.

15. "As the federal deficit continues to rise year after year," the politician said, "we have to ask ourselves what sort of **(spendthrifts / gravity)** we have representing us."

16. The **(spendthrift / gravity)** of the situation was so great that a national crisis was declared.

Hot and Cold:

Write the word from the lesson that is most nearly the *OPPOSITE* of the boldfaced word or words in each sentence below.

17. The **fragrant** smell of the blooming garden in spring must compete with the _____ stench of the cow's dung that fertilizes it.

18. Revolutionaries _____ democracy in the formerly feudal region while a cruel and oppressive dictator **ended** it.

19. Seeing many upset faces, Tim tried to alleviate the _____ of the situation by injecting some jokes and **levity** into his speech.

20. Marjory is a(n) _____ office assistant, but she makes a **skilled** driver.

21. While my business was successful I was quite the _____, lavishing myself and others with expensive (and needless) gifts, but now that we're nearly bankrupt, I've become quite the **penny-pincher**.

22. The monk believed that _____ led one to cling to money, career, and other aspects of life that he viewed as antithetical **to spiritual devotion**.

23. Lydia seemed tired and **sluggish** when surrounded by her young, _____ cousins.

24. The _____ fabric, large enough to serve as a circus tent, dwarfed the **miniscule** ballerina inside the costume.

Applying Yourself:

Choose the best word to complete each of the following sentences.

25. In the fall, he is going to _____ a new course of study, starting with a class in biochemistry.
    (A) initiate
    (B) proselytize
    (C) blandish
    (D) disparage
    (E) animate

26. A _____ must amend her ways if she is to endure these tough economic times.
    (A) spendthrift
    (B) initiation
    (C) materialist
    (D) ineptitude
    (E) gravity

27. Those who live near bogs must endure the scent of _____, rotting vegetation.
    (A) initiated
    (B) fetid
    (C) voluminous
    (D) materialistic
    (E) animated

28. I often think that Christmas has morphed from a celebration of family into a hallmark of costly _____.
    (A) materialism
    (B) spendthrift
    (C) gravity
    (D) ineptitude
    (E) volume

29. Our family could do without a(n) _____ house; instead, let's buy a smaller one with character.
    (A) initiated
    (B) voluminous
    (C) fetid
    (D) animated
    (E) inept

30. Disabuse yourself of your frivolous notions; at times such as these, we must look to the _____ of the situation with all seriousness.
    (A) gravity
    (B) materialism
    (C) volume
    (D) spendthrift
    (E) ineptitude

31. He talked in a(n) _____ way, always moving his hands and barely keeping his voice down.
    (A) fetid
    (B) initiated
    (C) materialistic
    (D) inept
    (E) animated

32. No one was surprised when his _____ attempt to repair the television failed completely.
    (A) inept
    (B) animated
    (C) voluminous
    (D) initiated
    (E) fetid

On Your Own:

Write one sentence using each word below to demonstrate your understanding of the word's meaning.

33. **fetid** _____

34. **materialism** _____

35. **animated** _____

36. **gravity** _____

37. **spendthrift** _____

38. **inept** _____

39. **initiate** _____

40. **voluminous** _____

C2 Advanced Vocabulary 22

First Impressions:

Using the example sentences below, write your own definition of each boldfaced word. Then write the letter of the definition from the box that best matches your definition.

A	verb: to pay part of the cost of something expensive	**C**	adjective: naturally occurring in a place
B	adjective: not biased; fair	**D**	adjective: wrinkled and shrunken, especially because of age

1. _____ The **wizened** old man slowly made his way from his doorstep to the mailbox.

WIZENED means: _____

2. _____ Olympic judges must be **impartial** when evaluating athletes.

IMPARTIAL means: _____

3. _____ The fast-growing Japanese vine kudzu is considered a pest in many parts of the United

States, as the transplanted species competes with and wipes out many plants **endemic** to the area.

ENDEMIC means: _____

4. _____ Mr. Lowell offered to give his daughter $1000 to help **defray** the cost of her first car.

DEFRAY means: _____

A	adjective: digressing; rambling; going off the subject	**C**	adjective: multiple; diverse; large in number
B	noun: a period of very low activity during a warm season	**D**	noun: an introduction, usually to a book or article

5. _____ At the candy shop, we faced **myriad** types of candy to choose from.

MYRIAD means: _____

6. _____ The African lungfish undergoes **estivation** during hot, dry seasons, lying inactive below a

dried stream bed for months until the waters return.

ESTIVATION means: _____

7. _____ The leader, known for **discursive** speeches that last hours, made a revolutionary move

on Wednesday by using a web service that limits messages to 140 characters.

DISCURSIVE means: _____

8. _____ The book's **preface** was written by the author and explained the novel's complex themes.

PREFACE means: _____

Divide and Conquer:
Choose the correct word to complete each of the following sentences.

9. The students sold cookies and popcorn to **(defray / preface)** the cost of the field trip.

10. It became obvious that the debate tournament judge had failed to be **(impartial / defrayed)** and let his personal beliefs in the debate subject cloud his decision when picking the winner.

11. There are **(wizened / myriad)** stars in the clear night sky.

12. The **(discursive / defrayed)** treatment of the topic led to lectures that were interesting but very long.

13. The **(myriad / preface)** to the novel explains that it was written in the span of only eight weeks.

14. The greater siren, an eel-like amphibian, undergoes occasional periods of **(preface / estivation)** during which it lies encased in a cocoon of mucus until the rains return.

15. We installed handrails in the first floor of the house when we learned our **(myriad / wizened)** grandmother would be living with us.

16. Before traveling overseas Dr. Ford had several vaccinations to protect against infections **(impartial / endemic)** to the rainforest.

Hot and Cold:
Write the word from the lesson that is most nearly the *OPPOSITE* of the boldfaced word or words in each sentence below.

17. Readers of the reclusive author's newest novel were confused, as he claimed different things about the book in his **afterword** than he did in his _____.

18. There are _____ ways to meet people, but only a **few** ways to keep in touch with the thousands of people you meet.

19. While this certain disease is _____ to the area, there's an **exogenic** virus, brought in by settlers, that has worsened its effects tenfold since the population has no natural immunity against it.

20. The insurance company promised to _____ the cost of my leg surgery, but in the end, they **foisted** the entire cost onto my family.

21. Grandfather's _____ face, lined with worry-lines and scars, seemed all the more ancient next to the fresh, **young** face of the little baby.

22. The professor's _____ lectures, constantly wandering off the subject at hand, made it difficult for students to take **concise** notes.

23. Though Randy tried to be _____ while settling disputes between his children, one of them usually accused him of being **unfair**.

Applying Yourself:
Choose the best word to complete each of the following sentences.

24. It will take me years to read the _____ books that line my bookshelf.
    - (A) prefaced
    - (B) myriad
    - (C) wizened
    - (D) discursive
    - (E) defrayed

25. The _____ of a book is a chance for the author to state his feelings about the book before it begins.
    - (A) defrayment
    - (B) impartiality
    - (C) dilettante
    - (D) estivation
    - (E) preface

26. If our judicial system were not _____, we would have many innocent people imprisoned for bad reasons.
    (A) defrayed
    (B) wizened
    (C) impartial
    (D) endemic
    (E) myriad

27. I wish to _____ the cost of my mother's purchase by paying half the balance by this time next year.
    (A) defray
    (B) sequester
    (C) preface
    (D) emigrate
    (E) inaugurate

28. Long delays are _____ to the road between Nirobi and Dodoma; truckers must often wait for several hours at the border while papers are processed.
    (A) impartial
    (B) myriad
    (C) wizened
    (D) defrayed
    (E) endemic

29. Yoda, a(n) _____ 900-year-old, shared the secrets of the Force with his apprentice.
    (A) myriad
    (B) wizened
    (C) defrayed
    (D) endemic
    (E) prefaced

30. His conversation was _____, starting with one topic and quickly moving onto the next.
    (A) wizened
    (B) myriad
    (C) endemic
    (D) defrayed
    (E) discursive

31. _____ overcame us during last year's heat wave, and we accomplished little for three days.
    (A) Dilettante
    (B) Defrayment
    (C) Impartiality
    (D) Estivation
    (E) Preface

On Your Own:
Write one sentence using each word below to demonstrate your understanding of the word's meaning.

32. **impartial** _____

33. **defray** _____

34. **endemic** _____

35. **preface** _____

36. **estivation** _____

37. **myriad** _____

38. **wizened** _____

39. **discursive** _____

C2 Advanced Vocabulary 23

First Impressions:

Using the example sentences below, write your own definition of each boldfaced word. Then write the letter of the definition from the box that best matches your definition.

A	verb: defamation; utterance of false and malicious statements	**C**	verb: to settle a disagreement by acting as a third party
B	noun: something that comes before and shows that another thing is approaching	**D**	adjective: strict about rules, manners, or ethics

1. _____ After failing to reach an agreement after a long debate, the students asked a teacher to **mediate** between them.

MEDIATE means: _____

2. _____ A professional lawyer must be extremely **punctilious**, as any minor violation of ethics will drastically impact his or her reputation.

PUNCTILIOUS means: _____

3. _____ The light drizzle on the rooftop was only a **precursor** to the heavy storm yet to come.

PRECURSOR means: _____

4. _____ Though the accusations were false, Aditya's reputation never recovered from the **slander**.

SLANDER means: _____

A	adjective: overpowering; having an irresistible effect	**C**	adjective: aggressive; savage and harsh
B	adjective: not easily changed; uncontrollable or unruly	**D**	noun: an argument or fight, usually in public

5. _____ Long-term pollution could have an **incorrigible** effect on wildlife, causing widespread birth defects and population decline for years to come.

INCORRIGIBLE means: _____

6. _____ Sergio and Frank were suspended for having a physical **altercation** in front of their school and were forced to apologize to each other.

ALTERCATION means: _____

7. _____ Although Mrs. Flamur wanted to believe her son, the presence of his baseball in all that broken glass was **compelling** evidence that it really had been he who had broken the window.

COMPELLING means: _____

8. _____ Expecting a verbal battle with several **truculent** youths, Mr. Bharathan was pleasantly surprised to find that his new students were quite easy-going and pleasant.

TRUCULENT means: _____

Divide and Conquer:

Choose the correct word to complete each of the following sentences.

9. Commentators must be careful to stick only to the facts when discussing specific politicians so as to avoid becoming guilty of **(altercation / slander)**.

10. The **(truculent / punctilious)** sports fans shouted loud insults as the opposing team passed by.

11. The Marine Corps relies upon the **(mediating / punctilious)** soldier who would never put his own interests above the regulations of the unit.

12. Although Blake was on a diet, the sight of the decadent brownie was too **(compelling / incorrigible)** for him to resist.

13. The **(altercation / precursor)** between the employee and customer was caught on tape, so it was impossible to hide who had started it.

14. Despite the headmistress's many efforts to reform Juliet, she remained **(incorrigible / punctilious)**.

15. The audience howled in appreciation as the trailer for the new film appeared, knowing that the short clip served as a **(mediation / precursor)** for the entire film.

16. A lawyer was called in to **(mediate / compel)** the dispute.

Hot and Cold:

Write the word from the lesson that is most nearly the *OPPOSITE* of the boldfaced word or words in each sentence below.

17. Numbness in the feet, one of the _____ to diabetes and an earlier indicator of problematic health, is a **result** of poor circulation.

18. Chandra's speech was rather _____ and had us all eager to follow the course of action she prescribed; it was much better than the **uninteresting** speeches we usually heard at these conferences.

19. A series of peace-making **reconciliations** has done little to reduce the number of _____ between gang members.

20. Praise, and not _____, will win you **friends** at your new post.

21. The **careless** custodian was replaced by a more _____ caretaker who would be sure that every sanitation regulation was followed.

22. We hoped Grandma's presence would help _____ the tension between the sides of the family, but it turned out that her presence only seemed to **exacerbate** everyone's temper.

23. The two kittens couldn't have been more different in temperament; Tiger, always _____, refused to learn to use his litter box, while the **obedient** Sage learned from the first time we showed her where she ought to go.

24. One _____ chimpanzee often started vicious fights with the more **peaceful** and cooperative members of his family.

Applying Yourself:

Choose the best word to complete each of the following sentences.

25. _____ warriors chased us through the hills, intent on sacrificing us to their god.
    (A) Mediated
    (B) Slandered
    (C) Truculent
    (D) Punctilious
    (E) Incorrigible

26. The author's argument that Shakespeare had written none of his famous plays, while probably false, was _____ enough to warrant more research.
    (A) truculent
    (B) compelling
    (C) incorrigible
    (D) slandered
    (E) mediated

27. Protests in the street were _____ to the broader revolution.
    (A) sagacity
    (B) mediation
    (C) slander
    (D) altercations
    (E) precursors

28. You can choose how to speak, but _____ against an honest man will only hurt both your reputations.
    (A) slander
    (B) precursor
    (C) mediation
    (D) altercation
    (E) sagacity

29. Cato the Younger, _____ to the end, required that a lesser general lead the fight against Julius Caesar because the Roman constitution demanded it.
    (A) punctilious
    (B) truculent
    (C) compelling
    (D) mediated
    (E) slandered

30. Because he had been spoiled all his life, Cindy's child had become _____, especially when it was time to clean his room.
    (A) slandered
    (B) mediated
    (C) incorrigible
    (D) truculent
    (E) punctilious

31. As the tension between the union and ownership heightened, the governor stepped in to _____ the dispute.
    (A) slander
    (B) mediate
    (C) matriculate
    (D) scintillate
    (E) compel

32. They got into a(n) _____ in a crowded bar and were both arrested as a result.
    (A) precursor
    (B) sagacity
    (C) altercation
    (D) slander
    (E) mediation

On Your Own:
Write one sentence using each word below to demonstrate your understanding of the word's meaning.

33. **precursor** _____

34. **altercation** _____

35. **incorrigible** _____

36. **punctilious** _____

37. **mediate** _____

38. **slander** _____

39. **compelling** _____

40. **truculent** _____

C2 Advanced Vocabulary 24

First Impressions:

Using the example sentences below, write your own definition of each boldfaced word. Then write the letter of the definition from the box that best matches your definition.

A	verb: to scold; to express strong disapproval	**C**	adjective: without proper manners or standards of politeness
B	noun: intended to belittle or criticize	**D**	adjective: unresisting; patiently submissive

1. _____ The child's **pejorative** comments, intended to hurt her little brother, earned her a sharp scolding from her mother.

PEJORATIVE means: _____

2. _____ He gave a **resigned** sigh, accepting the terrible lot he'd been given.

RESIGNED means: _____

3. _____ Rosa was harshly **rebuked** for her failure to give the dog water on such a hot day.

REBUKE means: _____

4. _____ The **crass** young woman wasn't invited back to the house for dinner, since her poor manners didn't sit well with the family.

CRASS means: _____

A	adjective: able to be maintained or defended against attack or objection; able to be used or held	**C**	noun: shrewdness, astuteness
B	adjective: exceedingly idealistic; unrealistic and impractical	**D**	adjective: silly and pointless

5. _____ I found many of the author's arguments to be rather **fatuous**, and so I was not able to take his book seriously.

FATUOUS means: _____

6. _____ The **perspicacity** of the investor allowed him to correctly choose profitable companies again and again.

PERSPICACITY means: _____

7. _____ My little brother's **quixotic** dreams probably won't last past middle school, but I try to encourage him anyway.

QUIXOTIC means: _____

8. _____ Unable to hold their position against the overwhelming forces, the captain ordered the troops to fall back to a more **tenable** position.

TENABLE means: _____

Divide and Conquer:

Choose the correct word to complete each of the following sentences.

9. The **(quixotic / crass)** students embarrassed the teacher with impolite questions.

10. **(Resigned / Pejorative)** speech of any kind will not be tolerated, as this is intended to be a space safe from criticism or hurtful words.

11. Rome's construction on a series of hills was ideal because it made the city **(tenable / quixotic)** even in the face of barbarian armies.

12. Manheim found the children's cartoon to be entirely **(fatuous / resigned)** and decided to spend his time on what he considered more important matters.

13. Some called her ideas **(pejorative / quixotic)**, but Margerie's "pay what you want" bakery has been quite successful.

14. Charles' **(resignation / perspicacity)** had allowed him to come up with plans to fit all potential contingencies.

15. Rather than praise me for my original thought, my team leader **(resigned / rebuked)** me for challenging her authority.

16. She told them in a **(resigned / pejorative)** voice that, since she had no power to hold them, they were free to go.

Hot and Cold:

Write the word from the lesson that is most nearly the *OPPOSITE* of the boldfaced word or words in each sentence below.

17. Juan's _____ jokes weren't fit for **polite** company.

18. Due to his sly smile, I couldn't tell if Ray's words were supposed to be **complimentary**, as they sounded, or rudely _____.

19. After much consideration, I decided my thesis was not _____ as it had too many weak points by which it could be **dismantled**; I revised it to make it more defensible.

20. Rinus was _____ by his friends and family, who did not **approve** of his getting involved in the notorious gang.

21. The _____ of this business plan is very impressive and indicative of a high level of mastery and the promise of success; it's far superior to the **short-sighted** and dull write-ups we've been reading.

22. Students must be **realistic**, not _____ about their chances for college acceptance; otherwise, they may be disappointed.

23. With a _____ sigh, the tired and overwhelmed teacher gave in to her students' passionately **determined** efforts to secure an extension on their papers.

24. Mother said my feelings for Annie were the result of a _____ obsession; she said it'd be more **practical** to pursue Margene, who was much more like me.

Applying Yourself:

Choose the best word to complete each of the following sentences.

25. Everett's _____ behavior at the dinner table made the others eating with him uncomfortable.
    - (A) quixotic
    - (B) crass
    - (C) pejorative
    - (D) tenable
    - (E) fatuous

26. The _____ old man thought that the windmills were giants and attacked them with a long spear.
    - (A) crass
    - (B) pejorative
    - (C) tenable
    - (D) quixotic
    - (E) fatuous

27. Fischer moved his bishop centrally to create a _____ position against his opponent's attack.
    (A) tenable
    (B) pejorative
    (C) fatuous
    (D) quixotic
    (E) crass

28. Richard Nixon endured a strong _____ from Congress due to his role in concealing the Watergate scandal.
    (A) resignation
    (B) pejorative
    (C) corollary
    (D) rebuke
    (E) malediction

29. I was shocked to learn that what I thought was a neutral term was actually often used as a hurtfully _____ slang word.
    (A) perspicacity
    (B) tenable
    (C) pejorative
    (D) fatuous
    (E) crass

30. _____ is essential when determining what possible consequences a policy will have.
    (A) Resignation
    (B) Malediction
    (C) Pejorative
    (D) Corollary
    (E) Perspicacity

31. His _____ look signaled that there would be no further objections to the dangerous plan.
    (A) tenable
    (B) pejorative
    (C) resigned
    (D) quixotic
    (E) crass

32. Children, while full of wonder and developing intelligence, can at the same time be _____ and crazy when given a dose of sugar.
    (A) crass
    (B) fatuous
    (C) pejorative
    (D) quixotic
    (E) rebuked

On Your Own:
Write one sentence using each word below to demonstrate your understanding of the word's meaning.

33. **resigned** _____

34. **quixotic** _____

35. **rebuke** _____

36. **pejorative** _____

37. **fatuous** _____

38. **tenable** _____

39. **crass** _____

40. **perspicacity** _____

C2 Advanced Vocabulary 25

First Impressions:

Using the example sentences below, write your own definition of each boldfaced word. Then write the letter of the definition from the box that best matches your definition.

A	verb: to say aloud for recording; to give orders	**C**	noun: a firmly held belief
B	adjective: utter; complete; total	**D**	noun: offense or annoyance

1. _____ Haeyoung took **umbrage** to Richard's disrespectful comments.

UMBRAGE means: _____

2. _____ It was amazing that Christie was never considered dishonest despite the fact that she told

outright lies often.

OUTRIGHT means: _____

3. _____ Michaela has deep **convictions** that all children should attend preschool for proper

cognitive development and socialization.

CONVICTION means: _____

4. _____ The chairwoman **dictated** the fundraising letter as her secretary diligently wrote down

every word.

DICTATE means: _____

A	adjective: light; heavenly; unusually refined	**C**	verb: to mock through parody
B	adjective: immature; lacking experience	**D**	verb: to approach or confront boldly

5. _____ Though his first novel was disappointingly **jejune**, by his third attempt the novelist had

developed a strong, mature voice.

JEJUNE means: _____

6. _____ Mr. Stephenson was offended at having been **accosted** by a complete stranger as he

walked to work.

ACCOST means: _____

7. _____ Witnesses to **ethereal** apparitions usually say they saw an angel or an alien spaceship.

ETHEREAL means: _____

8. _____ The comedian **lampooned** popular works of fiction with humorous skits titled "Lord of the

Onion Rings" and "Hairy Potter and the Sorcerer's Comb".

LAMPOON means: _____

Divide and Conquer:
Choose the correct word to complete each of the following sentences.

9. I speak with the (dictation / conviction) of someone who has examined her beliefs thoroughly and truly feels they are worth fighting for.

10. The film "Murder by Death" (lampoons / accosts) every clichéd trope of detective fiction to great comedic effect.

11. The firm made an (ethereal / outright) offer to buy me away from the company for which I currently work.

12. The police officer (accosted / lampooned) a man staggering down the street drunkenly, demanding to see his identification.

13. The students quickly wrote as their foreign language teacher (dictated / convicted) an exercise.

14. The CEO enjoyed reading the (dictated / jejune) imaginings in his old journals to see how much he had grown over the years.

15. The fog, illuminated by the street lights, gave the street an (ethereal / accosted) quality.

16. For a marriage to work, both parties cannot take (dictation / umbrage) at every minor idiosyncrasy.

Hot and Cold:
Write the word from the lesson that is most nearly the *OPPOSITE* of the boldfaced word or words in each sentence below.

17. I wish I hadn't agreed to the **partial** sale and had instead bought the house _____.

18. The high school poet's work seemed _____ to the experienced reader, but it was at least apparent that what the writer lacked in skill she could make up for with practice and eventually produce more **advanced** works.

19. It was strange to see someone _____ the old and widely-respected professor, whom most of us **revered** and would never dare mock.

20. We expected the president to _____ a message for us to write down and present at the press conference, but he **remained silent** and insisted he had nothing to say on the matter.

21. I took _____ with the fact that mother accused me of seeking only **pleasure** and joy when I should be facing the "facts of life"; she doesn't know me at all!

22. Always a pious dreamer, Ken seemed to be much more concerned with _____ matters, like the soul, than with **earthly** problems, like taking out the trash.

23. I'm sure a celebrity would much rather be **ignored** and treated like any other person than constantly _____ by aggressive fans on the street.

24. Even a protestor who seems to brim with _____ might experience serious **doubt**.

Applying Yourself:
Choose the best word to complete each of the following sentences.

25. The paparazzi _____ the celebrity after he emerged from the courtroom.
    (A) dictated
    (B) lampooned
    (C) dawdled
    (D) accosted
    (E) convicted

26. He ran for office to make sure that his _____ were represented in the government.
    (A) demagogues
    (B) dictations
    (C) umbrages
    (D) convictions
    (E) lampoons

27. Our orders _____ that we attack at dawn, so get ready.
    (A) lampoon
    (B) dawdle
    (C) dictate
    (D) accost
    (E) convict

28. *Scary Movie* is a(n) _____ of the ridiculous clichés common in more serious horror films.
    (A) demagogue
    (B) conviction
    (C) umbrage
    (D) lampoon
    (E) dictation

29. After the funeral, the family looked up at the night sky, imagining that the bright starlight reflected the _____ quality of Mom's spirit.
    (A) jejune
    (B) outright
    (C) ethereal
    (D) accosted
    (E) convicted

30. It's often better to buy a car _____ instead of paying for it in installments that gather interest.
    (A) jejune
    (B) ethereal
    (C) outright
    (D) accosted
    (E) convicted

31. Ming takes _____ against anyone who would unfairly soil her reputation.
    (A) dictation
    (B) umbrage
    (C) conviction
    (D) demagogue
    (E) lampoon

32. Just wait until the _____ team has a few more seasons under its belt; it will be a juggernaut.
    (A) convicted
    (B) lampooned
    (C) ethereal
    (D) jejune
    (E) accosted

On Your Own:

Write one sentence using each word below to demonstrate your understanding of the word's meaning.

33. **dictate** _____

34. **conviction** _____

35. **accost** _____

36. **outright** _____

37. **jejune** _____

38. **lampoon** _____

39. **ethereal** _____

40. **umbrage** _____

C2 Advanced Vocabulary 26

First Impressions:
Using the example sentences below, write your own definition of each boldfaced word. Then write the letter of the definition from the box that best matches your definition.

A	noun: lack of movement or change	**C**	adjective: occurring one after the other
B	noun: someone or something strongly upholding certain beliefs or principles; a feature of a fortress	**D**	verb: to praise

1. _____ The senator will be in town on Thursday to publicly **laud** the district's upgrade of a wastewater treatment plant.

LAUD means: _____

2. _____ I worked 20 hours for three **consecutive** days and was exhausted by the end.

CONSECUTIVE means: _____

3. _____ After Joanne graduated from college, her intellectual life entered a brief period of **stagnation** as she took on a dull job to pay her student loans.

STAGNATION means: _____

4. _____ Mrs. Wicks was the last **bastion** of students' rights at the school; her colleagues all treated young people like cattle to be moved along without incident.

BASTION means: _____

A	adjective: wasteful; reckless with money	**C**	verb: to distribute a collected resource among several parties
B	verb: to prove or demonstrate	**D**	verb: to reason without strong evidence; to guess

5. _____ Shannon had always been a **prodigal** spender; it seemed like she never had any money left at the end of the month.

PRODIGAL means: _____

6. _____ The board voted about how best to **allocate** the funds of the homeowner's association.

ALLOCATE means: _____

7. _____ Until we gather more data, we can only **surmise** the cause of the disturbance.

SURMISE means: _____

8. _____ He **evinced** an aptitude for chess during his early childhood.

EVINCE means: _____

Divide and Conquer:
Choose the correct word to complete each of the following sentences.

9. The parable of the **(prodigal / stagnant)** son tells the story of a young man who wastes all the money of his inheritance before returning home to his father, humble and repentant.

10. We **(evinced / surmised)** that Alli's lateness was due to her car, which appeared unreliable.

11. Many saw the bill as the last **(bastion / stagnation)** of defense of the controversial policy.

12. Jorge's impressive batting average **(lauds / evinces)** his dedication to practicing the fundamentals of baseball.

13. The board **(evinced / lauded)** the performance of the Vice President in successfully finding a solution to the crisis.

14. Because the fault line in New Jersey has demonstrated such **(allocation / stagnation)** over the last century, some seismologists predict a large earthquake soon.

15. The leader of the guild of beggars **(evinced / allocated)** a portion of the day's bread to each of the children.

16. The concerts were planned on **(consecutive / evinced)** days, so the band had to move very quickly from one city to the next.

Hot and Cold:
Write the word from the lesson that is most nearly the *OPPOSITE* of the boldfaced word or words in each sentence below.

17. In order to avoid _____, be sure to make positive **changes** in your life and commit yourself to new and rewarding challenges.

18. Ever _____ with his earnings, Rudolph will never be able to save as much money as his more **thrifty** brothers.

19. While the professor _____ that her student was failing due to problems at home, it was impossible to **conclude** without having a serious conversation with her.

20. The committee will discuss how to _____ funds to the individual departments and in what manner they will **collect** and analyze data from those departments.

21. Lisa preferred her college classes to be _____ rather than **dispersed** throughout the day.

22. The small, democratic nation was the _____ of freedom on the area, while the large area to the north was the region's **weak point** of personal liberty.

23. I tried to **conceal** the fact that I was laughing at him, but my smirk _____ my feelings.

24. I wished to _____ Craig for his several achievements this year, but my words must have come out wrong because he said all I ever do is **criticize** him.

Applying Yourself:
Choose the best word to complete each of the following sentences.

25. The Dutch, in trying to discover a northeast passage to Asia, _____ that a river or narrow sea would lead them through North America.
    - (A) lauded
    - (B) allocated
    - (C) evinced
    - (D) surmised
    - (E) stagnated

26. Lest you raise a(n) _____ child, you should make sure to bestow money only as a reward to show the value of a dollar.
    - (A) laudable
    - (B) evinced
    - (C) prodigal
    - (D) stagnated
    - (E) allocated

27. The trail lawyer masterfully _____ that her client had a solid alibi the night of the murder.
    (A) surmised
    (B) allocated
    (C) evinced
    (D) lauded
    (E) stagnated

28. Long a _____ of conservative politics, Indianapolis has, in recent years, established enclaves of liberalism.
    (A) surmise
    (B) laceration
    (C) skirmish
    (D) debauchery
    (E) bastion

29. Don't _____ me just yet; you haven't seen the negative aspects of what I've done.
    (A) laud
    (B) surmise
    (C) evince
    (D) allocate
    (E) stagnate

30. The division heads have _____ the general travel fund to meet the needs of all the traveling sales representatives.
    (A) surmised
    (B) evinced
    (C) allocated
    (D) lauded
    (E) stagnated

31. She was grateful for her job, but was displeased with the _____ of her place in the company, hoping as she had been for a promotion.
    (A) stagnation
    (B) laceration
    (C) bastion
    (D) debauchery
    (E) allocation

32. After six _____ losses, the coach decided that he might need a new strategy.
    (A) allocated
    (B) lauded
    (C) consecutive
    (D) prodigal
    (E) surmised

On Your Own:

Write one sentence using each word below to demonstrate your understanding of the word's meaning.

33. **prodigal** _____

34. **surmise** _____

35. **evince** _____

36. **consecutive** _____

37. **bastion** _____

38. **stagnation** _____

39. **laud** _____

40. **allocate** _____

C2 Advanced Vocabulary 27

First Impressions:

Using the example sentences below, write your own definition of each boldfaced word. Then write the letter of the definition from the box that best matches your definition.

A	noun: a sacred agreement between two or more individuals	**C**	adjective: sociable
B	verb: to reduce the negative effects of something without removing the cause	**D**	verb: to prevent in the course of action

1. _____ To many Christians, baptism is a **covenant** to give up an old, sinful life and take up a new

life dedicated to God.

COVENANT means: _____

2. _____ I was following my weight-loss regimen to the letter until my progress was **stymied** by

several weeks of delicious holiday food.

STYMIE means: _____

3. _____ The medication helped to **palliate** Stefanie's pain until the dentist was available to repair

her tooth.

PALLIATE means: _____

4. _____ Holloway is still a **gregarious** character, but he has put away the joke book and party hat

and remind everyone that there is a serious-minded football manager underneath it all.

GREGARIOUS means: _____

A	verb: to assent, submit, or agree without resistance	**C**	noun: the dried shell or withered remains of a living thing
B	adjective: related to soot or smoke	**D**	verb: to sincerely or passionately suggest a course of action

5. _____ The professor **exhorted** the students to begin studying early in order to fully prepare for

the exam.

EXHORT means: _____

6. _____ **Fuliginous** clouds billowed from the barn after the cow knocked over the burning oil lamp.

FULIGINOUS means: _____

7. _____ Nathan finally **acquiesced** to his punishment when he realized that his arguing was only

making the punishment worse.

ACQUIESCE means: _____

8. _____ She peeled away the **husk** so she could boil the corn for dinner.

HUSK means: _____

Divide and Conquer:
Choose the correct word to complete each of the following sentences.

9. I can't support your budget amendment if you attempt to **(acquiesce / stymie)** my nomination.

10. Roxanne pulled her car over to the side of the highway as **(fuliginous / palliated)** clouds wafted from the hood.

11. Victims would not **(acquiesce / exhort)** to any process aimed at facilitating an amnesty for the perpetrators who had escaped justice.

12. The **(husk / covenant)** of the seed will protect it through the harsh winter so it can take root next spring.

13. Josephine enjoyed her work as a face-to-face salesperson as it gave her a chance to exercise her **(fuliginous / gregarious)** nature.

14. The property deed of each condominium unit included a **(husk / covenant)** requiring the buyer to become part of the homeowners' association.

15. The public **(exhorted / palliated)** the painful budget cuts by running a successful fundraising campaign.

16. Harold respected Michael's right to make his own decision but **(palliated / exhorted)** him to at least consider other options.

Hot and Cold:
Write the word from the lesson that is most nearly the *OPPOSITE* of the boldfaced word or words in each sentence below.

17. It was surprising to see my cousin who once was so **withdrawn** acting in such a _____ fashion.

18. The lobbyist _____ the senator to take a strong stand against global warming and not to **show lukewarm enthusiasm** for environmental protection measures.

19. We will never _____; we will **fight** until we can win!

20. The opposed congressman hoped that _____ the discussion within the Capitol would **facilitate** his own ends.

21. The opiates my doctor prescribed _____ the pain of getting my wisdom teeth removed, but **worsened** the pain in my stomach until I was on the verge of vomiting.

Applying Yourself:
Choose the best word to complete each of the following sentences.

22. To me, our agreement was more than implicit; it was a(n) _____ designed to last a lifetime.
    (A) exhortation
    (B) husk
    (C) covenant
    (D) acquiescence
    (E) sage

23. Odysseus _____ his troops to scale the wall and bring about the ruin of Troy.
    (A) palliated
    (B) exhorted
    (C) stymied
    (D) acquiesced
    (E) waned

24. Even though his twin brother was shy and disliked crowds, Hank was rather _____.
    (A) gregarious
    (B) palliated
    (C) fuliginous
    (D) stymied
    (E) exhorted

25. My opponent _____ my attack on his bishop with a well-timed move of his rook.
    (A) waned
    (B) acquiesced
    (C) palliated
    (D) stymied
    (E) exhorted

26. He seemed to have aged until he was only a _____ of the man he once was.
    (A) covenant
    (B) matrimony
    (C) volition
    (D) husk
    (E) duration

27. We saw nothing but a(n) _____ black cloud rising from the smokestacks.
    (A) gregarious
    (B) stymied
    (C) acquiesced
    (D) fuliginous
    (E) palliated

28. We used a morphine drip to _____ Mom's discomfort until the merciful end came.
    (A) exhort
    (B) palliate
    (C) mock
    (D) wane
    (E) acquiesce

29. The governor won't _____ to the budget without a further tax break for the working poor.
    (A) palliate
    (B) acquiesce
    (C) debunk
    (D) exhort
    (E) confront

On Your Own:
Write one sentence using each word below to demonstrate your understanding of the word's meaning.

30. **covenant** _____

31. **palliate** _____

32. **acquiesce** _____

33. **husk** _____

34. **stymie** _____

35. **exhort** _____

36. **fuliginous** _____

37. **gregarious** _____

C2 Advanced Vocabulary 28

First Impressions:

Using the example sentences below, write your own definition of each boldfaced word. Then write the letter of the definition from the box that best matches your definition.

A	conjunction: although	**C**	adjective: in existence; part of reality; surviving
B	verb: to loiter or dawdle; to continue; to persist	**D**	adjective: doubtful; unsettled; questionable; perplexing

1. _____ An activist who pushed for a law on parental child abduction has a **problematic** past that some say includes involvement in a kidnapping case.

PROBLEMATIC means: _____

2. _____ What little **extant** evidence we have of Sumerian culture is hard to interpret.

EXTANT means: _____

3. _____ After class ended, my friends and I would **linger** around the carpool area while we waited for our parents to come pick us up.

LINGER means: _____

4. _____ She finished her work in a slow, **albeit** correct, manner.

ALBEIT means: _____

A	adjective: irrelevant; having nothing to do with the topic of discussion	**C**	noun: something that causes a large amount of suffering
B	noun: a state of permanent employment after a probationary period	**D**	verb: to drive or move forward; to urge onward

5. _____ The small wooden car was **propelled** forward by compressed air shot out of a canister.

PROPEL means: _____

6. _____ Whether or not you like the color blue is **immaterial** to the business deal.

IMMATERIAL means: _____

7. _____ The university offered the security of **tenure** to members of the faculty who have been professors in good standing for at least six years.

TENURE means: _____

8. _____ The plague of locusts was a **scourge** on the local population as it tore through the corn harvest.

SCOURGE means: _____

Divide and Conquer:
Choose the correct word to complete each of the following sentences.

9. HIV is a **(scourge / tenure)** on the population of certain groups.

10. The house was cozy, **(albeit / and)** small.

11. Your disagreement in this matter is **(problematic / tenured)**; we need everyone's enthusiasm before we can begin.

12. Despite the 2-year standstill, the new leader was able to **(linger / propel)** the project forward.

13. An energetic go-getter, David was not one to **(tenure / linger)** in bed after his alarm rang in the morning.

14. The professor earned **(scourge / tenure)** after, as a guest lecturer, he had published five books and authored several papers.

15. All **(extant / problematic)** files that survived the fire have been stored downtown.

16. As you are not an expert in this subject area, your objections are **(scourged / immaterial)**.

Hot and Cold:
Write the word from the lesson that is most nearly the *OPPOSITE* of the boldfaced word or words in each sentence below.

17. Whether or not your classmates followed the rules is _____: The important question here is whether or not you yourself **followed** them.

18. The sudden rainfall was a **blessing** after the _____ that was the decade-long drought.

19. There are very few _____ documents from the Library at Alexandria since most were **lost** hundreds of years ago.

20. Encouragement from her professors _____ Martha in her education, while her mother's negative attitude **hindered** her progress.

21. We hoped our guests would **disperse** after dinner; should they _____, we were bound to miss our train to the airport.

22. The question of how to intervene in the war-torn country remains _____, as a huge number of factors will influence the outcome of the conflict, but one fact remains obvious: Intervention is **necessary**.

Applying Yourself:
Choose the best word to complete each of the following sentences.

23. The weather is _____ since we will be playing the game inside.
    (A) problematic
    (B) lingering
    (C) immaterial
    (D) extant
    (E) tenured

24. There are few _____ documents from that long ago.
    (A) immaterial
    (B) propelled
    (C) problematic
    (D) extant
    (E) lingering

25. Our group _____ in the lounge for an hour after the concert ended, not wanting the night to end.
  (A) lingered
  (B) implemented
  (C) tenured
  (D) hoarded
  (E) propelled

26. She found herself in a(n) _____ situation when, after having tricked both her boyfriends into believing she was going on vacation, she found out both would be coming to her house to say good-bye.
  (A) problematic
  (B) propelled
  (C) immaterial
  (D) tenured
  (E) lingering

27. The powerful speech on government waste _____ the candidate into the newly vacated senate seat.
  (A) propelled
  (B) tenured
  (C) hoarded
  (D) lingered
  (E) implemented

28. Universities established the _____ system to protect outspoken professors against punishment by administrators.
  (A) extant
  (B) propelled
  (C) problematic
  (D) tenure
  (E) lingering

29. Some call malaria the "_____ of Africa."
  (A) linger
  (B) scourge
  (C) tenure
  (D) grandiloquence
  (E) pulchritude

30. We will succeed at this difficult project, _____ not without hard work.
  (A) therein
  (B) because
  (C) since
  (D) and
  (E) albeit

On Your Own:
Write one sentence using each word below to demonstrate your understanding of the word's meaning.

31. **propel** _____

32. **problematic** _____

33. **extant** _____

34. **albeit** _____

35. **linger** _____

36. **scourge** _____

37. **immaterial** _____

38. **tenure** _____

C2 Advanced Vocabulary 29

First Impressions:

Using the example sentences below, write your own definition of each boldfaced word. Then write the letter of the definition from the box that best matches your definition.

A	adjective: hidden; secret, especially "ulterior motives"	**C**	adjective: showing awareness and concern for the embarrassment or offense of others
B	adjective: inborn, or existing since birth; inherent	**D**	adjective: consistent and logically connected

1. _____ A therapist must be extraordinarily **tactful** and show discretion when hearing the personal

stories of his clients.

TACTFUL means: _____

2. _____ Though persuasive on an emotional level, the basic logic of the representative's speech

was barely **coherent**.

COHERENT means: _____

3. _____ Fran realized that Rob's **ulterior** motive in being nice to her was to get a job at her father's

business.

ULTERIOR means: _____

4. _____ It is unclear how much of one's personality is **innate** and how much is acquired through

experience.

INNATE means: _____

A	adjective: spending very little	**C**	adjective: indicating good in the future; inclined to forgive
B	adjective: dried out; dehydrated	**D**	adjective: dishonest, especially on an everyday basis

5. _____ What once had been a pristine lake had dried into an empty depression covered with the

desiccated skeletons of fish.

DESICCATED means: _____

6. _____ The sunny, warm morning was a **propitious** beginning to our beach trip.

PROPITIOUS means: _____

7. _____ The corporation lost most of its investors when the **mendacious** behavior of its CEO was

discovered and its credibility was subsequently ruined.

MENDACIOUS means: _____

8. _____ Thoreau's **frugal** living was made famous in his book "Walden," in which he describes

living for two years in a cabin that he built by hand and eating the food grown in his own garden.

FRUGAL means: _____

Divide and Conquer:
Choose the correct word to complete each of the following sentences.

9. Professor Farrell takes a(n) **(ulterior / tactful)** approach to freshmen who ask obvious questions, as he wants to encourage new students to be vocal.

10. The student read and reread the difficult book until it began to seem more **(coherent / tactful)**.

11. Throughout his life, he retained his innocence through his belief in the **(mendacious / innate)** goodness of humanity.

12. After the townspeople discovered just how **(mendacious / tactful)** Harold could be, no one was willing to do business with him.

13. The graduate student was so **(coherent / frugal)** that he lived largely on beans, rice, and other inexpensive but nourishing foods.

14. The archaeologist opened the sarcophagus, revealing the dusty and **(desiccated / tactful)** remains of one of Egypt's great pharaohs.

15. Even though he is already a promising young athlete, Thomas must work to improve his skills if he wants a **(mendacious / propitious)** first game.

16. I promise I have no **(ulterior / innate)** motive in asking you to come to the gym with me; I merely want your company.

Hot and Cold:
Write the word from the lesson that is most nearly the *OPPOSITE* of the boldfaced word or words in each sentence below.

17. Richard's father taught him to be _____ with his money and to avoid the extravagances associated with **spending** on credit and buying things he didn't need.

18. I thought that he had expressed **clear** reasons for going to the festival, but I found out later he had _____ motives.

19. The _____ little boy was accustomed to telling countless small lies throughout the day and didn't see any advantage to being **honest**.

20. The paper had a few _____ sentences that the professor not only understood but was impressed with, but on the whole both the logic and the grammar were **disjointed**.

21. We were glad Tina was able to attend the event; she was so supremely _____ that we knew she'd be able to salvage any difficult social situation the **insensitive** Frieda might get herself into.

22. The puppy was thin and _____ after being left alone without food or water for several days, but after spending some time with the loving family who found him, he was healthy and **hydrated** once more.

23. I don't believe in _____ abilities, and I am certain my talents in chess are 100% **learned**, not the result of some natural gift.

24. The tarot card reader indicated that the swordsman was a(n) _____ symbol, while the knave was rather **unlucky** and indicated something sinister on the horizon.

Applying Yourself:
Choose the best word to complete each of the following sentences.

25. The king's invitation was a(n) _____ sign that our family had returned to favor.
    (A) propitious
    (B) tactful
    (C) desiccated
    (D) frugal
    (E) ulterior

26. The _____ garden was marked by shriveled vegetables.
    (A) ulterior
    (B) coherent
    (C) desiccated
    (D) frugal
    (E) propitious

27. My only _____ motive in encouraging you to go to college is the desire to see you be independent.
   (A) mendacious
   (B) ulterior
   (C) tactful
   (D) propitious
   (E) coherent

28. _____ salesmen will say anything, true or false, to make sales on their daily rounds.
   (A) Mendacious
   (B) Tactful
   (C) Desiccated
   (D) Frugal
   (E) Propitious

29. Investment advisors bemoan the lack of _____ clients; it seems to them that all of their clients are careless with their funds.
   (A) tactful
   (B) propitious
   (C) desiccated
   (D) frugal
   (E) mendacious

30. Babies experience _____ leaps of logic at predicable internals in their lives; no one has to teach them how to walk, for instance.
   (A) frugal
   (B) tactful
   (C) ulterior
   (D) innate
   (E) propitious

31. LaRon's coaches were concerned that the blow had stunned him, but the athlete proved that he was still _____ by answering sensibly to questions.
   (A) coherent
   (B) propitious
   (C) desiccated
   (D) frugal
   (E) tactful

32. In a carefully _____ way, Sheila offered the recently laid-off workers her assistance in finding new jobs.
   (A) desiccated
   (B) innate
   (C) tactful
   (D) propitious
   (E) mendacious

On Your Own:

Write one sentence using each word below to demonstrate your understanding of the word's meaning.

33. **mendacious** _____

34. **desiccated** _____

35. **frugal** _____

36. **coherent** _____

37. **propitious** _____

38. **ulterior** _____

39. **tactful** _____

40. **innate** _____

C2 Advanced Vocabulary 30

First Impressions:

Using the example sentences below, write your own definition of each boldfaced word. Then write the letter of the definition from the box that best matches your definition.

A	noun: employment that yields significant rewards with little responsibility	**C**	adjective: mysterious; hidden; secret
B	adjective: arranged in order by time	**D**	adjective: not serious; intended to be humorous

1. _____ Harold's powerful friends in politics awarded him with a **sinecure** that allowed him to live a leisurely life of modest luxury.

SINECURE means: _____

2. _____ Though **chronological** order may seem traditional, some students prefer to study history by topic instead of by year.

CHRONOLOGICAL means: _____

3. _____ Though Richard had intended to be **facetious**, the entire class took his remark quite seriously.

FACETIOUS means: _____

4. _____ There was nothing **cryptic** about the message Nadira's stomach was sending her: "Feed me!"

CRYPTIC means: _____

A	verb: to corrupt; to lead into temptation	**C**	adjective: essential; inherent; built-in; natural
B	noun: lack of harmony; disagreement; war; a harsh noise	**D**	noun: something that is not in its correct historical time

5. _____ The horse-drawn buggy is an **anachronism** in modern transportation.

ANACHRONISM means: _____

6. _____ As a kid, I was often **seduced** into breaking the rules by a group of teenagers.

SEDUCE means: _____

7. _____ The relationship between the roommates was one of **discord** and constant argument.

DISCORD means: _____

8. _____ Buying or selling gold is difficult because no one can arrive at an **intrinsic** value of the precious metal.

INTRINSIC means: _____

Divide and Conquer:
Choose the correct word to complete each of the following sentences.

9. The speaker opened his talk with several **(intrinsic / facetious)** remarks before moving on to more serious matters.

10. The black-and-white portion of the film is told in **(chronological / cryptic)** order, but the portion in color begins at the end of the story and moves backward in time until the end of the film.

11. The partygoers followed one **(facetious / cryptic)** clue after another until they finally solved the mystery.

12. While holiday gatherings on Mario's side of the family were marked by **(anachronism / discord)**, get-togethers on Marissa's side were relatively calm and peaceful.

13. In such a well-research story it was jarring to come across such an obvious **(anachronism / discord)** as a reference to electricity in the 1100s.

14. Though at first the two customs seem quite remote from each other, they in fact have few **(intrinsic / discordant)** differences.

15. **(Seduced / Harangued)** by the lure of a large paycheck, Martin left the nonprofit organization to work for a large but disreputable company.

16. Bob enjoyed the **(sinecure / anachronism)** of "company morale officer" for so long that many assumed he had blackmailed one of the executives.

Hot and Cold:
Write the word from the lesson that is most nearly the *OPPOSITE* of the boldfaced word or words in each sentence below.

17. The digital watch was the one _____ on the set of **time-appropriate representations** of the 1870s.

18. Because Leon's face isn't very expressive, it's hard to tell whether his comments are meant to be _____ or **serious**.

19. He was **turned off** by the cult's strange practices, no matter how much they tried to _____ him.

20. Perhaps you came out of the womb with a compass in your head and your sense of direction is _____, but mine has been **learned** from years of studying maps.

21. Ever since our fight, I've felt a(n) _____ between Michelle and me, and I want nothing more than to regain our former **harmony**.

22. The therapist advised Mike to stop searching desperately for _____ meanings behind every word his father spoke and to take his words at their most **simple** meanings.

Applying Yourself:
Choose the best word to complete each of the following sentences.

23. After years of playing his college newspaper's crossword puzzle, whose clues were generally obvious synonyms, David thought the hints for the New York Times Sunday crossword were incredibly _____.
    (A) cryptic
    (B) intrinsic
    (C) facetious
    (D) chronological
    (E) discordant

24. Some people find Susan's _____ remarks off-putting in serious situations, but they are just an attempt to lighten the mood.
    (A) cryptic
    (B) intrinsic
    (C) discordant
    (D) facetious
    (E) anachronistic

25. She picked up the guitar for the first time and started playing the complicated piece, as though music were a(n) _____ part of her being.
    (A) cryptic
    (B) anachronistic
    (C) discordant
    (D) facetious
    (E) intrinsic

26. There are two ways to tell your story: thematically, grouping like topics together, or _____, starting from the birth of the protagonist to her death.
    (A) anachronistically
    (B) cryptically
    (C) facetiously
    (D) intrinsically
    (E) chronologically

27. Although the eclectic furnishings included _____ such as an oak icebox, we were charmed by the overall décor.
    (A) anachronisms
    (B) facetiousness
    (C) prefaces
    (D) sinecures
    (E) chronology

28. The secretive operation was meant to create _____ among the members government's elite circle, causing them to suspect one another.
    (A) facetiousness
    (B) anachronism
    (C) preface
    (D) discord
    (E) sinecure

29. I'm supposed to be on a diet, but your chocolate pie has _____ me.
    (A) languished
    (B) instigated
    (C) seduced
    (D) professed
    (E) supplanted

30. All the lazy kid hoped for in the years to come was a(n) _____ in which he could game all day and collect fat checks.
    (A) chronology
    (B) sinecure
    (C) preface
    (D) anachronism
    (E) facetiousness

On Your Own:
Write one sentence using each word below to demonstrate your understanding of the word's meaning.

31. **cryptic** _____

32. **facetious** _____

33. **chronological** _____

34. **seduce** _____

35. **sinecure** _____

36. **anachronism** _____

37. **discord** _____

38. **intrinsic** _____

C2 Advanced Vocabulary 31

First Impressions:
Using the example sentences below, write your own definition of each boldfaced word. Then write the letter of the definition from the box that best matches your definition.

A	noun: a small battle	**C**	verb: to expand and contract rhythmically; to vibrate
B	adjective: having sufficient, skill, knowledge, etc.; adequate	**D**	adjective: unselfishly generous; concerned for others

1. _____ Christmastime was Ethan's favorite time of year because it made him feel more **altruistic** and willing to help others.

ALTRUISTIC means: _____

2. _____ Though expert plumbers may charge more, the extra cost may be worthwhile because they are much more likely to be **competent**.

COMPETENT means: _____

3. _____ The **skirmishes** between the two gangs led up to a war later on.

SKIRMISH means: _____

4. _____ The surgeon watched with satisfaction as the transplanted heart began to **pulsate**.

PULSATE means: _____

A	verb: to drive away; to scatter; to cause to vanish	**C**	verb: to regularly give one's business; to treat with kindness that reveals a sense of superiority
B	adjective: slow; dull; sluggish	**D**	adjective: excessively emotional

5. _____ On one of his more **mawkish** days, Tim pulled all of his ex-girlfriends' letters from the box in his closet and read them while watching romantic dramas.

MAWKISH means: _____

6. _____ There was nothing to be done to **dispel** the rumor except to wait for people to grow tired of spreading it.

DISPEL means: _____

7. _____ The family members sat back in their chairs in a **torpid** state to digest their enormous Thanksgiving dinner.

TORPID means: _____

8. _____ Because she had **patronized** Sal's Diner for years, I was surprised to see Jiyoung at Marco's Eatery at dinnertime.

PATRONIZE means: _____

Divide and Conquer:

Choose the correct word to complete each of the following sentences.

9. Not only was she reliable, but she was also **(competent / dispelled)** and well-suited for the position, too.

10. Rather than issue a **(mawkish / patronized)** plea for donations, the director of the nonprofit organization released a sober and professional memo.

11. Sally was so **(altruistic / mawkish)** that she always considered the needs of others above her own.

12. While taciturn Sarah's portrait appeared dull and lifeless, exuberant Ehren produced artwork that seemed to **(skirmish / pulsate)** with energy.

13. The bright sunlight **(dispelled / pulsated)** the last shreds of fog drifting over the lake.

14. My six siblings and I got into many **(skirmishes / altruisms)** with each other over things as small as what to watch on T.V.

15. We cannot **(dispel / patronize)** a golf club that has restrictions against admitting female members.

16. Though he had slept and eaten well, Carlos felt **(torpid / mawkish)** at the start of the marathon.

Hot and Cold:

Write the word from the lesson that is most nearly the *OPPOSITE* of the boldfaced word or words in each sentence below.

17. Once quite **active** for his breed, my pet turtle has been so _____ that I'm sure he must be ill.

18. Though my employer says I'm perfectly _____ and that she's pleased with my work, I can't help but feel as though I am an **inadequate** worker who doesn't deserve my position.

19. The role of a skilled public relations officer is not to _____ rumors but to **create** and organize the rumors that are most useful.

20. Ever **stoic**, Joshua was repulsed by the _____ display of tears and begging showcased on the soap opera and was totally unmoved.

21. He hadn't been afraid of the _____ that he'd been in before, but this **large battle** that was about to start terrified him.

22. At first, I could make out the faint sound of the dying dog's heart _____, but soon enough it ceased and **beat no longer**.

23. I was tired of being _____ by my brothers, who call me their "dear sweet sis," implying that I don't know anything about the world; I want them to **respect** me.

24. I have grown _____ with age, but in my early life, I was a most **selfish** person, never wanting to let go of a penny that didn't directly benefit me.

Applying Yourself:

Choose the best word to complete each of the following sentences.

25. Although he wasn't amazing, the new employee was at least _____ enough to see the project through from beginning to end.
    (A) torpid
    (B) patronized
    (C) mawkish
    (D) pulsating
    (E) competent

26. Full of energy at the start of the marathon, Leslie's stride had become _____ by mile 15.
    (A) mawkish
    (B) torpid
    (C) patronized
    (D) altruistic
    (E) pulsating

27. Her presence caused my sense of loneliness to vanish; for a moment, my sadness was totally _____.
    (A) torpid
    (B) pulsating
    (C) altruistic
    (D) competent
    (E) dispelled

28. The _____ was over quickly and didn't lead to a full battle.
    (A) competence
    (B) enormity
    (C) pulse
    (D) skirmish
    (E) pinnacle

29. Don't _____ me for taking so long to assemble the furniture; the job is more complicated than it looks.
    (A) enervate
    (B) buttress
    (C) patronize
    (D) dispel
    (E) pulsate

30. John said that he finds romantic comedies _____ and unrealistic and only watches them when someone else wants to.
    (A) altruistic
    (B) mawkish
    (C) competent
    (D) pulsating
    (E) torpid

31. Those who give anonymous donations to the hospital are the most _____, as they care only for the good their money will do, not for the recognition.
    (A) torpid
    (B) altruistic
    (C) mawkish
    (D) competent
    (E) patronized

32. The lights in the club _____, creating a surreal, strobe-like pattern on the wall.
    (A) buttressed
    (B) patronized
    (C) enervated
    (D) skirmished
    (E) pulsated

On Your Own:
Write one sentence using each word below to demonstrate your understanding of the word's meaning.

33. **patronize** _____

34. **pulsate** _____

35. **altruistic** _____

36. **skirmish** _____

37. **mawkish** _____

38. **competent** _____

39. **torpid** _____

40. **dispel** _____

C2 Advanced Vocabulary 32

First Impressions:
Using the example sentences below, write your own definition of each boldfaced word. Then write the letter of the definition from the box that best matches your definition.

A	adjective: related to love, especially sexual love	**C**	noun: a feeling of strong dislike; strong hostility
B	verb: to name one thing as the cause of another	**D**	noun: likeness or resemblance; a shared characteristic

1. _____ The sisters glared at each other over the table, the **animosity** so great that their mother was compelled to separate them.

ANIMOSITY means: _____

2. _____ The mischievous twin sisters preferred each other's clothes to have a great **similitude** so that others could not tell them apart.

SIMILITUDE means: _____

3. _____ The engineers **imputed** the failure of the engine to a faulty seal.

IMPUTE means: _____

4. _____ It is considered highly inappropriate for an employer to make **amorous** advances toward one who is in his or her employ.

AMOROUS means: _____

A	adjective: profitable; making money	**C**	adjective: not easily bothered; unemotional
B	noun: composure and self-assurance	**D**	noun: one who lives outside of his or her native country

5. _____ During the emotional crisis, Denise was a **stolid** support for her spouse.

STOLID means: _____

6. _____ As a teenager, I started a **lucrative** lawn-mowing service that earned me $200 per week.

LUCRATIVE means: _____

7. _____ Before the election, Marvin jokingly said that he would have to become an **expatriate** and move to Canada if the president were reelected.

EXPATRIATE means: _____

8. _____ Such was Jeeves's **aplomb** that he reacted to even the most scandalous story with only a raised eyebrow and the words, "Indeed, sir?"

APLOMB means: _____

Divide and Conquer:
Choose the correct word to complete each of the following sentences.

9. The stuntman earned a lot of work for his **(similitude / animosity)** to Sylvester Stallone.

10. Protesters **(expatriated / imputed)** the pollution of the lake to the new manufacturing plant, but the owner maintained that the facility obeyed all environmental regulations.

11. The mediator was called in to settle the dispute without adding to the **(animosity / aplomb)** both parties felt.

12. Years of experience enabled the emergency medical technician to carry himself with **(expatriate / aplomb)** in even the most hectic circumstances.

13. Many associate the sonnet with **(amorous / lucrative)** writing, but many sonnets have nothing to do with romance.

14. The American **(animosities / expatriates)** met regularly in a café in Paris to share news of the old country.

15. Tourists often try to distract the palace guard in London, but the **(stolid / imputed)** members of that order maintain their composure.

16. The **(amorous / lucrative)** business managed its huge assets through a financial firm used to dealing with large sums of money.

Hot and Cold:
Write the word from the lesson that is most nearly the *OPPOSITE* of the boldfaced word or words in each sentence below.

17. The _____ between the identical twins was great enough that teachers often confused them, but their parents saw enough **dissimilarity** between them that they never to fail to tell them apart.

18. The challenge was to introduce **goodwill** into a relationship that formerly had been marked only by _____.

19. Since becoming a(n) _____ of Japan, I've become a Czech **national** after a long process of applying for citizenship there.

20. The doctors _____ my diet as the cause of my diabetes, but also said they couldn't **absolve** genetics as an important factor, too.

21. Vick handled most situations with great _____ and was known as a great navigator of social situations, much to the surprise of those who had witnessed his **maladroitness** in matters of romance.

22. Gretchen gave her husband a(n) _____ wink from across the room, but his **chaste** frown killed the spark of romance.

23. _____ as a statue, the woman merely nodded at the terrible news, surprising those who expected her to be more **emotional**.

24. Investors pulled their funding when they realized that the seemingly _____ business was highly **unprofitable**.

Applying Yourself:
Choose the best word to complete each of the following sentences.

25. I've often been told that there is much _____ between myself and Brad Pitt, so where's my movie deal?
    - (A) proclivity
    - (B) animosity
    - (C) expatriate
    - (D) similitude
    - (E) aplomb

26. Poker attracts players with _____ personalities; betraying frustration, glee, or anger can indicate mediocrity.
    - (A) exacting
    - (B) amorous
    - (C) stolid
    - (D) imputed
    - (E) lucrative

27. I yearned for my distant homeland until I discovered a community of fellow _____ in my neighborhood.
    (A) expatriates
    (B) aplomb
    (C) similitude
    (D) amorousness
    (E) proclivities

28. The _____ couple held each other with affectionate eyes, oblivious to their surroundings.
    (A) amorous
    (B) stolid
    (C) imputed
    (D) exacting
    (E) lucrative

29. The public _____ the president's unwillingness to enter into war as the cause of the tumult abroad.
    (A) collaborated
    (B) imputed
    (C) assailed
    (D) distinguished
    (E) expatriated

30. Investing in the stock market is not always _____; you can lose money just as easily as you can make it.
    (A) amorous
    (B) stolid
    (C) lucrative
    (D) exacting
    (E) imputed

31. The thief showed _____ when using carefully measured steps to evade the police.
    (A) animosity
    (B) expatriates
    (C) amorousness
    (D) aplomb
    (E) similitude

32. You could almost feel the _____ between the pair, both parties obviously bitter that the other had cheated.
    (A) proclivity
    (B) animosity
    (C) similitude
    (D) amorousness
    (E) aplomb

On Your Own:
Write one sentence using each word below to demonstrate your understanding of the word's meaning.

33. **expatriate** _____

34. **animosity** _____

35. **aplomb** _____

36. **lucrative** _____

37. **stolid** _____

38. **amorous** _____

39. **similitude** _____

40. **impute** _____

C2 Advanced Vocabulary 33

First Impressions:
Using the example sentences below, write your own definition of each boldfaced word. Then write the letter of the definition from the box that best matches your definition.

A	noun: someone prejudiced against women	**C**	noun: partiality; preference
B	adjective: done without conscious choice	**D**	noun: one particular aspect of something

1. _____ Two important **facets** of being a student are studying hard and organizing one's time.

FACET means: _____

2. _____ It appears that they have a **predilection** for trivialities rather than other, more pressing

   issues.

PREDILECTION means: _____

3. _____ Many governments are run by **misogynists** who restrict the rights of women.

MISOGYNIST means: _____

4. _____ In biology, we learned that the beating of the heart and the digestion of food are

   involuntary actions.

INVOLUNTARY means: _____

A	noun: one who donates generously to charity	**C**	noun: supporter; follower
B	adjective: easily approachable; obtainable	**D**	adjective: never stopping or lessening

5. _____ The Secret Service agents keep the president from becoming an **accessible** target to

   assassins.

ACCESSIBLE means: _____

6. _____ The **philanthropist** used his considerable wealth to build a new children's wing at the

   museum.

PHILANTHROPIST means: _____

7. _____ **Adherents** of both parties disagree on many issues, but they all have the people's best

   interests at heart.

ADHERENT means: _____

8. _____ The **unremitting** storm led flood waters to rise higher and higher over the course of the

   week.

UNREMITTING means: _____

Divide and Conquer:
Choose the correct word to complete each of the following sentences.

9. Most members of Carmilla's family have been **(adherents / misogynists)** of Catholicism for their entire lives, with some even entering church ministry.

10. Place the fire extinguisher in a(n) **(accessible / faceted)** spot so that we can quickly find it in an emergency.

11. The **(unremitting / accessible)** pounding of the great ram would eventually cause the thick gates of Minas Tirith to crack.

12. Because he had a **(predilection / misogyny)** for bending the rules, Peter was not promoted to management.

13. As they tested the man's brain, his arm jumped around with an **(involuntary / unremitting)** twitch.

14. Samantha was able to find success despite her **(misogynistic / faceted)** work environment by performing her job so well that her manager changed his unfair views of women.

15. Many of the country's first millionaires were also known as great **(predilections / philanthropists)** who donated money to the cities in which they resided.

16. The main **(facet / philanthropist)** of Gina's character is her generosity, but she's occasionally rude, too.

Hot and Cold:
Write the word from the lesson that is most nearly the *OPPOSITE* of the boldfaced word or words in each sentence below.

17. My older brother is quite the _____, while my younger sister is often a **miser**.

18. This area of the island, with its many bridges and roads to the mainland, is much more _____ than the remote western side, which is mostly jungle and **difficult to reach**.

19. Does the **whole** of history interest you, or is there a(n) _____ that you're more drawn to?

20. Gregory was searching for an _____ love that would never fade, so the **relenting** affections of Maria worried him.

21. Young children have a(n) _____ for sweet and salty foods, as these are the most calorie-dense, and an **aversion** toward bitter foods, which are often poisonous in the wild.

22. The _____ to the local faith are strong in their convictions and will tolerate no **opponents** attempting to prove them wrong.

23. People accused Dominic of being a(n) _____, but in truth he was a great **lover of women**.

24. The student insisted that his loud belch was _____, not **purposeful** as his teacher alleged.

Applying Yourself:
Choose the best word to complete each of the following sentences.

25. Peter was a true _____; he believed that no women should be allowed in the workplace.
    (A) philanthropist
    (B) misogynist
    (C) facet
    (D) predilection
    (E) adherent

26. This cove is just south of Playa Venao; other, smaller beaches in the area are only _____ at low tide.
    (A) acrimonious
    (B) accessible
    (C) juvenile
    (D) faceted
    (E) involuntary

27. I have closely examined every _____ of this situation, and I have yet to find one that I like.
    (A) adherent
    (B) philanthropist
    (C) facet
    (D) misogynist
    (E) predilection

28. Though the _____ gunfire caused us to hide in the basement, were confident that the ceasefire was coming.
    (A) accessible
    (B) faceted
    (C) unremitting
    (D) involuntary
    (E) juvenile

29. It's not difficult for anyone with a good soul to become a(n) _____ to a philosophy of nonviolence.
    (A) philanthropist
    (B) adherent
    (C) access
    (D) misogynist
    (E) predilection

30. I felt a(n) _____ twitch in my eye, probably caused by a lack of sleep.
    (A) unremitting
    (B) faceted
    (C) accessible
    (D) juvenile
    (E) involuntary

31. Jeanne, a born swimmer, had a strong _____ for water sports over sports that involve running.
    (A) predilection
    (B) facet
    (C) access
    (D) adherent
    (E) philanthropist

32. I hope one day to be rich enough to become a(n) _____ and donate all my money to curing the disease that killed my best friend.
    (A) misogynist
    (B) facet
    (C) predilection
    (D) access
    (E) philanthropist

On Your Own:
Write one sentence using each word below to demonstrate your understanding of the word's meaning.

33. **philanthropist** _____

34. **unremitting** _____

35. **adherent** _____

36. **accessible** _____

37. **involuntary** _____

38. **misogynist** _____

39. **predilection** _____

40. **facet** _____

C2 Advanced Vocabulary 34

First Impressions:

Using the example sentences below, write your own definition of each boldfaced word. Then write the letter of the definition from the box that best matches your definition.

A	noun: payment to compensate for wrongs or damages	**C**	verb: to force into submission; to force an emotion into becoming unconscious
B	noun: the quality of a situation or work that causes feelings of pity or compassion	**D**	adjective: showing heartfelt approval

1. _____ Some religious groups were severely **repressed** in Europe, where church divisions created much animosity between factions.

REPRESS means: _____

2. _____ Part of the peace treaty required that the invader pay **reparations** of hundreds of millions of dollars to repair the damage done to the invaded nation.

REPARATION means: _____

3. _____ Joni's **effusive** praise for her art students gave them the boost of confidence they needed.

EFFUSIVE means: _____

4. _____ The soft piano music and images of the lost child heightened the **pathos** of the film.

PATHOS means: _____

A	adjective: capable of being done, affected, or accomplished; probable; suitable; practical	**C**	adjective: constant; habitual; continuing over a long period
B	adjective: mocking	**D**	adjective: difficult to please; excessively particular, critical, or demanding

5. _____ Louise has **chronic** arthritis in her hands, which makes it difficult for her to write or type.

CHRONIC means: _____

6. _____ Ashley thought her mom was overly **fastidious** about the cleanliness of the house, which always had to be spotless.

FASTIDIOUS means: _____

7. _____ Using email to screen college students for major depressive disorder (MDD) appears to be a **feasible** and inexpensive way to detect MDD in this high-risk group.

FEASIBLE means: _____

8. _____ The show shocks people who think it's meant to be taken seriously, though the characters and plots are clearly **satirical**.

SATIRICAL means: _____

Divide and Conquer:
Choose the correct word to complete each of the following sentences.

9. The **(satirical / fastidious)** professor, who demanded nothing but excellence from his students, rarely gave out high marks.

10. Reading *Invisible Man* elicits in the reader feelings of **(pathos / satire)** for the narrator, who is routinely marginalized and ignored by the rest of society.

11. The unemployed workers shouted for **(reparations / repression)** from the bankers whose irresponsible speculation had caused the financial crisis.

12. He fails to come up with any **(feasible / chronic)**, long-term suggestions to solve what is quickly becoming a demographic time bomb.

13. He was able to endure occasional allergy symptoms, but it was more difficult for him to deal with his **(chronic / effusive)** cough.

14. **(Satirical / repressive)** works such as *A Modest Proposal* are darkly comedic criticisms of government.

15. Often **(repressive / effusive)** no matter what the occasion, my aunt becomes even more glowing and emotional at weddings and baby showers.

16. The king's guard quickly **(repressed / reproached)** the rebellion in the provincial city and restored order.

Hot and Cold:
Write the word from the lesson that is most nearly the *OPPOSITE* of the boldfaced word or words in each sentence below.

17. After attending a strict boarding school run by a particularly _____ headmaster, Rene found it difficult to adjust to life at a **lax** private school without half as many rules as he was used to.

18. The woman was so ridiculously over-the-top that most assumed her actions to be a(n) _____ take on upper-class life, but in fact, she was totally **sincere** in all her actions.

19. Linda's _____ support of her brother's career choice contrasted the **restrained** response from the siblings' parents.

20. Dennis wished his boss would assign him _____ tasks he could hope to accomplish instead of a mountain of assignments that was **impossible** to finish.

21. Is your stomach pain **acute**, occurring only once in awhile, or the kind of _____ pain that continues over a certain period of time?

22. Sometimes, it is better to **express** feelings of anger, as _____ these feelings may cause one to react more extremely later on.

Applying Yourself:
Choose the best word to complete each of the following sentences.

23. France and its allies required Germany to pay extensive _____ for damage caused during World War I.
    (A) satire
    (B) pathos
    (C) fastidiousness
    (D) reparations
    (E) effusions

24. Even if you disagree with its use in an anti-war campaign, you cannot deny the _____ of the photo of the baby bird covered in oil.
    (A) repression
    (B) satire
    (C) effusion
    (D) pathos
    (E) reparation

25. He was able to successfully _____ his urge to say something sarcastic, and instead just sat quietly.
    (A) revitalize
    (B) repress
    (C) litigate
    (D) lacerate
    (E) satire

26. His _____ handshake indicated how much he liked my speech.
    (A) repressed
    (B) effusive
    (C) chronic
    (D) feasible
    (E) fastidious

27. While Sarah's parents were particularly _____ and punished their daughter for even low A's, Soumya's parents were uncritical and didn't put much emphasis on grades.
    (A) fastidious
    (B) repressed
    (C) chronic
    (D) feasible
    (E) effusive

28. I disagree with arguments that say a fair justice system is _____ because I believe humans to be incapable of true objectivity.
    (A) feasible
    (B) chronic
    (C) fastidious
    (D) effusive
    (E) repressed

29. I opened the paper, only to witness the editors had issued a(n) _____ cartoon that depicted me with Pinocchio's nose.
    (A) chronic
    (B) satirical
    (C) fastidious
    (D) effusive
    (E) feasible

30. Undiagnosed Lyme disease renders the unfortunate victim with _____ back pain, often for the rest of his or her life.
    (A) repressed
    (B) chronic
    (C) effusive
    (D) feasible
    (E) satirical

On Your Own:

Write one sentence using each word below to demonstrate your understanding of the word's meaning.

31. **feasible** _____

32. **satirical** _____

33. **chronic** _____

34. **reparation** _____

35. **fastidious** _____

36. **pathos** _____

37. **repress** _____

38. **effusive** _____

C2 Advanced Vocabulary 35

First Impressions:
Using the example sentences below, write your own definition of each boldfaced word. Then write the letter of the definition from the box that best matches your definition.

A	noun: sameness leading to boredom	**C**	noun: a leader who gains influence through emotion and bias instead of clear reasoning
B	adjective: uncertain how to act; weak	**D**	noun: a basic principle that is accepted as true without proof

1. _____ The week spent on lab work and dissections was a pleasant break from the everyday **monotony** of lectures.

MONOTONY means: _____

2. _____ It's always good to have a back-up plan so you're not left **irresolute** if your original plan fails.

IRRESOLUTE means: _____

3. _____ Each **axiom** of geometry is necessary; if a single one of the basic principles is modified, entirely implausible results come into being.

AXIOM means: _____

4. _____ Joseph McCarthy is remembered as a **demagogue** who rose to prominence by claiming, without proof, that high positions in the government were "infested" with communists.

DEMAGOGUE means: _____

A	adjective: happening at the same time	**C**	adjective: not influenced by emotions; fair
B	verb: to ridicule; to imitate, often in derision	**D**	verb: to squander; to waste; to scatter

5. _____ The judge was **objective** in the case, placing the rule of the law over any emotional bias he felt during the parties' arguments.

OBJECTIVE means: _____

6. _____ The clown was able to **simultaneously** juggle 5 balls and ride a unicycle without dropping a single ball or falling out of the unicycle seat.

SIMULTANEOUS means: _____

7. _____ The staged fight was supposedly done to **mock** the incident that took place a year earlier.

MOCK means: _____

8. _____ Because Stefania did not carefully manage her finances, soon all of her savings had **dissipated**.

DISSIPATE means: _____

Divide and Conquer:

Choose the correct word to complete each of the following sentences.

9. The dancers moved in a(n) **(simultaneous / irresolute)** display of precision.

10. After struggling to defeat her sister in chess despite hours of practice, Mary was left **(monotony / irresolute)** as to how to proceed.

11. My firing came as a shock, but now that I have calmed down, I can use **(objective / mocking)** means to evaluate and improve myself.

12. Adolph Hitler was a highly successful **(monotony / demagogue)** who rallied an entire country to tolerate atrocity by calling on its national pride.

13. The fog slowly **(objectified / dissipated)** as it was warmed by the early morning sun.

14. The principle of fairness is a basic **(axiom / objectivity)** on which nearly all ethical rules are based.

15. Needing a break from the **(axiom / monotony)** of their jobs, Carrie and her pals embarked on a trip to Abu Dhabi.

16. She said that people shared their views and comments with each other but that no one had the right to **(mock / dissipate)** the holy personalities of any religion.

Hot and Cold:

Write the word from the lesson that is most nearly the *OPPOSITE* of the boldfaced word or words in each sentence below.

17. The sad feelings that had **accumulated** all day _____ when Michelle saw her smiling son's face.

18. The comparative _____ of the summer was surprising after the constant **unpredictability** of the school year.

19. Though Tony was _____ and seemed to be **unable to make up** his mind about which university to attend, he was sure that he would eventually make the right decision.

20. It was critical that each judge be _____, letting neither his or her politics nor personal life affect the decision-making process, but Judge Reiner kept injecting his **biased** opinions into the proceedings.

21. The review not only **praised** the new style of writing as fresh and unique, it _____ anything that reverted to older methods of expression.

22. The fact that we had a _____ reaction of laughter indicated that we were alike; if we had laughed **at different times**, it would indicate that we had slightly different senses of humor.

23. While the _____ was less reasonable than his opponents, he had a way of firing up a crowd that the more **rational leaders** could not compete with.

24. That "absence makes the heart grow fonder" is something of a(n) _____ rather than a **hypothesis**; it is often recited as a truism to comfort loved ones who have been split up.

Applying Yourself:

Choose the best word to complete each of the following sentences.

25. Even though the teacher expressed an authentic interest in all of his students, they still _____ him for his eccentric mannerisms.
    (A) objectified
    (B) capitulated
    (C) circumvented
    (D) dissipated
    (E) mocked

26. His mind told him that he was certain about which college he wanted to attend, but in his heart, he felt _____.
    (A) irresolute
    (B) simultaneous
    (C) objective
    (D) mocked
    (E) dissipated

27. The thirty-minute television show was an entertaining, refreshing break from the _____ of his calculus homework.
   (A) demagogue
   (B) irresolution
   (C) dissipation
   (D) monotony
   (E) axiom

28. Many philosophies revolve around a central _____, which opponents strive to disprove.
   (A) axiom
   (B) objectivity
   (C) demagogue
   (D) monotony
   (E) dissipation

29. Our daughters are playing in _____ games, so I will go to Jenn's soccer match, while James will attend Julie's basketball game.
   (A) objective
   (B) irresolute
   (C) mocking
   (D) simultaneous
   (E) monotonous

30. By the end of the year, not only had she spent her money without thought, but her time had _____ as well.
   (A) circumvented
   (B) capitulated
   (C) dissipated
   (D) mocked
   (E) objectified

31. Parents should remain _____ when settling quarrels between their children, or they will worsen the argument.
   (A) mocking
   (B) irresolute
   (C) objective
   (D) monotonous
   (E) dissipated

32. Cults have long centered around _____ who speak in assured tones but offer little in the way of wisdom.
   (A) objectivities
   (B) monotonies
   (C) axioms
   (D) causalities
   (E) demagogues

On Your Own:
Write one sentence using each word below to demonstrate your understanding of the word's meaning.

33. **monotony** _____

34. **objective** _____

35. **irresolute** _____

36. **demagogue** _____

37. **mock** _____

38. **axiom** _____

39. **simultaneous** _____

40. **dissipate** _____

C2 Advanced Vocabulary 36

First Impressions:
Using the example sentences below, write your own definition of each boldfaced word. Then write the letter of the definition from the box that best matches your definition.

A	verb: to promote growth; to cause to begin	C	verb: to change from one shape to another
B	verb: to make weak	D	noun: lengthy or idle discussion

1. _____ The tyrant sent his spies to discover and stop those who would **foment** rebellion.

FOMENT means: _____

2. _____ A personal scandal could seriously **debilitate** a politician's career, losing him support from several potential voters.

DEBILITATE means: _____

3. _____ Alchemists experimented at great length in order to find a way to **transmute** lead into gold.

TRANSMUTE means: _____

4. _____ I am eager to get to the point and have no interest in extending the **palaver** we've been engaged in this past hour.

PALAVER means: _____

A	noun: poor eyesight at long distances; lack of ability to plan for the future	C	noun: the unchanging, dull sound of a voice
B	noun: a person who establishes an organization, business, or other entity	D	verb: to cut off from additional supplies, especially with ships

5. _____ The organization's **founder** has finally been acknowledged for his selfless contribution to the Australian way of life.

FOUNDER means: _____

6. _____ The president ordered a **blockade** to the north to prevent hostile armies from gaining supplies.

BLOCKADE means: _____

7. _____ The senator announced that failing to fully fund disaster relief programs during times of plenty would be an instance of social **myopia** of the worst sort.

MYOPIA means: _____

8. _____ Speaking in a **monotone**, the teacher bored his students.

MONOTONE means: _____

Divide and Conquer:

Choose the correct word to complete each of the following sentences.

9. Tributes are pouring in for the company's **(founder / blockade)**, who died last week after a long illness.

10. The general was in charge of weakening the enemy supply line by setting up a **(blockade / debilitation)**.

11. The princess watched in wonder as the frog was **(debilitated / transmuted)** into a prince.

12. "If weightlifting is supposed to make me stronger," Brian thought, "why do I feel so **(debilitated / fomented)** every time I leave the gym?"

13. Our **(transmutation / myopia)** is such that we ignore the consequences of global warming in favor of short-term gain.

14. The school bell, sounding in a seemingly endless **(monotone / founder)**, annoyed both students and teachers.

15. The unwanted change in policies **(transmute / fomented)** discontent among the members of the association.

16. We feel the time to **(foment / palaver)** over the issue has passed; it's time for action.

Hot and Cold:

Write the word from the lesson that is most nearly the *OPPOSITE* of the boldfaced word or words in each sentence below.

17. The passionate speaker sought to _____ discontent and rebellion where the government had long **suppressed** it.

18. It was fortunate that the company's _____ wasn't present to watch the **liquidators** sell off every last bit of the business he had built.

19. Mrs. Norris _____ Diefer in the bathroom, not wishing to **grant access** to the freshly cleaned living room.

20. After his body was _____ by the coma, the athlete took several weeks to **recover** and strengthen his muscles.

21. The signal from outer space switched between a high-pitched _____ and a series of **variable pitches**.

22. The tense atmosphere in the room made any _____ distasteful to the stressed inhabitants, who only cared for **relevant discussion**.

23. Jasmine gave up believing that kissing a frog would _____ it into a prince and accepted that no matter how much she smooched it, a frog would **keep its shape**.

24. Glenda's _____ in planning the project meant that she didn't plan for the long-term results of her proposal and proved herself less capable than her **farsighted** peers.

Applying Yourself:

Choose the best word to complete each of the following sentences.

25. Alchemists strove to _____ lead into gold and were paid handsomely by greedy monarchs who hoped their research was valid.
    (A) palaver
    (B) debilitate
    (C) transmute
    (D) foment
    (E) blockade

26. In a hostile buyout, Mr. Wallace, a longtime adversary of our company's _____, all but destroyed our chances at keeping the business.
    (A) palaver
    (B) founder
    (C) debilitation
    (D) blockade
    (E) monotone

27. We _____ the plan to revitalize our downtown by instilling tax incentives for new businesses.
    (A) palavered
    (B) fomented
    (C) debilitated
    (D) transmuted
    (E) blockaded

28. Many accuse American politicians of _____ regarding the national debt; they seem to spend with no regard for the burden of future generations.
    (A) founder
    (B) blockade
    (C) monotone
    (D) palaver
    (E) myopia

29. The boxer was now suffering from Alzheimer's, which is a terribly _____ disease.
    (A) monotonous
    (B) transmuted
    (C) debilitating
    (D) blockaded
    (E) myopic

30. Cut off on our island, we were unable to get supplies past the _____.
    (A) palaver
    (B) founder
    (C) myopia
    (D) blockade
    (E) monotone

31. Mick was bored with the room's endless _____ and sought a more exciting discussion elsewhere.
    (A) founder
    (B) palaver
    (C) transmutation
    (D) myopia
    (E) blockade

32. The famous comedian spoke in a _____, making his audiences laugh by saying ridiculous things without changing his tone of voice.
    (A) myopia
    (B) palaver
    (C) founder
    (D) monotone
    (E) transmutation

On Your Own:

Write one sentence using each word below to demonstrate your understanding of the word's meaning.

33. **founder** _____

34. **debilitate** _____

35. **palaver** _____

36. **foment** _____

37. **myopia** _____

38. **monotone** _____

39. **blockade** _____

40. **transmute** _____

C2 Advanced Vocabulary 37

First Impressions:
Using the example sentences below, write your own definition of each boldfaced word. Then write the letter of the definition from the box that best matches your definition.

A	adjective: very important	**C**	noun: harmony; agreement
B	adjective: stubborn	**D**	noun: wandering away from the subject

1. _____ The teacher made so many **digressions** in his lecture that students had trouble finding

the central theme of the talk.

DIGRESSION means: _____

2. _____ The rival factions at last reached an **accord** after twenty years or bitter disputes.

ACCORD means: _____

3. _____ It would not be in the Democrats' interests to refuse to support the Republicans because

of **obdurate** party loyalty.

OBDURATE means: _____

4. _____ Many see the first manned landing on the moon in 1969 as the most **momentous** event of

the decade.

MOMENTOUS means: _____

A	adjective: dry; lacking in water	**C**	adjective: impossible to satisfy
B	noun: the tendency or act of being compassionate or merciful	**D**	adjective: friendly

5. _____ The general's desire for land was **implacable**; he conquered territory after territory until he

was finally stopped by force.

IMPLACABLE means: _____

6. _____ The **amiable** old dog loved both cats and children.

AMIABLE means: _____

7. _____ Judge Bonny was upset to learn that the man she had granted **clemency** to during the

previous week had been arrested a second time.

CLEMENCY means: _____

8. _____ The **arid** desert hadn't seen rain in months.

ARID means: _____

Divide and Conquer:

Choose the correct word to complete each of the following sentences.

9. A(n) **(implacable / digressive)** curiosity led Joseph to discoveries in several different branches of science.

10. After many **(digressions / accords)**, the teacher forgot the original topic of his lecture.

11. The plan went into action smoothly, as the heads of each of the major campus organizations were in a(n) **(clemency / accord)** on the decision.

12. Benjamin, one of the most **(amiable / obdurate)** people I know, gets along with just about everyone.

13. May 25th was chosen to commemorate the premiere of Star Wars in 1977, a day in history that fans have considered quite **(arid / momentous)**.

14. The air in the room was hot and **(obdurate / arid)**, making the students extremely thirsty.

15. The president rejected a request from a political terrorist for **(accord / clemency)**.

16. Benji's **(obdurate / amiable)** dog refused to enter the car peacefully, instead wedging himself under the bed.

Hot and Cold:

Write the word from the lesson that is most nearly the *OPPOSITE* of the boldfaced word or words in each sentence below.

17. The **unsociable** cat had a much harder time being adopted than his _____ siblings.

18. A graduation is no **minor** event like a dentist appointment or a trip to the grocery store; it's a(n) _____ occasion at which we get to celebrate your success.

19. The **humid** air of the South is quite different from the _____ air here in the West.

20. The _____ within our group was broken when one member admitted that she had actually been in strong **disagreement** with us throughout the years.

21. Between Maya's _____ inability to compromise and Missy's **flexible** willingness to bend the rules as each situation demanded, the two ladies made an interesting duo.

22. Because our English teacher last year was **easily pleased** by our minimal efforts, we weren't prepared for the quality of work demanded by our seemingly _____ new teacher.

23. The **consistencies** in the second speaker's presentation—the way he developed his point without deviation—made up for the numerous irrelevant _____ in the previous speaker's presentation.

24. Known for his _____, the governor pardoned 10 death row inmates during his tenure; his successor, pardoning none, was accused of **ruthlessness**.

Applying Yourself:

Choose the best word to complete each of the following sentences.

25. What's the point of working hard if your _____ boss refuses to recognize any work well done?
    (A) arid
    (B) implacable
    (C) amiable
    (D) momentous
    (E) digressive

26. Due to gridlock in congress, it feels as though the two parties will never reach a(n) _____ over the debt ceiling.
    (A) accord
    (B) catharsis
    (C) amiability
    (D) digression
    (E) clemency

27. Shira envied her friends' easily manageable acne, for hers was particularly _____, even after she tried numerous treatments.
    - (A) obdurate
    - (B) amiable
    - (C) implacable
    - (D) digressive
    - (E) arid

28. The invention of penicillin was a(n) _____ achievement; it allowed, for the first time, doctors to combat infection in a consistently effective way.
    - (A) obdurate
    - (B) digressive
    - (C) momentous
    - (D) amiable
    - (E) arid

29. _____ should not be granted out of charity, but out of a desire to right injustice.
    - (A) Accords
    - (B) Clemency
    - (C) Amiability
    - (D) Catharsis
    - (E) Digression

30. "I'd love to come along," George said with a(n) _____ smile.
    - (A) digressive
    - (B) amiable
    - (C) implacable
    - (D) momentous
    - (E) arid

31. It is difficult for plants to survive in a(n) _____ desert environment.
    - (A) obdurate
    - (B) digressive
    - (C) amiable
    - (D) arid
    - (E) implacable

32. Her sudden _____ led them to believe that she was uncomfortable talking through the issue.
    - (A) accord
    - (B) catharsis
    - (C) digression
    - (D) amiability
    - (E) clemency

On Your Own:
Write one sentence using each word below to demonstrate your understanding of the word's meaning.

33. **clemency** _____

34. **digression** _____

35. **amiable** _____

36. **arid** _____

37. **implacable** _____

38. **momentous** _____

39. **accord** _____

40. **obdurate** _____

C2 Advanced Vocabulary 38

First Impressions:

Using the example sentences below, write your own definition of each boldfaced word. Then write the letter of the definition from the box that best matches your definition.

A	adjective: not able to be tolerated by the conscience	**C**	verb: to assemble; to gather into one place or source; to make of materials from various sources
B	noun: free will; personal choice	**D**	adjective: capable of being broken or damaged

1. _____ A court convened to place the general on trial for his **unconscionable** acts during the war.

UNCONSCIONABLE means: _____

2. _____ Mr. Thibodaux was impressed to see the children studying diligently of their own **volition**, even without being told to do so.

VOLITION means: _____

3. _____ The school psychologist will **compile** results from the larger survey this summer and report back to the school board.

COMPILE means: _____

4. _____ The desk looked sturdy, but its shoddy construction meant it was actually quite **frangible**.

FRANGIBLE means: _____

A	adjective: hopeless or pitiful	**C**	verb: to indulge in a luxury; to spend money unnecessarily
B	verb: to scold	**D**	adjective: empty; lacking ideas or content

5. _____ The principal **castigated** Shayshay for yelling at her teacher and nearly sent her home.

CASTIGATE means: _____

6. _____ Compared to the deep and insightful commentary of his later years, Jorge's early critical work seems rather **vacuous**.

VACUOUS means: _____

7. _____ No matter how little money was in her bank account, Rhona would always **splurge** on a massage once a month.

SPLURGE means: _____

8. _____ Kevin spent a few weekends every year volunteering at a local shelter to help those who were in **abject** poverty.

ABJECT means: _____

Divide and Conquer:
Choose the correct word to complete each of the following sentences.

9. Dr. Carson dedicated his work to the improvement of human beings of all social classes, from the most **(vacuous / abject)** to the most powerful.

10. I'll **(compile / splurge)** the most notable comments from this thread into an easy-to-read document.

11. The motivational speaker taught that each person is free to choose, to act according to his own **(volition / frangibility)**.

12. Unless the professor emphasizes the rigor of logic, philosophy classes can degenerate into **(vacuous / splurged)** forums of empty assertions.

13. Loopholes in the criminal code occasionally allow those who have committed **(frangible / unconscionable)** acts their freedom.

14. We were all **(castigated / compiled)** by our parents for teasing our youngest sibling.

15. Mrs. Wickham's **(splurging / compiling)** on a new, designer-brand suit surprised her friends, as she had gained a reputation for being miserly.

16. Clay pigeons are highly **(frangible / abject)** disks that are designed to break apart easily when impacted by shotgun pellets.

Hot and Cold:
Write the word from the lesson that is most nearly the *OPPOSITE* of the boldfaced word or words in each sentence below.

17. The thing that drives me crazy about Richard is that when we fight, he gives me the most _____ responses, devoid of any **intelligent** thought.

18. Ever the believer in free will, Sandra insisted that her success was due to her own _____ and that **fate** had less than nothing to do with how her life had turned out.

19. After we _____ these sources into one long list, we'll have to **disassemble** it and put each piece of research material into its own category.

20. An object that is rigid but _____ will be less likely to withstand a storm than one that is weak but **pliable**.

21. Throughout college I've learned to **save** my money very well, but now that graduation nears, I think I'll _____ on an expensive new swimsuit I've had my eye on.

22. Veronika felt _____ after being rejected by Juan, but she very soon received the **fantastic** news that she'd been offered her dream job.

23. The regime had committed _____ acts against its own people and would have to answer to a tribunal responsible for trying those in violation of **ethical** wartime behavior.

24. If you want people to **praise** you, don't give them cause to _____ you instead.

Applying Yourself:
Choose the best word to complete each of the following sentences.

25. The movie's plot revolved around transporting a(n) _____ vase from an earthquake-prone area to one of safety.
   (A) frangible
   (B) abject
   (C) castigated
   (D) vacuous
   (E) unconscionable

26. Sadly, even the most brilliant minds in the third-world country cannot escape the _____ poverty that comes with a lack of opportunity.
   (A) compiled
   (B) splurged
   (C) castigated
   (D) abject
   (E) unconscionable

27. We _____ evidence over several months to suggest that the results of our experiment were more than just circumstantial.
    (A) circumvented
    (B) castigated
    (C) compiled
    (D) proselytized
    (E) splurged

28. After his mother _____ him for staying out late, Henry promised he'd be home on time from then on.
    (A) compiled
    (B) proselytized
    (C) circumvented
    (D) splurged
    (E) castigated

29. He cannot blame his predicament on anyone else because he acted of his own _____.
    (A) splurge
    (B) compilation
    (C) quisling
    (D) affinity
    (E) volition

30. It's okay to _____ occasionally when you are diligently saving money.
    (A) proselytize
    (B) castigate
    (C) circumvent
    (D) compile
    (E) splurge

31. For years, the umpire Jim Joyce felt _____ about blowing a call that would have given the pitcher a perfect game.
    (A) frangible
    (B) compiled
    (C) vacuous
    (D) unconscionable
    (E) abject

32. Sadly, my date last night was _____, as every one of his "thoughts" was taken directly from television shows.
    (A) abject
    (B) frangible
    (C) castigated
    (D) vacuous
    (E) compiled

On Your Own:

Write one sentence using each word below to demonstrate your understanding of the word's meaning.

33. **unconscionable** _____

34. **frangible** _____

35. **splurge** _____

36. **compile** _____

37. **vacuous** _____

38. **volition** _____

39. **castigate** _____

40. **abject** _____

C2 Advanced Vocabulary 39

First Impressions:

Using the example sentences below, write your own definition of each boldfaced word. Then write the letter of the definition from the box that best matches your definition.

A	noun: the creation of agreement or compatibility between two or more things	**C**	noun: one who helps another, who is less experienced, to grow and learn
B	verb: to worsen; to deteriorate	**D**	adjective: marvelous; enormous

1. _____ It is interesting how national beauty pageants can **degenerate** into platforms for controversy and juicy gossip.

DEGENERATE means: _____

2. _____ The part of his job that Professor Sherwood enjoyed the most was acting as a **mentor** to older students who were about to leave school and enter the job market.

MENTOR means: _____

3. _____ The **reconciliation** of the two brothers after years of bitterness was a source of great joy and relief to their parents.

RECONCILIATION means: _____

4. _____ Even weeks after the accident, the well was still spouting **prodigious** amounts of oil into the water.

PRODIGIOUS means: _____

A	adjective: theoretical; existing as an idea, but not in reality; difficult to understand	**C**	adjective: real; genuine; reliable; not false or copied
B	adjective: lowered in intensity or strength; not marked by any special features; quiet; controlled	**D**	noun: a sacred offering

5. _____ The priest placed the **oblation** of rice and chicken into the sacred flame.

OBLATION means: _____

6. _____ The symptoms of allergies are similar to those caused by a severe head cold, but in a milder, more **subdued** form.

SUBDUED means: _____

7. _____ I have trouble imagining **abstract** ideas and much prefer to have some kind of physical example for what I'm supposed to be thinking about.

ABSTRACT means: _____

8. _____ Lyra wasn't sure whether the funny picture on the Internet was **authentic** or fake.

AUTHENTIC means: _____

Divide and Conquer:

Choose the correct word to complete each of the following sentences.

9. The Trojan army would leave a(n) **(mentor / oblation)** on the altar at the temple of Apollo to gain favor with the god on the eve of the battle.

10. Rubin amazed everyone with his **(degenerate / prodigious)** intellect by getting a perfect score on the SAT.

11. Under the tutelage of his **(subdual / mentor)**, Jim quickly learned the ropes of corporate finance and eventually became an industry leader.

12. Checkers is a(n) **(abstract / prodigious)** strategy game; unlike the bishops and knights of chess, checkers pieces do not represent any real-world items.

13. Over time the patient's condition **(degenerated / authenticated)** as the disease took hold.

14. The curator of the museum decided to consult an expert to determine whether the newly-discovered painting was **(authentic / abstract)** or spurious.

15. The **(oblation / reconciliation)** between the Hatfields and the McCoys may never occur; their mutual hatred is too great.

16. Our celebration became **(abstract / subdued)** when the neighbors complained about the noise.

Hot and Cold:

Write the word from the lesson that is most nearly the *OPPOSITE* of the boldfaced word or words in each sentence below.

17. Though Lisa's desire to do well in school is _____, her claim that she'll be able to change her poor study habits overnight seems misguided if not entirely **false**.

18. While I enjoy calculus, its _____ concepts occasionally confuse me to the point where I want to run screaming back to the **concrete** world of arithmetic.

19. Hungry for **conflict**, Shawn refused all of my attempts at _____ and would not allow his bruised ego to be mollified in any way.

20. After our **paltry** breakfast of toast and water, the _____ dinner of meats, cooked vegetables, casseroles, and desserts before us was utterly spectacular.

21. As my physical health _____ and I grew less capable of taking care of myself, I found that my mental clarity **improved** and I was able to process more complex information than ever before.

22. Mr. Allen, my _____ for many years, has told me that it has been enjoyable for him to share his knowledge and experience with me, his favorite **pupil**.

23. The atmosphere of the party was surprisingly _____ compared to the prior week's **rowdy** gathering.

Applying Yourself:

Choose the best word to complete each of the following sentences.

24. We had to review July's expenditures before the _____ between the two differing accounts could occur.
    (A) oblation
    (B) abstraction
    (C) subdual
    (D) reconciliation
    (E) mentor

25. The Aztecs practiced human _____, thinking that the death of a person would satisfy the gods and ensure a bountiful harvest.
    (A) subdual
    (B) oblation
    (C) reconciliation
    (D) abstraction
    (E) mentor

26. The happy atmosphere in the room became
    _____ when the dour news arrived.
    (A) degenerated
    (B) authentic
    (C) subdued
    (D) prodigious
    (E) abstract

27. The guys down at Jewelry Central can examine
    your coin to determine whether or not it is
    _____.
    (A) authentic
    (B) prodigious
    (C) subdued
    (D) degenerate
    (E) abstract

28. Her _____ stamina allowed her to finish the
    marathon in record time.
    (A) subdued
    (B) abstract
    (C) prodigious
    (D) authentic
    (E) degenerated

29. Macon preferred to deal with concrete
    problems, such as financial accounting, and
    didn't take well to _____ fields of study like
    theoretical physics.
    (A) prodigious
    (B) abstract
    (C) subdued
    (D) authentic
    (E) prodigious

30. This was a sign not of progress, but of how we
    have let our forward-thinking _____ into militant
    progressivism.
    (A) subdue
    (B) blandish
    (C) culminate
    (D) authenticate
    (E) degenerate

31. Learn to adopt a(n) _____ and rely on her, and
    you won't have to reinvent the wheel in
    everything you do.
    (A) mentor
    (B) reconciliation
    (C) abstraction
    (D) subdual
    (E) oblation

On Your Own:
Write one sentence using each word below to demonstrate your understanding of the word's meaning.

32. **reconciliation** _____

33. **authentic** _____

34. **mentor** _____

35. **oblation** _____

36. **prodigious** _____

37. **degenerate** _____

38. **subdued** _____

39. **abstract** _____

C2 Advanced Vocabulary 40

First Impressions:

Using the example sentences below, write your own definition of each boldfaced word. Then write the letter of the definition from the box that best matches your definition.

A	adjective: fervent; passionate; devoted	C	noun: an idea contrary to popular belief or accepted religion
B	noun: a rule or principle for evaluating or testing something	D	noun: hatred; spite

1. _____ Copernicus' burial in an anonymous grave in the 16th century was not, as some claim, linked to the fact that the church accused him of **heresy**.

HERESY means: _____

2. _____ Tony is an **avid** comic book fan who collects every issue of Superman comics he can find.

AVID means: _____

3. _____ Teachers should never play favorites; they should always use the same **criterion** to grade their students' work.

CRITERION means: _____

4. _____ Sam's **malice** towards Sofia was so strong that he couldn't even bear to be in the same room with her.

MALICE means: _____

A	noun: happiness; a source of happiness	C	noun: disrespectful boldness
B	noun: a small amount	D	noun: something new; newness

5. _____ Feeling that his predecessor's decision lacked "even a **modicum** of good sense", the judge overturned the earlier ruling.

MODICUM means: _____

6. _____ The **novelty** of the new product wore off quickly when a competitor came out with a similar, but flashier, version of it.

NOVELTY means: _____

7. _____ Dr. Stephenson was unwilling to tolerate such **effrontery** and demanded that his colleague apologize for such lack of proper respect.

EFFRONTERY means: _____

8. _____ The students enjoyed a period of **felicity** after it was announced that their school would be visited by a famous and popular comedian.

FELICITY means: _____

Divide and Conquer:

Choose the correct word to complete each of the following sentences.

9. The principal was temporarily surprised by the **(modicum / effrontery)** of the student who took the pen from her hand to write with.

10. The teacher remarked that the phrase "they all lived happily ever after" is more traditional than "each individual dwelt in enduring **(felicity / modicum)**."

11. While some praised the new model as an important innovation, others denounced it as **(novelty / heresy)**.

12. A(n) **(avid / malicious)** reader, Sam has read over 15 books this summer.

13. The police officer determined that the broken window was the result of an accident rather than **(malice / effrontery)**.

14. When films were first invented, the **(novelty / felicity)** of the new medium shocked audiences so much that some viewers fainted when they saw a clip of a train moving towards them.

15. The website clearly listed each **(effrontery / criterion)** of the hiring process for new candidates.

16. Even a **(heresy / modicum)** of sense should prevent someone from playing with matches.

Hot and Cold:

Write the word from the lesson that is most nearly the *OPPOSITE* of the boldfaced word or words in each sentence below.

17. It is strange that the people for whom we show the most **love** can also be the people for whom we feel the greatest _____.

18. The easily offended master demanded complete **meekness** from his students and would tolerate no hint of _____ on their parts.

19. I'd appreciate even the smallest _____ of decency among the **abundance** of disrespect with which you've been regarding me recently.

20. The child showed her **displeasure** by grimacing intently and her _____ by letting out big, happy laughs.

21. The _____ of travel may be exciting at first, but you might soon come to realize that you miss the **familiarity** of home.

22. Claire was **indifferent** to Jeremy's _____ interest in her.

23. The traditions of the **orthodoxy** are long-held, and those who uphold them are suspicious of any act of _____ that might challenge old beliefs.

Applying Yourself:

Choose the best word to complete each of the following sentences.

24. The scientist's new writings, which introduced radical new ideas about the solar system, were declared by the Church to be _____.
    (A) modicum
    (B) malice
    (C) effrontery
    (D) criterion
    (E) heresy

25. Our _____ for acceptance is simple: at least one year of experience.
    (A) criterion
    (B) heresy
    (C) modicum
    (D) felicity
    (E) effrontery

26. Even though you hate your aunt, try to show more than a _____ of respect while you are at her house.
(A) modicum
(B) novelty
(C) criterion
(D) felicity
(E) heresy

27. Respecting your opponent, rather than showing _____, is a sure way to curry favor with the voters.
(A) effrontery
(B) novelty
(C) heresy
(D) malice
(E) felicity

28. Should you wish to pass others on the corporate ladder, show discipline and respect, rather than _____, in all your dealings.
(A) effrontery
(B) modicum
(C) criterion
(D) heresy
(E) felicity

29. Her dramatic monologues were known for their _____ and original characters.
(A) heresy
(B) novelty
(C) malice
(D) modicum
(E) effrontery

30. A(n) _____ science fiction fan, she read dozens of novels per month.
(A) felicitous
(B) avid
(C) heretical
(D) novel
(E) malicious

31. My daughter is my _____: an eternal light on even the dreariest of days.
(A) effrontery
(B) heresy
(C) felicity
(D) modicum
(E) malice

On Your Own:
Write one sentence using each word below to demonstrate your understanding of the word's meaning.

32. **effrontery** _____

33. **novelty** _____

34. **heresy** _____

35. **criterion** _____

36. **avid** _____

37. **felicity** _____

38. **modicum** _____

39. **malice** _____

C2 Advanced Vocabulary 41

First Impressions:

Using the example sentences below, write your own definition of each boldfaced word. Then write the letter of the definition from the box that best matches your definition.

A	adjective: peaceful; able to be trained or controlled	**C**	adjective: ridiculous; intended to amuse through an absurd situation
B	noun: the lowest point	**D**	verb: to reach the final stage or highest point

1. _____ The many minor celebrations **culminated** in a giant stage show in the town square.

CULMINATE means: _____

2. _____ The actor launched his career with a **farcical** comedy that poked fun at the lives of

powerful businessmen.

FARCICAL means: _____

3. _____ After two years spent teaching unruly kindergarteners, Mrs. Katz found working with the

relatively **docile** junior class to be a refreshing change of pace.

DOCILE means: _____

4. _____ After it reached its **nadir**, the economy had no direction to go but up.

NADIR means: _____

A	verb: to avoid or escape, especially to avoid capture	**C**	adjective: conscientious; extremely thorough
B	verb: to be successful over an opponent	**D**	verb: to give a false appearance

5. _____ We must be steadfast in our training if we hope to **prevail** at the state finals next year.

PREVAIL means: _____

6. _____ The **scrupulous** worker stayed late to finish inputting data and then checked the chart

once he was done to make sure there were no mistakes.

SCRUPULOUS means: _____

7. _____ The point of "hide and seek" is to **elude** whoever is "it" for as long as possible.

ELUDE means: _____

8. _____ As we move forward with this controversial measure, it is important that we not

dissemble, but rather be clear and frank in our intentions.

DISSEMBLE means: _____

Divide and Conquer:

Choose the correct word to complete each of the following sentences.

9. While helium **(prevails / dissembles)** as the second-most common element in the universe, on Earth it is becoming more and more scarce.

10. Jacob's many efforts to improve education **(culminated / dissembled)** in his founding of an online university late in his career.

11. The **(culmination / nadir)** of the mailman's day wasn't the moment when he was bitten by the dog; it occurred when the dog ran away with his pants in its teeth.

12. Ashley felt no need to **(dissemble / prevail)** happiness; she was genuinely excited to hear the news.

13. After a heavy meal the vicious dog became sluggish and **(docile / farcical)**.

14. The manager of the store promoted Cecile to assistant front manager due to her **(docile / scrupulous)** work as a cashier: she always arrived on time and worked hard during all of her hours.

15. The students wrote a **(dissembled / farcical)** play in which the teachers of the school were detectives trying to find missing pets.

16. The rare frog has **(prevailed / eluded)** capture for years, so researchers have had very little chance to study it directly.

Hot and Cold:

Write the word from the lesson that is most nearly the *OPPOSITE* of the boldfaced word or words in each sentence below.

17. Knowing my parents' views on schooling, I found it necessary to _____ like I was still in college rather than **proclaim** that I had started my own business.

18. Seeing Ralph's career _____ in the appointment to such a prestigious position shocked those who had witnessed his influence **decline** over the years.

19. Truth and honor may be righteous, but they don't always _____ over lies and selfishness; indeed, sometimes the best virtues **lose** to the most wicked.

20. The once **ill-tempered** mare had grown _____ with age, letting even children ride her where once she would have reared up at the mere sight of anyone but her trainer.

21. The _____ play made half the audience, who knew it was supposed to be a joke, laugh, and confused those who assumed the play would be seriously **straightforward**.

22. As much as the fox tried to _____ the farmer, it was **caught** after 4 months of stealing chickens.

23. I didn't have time to make a(n) _____ or even remotely careful critique of the work; given the short deadline, the best I could manage was a somewhat **careless** review of whether or not the book had appealed to me.

24. The _____ of our business' profits occurred during 2008, the year of the economic crash, while its **zenith** was at the height of the housing boom in the early 2000s.

Applying Yourself:

Choose the best word to complete each of the following sentences.

25. To _____ over the Heat, the Lakers must play perfect basketball.
    (A) culminate
    (B) prevail
    (C) liquefy
    (D) elude
    (E) dissemble

26. Pessimists don't view a bad situation as _____ in their lives; they believe that things can always get worse.
    (A) farces
    (B) culminations
    (C) nadirs
    (D) scruples
    (E) pathologies

27. Unlike his _____ sister, Robert, an underachiever, received poor grades and never paid much attention to his responsibilities.
    (A) docile
    (B) culminated
    (C) dissembled
    (D) farcical
    (E) scrupulous

28. It was impossible to _____ the police; they caught up with us in minutes.
    (A) elude
    (B) dissemble
    (C) culminate
    (D) liquefy
    (E) prevail

29. _____ material has traditionally been the domain of situation comedies.
    (A) Dissembled
    (B) Scrupulous
    (C) Farcical
    (D) Eluded
    (E) Docile

30. Our journey to the Himalayas _____ in reaching the summit of Mt. Everest.
    (A) eluded
    (B) prevailed
    (C) culminated
    (D) liquefied
    (E) dissembled

31. After months of training, the attack dog was rendered _____ to the point that its owners allowed their toddler to play with it.
    (A) eluded
    (B) culminated
    (C) docile
    (D) farcical
    (E) scrupulous

32. I _____ and feigned disappointment when my wife's irritating friend couldn't make it to the party.
    (A) liquefied
    (B) eluded
    (C) dissembled
    (D) culminated
    (E) prevailed

On Your Own:
Write one sentence using each word below to demonstrate your understanding of the word's meaning.

33. **dissemble** _____

34. **scrupulous** _____

35. **farcical** _____

36. **culminate** _____

37. **elude** _____

38. **prevail** _____

39. **nadir** _____

40. **docile** _____

C2 Advanced Vocabulary 42

First Impressions:
Using the example sentences below, write your own definition of each boldfaced word. Then write the letter of the definition from the box that best matches your definition.

A	adjective: extremely small	**C**	noun: deep disgrace; shame; dishonor
B	noun: the inability to sleep	**D**	verb: to struggle; to compete; to assert passionately

1. _____ Valuable metals like gold can be found dissolved in plain ocean water, though in amounts so **miniscule** as not to be worth the effort needed to retrieve them.

MINUSCULE means: _____

2. _____ Collins' team will avoid the **ignominy** of having lost the gold medal.

IGNOMINY means: _____

3. _____ Crowds of fans poured into the stadium to watch the finalists **contend** for the championship title.

CONTEND means: _____

4. _____ Craig finally cured his **insomnia** by seeing a therapist and learning better sleeping habits.

INSOMNIA means: _____

A	noun: an event that has significance to many members of a group	**C**	verb: to increase in number; to reproduce
B	adjective: young and immature	**D**	adjective: argumentative; fond of arguing

5. _____ Atomic weapons **proliferated** at an alarming rate during the Cold War as the United States and Soviet Union competed to become the dominant world power.

PROLIFERATE means: _____

6. _____ The brothers always seemed to be arguing about something; they were a rather **disputatious** pair.

DISPUTATIOUS means: _____

7. _____ Krista's **juvenile** response to the insult convinced her parents that she wasn't nearly as mature as they'd thought.

JUVENILE means: _____

8. _____ The tragic attack on the World Trade Center and the Pentagon on 9/11 serve as a **touchstone** for many Americans who were born in the 1970s or 1980s.

TOUCHSTONE means: _____

Divide and Conquer:
Choose the correct word to complete each of the following sentences.

9. The storming of the Bastille is a(n) **(ignominy / touchstone)** for French citizens who struggle with the excesses of authority.

10. The brothers were so **(disputatious / miniscule)** that it was a refreshing rarity to find them agreeing on any topic.

11. The young new mayor was forced to **(contend / proliferate)** with the diehards of the former political regime.

12. The **(juvenile / disputatious)** zebra became separated from its mother and barely survived the night.

13. The bubonic plague **(proliferated / contended)** as merchants unwittingly carried the disease across Europe.

14. The worm is so **(contentious / minuscule)** that biologists need a powerful microscope to see it.

15. So great was the **(contention / ignominy)** of the offense that the leader was forced to leave the clan in shame.

16. Suffering from **(insomnia / proliferation)** for 20 years, my mother has never been able to get a good night's sleep.

Hot and Cold:
Write the word from the lesson that is most nearly the *OPPOSITE* of the boldfaced word or words in each sentence below.

17. Some regarded Joan of Arc with the _____ deserving a traitor; others conferred her with the **honor** of sainthood.

18. It is important for _____ students to have respect for their **elders**.

19. One of the _____ of Christianity is lauding the resurrection, while seeing parts of the Old Testament as **inconsequential events**.

20. While this warm weather has caused heat-loving algae to _____, it has caused the Thurman's minnow, which prefers the cold, to **die off**.

21. The _____ amount of effort it took to prepare a small breakfast for me is a drop in the bucket compared to the **huge amount** of energy it will take to prepare the food for the party's 100 guests.

22. Though he was accused of being _____ and arguing just for the love of drama, Craig insisted that he only challenged others so often because no progress came from a **conciliatory** attitude.

23. The **restfulness** of the others in the cabin mocked me and my terrible _____.

24. Our history professor would _____ that anyone who refused to study history had no place in it; he would heatedly debate anyone who did not **accept** his position.

Applying Yourself:
Choose the best word to complete each of the following sentences.

25. I lay awake in bed all night, suffering from _____.
   (A) insomnia
   (B) proliferation
   (C) touchstones
   (D) contention
   (E) ignominy

26. Certain events on television, such as the finale of *Lost*, serve as cultural _____ for members of a certain generation.
   (A) touchstones
   (B) insomnia
   (C) ignominy
   (D) proliferation
   (E) contention

27. Even a(n) _____ amount of dust can contaminate the entire experiment.
    (A) proliferated
    (B) minuscule
    (C) ignominious
    (D) juvenile
    (E) disputatious

28. The Cold War had escalated to the point that both the USA and the USSR _____ their nuclear arsenals.
    (A) contended
    (B) proliferated
    (C) infringed
    (D) corroborated
    (E) scintillated

29. Unwilling to debate with Michael, who _____ his arguments so forcefully that his opponents almost always lost, she opted to practice with another club member.
    (A) corroborated
    (B) infringed
    (C) scintillated
    (D) proliferated
    (E) contended

30. The twins were complete opposites: one was very shy and fearful of causing problems while the other was rather _____.
    (A) disputatious
    (B) juvenile
    (C) miniscule
    (D) proliferated
    (E) ignominious

31. We felt a sense of deep mutual _____ for lying to our friend about our whereabouts.
    (A) ignominy
    (B) adversity
    (C) touchstone
    (D) contention
    (E) jubilation

32. She found his sense of humor _____; the only things he seemed to find funny were fart jokes.
    (A) ignominious
    (B) miniscule
    (C) juvenile
    (D) proliferating
    (E) disputatious

On Your Own:

Write one sentence using each word below to demonstrate your understanding of the word's meaning.

33. **juvenile** _____

34. **proliferate** _____

35. **contend** _____

36. **touchstone** _____

37. **disputatious** _____

38. **insomnia** _____

39. **minuscule** _____

40. **ignominy** _____

C2 Advanced Vocabulary 43

First Impressions:
Using the example sentences below, write your own definition of each boldfaced word. Then write the letter of the definition from the box that best matches your definition.

A	verb: to prohibit something that is seen as harmful	**C**	adjective: freely exchangeable or replaceable
B	noun: cheerful readiness for action	**D**	noun: a puzzle; a mystery

1. _____ The soldier responded to every order with **alacrity**, quickly fulfilling whatever duty was required.

ALACRITY means: _____

2. _____ Sherlock Holmes is known for solving many **enigmas** deemed unsolvable by the police or those involved in them.

ENIGMA means: _____

3. _____ Crude oil is a **fungible** resource: one barrel of oil has nearly exactly the same properties as any other.

FUNGIBLE means: _____

4. _____ The city council created an ordinance to **proscribe** the sale of aerosol paint cans to minors in order to reduce the appearance of graffiti.

PROSCRIBE means: _____

A	verb: to wander aimlessly, physically or mentally	**C**	verb: to make a sudden movement due to shock or pain
B	adjective: burdensome; heavy and awkward	**D**	verb: to agree; to cooperate; to happen at the same time

5. _____ I **flinched** as the zookeeper draped the snake over my shoulders.

FLINCH means: _____

6. _____ Robert was prone to **ramble** in the courtroom; twice the judge had to remind him to stick to the case at hand while making his statement.

RAMBLE means: _____

7. _____ The **cumbersome** books were difficult to carry down the stairs.

CUMBERSOME means: _____

8. _____ I **concur** that the book was fantastic, although I disagree that the best part was the introduction.

CONCUR means: _____

Divide and Conquer:

Choose the correct word to complete each of the following sentences.

9. The puppy **(concurred / flinched)** sharply when I shook him awake.

10. Because the new employee answered each challenge with **(alacrity / enigma)**, he was quickly promoted to a position of authority.

11. It will be difficult to hike with such a **(cumbersome / rambling)** pack, but I look forward to the challenge.

12. Though few take the idea of the Bermuda Triangle seriously, the disappearance of several ships off the coast of Florida remains a(n) **(concurrence / enigma)**.

13. The fire code **(rambles / proscribes)** the use of fireworks except by approved groups.

14. Many raw materials are **(proscribed / fungible)** resources; after they have been turned into manufactured products it is impossible to determine their origin.

15. I started to make a grocery list as my roommate **(rambled / concurred)** about yet another inane topic.

16. We are in broad agreement with the recommendations and **(concur / flinch)** with the conclusions on the key issues as identified.

Hot and Cold:

Write the word from the lesson that is most nearly the *OPPOSITE* of the boldfaced word or words in each sentence below.

17. During the 1920s, alcohol was _____ in the United States as it was seen as the cause of disease and unemployment; only alcohol as **prescribed** by a doctor was permitted.

18. The new student's _____ enthused her teacher, who was accustomed to the **wariness** and educational timidity of her current class.

19. Some historical facts are obvious **truths**, while others remain _____ due to the lack of proof or evidence surrounding them.

20. As far as I could see, the puppies were _____; none of them were **distinguishable** from any others.

21. The CEO _____ that big changes had to be made—in fact, she said that this fact was indisputable—but she **disagreed** that the solution was to cut wages and asked the board to think of an alternative solution.

22. Rodney **remained stony-faced** during the examination, but Lyle _____ when the doctor pricked his skin.

23. Do not _____; restrain yourself to **speaking directly and relevantly**.

24. The _____ penguin waddled along the ice while the **graceful** seal swam below.

Applying Yourself:

Choose the best word to complete each of the following sentences.

25. The issue of whether or not to _____ assault rifles has formed a rift between some community leaders and gun advocates.
    (A) flinch
    (B) encumber
    (C) ramble
    (D) concur
    (E) proscribe

26. Shelpa demonstrated her _____ for the trip when she packed her bag a week before the departure date.
    (A) ramble
    (B) concurrence
    (C) alacrity
    (D) flinch
    (E) proscription

27. Lefty asked me to retrieve his bat from the rack, but it didn't stand out among the many _____ bats lined up there.
    (A) proscribed
    (B) cumbersome
    (C) fungible
    (D) flinching
    (E) rambling

28. Since they had the whole day off, they leisurely _____ through the shops until closing time.
    (A) flinched
    (B) concurred
    (C) proscribed
    (D) allocated
    (E) rambled

29. Compared to the previous case study, which had been very definite, this one was a(n) _____.
    (A) encumbrance
    (B) alacrity
    (C) flinch
    (D) enigma
    (E) vestige

30. Hauling my _____ backpack around all day is exhausting.
    (A) enigmatic
    (B) proscribed
    (C) cumbersome
    (D) rambling
    (E) fungible

31. Even though I have reservations about the proposed military attack, I _____ that we must intervene.
    (A) flinch
    (B) ramble
    (C) proscribe
    (D) concur
    (E) encumber

32. Startled, I _____ when he came up behind me without warning.
    (A) rambled
    (B) flinched
    (C) encumbered
    (D) concurred
    (E) proscribed

On Your Own:
Write one sentence using each word below to demonstrate your understanding of the word's meaning.

33. **concur** _____

34. **cumbersome** _____

35. **proscribe** _____

36. **enigma** _____

37. **ramble** _____

38. **alacrity** _____

39. **fungible** _____

40. **flinch** _____

C2 Advanced Vocabulary 44

First Impressions:
Using the example sentences below, write your own definition of each boldfaced word. Then write the letter of the definition from the box that best matches your definition.

A	noun: something disliked universally	**C**	noun: a long period of historical time
B	verb: to completely erase	**D**	adjective: showing sudden irritation to minor annoyances

1. _____ Before the Earth had its current climate, it underwent an **epoch** of extreme cold.

EPOCH means: _____

2. _____ The **petulant** child refused to sit in the chair because it was not blue.

PETULANT means: _____

3. _____ Though members of different political parties disagree about many things, topics like child

abuse are **anathema** to all.

ANATHEMA means: _____

4. _____ After it was learned that Robert had been wrongfully charged with the robbery, his criminal

record was **expunged**.

EXPUNGE means: _____

A	adjective: considerate; thoughtful; paying attention; polite	**C**	verb: to perform difficult labor
B	noun: an order or command	**D**	adjective: uncalled for; unnecessary

5. _____ Evelyn appreciated her friend's **attentive** tutoring the night before her final exam.

ATTENTIVE means: _____

6. _____ The principal issued the **mandate** that all teachers would have to include more reading in

their curricula.

MANDATE means: _____

7. _____ The farmers **moiled** for hours in the hot sun to bring in the harvest.

MOIL means: _____

8. _____ The strict parents often gave their children **undue** punishments for minor offenses.

UNDUE means: _____

Divide and Conquer:
Choose the correct word to complete each of the following sentences.

9. Some say that the time of the Roman Empire was a(n) **(petulance / epoch)** of simultaneous peace and constant war in European and African history.

10. Janet tried to leave the party without calling **(undue / attentive)** attention to herself.

11. The Stewarts spend very little on fresh produce, as green vegetables are **(anathema / moil)** to the members of the family.

12. The detective suspected that someone had covered up a crime when he discovered that several specific records had been **(mandated / expunged)**.

13. It's important to be **(attentive / mandated)** during class so that you will be alert and ready to answer any questions.

14. The **(petulant / undue)** girl became cranky at the smallest irritations.

15. Relief workers **(expunged / moiled)** in the quagmire to help the area recover from the hurricane.

16. Charlie received a(n) **(mandate / epoch)** from his employer to take his vacation time before Christmas.

Hot and Cold:
Write the word from the lesson that is most nearly the *OPPOSITE* of the boldfaced word or words in each sentence below.

17. Janet felt she'd be more willing to cooperate with her parents if they'd _____ less and **request** more.

18. Fearful of ever being **inconsiderate** of her guests' needs, Kesha did her best to be as _____ as possible and anticipate anything they might need to feel comfortable.

19. I hope he didn't cause you a(n) _____ amount of trouble tonight; he's typically quite **reasonable**.

20. After the graffiti was _____ from the outside of the building, its walls were **inscribed** with ornate decorations to discourage further "adornment".

21. Conservative ideals were a(n) _____ to Thomas, as he had long cherished the **blessing** of progressivism.

22. Because she was so **easygoing** and refused to get angry, Sharon often annoyed her _____ roommate, who expected everyone to be as high-strung as he was.

23. While the men outside _____ over the back-breaking building project, the landowner **luxuriated** with a glass of expensive champagne.

24. Each historical _____ is composed of the **moments** that make it meaningful.

Applying Yourself:
Choose the best word to complete each of the following sentences.

25. The dinosaurs lived many _____ ago.
    (A) exigencies
    (B) epochs
    (C) mandates
    (D) anathemas
    (E) legerdemains

26. They chatted for some time before ordering, sending the _____ waiter away several times.
    (A) expunged
    (B) mandated
    (C) attentive
    (D) moiled
    (E) undue

27. True, it is best to be tolerant, but we can agree that some _____ are too repugnant to be accepted.
    (A) exigencies
    (B) mandates
    (C) epochs
    (D) legerdemains
    (E) anathemas

28. I did feel that the praise I received was _____ as my contributions to the project were minimal.
    (A) moiled
    (B) undue
    (C) attentive
    (D) mandated
    (E) petulant

29. The chain gang _____ for hours, breaking rocks with pickaxes, until the project was done.
    (A) harangued
    (B) palliated
    (C) relegated
    (D) moiled
    (E) expunged

30. My husband turns from an easygoing guy to a(n) _____, whiny child when he gets a cold.
    (A) petulant
    (B) expunged
    (C) undue
    (D) attentive
    (E) moiled

31. In the military, it is treasonous to disobey your commander's _____.
    (A) mandates
    (B) exigencies
    (C) epochs
    (D) anathemas
    (E) legerdemains

32. We tried to find proof that the evidence had been tampered with, but the needed documentation had been _____ from the record.
    (A) expunged
    (B) mandated
    (C) harangued
    (D) moiled
    (E) relegated

On Your Own:

Write one sentence using each word below to demonstrate your understanding of the word's meaning.

33. **expunge** _____

34. **epoch** _____

35. **undue** _____

36. **moil** _____

37. **mandate** _____

38. **petulant** _____

39. **anathema** _____

40. **attentive** _____

C2 Advanced Vocabulary 45

First Impressions:

Using the example sentences below, write your own definition of each boldfaced word. Then write the letter of the definition from the box that best matches your definition.

A	adjective: typical or customary	**C**	adjective: pompous; making unjustified claims; overambitious
B	noun: to view with scorn or contempt; to consider unworthy of notice or response	**D**	adjective: understood, but not stated

1. _____ Because their agreement was only **implicit** instead of written and signed, it was

impossible for Roger to sue Linda for the money she owed him.

IMPLICIT means: _____

2. _____ The seniors **disdained** the freshman students, refusing even to listen to their opinions.

DISDAIN means: _____

3. _____ At first Suelgi impressed everyone with her boasting and ambition, but after she failed to

deliver results they realized that she was merely **pretentious**.

PRETENTIOUS means: _____

4. _____ **Conventional** methods are of no use here; we must experiment to find innovative

solutions to the new problems that we face.

CONVENTIONAL means: _____

A	verb: to do without; to refrain from	**C**	noun: the place where two things meet
B	noun: a traditional saying that teaches a lesson	**D**	adjective: arousing anger or interest; annoying

5. _____ At the **junction** of 1st Street and Main, someone is building a coffee shop.

JUNCTION means: _____

6. _____ "A stitch in time saves nine" is an **adage** with parallels in many different cultures.

ADAGE means: _____

7. _____ I advise everyone to avoid rabble-rousing and making **provocative** statements.

PROVOCATIVE means: _____

8. _____ In order to save money, Ashish decided to **forgo** eating at restaurants for a few months.

FORGO means: _____

Divide and Conquer:
Choose the correct word to complete each of the following sentences.

9. The speaker began by relating a simple **(provocation / adage)** she had learned from her grandmother that had guided her through many important decisions in her life.

10. **(Conventional / Implicit)** wisdom tells us that grains should make up the basis of a sound diet, but some nutritionists disagree with this traditional notion.

11. The author arrogantly refused to take part in book signings, **(forgoing / disdaining)** the very public that was responsible for his success.

12. Christine decided to **(forgo / disdain)** eating sweets as part of her resolutions for the new year.

13. As the **(junction / adage)** of two major railroad routes, the city quickly became a prosperous part of the trade route.

14. **(Pretentious / Implicit)** in the new policy is an understanding that success is a goal shared by the entire faculty.

15. The club's advisor thought that it was **(provocative / pretentious)** of Samuel, who had just joined the group, to ask to be chosen as president.

16. Salvador Dali once produced a film that was so **(conventional / provocative)** that before the premier he filled his pockets with stones in case he needed to throw them at angry audience members.

Hot and Cold:
Write the word from the lesson that is most nearly the *OPPOSITE* of the boldfaced word or words in each sentence below.

17. The first presentation was quite _____, causing many arguments to break out within the classroom; the second was much more **calming**, dealing in universal truths everyone agreed upon.

18. Though her words were not **direct**, Marcia's stern expression was enough to convey the _____ message that she was very unhappy with us.

19. We celebrate not only a(n) _____ Christmas with a tree and eggnog, but also a **unique** family holiday called "Merrynight" during which we each get to do exactly what we want all evening.

20. Rachel was willing to _____ such luxuries as a hot shower and indoor toilet, but she absolutely **required** access to clean, filtered water.

21. The _____ I felt for my lying classmates was matched only by the **appreciation** I had for the one among them who stood up and told the truth.

22. In each of my college classes, there has been one _____ student who hijacks the discussion from more **contemplative** ones with his constant, overconfident assessments of the topic at hand.

23. I feel that I am now at the _____ of childhood and adulthood; past this moment in my life is the **divergence** of these two realities.

Applying Yourself:
Choose the best word to complete each of the following sentences.

24. The action movie was so _____ that we knew the plot within the first ten minutes.
    - (A) conventional
    - (B) provocative
    - (C) pretentious
    - (D) implicit
    - (E) disdainful

25. The accident occurred at the _____ of those two roads.
    - (A) convention
    - (B) implicitness
    - (C) adage
    - (D) disdain
    - (E) junction

26. The president treated the Soviet offer with _____ and refused to acknowledge the comments he had made.
    (A) junction
    (B) implicitness
    (C) convention
    (D) adage
    (E) disdain

27. Don't abandon all your financial dreams for the sake of saving up; instead, _____ all things unnecessary.
    (A) discriminate
    (B) forgo
    (C) ramble
    (D) disdain
    (E) disparage

28. Although the teacher never specified if students could leave the classroom to use the bathroom without asking, her imposing demeanor and strict adherence to order let the class _____ know they should ask before leaving.
    (A) implicitly
    (B) conventionally
    (C) provocatively
    (D) disdainfully
    (E) pretentiously

29. The _____ "don't cry over spilled milk" tells us to avoid worrying about minor inconveniences.
    (A) junction
    (B) convention
    (C) provocation
    (D) adage
    (E) pretentiousness

30. The _____ scientists made the false claim that they had perfected cold fusion, which, if true, would have solved the world's energy crisis.
    (A) conventional
    (B) disdainful
    (C) implicit
    (D) pretentious
    (E) provocative

31. Many view the new film as unnecessarily _____, as it portrays Martin Luther King Jr. in an unfavorable light.
    (A) disdainful
    (B) conventional
    (C) implicit
    (D) pretentious
    (E) provocative

On Your Own:
Write one sentence using each word below to demonstrate your understanding of the word's meaning.

32. **adage** _____

33. **provocative** _____

34. **junction** _____

35. **forgo** _____

36. **pretentious** _____

37. **implicit** _____

38. **disdain** _____

39. **conventional** _____

C2 Advanced Vocabulary 46
First Impressions:
Using the example sentences below, write your own definition of each boldfaced word. Then write the letter of the definition from the box that best matches your definition.

A	noun: hatred	**C**	noun: forgiveness for wrongdoings, especially when granted by a government
B	noun: a basic rule of proper behavior	**D**	verb: to analyze; to test out

1. _____ She decided to carefully **assess** the situation before jumping into it headfirst.

ASSESS means: _____

2. _____ The new law would grant **amnesty** to illegal aliens and offer them a path to gaining full

citizenship.

AMNESTY means: _____

3. _____ Hikari felt a great **enmity** towards her brother because he sold their videogames without

asking her first.

ENMITY means: _____

4. _____ Many consider the Ten Commandments to be the fundamental **precepts** of Judeo-

Christian ethics.

PRECEPT means: _____

A	adjective: respectful	**C**	verb: to scold
B	noun: an abnormal narrowing; a restriction	**D**	noun: excessive pride that leads to downfall

5. _____ The Tower of Babel is a biblical tale of mankind's **hubris**: When the citizens of a great city

attempt to build a tower reaching to heaven, their language is confounded as punishment for their

pride.

HUBRIS means: _____

6. _____ The recent **stricture** on new memberships to the club was intended to halt overcrowding.

STRICTURE means: _____

7. _____ The **reverent** attendees of the court dropped to the ground when their king entered.

REVERENT means: _____

8. _____ The principal **admonished** Shayshay for yelling at her teacher and nearly sent her home.

ADMONISH means: _____

Divide and Conquer:
Choose the correct word to complete each of the following sentences.

9. Before opening her mouth, Alex calmly **(assessed / admonished)** the situation and tried to decide whether she were right or wrong.

10. The library held a(n) **(stricture / amnesty)** day on which patrons could return their overdue books without paying any fines.

11. After spending several days alone in the woods, Matthew developed an appreciation and **(stricture / reverence)** for nature's beauty and calming effects.

12. Members of the two warring tribes felt strong **(enmity / admonishment)** toward each other.

13. Winnie the Pooh **(assessed / admonished)** Piglet for spilling the honey.

14. Taking proper notes and completing papers on time are **(precepts / admonishments)** for this class.

15. The **(hubris / reverence)** of the soldier led him to charge a bunker alone in the belief that he could singlehandedly change the outcome of the battle.

16. Exposure to corn causes a **(stricture / hubris)** in Alyssa's breathing canals, so she keeps an inhaler of medicine with her at all times.

Hot and Cold:
Write the word from the lesson that is most nearly the *OPPOSITE* of the boldfaced word or words in each sentence below.

17. The government of the northern country granted _____ to the child soldiers involved in the war and heavily **sanctioned** the militia responsible for forcing these children to commit unspeakable acts.

18. While one group wanted to _____ the scientific journal's claims, the other preferred to **accept** without question any theory put forth as fact.

19. I fell victim to my own _____ and failed the test I thought I was too smart to study for, proving that **humility** is more useful than pride.

20. There was some left over _____ between my parents as a result of their bitter divorce, but their **love** for me overshadowed the ill-will they held for each other.

21. Leann felt a(n) _____ appreciation for her history teacher and wouldn't stand for any **disrespectful** comments toward him.

22. The teacher's severe _____ were difficult to deal with for children used to much praise and **positivity** from their superiors.

23. Rather than being **praised** for telling the truth about what he'd done, John was _____ for roughhousing indoors and breaking the lamp..

Applying Yourself:
Choose the best word to complete each of the following sentences.

24. The president has the power to grant _____ to prisoners who he feels have been railroaded.
    (A) admonishments
    (B) assessments
    (C) hubris
    (D) amnesty
    (E) strictures

25. The _____ between cats and mice is easy to spot; there is no love between animals of these species.
    (A) amnesty
    (B) hubris
    (C) enmity
    (D) assessment
    (E) admonishment

26. Hall's brash manner can be attributed to _____; because he was an award-winning rock climber, he assumed that no tragedy could ever befall him.
    (A) hubris
    (B) assessment
    (C) reverence
    (D) precept
    (E) stricture

27. Her mother was constantly _____ her to do her chores.
    (A) assessing
    (B) revering
    (C) evincing
    (D) alienating
    (E) admonishing

28. Be _____ toward your grandfather, for he endured much during tough times in order to improve our family's lot.
    (A) primal
    (B) alienating
    (C) admonishing
    (D) assessed
    (E) reverent

29. In an attempt to _____ the effectiveness of the dishwashing fluid, the testers tried in on several varieties of stains.
    (A) alienate
    (B) assess
    (C) admonish
    (D) evince
    (E) revere

30. The town's _____ against dogs on the beach left us feeling that no one on the city council was an animal lover.
    (A) stricture
    (B) enmity
    (C) assessment
    (D) hubris
    (E) reverence

31. Following the _____ of the company includes dressing conservatively, staying off social media, and respecting coworkers.
    (A) reverence
    (B) admonishment
    (C) strictures
    (D) hubris
    (E) precepts

On Your Own:
Write one sentence using each word below to demonstrate your understanding of the word's meaning.

32. **stricture** _____

33. **hubris** _____

34. **admonish** _____

35. **enmity** _____

36. **reverent** _____

37. **precept** _____

38. **amnesty** _____

39. **assess** _____

C2 Advanced Vocabulary 47

First Impressions:

Using the example sentences below, write your own definition of each boldfaced word. Then write the letter of the definition from the box that best matches your definition.

A	verb: to call forth or summon	**C**	noun: a fictional creature made from parts of different animals; an unlikely product of imagination
B	verb: to weaken; to disturb the composure of; to faze	**D**	adjective: filled with unreasonable fascination

1. _____ Jason became **infatuated** with a new author every month, declaring each to be the greatest writer since Shakespeare.

INFATUATED means: _____

2. _____ Though recent events have been difficult, we cannot let them **enervate** us as we strive to bring about change.

ENERVATE means: _____

3. _____ The wizard **conjured** a fiery spirit to do combat with the rival magician.

CONJURE means: _____

4. _____ While Lavanya was convinced that one day she would find a medicine that would cure any viral disease, other researchers thought that this notion was a mere **chimera**.

CHIMERA means: _____

A	verb: to enroll in a school or university	**C**	noun: approval, especially from an official source
B	verb: to express disapproval to someone	**D**	noun: the group of members of society who are highly educated or literate

5. _____ With the **approbation** of the city council, Manthan was able to move forward with his plans to construct a conference center.

APPROBATION means: _____

6. _____ Ms. Williams gently **reproached** her student for giving up on the assignment five minutes after he started.

REPROACH means: _____

7. _____ Phillip **matriculated** as an undergraduate in 2006, but he was not to complete his time at the university until he received his PhD in 2013.

MATRICULATE means: _____

8. _____ During his purge, the new dictator eliminated many members of the **clerisy**, as he believed that these intellectuals were in the best position to challenge his power.

CLERISY means: _____

Divide and Conquer:
Choose the correct word to complete each of the following sentences.

9. After graduating from high school, Siwon (**infatuated / matriculated**) at Yale.

10. Some argue about whether the educational system is designed to prepare effectively students for life or to create needlessly more members of the (**clerisy / approbation**).

11. Roger was deeply (**infatuated / conjured**) with the culture of fitness, but sadly, his deep interest did not extend to actual exercise.

12. Without the (**approbation / chimera**) of the city, citizens who take the law into their own hands are mere vigilantes.

13. Though his colleagues dismiss the notion of cold fusion as a(n) (**chimera / approbation**), Professor Herbert feels that his research is close to a breakthrough.

14. The writer skillfully (**conjures / enervates**) images of lazy summers in a small Midwestern town.

15. The tragedy failed to (**enervate / reproach**) Sabrina; rather, she was filled with energy and resolve to accomplish her goals.

16. His parents (**reproached / infatuated**) his decision to drop out of school.

Hot and Cold:
Write the word from the lesson that is most nearly the *OPPOSITE* of the boldfaced word or words in each sentence below.

17. Walking through the gallery and seeing so many talented artists showcasing their work at first _____ my belief in my own abilities, but after a while, the accumulation of beauty and success **strengthened** my resolve.

18. Though Hans received plenty of _____ from his superiors for a job well done, all the praise in the world couldn't make up for the **censure** he received from his family for having worked late every day for a month.

19. While she _____ the boys' silly attitudes, the old piano teacher **approved** of the fact that they nevertheless did their homework and seemed to be improving in their skills.

20. Unfortunately, certain family circumstances are causing me to **drop out** of school only a few months after I _____.

21. The sight of the waves _____ peace and serenity in my heart and **banished** the anxiety I had so recently felt.

22. Though I knew the Boogieman was a mere _____ and couldn't possibly hurt me, to my young mind he seemed an absolute **realism**.

23. The _____ held great power over the **peasantry** since the former had access to education while the latter only labored from sun up to sun down.

24. Though I was _____ with the idea of space travel, which seemed to consume my every waking thought, I was **bored** by the study of astrophysics itself.

Applying Yourself:
Choose the best word to complete each of the following sentences.

25. The monster was a(n) _____ of Dr. Frankenstein's genius; it contained the most beautiful parts of many deceased persons.
    (A) chimera
    (B) approbation
    (C) infatuation
    (D) matriculation
    (E) clerisy

26. W.E.B Dubois believed in the "talented tenth", a(n) _____ that would lead the less educated classes of African-American society to equality.
    (A) approbation
    (B) chimera
    (C) infatuation
    (D) matriculation
    (E) clerisy

27. After she finished her marathon run, Stephanie felt extremely _____ and wanted to sleep for an entire day.
   (A) infatuated
   (B) enervated
   (C) matriculated
   (D) conjured
   (E) reproached

28. After acing the SAT, getting straight A's, and serving as president of three clubs, Sean had earned the right to _____ into his dream college.
   (A) conjure
   (B) reproach
   (C) infatuate
   (D) matriculate
   (E) enervate

29. We don't have time to wait for _____ from our commanding officer; we must attack now.
   (A) clerisy
   (B) enervation
   (C) approbation
   (D) chimera
   (E) infatuation

30. _____ a rabbit out of thin air is an old magician's trick.
   (A) Conjuring
   (B) Matriculation
   (C) Reproaching
   (D) Enervating
   (E) Infatuation

31. Rivals attempted to insult her methods, but her research proved beyond _____.
   (A) approbation
   (B) clerisy
   (C) matriculation
   (D) reproach
   (E) infatuation

32. I'm so _____ with the new president that I'm willing to overlook any of his faults.
   (A) reproached
   (B) approbated
   (C) infatuated
   (D) enervated
   (E) conjured

On Your Own:
Write one sentence using each word below to demonstrate your understanding of the word's meaning.

33. **reproach** _____

34. **approbation** _____

35. **infatuated** _____

36. **conjure** _____

37. **chimera** _____

38. **clerisy** _____

39. **enervate** _____

40. **matriculate** _____

C2 Advanced Vocabulary 48

First Impressions:
Using the example sentences below, write your own definition of each boldfaced word. Then write the letter of the definition from the box that best matches your definition.

A	noun: a short account of an amusing or interesting event	**C**	adjective: impatient; easily angered
B	noun: care for and maintenance of crops, livestock, or a household	**D**	adjective: causing or involving argument or controversy

1. _____ Remember to include more than just personal **anecdotes** in your SAT essay: your life's story might not completely support your thesis.

ANECDOTE means: _____

2. _____ The rise of animal **husbandry** greatly improved agriculture by allowing plows to be drawn by beasts of burden instead of by man.

HUSBANDRY means: _____

3. _____ Because Theodore was highly **choleric**, his friends tended to avoid him when he was having a bad day.

CHOLERIC means: _____

4. _____ The cutting of funds for student loans was the most **contentious** item in the budget, causing mass protests from the student population.

CONTENTIOUS means: _____

A	noun: treachery or faithlessness	**C**	adjective: insignificant; petty; trifling
B	noun: extreme wealth; luxuriousness; abundance	**D**	verb: to cause; to produce; to create

5. _____ The father served a **paltry** breakfast of a single boiled egg.

PALTRY means: _____

6. _____ For his **perfidy** during the Revolutionary War, Benedict Arnold has gone down in American history as a traitor.

PERFIDY means: _____

7. _____ The wealthy merchant surrounded himself with fine wines, expensive suits, and all the other trappings of **opulence**.

OPULENCE means: _____

8. _____ The group performed a series of team-building exercises to **engender** a more familiar relationship.

ENGENDER means: _____

Divide and Conquer:
Choose the correct word to complete each of the following sentences.

9. The teacher shared many **(contentions / anecdotes)** with the class of his former life as a CIA agent.

10. Robert F. Kennedy established the Peace Corps in order to **(oust / engender)** a favorable view of American culture abroad.

11. Through careful **(anecdotes / husbandry)** over several generations, many dangerous wild animals became manageable domestic livestock.

12. Religion and politics tend to be **(opulent / contentious)** subjects, so it is often considered impolite to discuss them at the dinner table.

13. Don't trust Binh to support you; his **(perfidy / anecdote)** is well documented.

14. Stewart had so much success overcoming his **(choleric / contentious)** tendencies that he decided to become an anger management counselor.

15. I had hoped for a large raise in salary, so I was disappointed by the **(paltry / husbandry)** increase in wages.

16. After leaving the impoverished countryside, Kristine was amazed by the comparative **(opulence / perfidy)** of the city.

Hot and Cold:
Write the word from the lesson that is most nearly the *OPPOSITE* of the boldfaced word or words in each sentence below.

17. The author accused the screenwriter of _____ against the original novel and claimed that the screenplay lacked an ounce of **faithfulness** to the original text.

18. The prospect of a job interview _____ hope of a brighter future within me and **diminished** the terrible feeling that I'd be unemployed forever.

19. Marv has a special talent of turning what could be a delightful little _____ about something funny that happened to him into a great **epic** that takes hours to recount.

20. While the article was mostly **pacifying** in both tone and content—seeking, as it was, to mend old political rivalries—it made a few _____ remarks that left the gates of controversy wide open.

21. The _____ baby disliked being touched, talked to, or even looked at; it had been months since he was totally **mellow**.

22. This occasion calls for a **generous** feast, not a _____ meal.

23. The _____ of the resort island, with its crystal pools and air-conditioned walkways, stood out against the sparse majority of the archipelago, fraught with **poverty** and disease.

Applying Yourself:
Choose the best word to complete each of the following sentences.

24. While I think Devin's actions harm the group, to call them acts of _____ goes a bit far.
    (A) anecdote
    (B) perfidy
    (C) contention
    (D) husbandry
    (E) opulence

25. He brought a sense of excitement to the team and _____ deep loyalty in his teammates.
    (A) contended
    (B) ousted
    (C) engendered
    (D) infringed
    (E) plodded

26. Her contribution was rather significant, unlike his _____ one.
    (A) anecdotal
    (B) opulent
    (C) paltry
    (D) contentious
    (E) perfidious

27. The community's identity had been founded upon _____; once the malls and developers encroached on our farmlands, we felt like we had lost something sacred.
    (A) contention
    (B) anecdotes
    (C) husbandry
    (D) opulence
    (E) perfidy

28. My tendency to be too _____ often results in heated arguments that end badly.
    (A) choleric
    (B) opulent
    (C) paltry
    (D) contentious
    (E) engendered

29. Chase felt ashamed that he had spent so much on the _____ of his apartment when so many in the city were hungry.
    (A) anecdotes
    (B) opulence
    (C) contention
    (D) perfidy
    (E) husbandry

30. So _____ was his demeanor that he snapped at even the slightest delay.
    (A) opulent
    (B) contentious
    (C) perfidious
    (D) engendered
    (E) choleric

31. Brian is great at parties; his _____ of last year's eventful trip to France can keep an audience entertained for hours.
    (A) anecdotes
    (B) contention
    (C) opulence
    (D) perfidy
    (E) husbandry

On Your Own:

Write one sentence using each word below to demonstrate your understanding of the word's meaning.

32. **paltry** _____

33. **engender** _____

34. **perfidy** _____

35. **opulence** _____

36. **contentious** _____

37. **choleric** _____

38. **husbandry** _____

39. **anecdote** _____

C2 Advanced Vocabulary 49

First Impressions:
Using the example sentences below, write your own definition of each boldfaced word. Then write the letter of the definition from the box that best matches your definition.

A	adjective: completely see-through; obvious	**C**	verb: to bend light by passing from one medium to another
B	noun: humble submission or respect	**D**	verb: to interpret or understand in a particular way

1. _____ Helen's prism **refracted** the sunlight and caused it to split into a rainbow of colors.

REFRACT means: _____

2. _____ In **deference** to the minister, please do not take pictures during the sermon.

DEFERENCE means: _____

3. _____ That shirt is nearly **transparent**; you need to wear a tank top underneath it.

TRANSPARENT means: _____

4. _____ It is important to speak clearly so that your listeners do not **construe** your words

incorrectly.

CONSTRUE means: _____

A	verb: to establish truth or accuracy; to settle; to establish	**C**	adjective: showing off learning; bookish
B	noun: energy and love of life; vitality	**D**	verb: to revoke, formally withdraw from, or annul

5. _____ Jennifer checked her plane ticket to **confirm** that her seat was in row 14.

CONFIRM means: _____

6. _____ Richard corrected other people's grammar so often that his friends labeled him as

pedantic.

PEDANTIC means: _____

7. _____ The community leader led the campaign to **repeal** the discriminatory voting laws, winning

him much support.

REPEAL means: _____

8. _____ Andrea's **joie de vivre** was infectious; everyone around her felt happier and more alive.

JOIE DE VIVRE means: _____

Divide and Conquer:
Choose the correct word to complete each of the following sentences.

9. When the members of the judicial council learned that the evidence upon which they had based their decision was faulty, they **(repealed / refracted)** their earlier judgment.

10. She will see to it that all due **(confirmation / deference)** be paid to their teachers by her pupils.

11. I issued a silent cry when the **(pedantic / transparent)** person sitting next to me at the reception assaulted me with an hour-long speech on the merits of adobe as a building material.

12. The professor possessed a **(confirmation / joie de vivre)** that surprised and refreshed the tired students.

13. The child's motives were **(transparent / pedantic)**: she merely wanted to sleep in her parents' bed, not to "test their mattress' strength" as she'd said.

14. I hope that you don't **(construe / repeal)** my interruptions as intentionally offensive!

15. The impressive features displayed in the advertisement **(refracted / confirmed)** rumors that the company had secretly been developing new technology for months.

16. Telescopes **(refract / defer)** light and bring it into focus, much like a magnifying glass.

Hot and Cold:
Write the word from the lesson that is most nearly the *OPPOSITE* of the boldfaced word or words in each sentence below.

17. The government _____ that it did indeed possess a stash of chemical weapons but **denied** that it would use them, hoping to stave off foreign intervention.

18. The professor may appear _____ as he stands at his podium espousing his knowledge, but in truth, he's a very **humble** fellow who believes he can learn something from everyone he meets.

19. The illness seemed to suck every bit _____ for which Sam was known and replaced it with melancholic **lethargy**.

20. Before the new law can be **enacted**, the one prohibiting its measures must be _____.

21. Though I tried my best to _____ what she meant, my efforts were **obscured** by her use of archaic vocabulary.

22. The court treated the king with _____, constantly keeping his needs and wishes in mind, but those same people thought nothing of regarding the kind's assistant with utmost **inconsideration**.

23. I bought new sunglasses that change color depending on the light: they're _____ inside and **dark** in the sun.

Applying Yourself:
Choose the best word to complete each of the following sentences.

24. The window filled with argon gas _____ the light into another direction.
    (A) confirmed
    (B) refracted
    (C) construed
    (D) deferred
    (E) repealed

25. The most respected scholars let their research do the talking, as opposed to engaging in _____ speeches.
    (A) transparent
    (B) construed
    (C) refracted
    (D) pedantic
    (E) repealed

26. Show due _____ to the professor emeritus, as his views have proven wise over the decades.
    (A) confirmation
    (B) refraction
    (C) joie de vivre
    (D) transparency
    (E) deference

27. Express _____ in all that you do; spare yourself the lethargy and sadness.
    (A) deference
    (B) joie de vivre
    (C) refraction
    (D) confirmation
    (E) transparency

28. The friends looked forward to using their backstage passes, only to find at the door that the passes had been _____.
    (A) deferred
    (B) construed
    (C) repealed
    (D) confirmed
    (E) refracted

29. We _____ his subtle limp as evidence that his injury was worse than had been reported.
    (A) construed
    (B) deferred
    (C) confirmed
    (D) repealed
    (E) refracted

30. Stacy, who went to Dr. Wilson to have him _____ her pregnancy test findings, was disappointed when his tests revealed the opposite result.
    (A) confirm
    (B) repeal
    (C) construe
    (D) refract
    (E) defer

31. Barb tried to hide her emotions, but her true feelings were quite _____.
    (A) refracted
    (B) repealed
    (C) construed
    (D) transparent
    (E) deferred

On Your Own:

Write one sentence using each word below to demonstrate your understanding of the word's meaning.

32. **transparent** _____

33. **joie de vivre** _____

34. **deference** _____

35. **confirm** _____

36. **pedantic** _____

37. **refract** _____

38. **repeal** _____

39. **construe** _____

C2 Advanced Vocabulary 50

First Impressions:
Using the example sentences below, write your own definition of each boldfaced word. Then write the letter of the definition from the box that best matches your definition.

A	adjective: severely critical; eager to find fault	**C**	adjective: long and tiresome; wordy so as to cause boredom
B	verb: to spread a message in order to win others to one's point of view	**D**	adjective: rude and disrespectful

1. _____ He is an extremely careful worker and never leaves a job unfinished, regardless of how difficult, **tedious**, or time consuming.

TEDIOUS means: _____

2. _____ **Impertinent** behavior will not be tolerated; students must show teachers proper respect.

IMPERTINENT means: _____

3. _____ Many Mormon youths devote two years of their lives to **proselytizing** to others around the world.

PROSELYTIZE means: _____

4. _____ Chloe's father seemed overly **censorious** of her English report: every time she would bring it to him, he would find something else that she needed to fix.

CENSORIOUS means: _____

A	noun: corruption; wickedness	**C**	adjective: shining brilliantly
B	adjective: in agreement; consistent	**D**	adjective: favorable of success

5. _____ **Effulgent** beams burst forth into the room as the lantern was uncovered.

EFFULGENT means: _____

6. _____ I was pleased to find that the manager's values were **consonant** with my own.

CONSONANT means: _____

7. _____ The level of **depravity** to which our youths have descended was made evident by the shocking discovery that was made.

DEPRAVITY means: _____

8. _____ The voyage at sea began well with an **auspicious** breeze and a bright blue sky.

AUSPICIOUS means: _____

Divide and Conquer:
Choose the correct word to complete each of the following sentences.

9. The game against Baltimore was tough to watch at times, especially a(n) **(tedious / effulgent)** first half that saw just one shot in its dying seconds.

10. The political group **(censored / proselytized)** their viewpoint in many ways, including advertising and direct contact with the voters.

11. The team's effortless victory in the first match was an **(auspicious / impertinent)** start to the tournament.

12. The **(effulgence / depravity)** of the warlord shocked the members of the international community.

13. Tae studied carefully to find a presidential candidate whose views were **(consonant / depraved)** with his own.

14. The orchestra conductor's continuously **(tedious / censorious)** comments ended up destroying his students' confidence instead of motivating them to improve.

15. The **(consonant / effulgent)** sun rose above the clouds, shedding its light across the land.

16. The new recruit was punished for **(impertinent / proselytized)** behavior and quickly learned to show respect for his commanding officers.

Hot and Cold:
Write the word from the lesson that is most nearly the *OPPOSITE* of the boldfaced word or words in each sentence below.

17. My father's and my teacher's expectations are _____, but my mother has an **inconsistent** idea of what I should be able to achieve.

18. The seer, observing the tea leaves, proclaimed that Martha's leaves showed _____ symbols, while mine demonstrated an **unlucky** pattern.

19. The _____ star at the top of the tree was lit by several smaller lights, making it glow like a beacon of hope over the **dull**, rural plain below it.

20. A(n) _____ lecture only serves to put me to sleep; I much prefer reviewing a **concise** summary.

21. The _____ of the prior regime—the parties, the rampant corruption—was incomparable to the prudent, **straight-laced** congress that took over afterward.

22. One branch of the faith encourages its members to _____ by going door-to-door to discuss scripture with strangers; the other urges followers to **keep quiet** about their beliefs and simply live as an example to others.

23. Lynn's _____ attitude toward her parents showed the harshness with which she judged those closest to her; indeed, she was more **charitable** toward complete strangers.

24. Glenda refused to answer such a(n) _____ question as why her children were so poorly behaved and demanded more **tact** from her interviewers.

Applying Yourself:
Choose the best word to complete each of the following sentences.

25. We viewed the clear sky and temperate weather as a(n) _____ sign for a successful climb.
    (A) depraved
    (B) tedious
    (C) auspicious
    (D) proselytized
    (E) consonant

26. Roberta, the new line chef, preferred the hectic kitchen to the _____ hostess' stand.
    (A) depraved
    (B) proselytized
    (C) consonant
    (D) tedious
    (E) auspicious

27. The _____ testimony foiled the attorney, who had hoped to find inconsistencies between the witnesses.
    (A) consonant
    (B) depraved
    (C) effulgent
    (D) impertinent
    (E) proselytized

28. Due to the _____ of his crime, the judge ruled a maximum penalty for the convict.
    (A) consonance
    (B) depravity
    (C) tedium
    (D) impertinence
    (E) auspiciousness

29. The White House is a place where decorum must be observed, so _____ speech of any kind is frowned upon.
    (A) proselytized
    (B) impertinent
    (C) depraved
    (D) censorious
    (E) consonant

30. On clear and moonless nights, the _____ stars in the country are all the illumination we need.
    (A) tedium
    (B) consonance
    (C) auspiciousness
    (D) depravity
    (E) effulgent

31. What could have possessed Steven to _____ so forcefully to those of us who didn't agree with him?
    (A) squander
    (B) proselytize
    (C) deplete
    (D) proscribe
    (E) capitulate

32. A boss cannot succeed while being constantly _____ and never showing appreciation.
    (A) depraved
    (B) auspicious
    (C) consonant
    (D) impertinent
    (E) censorious

On Your Own:

Write one sentence using each word below to demonstrate your understanding of the word's meaning.

33. **auspicious** _____

34. **censorious** _____

35. **impertinent** _____

36. **effulgent** _____

37. **depravity** _____

38. **proselytize** _____

39. **consonant** _____

40. **tedious** _____

C2 Advanced Vocabulary 51

First Impressions:

Using the example sentences below, write your own definition of each boldfaced word. Then write the letter of the definition from the box that best matches your definition.

A	verb: to close; to stop up; to shut something in, out, or off	**C**	adjective: most reliable or complete; fully developed
B	adjective: deserving blame	**D**	adjective: abundant; sufficient; many

1. _____ The pipeline spilled over 100 gallons of oil before technicians were able to **occlude** the leak.

OCCLUDE means: _____

2. _____ To many, the 1611 Authorized King James Version of the Bible is the **definitive** text--no other translation will do.

DEFINITIVE means: _____

3. _____ Using a tragic event like this as a platform for personal propaganda is **reprehensible**.

REPREHENSIBLE means: _____

4. _____ We should have no problems funding the project because we have **ample** resources.

AMPLE means: _____

A	noun: impertinence; insolence; disrespect	**C**	adjective: suitable to achieve a particular end; practical; politic
B	noun: a brief but complete collection of a body of knowledge	**D**	verb: to blame, criticize, or disapprove harshly

5. _____ Carter didn't know why his parents were **censuring** him just for going out last night; it wasn't as though he'd been out drinking for hours.

CENSURE means: _____

6. _____ The disappearing encyclopedia was once valued as a **compendium** of human knowledge that could fit on a shelf.

COMPENDIUM means: _____

7. _____ Although Gabriel wanted to play a game, he realized that it would be more **expedient** to get his homework done first.

EXPEDIENT means: _____

8. _____ Dmitri felt so insulted that he got out of the limo and berated the drive-thru cashier for his **impudence**.

IMPUDENCE means: _____

Divide and Conquer:

Choose the correct word to complete each of the following sentences.

9. The stern teacher refused to give credit for the late project, saying that the student had had (**ample / impudent**) time to complete it.

10. Powerful governments are limiting progress in international justice by acting only when it is politically (**expedient / reprehensible**).

11. When most people think of New York rock stars, they think of the savvy (**compendium / impudence**) of the likes of Lou Reed, who flouted authority often.

12. We (**occluded / censured**) the pipe so that we could repair the damage to the plumbing without the hazard of incoming water.

13. With its revisions based on actual manuscripts, the latest edition of the poet's work promises to be (**definitive / ample**).

14. Lying to protect yourself, rather than telling the truth to preserve the sanctity of your office, is a (**censured / reprehensible**) action.

15. The network executives decided to (**occlude / censure**) the show's producer when they received thousands of phone calls complaining about immoral messages and explicit visuals.

16. The general asked his aide to prepare a (**compendium / censure**) of the staff's reports to present before the committee.

Hot and Cold:

Write the word from the lesson that is most nearly the *OPPOSITE* of the boldfaced word or words in each sentence below.

17. Though the ship's engineers insisted that it was equipped with _____ life boats, the number turned out to be **insufficient** when several passengers were left without a way to exit the sinking ship.

18. It would have been _____ had the embassy issued my visa on time; instead, the embassy made the most **unhelpful** decision to delay my immigration hearing another month.

19. The city council denied and _____ the measure to cut funds from special-needs schools, claiming it was an atrocity, but heartily **approved** a measure to cut similar funds from an all-girls' school.

20. No _____ will be tolerated; we demand the **respect** of all members of the organization.

21. The mass has _____ Jean's small intestine, preventing food from passing through it, so the doctor intends to perform surgery to **open** the passage.

22. This book is intended to be a _____ collection of the band's song lyrics and will be far more thorough than the **incomplete** volumes that came before it.

23. While the committee's actions are indeed _____, its lower-ranking members appear to be **innocent** as they had no idea what kind of terrible acts their seniors were planning.

24. The editors had taken all the **scattered knowledge** in the field and compiled it into a _____ that could be accessed by anyone with an interest in the subject.

Applying Yourself:

Choose the best word to complete each of the following sentences.

25. At last, we have a(n) _____ biography of Churchill, one that clarifies all mysteries and that cannot be improved upon.
    (A) definitive
    (B) ample
    (C) occluded
    (D) impudent
    (E) censured

26. We rushed to _____ the water supply when a pipe burst and flooded the bathroom.
    (A) define
    (B) censure
    (C) occlude
    (D) expedite
    (E) reprehend

27. Negotiations collapsed when the _____ of the visiting delegation's leader proved too insulting to bear.
   (A) impudence
   (B) definition
   (C) compendium
   (D) censure
   (E) occlusion

28. A good product will be accompanied by a(n) _____ describing in simple terms how to perform every one of the product's functions.
   (A) censure
   (B) impudence
   (C) compendium
   (D) definition
   (E) expedience

29. Congress _____ President Clinton after he had lied under oath.
   (A) censured
   (B) occluded
   (C) expedited
   (D) reprehended
   (E) defined

30. The tutor taught Shikha a more _____ and quick way of finding the answer to her math problems.
   (A) definitive
   (B) expedient
   (C) reprehensible
   (D) impudent
   (E) ample

31. _____ evidence exists to suggest that global warming is being radically accelerated by pollution.
   (A) Reprehensible
   (B) Expedient
   (C) Ample
   (D) Impudent
   (E) Censured

32. Despite claims that they were only following orders, the members of the accused Nazi leadership were convicted for their _____ actions.
   (A) occluded
   (B) censured
   (C) expedient
   (D) reprehensible
   (E) ample

On Your Own:
Write one sentence using each word below to demonstrate your understanding of the word's meaning.

33. **impudence** _____

34. **definitive** _____

35. **reprehensible** _____

36. **ample** _____

37. **occlude** _____

38. **compendium** _____

39. **expedient** _____

40. **censure** _____

C2 Advanced Vocabulary 52

First Impressions:

Using the example sentences below, write your own definition of each boldfaced word. Then write the letter of the definition from the box that best matches your definition.

A	adjective: sharp and harsh; caustic like acid	**C**	adjective: dependent on something else
B	noun: certainty; freedom from doubt	**D**	verb: to make amends for a crime or sin

1. _____ Such **vitriolic** comments were surprising from someone who is usually so calm and gentle.

VITRIOLIC means: _____

2. _____ The former burglar spent his weekends volunteering at the hospital in an attempt to **atone** for his misdeeds.

ATONE means: _____

3. _____ Her early acceptance to college is **contingent** on her grades this final semester.

CONTINGENT means: _____

4. _____ While Fiona was confident in the **certitude** of her faith, Evelyn was having doubts.

CERTITUDE means: _____

A	noun: a loud, unpleasant mixture of sounds	**C**	noun: a document stating the principles of an organization or movement
B	adjective: unruly; noisy; difficult to control	**D**	noun: the belief that no god or gods exist

5. _____ Discriminated against because of his **atheism**, Mark was barred from holding local office until he declared he believed in a god.

ATHEISM means: _____

6. _____ The revolutionaries sent to each major newspaper a copy of the **manifesto** outlining their principles.

MANIFESTO means: _____

7. _____ A **cacophony** blared from the garage as the members of the heavy metal band tuned their heavily-distorted instruments.

CACOPHONY means: _____

8. _____ When a few **obstreperous** students disrupted the assembly, the principal assigned each to detention.

OBSTREPEROUS means: _____

Divide and Conquer:
Choose the correct word to complete each of the following sentences.

9. A(n) (**atheist / manifesto**) has little reason to attend a religious service.

10. The plans for the outdoor picnic are (**vitriolic / contingent**) on the continuation of this nice weather.

11. Many suspect that (**contingent / obstreperous**) children have become so because of lenient and indulgent parenting.

12. Casey's reaction to our subpar performance was critical, even bordering on (**atheistic / vitrolic**).

13. The revolutionary leaders released a (**vitriolic / manifesto**) on the internet describing their intentions.

14. To avoid the dangers of internet scams, you should never enter your credit card number on a site unless you have (**certitude / vitriolic**) that the site is genuine.

15. From the busy city streets rose a(n) (**cacophony / atheism**) of horns, shouts, cellphone conversations, and roaring diesel engines.

16. Jae's guilty conscience told him that nothing could (**atheism / atone**) for his crimes.

Hot and Cold:
Write the word from the lesson that is most nearly the *OPPOSITE* of the boldfaced word or words in each sentence below.

17. The priest insisted I had to _____ for my sins and repent, or else I would continue to **exacerbate my guilt**.

18. While the majority of the population practices some form of **piety**, _____ is a growing form of belief in many countries.

19. Kev's _____ attitude toward Fredo's success suggested that he was jealous and perhaps needed to hear some **gentle remarks** about his own victories, too.

20. Whether or not I go to London is _____ on whether you'll come with me, and I am unable to make **independent** plans.

21. After spending all day listening to the horrible _____ of construction equipment, the **soothing sound** of my wife gently humming made me forget the stressful day.

22. I'd rather deal with the **meek and respectful** children of my friends than with my own obnoxiously _____ brood.

23. I am as confident in my **doubtfulness** in my ability to be a good father as you are in your _____ that the sky is blue and grass is green.

Applying Yourself:
Choose the best word to complete each of the following sentences.

24. We cannot completely _____ for our past mistakes, but issuing a formal apology is the first step toward reconciliation.
    (A) dispute
    (B) proliferate
    (C) contend
    (D) atone
    (E) relegate

25. The fans, though enthusiastic, grew _____ to the point of disrupting the enjoyment of all around them.
    (A) contingent
    (B) obstreperous
    (C) vitriolic
    (D) atheistic
    (E) atoned

26. We noticed the untrained understudies had taken the place of the regular musicians when a(n) _____ emerged from the orchestral pit.
   (A) cacophony
   (B) manifesto
   (C) atheism
   (D) vitriol
   (E) contingent

27. As science discovered more and more about the way the world works in the early twentieth century, the rise of _____ began.
   (A) cacophony
   (B) obstreperousness
   (C) atheism
   (D) manifesto
   (E) atonement

28. _____ statements aren't effective ways to solve arguments; try a calmer approach instead.
   (A) Atoning
   (B) Contingent
   (C) Vitriolic
   (D) Certain
   (E) Atheistic

29. Since my plans are _____ on your own, it's crucial that you let me know set dates for your arrival and departure.
   (A) vitriolic
   (B) obstreperous
   (C) contingent
   (D) cacophonous
   (E) atoned

30. After the exhaustive, three-year survey, I can say with _____ that the number of parents needing subsidized childcare is increasing.
   (A) contingency
   (B) atonement
   (C) manifesto
   (D) certitude
   (E) cacophony

31. The bomber had a(n) _____ detailing the reasons for his actions posted to an anonymous website.
   (A) obstreperousness
   (B) manifesto
   (C) contingency
   (D) atonement
   (E) vitriol

On Your Own:
Write one sentence using each word below to demonstrate your understanding of the word's meaning.

32. **vitriolic** _____

33. **certitude** _____

34. **cacophony** _____

35. **contingent** _____

36. **atheism** _____

37. **manifesto** _____

38. **atone** _____

39. **obstreperous** _____

C2 Advanced Vocabulary 53

First Impressions:

Using the example sentences below, write your own definition of each boldfaced word. Then write the letter of the definition from the box that best matches your definition.

A	adjective: yellow in color	**C**	adjective: drowsy; dull
B	adjective: aggressive, especially in a physical way	**D**	adjective: ambiguous; intentionally misleading

1. _____ Although calculus sometimes seems to be somewhat **equivocal**, it's very straightforward once you understand it.

EQUIVOCAL means: _____

2. _____ The artist colored the autumn leaves with goldenrod, amber, honey, lemon, and other **xanthic** hues.

XANTHIC means: _____

3. _____ Maurice worried that **pugnacious** son would end up as a bully later in his school years.

PUGNACIOUS means: _____

4. _____ While recovering from the surgery, Albert felt extremely **lethargic** and spent most of his time sleeping.

LETHARGIC means: _____

A	noun: a light breeze	**C**	verb: to recognize differences between items
B	noun: a rigid disciplinarian; a strict military officer; someone who holds strictly to rules and regulation	**D**	adjective: critical of and seeking to change existing institutions

5. _____ A pleasant **zephyr** rustled the leaves on the trees.

ZEPHYR means: _____

6. _____ Coach Jones shouted orders at us like a **martinet**.

MARTINET means: _____

7. _____ The military intelligence agent uncovered a **subversive** plot to undermine the government's authority.

SUBVERSIVE means: _____

8. _____ In strong light, the human eye can **distinguish** about 10 million different colors, but in dim light, there is not enough data to tell the difference between similar shades.

DISTINGUISH means: _____

Divide and Conquer:

Choose the correct word to complete each of the following sentences.

9. Most individuals suffering from colorblindness can actually (**equivocate / distinguish**) a few shades; only a few people have absolutely no ability to recognize colors.

10. The old mentor's (**subversive / equivocal**) advice merely confused the hero, who was seeking straightforward guidance.

11. After a heavy dinner Harold was feeling (**xanthic / lethargic**) and fell asleep in his chair.

12. The chemical reaction removed the blue coloring from the green mixture, leaving a pale, (**zephyr / xanthic**) residue.

13. By midday, the ferocious storm's winds had dissipated into (**zephyrs / martinets**).

14. Certain (**subversive / distinguished**) elements of the board are working to replace the chairwoman and her ally, the CEO.

15. Jared, who had a very strict father, was used to listening to a (**martinet / zephyr**) and had no trouble adjusting to life in military school.

16. The (**pugnacious / equivocal**) fighter took the center of the ring, hoping to overwhelm his cautious opponent.

Hot and Cold:

Write the word from the lesson that is most nearly the *OPPOSITE* of the boldfaced word or words in each sentence below.

17. One of the school prefects, a _____ through and through, would hand out citations for any small infraction; the other, a **liberal** in matters of rule-enforcement, let anything slide as long as it wasn't damaging to people or property.

18. The _____ opinions of the board, proclaiming neither approval nor disapproval of the proposal, were not enough to form a **definite** action plan.

19. The _____ literature, which called for ordinary citizens to rally against the current government, was detested by **conservative** loyalists.

20. Because I could not _____ individual words without my eyeglasses, I merely **glossed over** the page to give the illusion that I was reading.

21. The **timid** younger children were easily intimidated by the _____ older kids, who knew they could easily take whatever they wanted from those smaller than themselves.

22. While she would have normally responded with an **energetic** wave, Maya, having pulled an all-nighter, could only muster a _____ nod.

Applying Yourself:

Choose the best word to complete each of the following sentences.

23. His answer was somewhat _____, even though her question was very clear.
   (A) pugnacious
   (B) subversive
   (C) equivocal
   (D) distinguished
   (E) xanthic

24. Should the lime appear _____, wait until it ripens into a deep green color before slicing it open.
   (A) pugnacious
   (B) equivocal
   (C) subversive
   (D) xanthic
   (E) distinguished

25. _____ words are tolerated, if not encouraged in democracies; in dictatorships, however, they are forbidden.
    (A) Equivocal
    (B) Subversive
    (C) Xanthic
    (D) Lethargic
    (E) Pugnacious

26. How unlucky it was that we received a(n) _____, who makes us run ten miles each morning, as a commanding officer.
    (A) martinet
    (B) lethargy
    (C) zephyr
    (D) subversion
    (E) equivocation

27. _____ behavior is uncalled for on the practice field; save it for our hated rivals.
    (A) Lethargic
    (B) Xanthic
    (C) Subversive
    (D) Pugnacious
    (E) Equivocal

28. Only experts can _____ between an expertly counterfeited bill and the genuine article.
    (A) equivocate
    (B) subvert
    (C) distinguish
    (D) atone
    (E) deviate

29. After being stuck in the cramped room for hours, stepping outside to a soft sun and a light _____ blowing against my skin was like stepping into heaven.
    (A) contingency
    (B) zephyr
    (C) lethargy
    (D) martinet
    (E) manifesto

30. I feel very _____ after eating a Christmas dinner, even though the holiday is supposed to represent a very exciting time.
    (A) xanthic
    (B) equivocal
    (C) distinguished
    (D) pugnacious
    (E) lethargic

On Your Own:

Write one sentence using each word below to demonstrate your understanding of the word's meaning.

31. **pugnacious** _____

32. **xanthic** _____

33. **martinet** _____

34. **lethargic** _____

35. **equivocal** _____

36. **distinguish** _____

37. **subversive** _____

38. **zephyr** _____

C2 Advanced Vocabulary 54

First Impressions:
Using the example sentences below, write your own definition of each boldfaced word. Then write the letter of the definition from the box that best matches your definition.

A	verb: to assemble; to place in order or position	**C**	verb: to avoid; to dodge
B	noun: excessive greed for wealth	**D**	adjective: universal; involving a wide range of tastes or ideas

1. _____ The cartoon villain was a caricature of **avarice**: he threw an entire village of cute, fluffy bunnies out of their homes in order to obtain the buried pirate gold.

AVARICE means: _____

2. _____ His interests in music are **catholic**, ranging from jazz to j-pop to polka.

CATHOLIC means: _____

3. _____ The general **marshaled** the troops for one last charge.

MARSHAL means: _____

4. _____ She **sidestepped** responsibility by claiming she was out of the town when the mistake was made.

SIDESTEP means: _____

A	noun: an expression or idea that is very common or unoriginal	**C**	adjective: hazy and light; nearly transparent
B	adjective: related to glass; transparent	**D**	verb: to waver; to change repeatedly

5. _____ Dracula's aristocratic bearing was new and fresh in Bela Lugosi's 1931 film, but over time this image of a vampire has become a **cliché**.

CLICHÉ means: _____

6. _____ The **vitreous** humour of the eye is so named because it allows light to flow freely through the eyeball to the retina.

VITREOUS means: _____

7. _____ Your grades will not **fluctuate** if you are consistent in your study habits.

FLUCTUATE means: _____

8. _____ The choreographer created a dreamlike effect by having the dancers spin behind a **diaphanous** curtain.

DIAPHANOUS means: _____

Divide and Conquer:

Choose the correct word to complete each of the following sentences.

9. Once a year Nikolai overcame his (**avarice / cliché**) and made a large donation to charity.

10. No one could accuse her of spouting (**clichés / fluctuations**); in fact, her ideas are some of the most innovative and controversial in her field.

11. The value of a stock (**marshals / fluctuates**) during the course of the day as confidence in the market rises or falls.

12. The wall, although opaque, was painted in such a style as to have a (**vitreous / catholic**) quality.

13. The politician would (**marshal / sidestep**) issues by answering questions that hadn't even been asked.

14. The chief (**marshaled / fluctuated**) the fire fighters beside the blazing building.

15. Light passed easily through the (**diaphanous / cliché**) wings of the butterfly.

16. The term "university" suggests an education that is universal in its disciplines and (**cliché / catholic**) in its scope.

Hot and Cold:

Write the word from the lesson that is most nearly the *OPPOSITE* of the boldfaced word or words in each sentence below.

17. The amount of time we are able to spend together may _____, but my feelings for you are as **constant** as the North Star.

18. Gathering courage, I _____ every bit of my will to take control of the project and refused to **submit to orders** any longer.

19. Some find Buddhist teachings, which require no adherence to a **narrow path** of salvation, to be the most _____, since they include coping and meditative strategies that may be adopted by followers of any other faith.

20. The fencer lightly _____ his opponent's thrust and **moved straight** into the center of the arena.

21. The _____ of moneylenders led to a recession that might only be solved by the **generous** wealthy who might contribute to the lessening of the economic downturn.

22. Lacy's _____ gown seemed to dance and float; compared to her old **thick** velvet gown, it was light as a feather.

23. The works of Shakespeare are filled with terms and phrases that were **neologisms** when he wrote them, but due to the popularity of his works, have since become _____.

24. The _____ pane seemed to pass light from a farther room, but it was in fact an **opaque** mirror that one couldn't see through at all.

Applying Yourself:

Choose the best word to complete each of the following sentences.

25. Must we endure another film with endless _____, such as boring car chases and long-winded inspirational speeches?
    (A) avarice
    (B) sidestepping
    (C) clichés
    (D) catholicism
    (E) marshaling

26. The door's _____ panels allowed sunlight to bathe the entryway.
    (A) diaphanous
    (B) vitreous
    (C) catholic
    (D) cliché
    (E) sidestepped

27. _____ clouds filled the night sky, and it was possible to see Mars even as the clouds wafted by.
  (A) Avaricious
  (B) Sidestepped
  (C) Diaphanous
  (D) Catholic
  (E) Vitreous

28. The Persian Empire was a bazaar of _____ ideas: from one corner, a new food would spread to the known world, and from the other, a technique for crafting stronger weapons.
  (A) avaricious
  (B) diaphanous
  (C) catholic
  (D) vitreous
  (E) sidestepped

29. I prefer to _____ the issue of payment until I'm sure a worker can handle the job.
  (A) deviate
  (B) equivocate
  (C) marshal
  (D) fluctuate
  (E) sidestep

30. Melissa's favorite ice cream _____ from week to week, so it's best to check with her before you buy a pint.
  (A) sidesteps
  (B) fluctuates
  (C) marshals
  (D) atones
  (E) distinguishes

31. We _____ support for our plan to the tune of thousands of signatures.
  (A) lauded
  (B) fluctuated
  (C) sidestepped
  (D) marshaled
  (E) deviated

32. The credit crisis was caused by one central factor: short-term _____ by Wall Street bankers to the tune of eight-figure bonuses.
  (A) avarice
  (B) catholicism
  (C) clichés
  (D) fluctuation
  (E) marshaling

On Your Own:
Write one sentence using each word below to demonstrate your understanding of the word's meaning.

33. **cliché** _____

34. **avarice** _____

35. **sidestep** _____

36. **catholic** _____

37. **fluctuate** _____

38. **diaphanous** _____

39. **vitreous** _____

40. **marshal** _____

C2 Advanced Vocabulary 55

First Impressions:
Using the example sentences below, write your own definition of each boldfaced word. Then write the letter of the definition from the box that best matches your definition.

A	adjective: vigorous; strong	**C**	adjective: widespread, usually in a negative way
B	adjective: talkative	**D**	adjective: odd or unusual in behavior

1. _____ The scientist was a kind but **eccentric** man whose behavior never followed the norm.

ECCENTRIC means: _____

2. _____ The troops drove back the invaders with a **robust** defense.

ROBUST means: _____

3. _____ The dandelion is a **rampant** weed that is choking out my entire garden.

RAMPANT means: _____

4. _____ A normally **loquacious** Environment Minister was surprisingly quiet on Tuesday as he

refused to utter even one word on his recent statements on the government's policy on China.

LOQUACIOUS means: _____

A	verb: to walk extremely slowly, with heavy steps	**C**	adjective: doubting; examining evidence before deciding
B	noun: an uncultured person, especially one who is hostile towards high culture	**D**	noun: a perfect, harmonious society, especially an unlikely one

5. _____ The curator of the museum saw himself as a crusader engaged in the fight to bring

civilization to the **philistines** of the city.

PHILISTINE means: _____

6. _____ Though he knew not to promise a **utopia**, the senator outlined several surprisingly

idealistic projects in his speech.

UTOPIA means: _____

7. _____ The drug company faces an uphill battle persuading **skeptical** physicians to give their

expensive new treatment a chance.

SKEPTICAL means: _____

8. _____ The turtle **plods** slowly across the sand.

PLOD means: _____

Divide and Conquer:
Choose the correct word to complete each of the following sentences.

9. News director Ron Breeding decided he needed a couple of (**loquacious / philistine**) analysts to help him keep the airtime filled.

10. Jenny tried to tear down Lisa's fort, but the structure was too (**robust / philistine**).

11. Ironically, the abandoned city became a(n) (**eccentricity / utopia**) for new artists, who found the clash of concrete jungles and perfect quiet ideal for their work.

12. The old lady has become more (**eccentric / utopian**) over the years, wearing furs coats even in the summer and addressing total strangers as "Marco".

13. Holden amassed a fortune by making bold but risky investments that his more (**loquacious / skeptical**) peers avoided.

14. Mrs. Jackson had to crack down on the (**rampant / robust**) cheating that had plagued her classroom.

15. Sometimes I wonder that the (**philistines / eccentrics**) who deride modern art don't walk around chewing on half-cooked mutton legs while wearing animal skins for warmth.

16. The penguin (**plodded / occluded**) slowly on the ice, careful to avoid falling through.

Hot and Cold:
Write the word from the lesson that is most nearly the *OPPOSITE* of the boldfaced word or words in each sentence below.

17. The quiet, crime-free suburb felt like a(n) _____ compared to the squalid **hell-hole** in which I grew up.

18. The government institutes quarantines to keep diseases **confined** to one area and prevent those illnesses from becoming _____.

19. Ninjas, despite their reputation for being **nimble**, sometimes _____ along like the rest of us.

20. Though initially _____, after investigating the evidence, the team became **trusting**.

21. The _____ businessman never responded in a **predictable** fashion.

22. After three months in bed feeling **sick and weak**, Arthur was glad to return to work feeling _____ and healthy as ever.

23. Rhonda resented her _____ parents, who banned classical music and fine art from the home, and swore to grow up to be a fully **cultured** woman.

24. One group made a _____ and detailed explanation of its point of view, while the other chose a few **terse** words to explain its position.

Applying Yourself:
Choose the best word to complete each of the following sentences.

25. Her carefully chosen words were always worth listening to, unlike those of her _____ and shallow husband.
    (A) loquacious
    (B) rampant
    (C) philistine
    (D) utopian
    (E) robust

26. The school knew that it had to do something about the _____ cheating that was affecting every class.
    (A) philistine
    (B) rampant
    (C) eccentric
    (D) robust
    (E) plodding

27. After being treated badly by people his entire life, Nate has become a(n) _____ and doubts the good intentions of others.
    (A) skeptic
    (B) philistine
    (C) utopia
    (D) eccentric
    (E) manifesto

28. We _____ through the snow with our heavy snow shoes until my feet ached.
    (A) expedited
    (B) plodded
    (C) reprehended
    (D) occluded
    (E) plodded

29. Though we in the country are so often branded as _____, we do in fact maintain a high order of social debate.
    (A) utopias
    (B) skeptics
    (C) eccentrics
    (D) philistines
    (E) martinets

30. The travelers had thought that the hidden city was a(n) _____, but they soon realized that it harbored a dark secret.
    (A) philistine
    (B) skeptic
    (C) utopia
    (D) eccentric
    (E) chimera

31. His outfit was highly _____; he wore a top hat and a bathing suit.
    (A) robust
    (B) loquacious
    (C) eccentric
    (D) philistine
    (E) rampant

32. A skunk lets off a very strong smell, and only another _____ odor can combat its stench.
    (A) philistine
    (B) loquacious
    (C) skeptical
    (D) utopian
    (E) robust

On Your Own:

Write one sentence using each word below to demonstrate your understanding of the word's meaning.

33. **robust** _____

34. **plod** _____

35. **rampant** _____

36. **utopia** _____

37. **philistine** _____

38. **skeptical** _____

39. **eccentric** _____

40. **loquacious** _____

C2 Advanced Vocabulary 56

First Impressions:

Using the example sentences below, write your own definition of each boldfaced word. Then write the letter of the definition from the box that best matches your definition.

A	adjective: related to the rule of one area by an outside nation	**C**	noun: proper manners or conduct
B	verb: to urge; to support	**D**	noun: stiff hairs growing along the mouths of many animals that aid in sensation; whiskers

1. _____ At the height of Great Britain's **imperial** period, England ruled one-fifth of the world's population via countless colonies throughout the world.

IMPERIAL means: _____

2. _____ The animal rights organization strongly **advocates** the ethical treatment of animals.

ADVOCATE means: _____

3. _____ The **vibrissae** of a cat are not simple hairs; they actually help the animal to navigate in total darkness.

VIBRISSAE means: _____

4. _____ Jaemin instructed the students at the charm school to be respectful, kind, and polite, and to observe proper **rectitude** in all interactions.

RECTITUDE means: _____

A	adjective: deep; not superficial; complete	**C**	adjective: tireless
B	noun: the state of being alone; seclusion	**D**	verb: to push aside; to redirect

5. _____ Wile E. Coyote is **indefatigable** in his hunt for Road Runner, having spent decades trying to capture the bird.

INDEFATIGABLE means: _____

6. _____ Many seek the **solitude** of wilderness as a temporary break from crowded city life.

SOLITUDE means: _____

7. _____ Anticipating crashing with the grocery cart in front of me, I **shunted** my cart to the left.

SHUNT means: _____

8. _____ The professor's **profound** insights on the novel made the students realize that despite having already read the book, they missed the subtle messages of the author.

PROFOUND means: _____

Divide and Conquer:
Choose the correct word to complete each of the following sentences.

9. The young man (**advocated / shunted**) his brother out of the way as the bus approached.

10. Napoleon exercised his (**indefatigable / imperial**) ambitions by invading and conquering several other nations.

11. Prisons use forced (**solitude / rectitude**) as punishment because all humans crave company.

12. The group (**advocates / shunts**) their specialized approach in teaching by sending pamphlets to schools across the nation.

13. The documentary's insightful ending served as a(n) (**profound / indefatigable**) reminder that we often hide our biases from even ourselves.

14. The raccoon's (**solitude / vibrissae**) retracted toward the animal's face when the predator approached.

15. In a remarkable lack of (**solitude / rectitude**), Jack put his feet on the table and yelled for his host to bring more chicken.

16. The (**indefatigable / imperial**) relief workers toiled on into the late hours of the night without complaint.

Hot and Cold:
Write the word from the lesson that is most nearly the *OPPOSITE* of the boldfaced word or words in each sentence below.

17. Casting an _____ stare about her, the cat seemed a haughty queen compared to the **goofy** dog chasing its tail on the ground below her.

18. Leonard tried to engage his children with _____ questions, but their **short and shallow** answers indicated that they were not interested.

19. The priest's holy _____ feels out of place among the **crassness** of the drunkards at the local pub.

20. I dashed into the street and _____ the child so that he wouldn't be **standing directly** in the oncoming traffic.

21. The **bustling environment** I enjoyed while aboard the cruise ship felt so refreshing after the _____ I'd had for two weeks.

22. Though he felt **weary** of arguing and did not look forward to continuing the debate, the president was spurred on by his _____ desire to get the bill passed.

23. How can I _____ in favor of something I have **castigated** so passionately in the past?

Applying Yourself:
Choose the best word to complete each of the following sentences.

24. Should you wish to read _____ thoughts, pick up a copy of the Tao Te Ching, which dispenses advice about how to live a good life.
    (A) loquacious
    (B) imperial
    (C) advocated
    (D) profound
    (E) indefatigable

25. Most experts _____ consistency over cramming for learning vocabulary; a certain number of minutes each day usually suffices.
    (A) advocate
    (B) shunt
    (C) plod
    (D) censure
    (E) culminate

26. The man, moving quickly, _____ me to the left and continued speed-walking down the sidewalk.
    (A) advocated
    (B) shunted
    (C) occluded
    (D) reprehended
    (E) engendered

27. A cat's _____ supplement the touch felt by the animal's skin.
    (A) vibrissae
    (B) profundities
    (C) advocates
    (D) manifestos
    (E) martinets

28. His loneliness was largely the result of having spent his childhood years in _____.
    (A) profundity
    (B) advocacy
    (C) vibrissae
    (D) indefatigability
    (E) solitude

29. Eating with royalty requires perfect _____, so remember to keep your elbows off the table.
    (A) advocacy
    (B) indefatigability
    (C) profundity
    (D) rectitude
    (E) solitude

30. The group had hiked without stopping for hours, _____ in its desire to reach the summit.
    (A) profound
    (B) indefatigable
    (C) shunted
    (D) solitary
    (E) advocated

31. Franklin, Adams, Washington, and Jefferson led the revolution from the _____ rule of Britain.
    (A) imperial
    (B) profound
    (C) shunted
    (D) solitary
    (E) indefatigable

On Your Own:
Write one sentence using each word below to demonstrate your understanding of the word's meaning.

32. **profound** _____

33. **advocate** _____

34. **imperial** _____

35. **rectitude** _____

36. **solitude** _____

37. **indefatigable** _____

38. **shunt** _____

39. **vibrissae** _____

C2 Advanced Vocabulary 57

First Impressions:
Using the example sentences below, write your own definition of each boldfaced word. Then write the letter of the definition from the box that best matches your definition.

A	adjective: modest and reserved	**C**	verb: to shun or renounce
B	verb: to advance; to improve	**D**	verb: to cause great shame or embarrassment

1. _____ Next to her sister's sparkling gold cocktail dress, Brienne's simple gray suit looked quite **demure**.

DEMURE means: _____

2. _____ Susan mother's attempts to act "hip" in front of her friends **mortified** her daughter.

MORTIFY means: _____

3. _____ The monk **abjured** the material pleasures of the world in order to build his inner strength and spirituality.

ABJURE means: _____

4. _____ The chef added several exotic spices to **enhance** the flavor of the dish.

ENHANCE means: _____

A	verb: to postpone; to delay or put off	**C**	adjective: tending to include everything
B	verb: to adopt; to support	**D**	adjective: involving a discussion between people of different points of view to arrive at a common ground

5. _____ Jim wanted to know whether the test was all-**inclusive** or only covered a few of the subjects the class had studied.

INCLUSIVE means: _____

6. _____ The social network rarely misses an opportunity to **espouse** the benefits of sharing.

ESPOUSE means: _____

7. _____ Divya enjoyed learning from **dialectical** discussions with people of varied backgrounds.

DIALECTICAL means: _____

8. _____ While registering for classes can be a hassle, students are encouraged not to **procrastinate** due to high numbers of enrollment and limited space in classes.

PROCRASTINATE means: _____

Divide and Conquer:
Choose the correct word to complete each of the following sentences.

9. My mother (**espoused** / **mortified**) me when she told my date stories of how I had been afraid of the dark until I was ten.

10. I made sure I did my homework two nights in advance and didn't (**procrastinate** / **espouse**).

11. The platform that the party (**abjured** / **espoused**) was so controversial that it was talked about in nearly every home.

12. Harold had always felt that a (**demure** / **dialectical**) approach would yield more solutions than endless bickering would.

13. The organization is taking measures to (**enhance** / **mortify**) users' privacy by rolling out two new security features.

14. Roberta, who was usually extremely bold and forward, became (**inclusive** / **demurred**) in the presence of her favorite movie star.

15. Long, careful study led the scientist to (**abjure** / **procrastinate**) several theories that he once had held quite strongly.

16. Though some early political parties refused to admit people of certain ethnic backgrounds, others were more (**inclusive** / **dialectical**).

Hot and Cold:
Write the word from the lesson that is most nearly the *OPPOSITE* of the boldfaced word or words in each sentence below.

17. The conversation was _____ and, by nature, involved some disagreement, but the two parties eventually overcame the **stubborn paradigm** of political entrenchment and reached an accord.

18. I find that listening to classical music while working _____ my productivity, while listening to anything with words **diminishes** it because I focus more on what's being said than on the task at hand.

19. I meant to impress my in-laws with a respectfully _____ greeting, but I was so nervous I accidentally stuck out my hand forcefully and barked a **brazen** "How's it goin'?"

20. Hank was _____ by the fact that his embarrassing childhood photos were made public, but in fact the photos of him as an innocent child **exulted** him in the eyes of most.

21. Aunt Carla enthusiastically _____ the beliefs of the minister at her local church and **rejects** as heresy any other interpretation of scripture that she may come across.

22. The club preferred to hold _____ events to which every student—even those belonging to rival clubs—was invited instead of **exclusive** affairs that boasted a selective guest list.

23. I tend to _____ my own work, leaving it until the very last moment, and **prioritize** things I've promised to do for others, completing them well in advance of their deadlines.

24. The new minister _____ any form of secularism as against God's word and **venerated** earlier versions of the religion that strictly adhered to the holy text.

Applying Yourself:
Choose the best word to complete each of the following sentences.

25. I _____ the candidate's bond initiative, as it will help the poor immensely.
    (A) espouse
    (B) demur
    (C) abjure
    (D) enhance
    (E) mortify

26. The terrible condition of my room _____ me, so I refuse to have any visitors.
    (A) abjures
    (B) shunts
    (C) enhances
    (D) mortifies
    (E) espouses

27. My encroaching blindness, though depressing, has actually _____ my other senses and I can now smell garlic from two rooms away.
    (A) procrastinated
    (B) abjured
    (C) espoused
    (D) mortified
    (E) enhanced

28. Our company wants the decision to take on the project to be _____, so everyone should offer their opinions.
    (A) inclusive
    (B) mortified
    (C) dialectical
    (D) demure
    (E) abjured

29. The politician _____ his former party, which he thought had become bitterly partisan.
    (A) enhanced
    (B) espoused
    (C) mortified
    (D) abjured
    (E) procrastinated

30. _____ discussions are increasingly rare in a polarized congress more concerned with party loyalty than with solving problems.
    (A) Mortified
    (B) Abjured
    (C) Dialectical
    (D) Enhanced
    (E) Demure

31. Because Jason would always _____ instead of doing his assignments on time, his assignments were usually turned in late.
    (A) demurs
    (B) enhances
    (C) abjures
    (D) procrastinate
    (E) enhances

32. The company has no need for _____ salespeople, so be aggressive in your pitches.
    (A) inclusive
    (B) demure
    (C) mortified
    (D) enhanced
    (E) dialectical

On Your Own:
Write one sentence using each word below to demonstrate your understanding of the word's meaning.

33. **enhance** _____

34. **mortify** _____

35. **dialectical** _____

36. **espouse** _____

37. **procrastinate** _____

38. **demure** _____

39. **abjure** _____

40. **inclusive** _____

C2 Advanced Vocabulary 58

First Impressions:

Using the example sentences below, write your own definition of each boldfaced word. Then write the letter of the definition from the box that best matches your definition.

A	adjective: practical, as opposed to idealistic; dealing with the practical worth of something	**C**	adjective: marked by strong resentment or bitterness
B	noun: a natural consequence; an obvious result	**D**	adjective: irritable and complaining

1. _____ Though Christine loved the idea of becoming a traveling artist, she took a **pragmatic** approach and decided to study accounting.

PRAGMATIC means: _____

2. _____ The **fractious** tempers of the children were only soothed when the teacher gave them treats.

FRACTIOUS means: _____

3. _____ "Why so **acrimonious**?" Leander asked, noticing his friend's hostile stance and sour expression.

ACRIMONIOUS means: _____

4. _____ As a **corollary** to the lowered tax rate, individuals will have more money available to invest in new businesses.

COROLLARY means: _____

A	adjective: extremely sacred; not able to be criticized	**C**	verb: to honor the memory of; to serve as a memorial or reminder of
B	adjective: extremely cold; happening or moving very slowly	**D**	noun: one who enjoys spending time with others

5. _____ She delivered the remarks today at a ceremony to **commemorate** Memorial Day.

COMMEMORATE means: _____

6. _____ As an **extrovert**, Maurice loved the opportunity that his job gave him to meet many people from all walks of life.

EXTROVERT means: _____

7. _____ The **glacial** temperatures of Antarctica make living difficult for scientists and explorers.

GLACIAL means: _____

8. _____ The comedian would criticize any topic, no matter how taboo; to him, nothing was **sacrosanct**.

SACROSANCT means: _____

Divide and Conquer:
Choose the correct word to complete each of the following sentences.

9. Isabel and Francine were far from (**fractious / sacrosanct**); in fact, they were among the most pleasant people one was likely to meet.

10. Continuous fighting has led to such (**acrimonious / pragmatic**) feelings between the two nations that it is difficult to envision a peace.

11. A true (**sacrosanct / extrovert**), Janice spent nearly every weekend throwing or attending a large party.

12. The notion that the famous leader was perfect was (**glacial / sacrosanct**); no one would admit that he was corrupt as well as visionary.

13. New claims for jobless benefits are expected to continue their (**glacial / commemorated**) but steady improvement, trickling away by 20 per week.

14. The senator pointed out that tax cuts, while popular, bear the inescapable (**pragmatism / corollary**) of reducing government revenues.

15. The purpose of Memorial Day is to (**commemorate / occlude**) soldiers who died while in the service of their country.

16. He judged the action by its beauty rather than by its (**pragmatic / glacial**) virtues.

Hot and Cold:
Write the word from the lesson that is most nearly the *OPPOSITE* of the boldfaced word or words in each sentence below.

17. Weight loss is a _____ to decreasing caloric intake and increasing physical activity, but a decrease in self-esteem is, at times, an **unexpected consequence** of rapid weight loss as people adjust to their new self-images.

18. I may come off as a(n) _____ with many friends, but the reality is that I'm an **introvert** who would much rather spend my time in solitude.

19. Reuben decided that it was time to become more _____ and put aside his **fanciful** and idealistic ways.

20. I thought my hometown's bureaucracy moved at a frustratingly _____ pace, but it was downright **speedy** compared to that of the country I visited this summer.

21. I'm certain that a hug is all Jane needs to heal her _____ mood and go back to the **mellow** person we once knew.

22. Family gatherings have always been _____ affairs, since one half tends constantly to be angry at the other, but the birth of Mary's baby inspired us to be **sweet** with one another for the first time in years.

23. After the national tragedy, a memorial was erected to _____ those lost and to ensure that the collective public would never **forget** the tragedy.

24. The religious among them felt that the book was _____ and that none may injure it, but the **secular** members of the group felt it was merely a collection of words like any other.

Applying Yourself:
Choose the best word to complete each of the following sentences.

25. We _____ the death of those in our unit with an annual reunion.
    - (A) commemorate
    - (B) subordinate
    - (C) prepossess
    - (D) posit
    - (E) efface

26. The church members, while divided over certain policies of their church, tend not to denounce their leader, whom they view as _____.
    - (A) pragmatic
    - (B) sacrosanct
    - (C) glacial
    - (D) acrimonious
    - (E) extroverted

27. _____ tend to dominate fundraisers, where making friends and influencing people through lively behavior is vital.
    (A) Extroverts
    (B) Commemoration
    (C) Pragmatism
    (D) Acrimoniousness
    (E) Fractiousness

28. While choosing a major, Zack, who daydreamed of becoming of actor, was often at odds with his father, who urged his son to choose a more _____ career.
    (A) pragmatic
    (B) acrimonious
    (C) glacial
    (D) sacrosanct
    (E) fractious

29. Doing well on the SAT's critical reading section is a(n) _____ of habitual reading.
    (A) commemoration
    (B) acrimoniousness
    (C) extrovert
    (D) pragmatism
    (E) corollary

30. The attention shown to the player who lost the game has been _____; even today, he must walk around Chicago in disguise to avoid derision.
    (A) commemorated
    (B) sacrosanct
    (C) pragmatic
    (D) glacial
    (E) acrimonious

31. Jenny could hardly tolerate her husband's _____ look while he sat in the dentist's chair—it was as though she were forcing him to eat dirt rather than get a root canal.
    (A) fractious
    (B) glacial
    (C) commemorated
    (D) sacrosanct
    (E) pragmatic

32. While Susan expected to be done quickly, the _____ pace of the cashier at the checkout lane delayed her by twenty minutes.
    (A) fractious
    (B) glacial
    (C) pragmatic
    (D) acrimonious
    (E) sacrosanct

On Your Own:
Write one sentence using each word below to demonstrate your understanding of the word's meaning.

33. **sacrosanct** _____

34. **corollary** _____

35. **glacial** _____

36. **commemorate** _____

37. **acrimonious** _____

38. **pragmatic** _____

39. **extrovert** _____

40. **fractious** _____

C2 Advanced Vocabulary 59

First Impressions:
Using the example sentences below, write your own definition of each boldfaced word. Then write the letter of the definition from the box that best matches your definition.

A	noun: a waterfall; something that resembles a waterfall	**C**	adjective: having the appearance of merit, but actually lacking it
B	noun: a lack of seriousness; lightness	**D**	adjective: acting on instinct without much thought

1. _____ Amy always felt a wonderful **levity** when she was in the water, able to float and flip and do other such things she couldn't do on land.

LEVITY means: _____

2. _____ The closet was so haphazardly packed with toys that when I opened it, the toys poured out in a **cascade** of plastic.

CASCADE means: _____

3. _____ The training program for bank examiners requires applicants to tell the difference between bonds that are **specious** and those that are genuine.

SPECIOUS means: _____

4. _____ Most animals are **impetuous** and act on instinct more than higher reason.

IMPETUOUS means: _____

A	noun: any person that is harmed as a result of an event	**C**	noun: false testimony under oath
B	adjective: obnoxious and stubborn	**D**	verb: to surrender unconditionally

5. _____ A witness who lies in court is guilty of **perjury**.

PERJURY means: _____

6. _____ The nation was forced to **capitulate** when its military ran out of supplies.

CAPITULATE means: _____

7. _____ Penelope, who was laid off last week, is just the latest **casualty** of her company's downsizing.

CASUALTY means: _____

8. _____ Dan's **boorish** behavior led the rest of the team to avoid him and even compelled one coworker to complain to their boss about him.

BOORISH means: _____

Divide and Conquer:
Choose the correct word to complete each of the following sentences.

9. He behaved (**impetuously / boorishly**), spilling food and chewing with his mouth open even after the other guests protested.

10. Emilia later regretted her (**boorish / impetuous**) decision to leave home and wished she had planned her steps more carefully.

11. Rather than (**perjure / capitulate**) to old age, Stefanie embarked on a stringent diet and exercise regimen.

12. Many have objected to the terms "friendly fire" and "collateral damage", feeling that (**casualties / perjuries**) of war should not be euphemized.

13. Mr. Mason accused the witness of (**perjury / levity**) after noticing that he had changed his testimony.

14. The atmosphere of the typically somber business meeting was marked by an unusual (**levity / boorishness**).

15. The water from the broken hydrant fell over the road in a (**perjury / cascade**).

16. (**Specious / Boorish**) claims of UFOs waste a lot of time, as government officials lose countless hours researching and explaining those sightings.

Hot and Cold:
Write the word from the lesson that is most nearly the *OPPOSITE* of the boldfaced word or words in each sentence below.

17. Peter was embarrassed by Colin's _____ behavior at the swimming pool, so he felt it only **polite** to apologize to the lifeguards.

18. The speaker added _____ to an otherwise **dry** lecture with his self-deprecating humor.

19. Samantha was well-known for her **honesty**, so it was a shock when she was accused of _____ .

20. Because the senator's few **veracious** statements were sprinkled among countless _____ ones, it was difficult for voters to distinguish fact from fiction.

21. The first castle under siege _____ quickly, as it did not have the resources to face an attack, but the second **held out** for two months and gave the attacking army a run for its money.

22. Our **calculating** chemistry teacher is never given to _____ shows of emotion.

23. Low-level employees will be the main _____ of this merger, as it will eliminate 1,000 positions, but top management, the primary **beneficiaries**, will receive significant raises.

Applying Yourself:
Choose the best word to complete each of the following sentences.

24. Giving in to aggressive nations may seem to serve the peace, but the act is _____ in the long term.
    (A) impetuous
    (B) capitulated
    (C) specious
    (D) boorish
    (E) cascading

25. The comedian felt stoic and tense before the set, but as he was introduced, the room's _____ won him over.
    (A) levity
    (B) speciousness
    (C) boorishness
    (D) perjury
    (E) capitulation

26. The report indicates the expected _____, both civilian and military, of the ordered strike against the rogue nation's capital.
    (A) levity
    (B) casualties
    (C) cascades
    (D) impetuousness
    (E) boorishness

27. Though he was accused of _____, Mr. Mason swore that he had never told anything but the truth.
    (A) levity
    (B) cascading
    (C) perjury
    (D) capitulation
    (E) boorishness

28. No one appreciated the _____ behavior of the boys who crashed the party.
    (A) capitulating
    (B) impetuous
    (C) cascading
    (D) specious
    (E) boorish

29. Niagara Falls, while not the tallest _____ in the world, carries the most water over a cliff that separates Canada from the United States.
    (A) impetuousness
    (B) casualty
    (C) boor
    (D) perjury
    (E) cascade

30. If you act _____, eventually you will run into problems with a situation that you have not thought through.
    (A) boorish
    (B) pragmatically
    (C) extroverted
    (D) speciously
    (E) impetuously

31. I cannot _____ to your wish to paint the bathroom pink, so let's compromise by using brown instead.
    (A) capitulate
    (B) perjure
    (C) cascade
    (D) distinguish
    (E) abjure

On Your Own:
Write one sentence using each word below to demonstrate your understanding of the word's meaning.

32. **perjury** _____

33. **levity** _____

34. **casualty** _____

35. **impetuous** _____

36. **boorish** _____

37. **specious** _____

38. **cascade** _____

39. **capitulate** _____

C2 Advanced Vocabulary 60

First Impressions:

Using the example sentences below, write your own definition of each boldfaced word. Then write the letter of the definition from the box that best matches your definition.

A	noun: urgent need or situation	**C**	noun: an accusation in response to another's accusation
B	verb: to prepare for a purpose; to supply with information	**D**	noun: someone who eats too much; a greedy person

1. _____ Which of those **gluttons** ate the cookies I made for Sang Min's party?

GLUTTON means: _____

2. _____ The assistant **primed** his boss on the name of his next appointment and the nature of the

meeting.

PRIME means: _____

3. _____ Roland responded to the insult with a long list of **recriminations** against his challenger.

RECRIMINATION means: _____

4. _____ Emergency Medical Technicians are trained to respond to any medical **exigency**.

EXIGENCY means: _____

A	noun: a loud noise	**C**	verb: to free from blame
B	adjective: related to the senses	**D**	noun: a fear of being in enclosed or narrow places

5. _____ Hei Ryung reached quickly to stop the **clamor** of her alarm clock.

CLAMOR means: _____

6. _____ The robot could process readings from a camera, microphone, and other **sensory** input

devices in order to make decisions.

SENSORY means: _____

7. _____ After a lengthy trial, the court **exculpated** Henry due to a lack of sufficient evidence

needed to convict him.

EXCULPATED means: _____

8. _____ Because of her **claustrophobia**, Frida's palms would get sweaty and her head would

ache whenever she used an elevator.

CLAUSTROPHOBIA means: _____

Divide and Conquer:
Choose the correct word to complete each of the following sentences.

9. No amount of penance could (**prime / exculpate**) the mob boss from his crimes.

10. Persons suffering from (**claustrophobia / gluttony**) should avoid becoming magicians' assistants, as the work frequently requires hiding in small, cramped spaces.

11. The football team (**recriminated / primed**) itself with hours of film study in preparation for the game.

12. A (**glutton / clamor**) arose from the kennel as a cat ran past the cages of barking dogs.

13. Asher was a (**glutton / clamor**) for sweets and regularly asked his mother to bake cookies or brownies.

14. The blinding light created temporary (**sensory / exigent**) overload for those looking west.

15. Mr. Penniman's accusation that Mr. Lee's dog had ruined his lawn brought a (**recrimination / glutton**) that Mr. Penniman had lured the dog over with a juicy bone.

16. The ratio between public debt and gross domestic product in the United States was at its peak in the 1940s, when the (**gluttons / exigencies**) of World War II required vast funds.

Hot and Cold:
Write the word from the lesson that is most nearly the *OPPOSITE* of the boldfaced word or words in each sentence below.

17. Rather than respond with an endless volley of _____, I chose to **accept quietly** the blame and refused to point a finger at anyone else.

18. I prefer novels that offer me _____ details I can picture rather than **abstract** concepts I can hardly picture, much less understand.

19. Tran hoped that the new evidence would _____ him, but instead, it **made him seem even more guilty**.

20. I'd rather be something of a _____ when it comes to the things I enjoy than an **ascetic** who sits alone in the corner looking sourly at those who would enjoy themselves.

21. After spending all day listening to the _____ of the kindergarten, Fred loved to retreat to the **quiet** of his secluded bedroom.

22. West End's candidate had been _____ for the interview portion of the competition and sailed through it with ease; Newburg's had been **left unprepared** and struggled to think of answers for each question.

23. Compared to the _____ of deciding which hospital to send your sister to, the question of what to have for dinner seems like an **afterthought** indeed.

Applying Yourself:
Choose the best word to complete each of the following sentences.

24. My puppy is a(n) _____, so we must carefully ration his every bite.
    (A) glutton
    (B) sense
    (C) exculpation
    (D) recrimination
    (E) exigency

25. The _____ of Hurricane Sandy requires that we transfer resources to disaster preparation.
    (A) sense
    (B) exculpation
    (C) exigency
    (D) gluttony
    (E) recrimination

26. Aaron protested his innocence in an attempt to _____ himself.
    (A) glut
    (B) prime
    (C) clamor
    (D) recriminate
    (E) exculpate

27. Casey had to wait for hours for the anesthesia to wear off and her _____ faculties to return; until then, her sight was bleary and she could hardly hear the voices of those who addressed her.
    (A) primed
    (B) sensory
    (C) gluttonous
    (D) exigent
    (E) claustrophobic

28. We _____ the president with information about the crisis before he entered the situation room.
    (A) clamored
    (B) glutted
    (C) recriminated
    (D) primed
    (E) exculpated

29. The long ride in the small elevator kindled my latent _____.
    (A) claustrophobia
    (B) gluttony
    (C) exigency
    (D) exculpation
    (E) recrimination

30. Exposing corruption in government too often leads to _____ by those in power against the accuser.
    (A) exculpation
    (B) recrimination
    (C) claustrophobia
    (D) exigency
    (E) priming

31. She much preferred hearing the quiet crackling of the fire and reading a book than navigating the crowd and _____ of this night club.
    (A) exculpation
    (B) recrimination
    (C) exigency
    (D) gluttony
    (E) clamor

On Your Own:

Write one sentence using each word below to demonstrate your understanding of the word's meaning.

32. **sensory** _____

33. **prime** _____

34. **clamor** _____

35. **glutton** _____

36. **exigency** _____

37. **claustrophobia** _____

38. **recrimination** _____

39. **exculpate** _____

C2 Advanced Vocabulary 61

First Impressions:

Using the example sentences below, write your own definition of each boldfaced word. Then write the letter of the definition from the box that best matches your definition.

A	adjective: moving towards death or extinction	**C**	adjective: odd; unpredictable; wandering
B	adjective: lacking proper seriousness	**D**	noun: reconstruction in order to make something like new

1. _____ Any new storage medium is **moribund** from the day it is created because it will inevitably be replaced by a more efficient alternative.

MORIBUND means: _____

2. The **renovation** of the old home was an expensive but worthwhile effort requiring three carpenters, an electrician, and a stonemason.

RENOVATION means: _____

3. _____ With a casual smirk, Michael gave a **flippant** response that only increased his parents' suspicion of him.

FLIPPANT means: _____

4. _____ The security officer was trained to recognize the **erratic** behavior indicative of shoplifters.

ERRATIC means: _____

A	adjective: having the same or proportional measures	**C**	noun: a natural liking; a similarity
B	noun: an individual who sacrifices principles for expediency by taking advantage of circumstances	**D**	adjective: famous due to a bad reputation

5. _____ The trial has begun for Chicago's **infamous** former police commander who is believed to have tortured hundreds of suspects during his career.

INFAMOUS means: _____

6. _____ Marcian was a political **opportunist** who would do or say whatever it took to get elected, regardless of his true beliefs.

OPPORTUNIST means: _____

7. _____ Sarika became a teacher because she found that she had an **affinity** for children.

AFFINITY means: _____

8. _____ It is generally accepted that an increase in responsibility should be matched with a **commensurate** increase in salary.

COMMENSURATE means: _____

Divide and Conquer:
Choose the correct word to complete each of the following sentences.

9. Robin was pleased to find that an increase in her study time was reflected by a(n) (**commensurate** / **erratic**) rise in test scores.

10. The Deepwater Horizon oil spill is the worst in American history, having surpassed even the (**infamous** / **opportunistic**) Exxon Valdez spill.

11. (**Renovations** / **Affinities**) gave the theater new fixtures but left its antique features intact.

12. If you sacrifice loyalty for money at the first sign of potential gain, you will be branded as a(n) (**renovation** / **opportunist**).

13. Berenice, who had always had a(n) (**opportunist** / **affinity**) for science, surprised everyone by studying art in college.

14. Several ingenious innovations brought energy back to the (**erratic** / **moribund**) industry.

15. The manager decided not to hire the potential employee who had made several (**flippant** / **infamous**) remarks during the interview.

16. The intoxicated man wandered down the street in a(n) (**moribund** / **erratic**) pattern.

Hot and Cold:
Write the word from the lesson that is most nearly the *OPPOSITE* of the boldfaced word or words in each sentence below.

17. Carrie's _____ attitude toward her principal's stern warning indicated that Carrie had little **respect** for the institution he represented.

18. Dan, the **altruist** in the family, dedicated his life to serving the poor, while Shelly, the _____, moved to a developing country to use her business acumen to seize control of a local economy.

19. Jan's _____ for city life contrasts with her husband's **aversion** to tall buildings, crowded streets, and traffic pollution.

20. This job advertisement claims that pay will be _____ with experience, but I find that the salary is rather **disproportional** for someone with my level of skill and expertise.

21. Though he is an _____ cheater among the members of the card-playing community, Logan is **widely respected** as a classical pianist.

22. The snake's _____ movements frightened its handler, who was used to a more **predictable** temperament from the animal and feared it would become agitated and violent.

23. The _____ old city, with only a run-down bank and a few houses, is a sad sight compared to the economically **invigorated** town up the road, whose population increases every day.

24. When it came to old buildings, the city council refused to consider _____, citing the expense, and preferred **demolition** of even the oldest, most historically unique buildings.

Applying Yourself:
Choose the best word to complete each of the following sentences.

25. John Dillinger, the _____ gangster, was considered a hero by the common people, even though he was on every police department's "Most Wanted" list.
    (A) infamous
    (B) opportunistic
    (C) erratic
    (D) flippant
    (E) moribund

26. Her fondness for chocolate was only eclipsed by her _____ for pillow fights.
    (A) renovation
    (B) infamy
    (C) opportunity
    (D) affinity
    (E) commensuration

27. Although he had promised his boss that he could work at the restaurant for at least four months, Grant, a(n) _____, quit the job as soon as he found a better offer.
    (A) affinity
    (B) opportunist
    (C) renovation
    (D) commensuration
    (E) infamy

28. Good writers are happy that tired clichés are becoming _____ in the English language.
    (A) flippant
    (B) commensurate
    (C) moribund
    (D) infamous
    (E) opportunistic

29. The musician produced a(n) _____ album; the songs seemed alternately inspired and derivative.
    (A) infamous
    (B) opportunistic
    (C) moribund
    (D) flippant
    (E) erratic

30. The house requires an extensive _____, starting with the dated kitchen.
    (A) renovation
    (B) affinity
    (C) flippancy
    (D) infamy
    (E) commensuration

31. His _____ speech caused great discomfort during the memorial service for the car crash victims.
    (A) opportunistic
    (B) flippant
    (C) moribund
    (D) commensurate
    (E) erratic

32. The punishment will be _____ with the severity of the crime.
    (A) erratic
    (B) commensurate
    (C) flippant
    (D) renovated
    (E) moribund

On Your Own:
Write one sentence using each word below to demonstrate your understanding of the word's meaning.

33. **commensurate** _____

34. **opportunist** _____

35. **erratic** _____

36. **infamous** _____

37. **flippant** _____

38. **affinity** _____

39. **renovation** _____

40. **moribund** _____

C2 Advanced Vocabulary 62

First Impressions:
Using the example sentences below, write your own definition of each boldfaced word. Then write the letter of the definition from the box that best matches your definition.

A	adjective: mockingly sarcastic	**C**	adjective: changeable; explosive; evaporating rapidly
B	verb: to rear; to encourage; to nurture	**D**	noun: food and other necessary provisions

1. _____ The **volatile** nature of the market means it is impossible to predict whether or not it will be profitable to invest.

VOLATILE means: _____

2. _____ The teacher scolded the bully for making **sardonic** comments about another student.

SARDONIC means: _____

3. _____ The teacher sought to **foster** an appreciation of learning in all her students.

FOSTER means: _____

4. _____ Because we were running low on **victuals**, my mother sent me to the store to get more flour, eggs, milk, and bacon.

VICTUALS means: _____

A	noun: laziness	**C**	noun: the quality of being frank, open, and sincere
B	noun: one who rebels against an authority, often violently	**D**	adjective: poor

5. _____ Throughout history, whenever a foreign invader has occupied a country, **insurgents** have fought to expel the foreigners and reestablish independent rule.

INSURGENT means: _____

6. _____ Although life in the United States is comfortable for most, there are several **impoverished** areas within the nation.

IMPOVERISHED means: _____

7. _____ Offended to see the results of such **sloth**, Manthan's father told him to stop watching television at once and clean his room.

SLOTH means: _____

8. _____ Kayla wished that the politicians would speak with **candor** for once instead of constantly polling to find out what everyone else thought before giving their opinions on each and every subject.

CANDOR means: _____

Divide and Conquer:

Choose the correct word to complete each of the following sentences.

9. (**Impoverished** / **Slothful**) settlers gathered in makeshift shelters of discarded plastic and plywood.

10. The FBI monitors distribution of nitroglycerin, a (**sardonic** / **volatile**) compound that can be dangerous in the wrong hands.

11. We must (**impoverish** / **foster**) the economic policies that we have created so that they grow into sea-changing waves in our financial culture.

12. Dr. Humphreys encouraged his son to give up his life of (**candor** / **sloth**) and take up a position of responsibility.

13. Make sure to pack (**insurgents** / **victuals**) that won't spoil because we won't reach the next cabin for a week.

14. The company representative's (**insurgent** / **candor**) was refreshing; most of the listeners had expected to hear only doubletalk and vague promises.

15. The (**insurgent** / **candor**) roused a militia in order to express disdain for the new laws.

16. The oddly-dressed man received jeers and (**impoverished** / **sardonic**) calls of "looking good!" as he walked down the street.

Hot and Cold:

Write the word from the lesson that is most nearly the *OPPOSITE* of the boldfaced word or words in each sentence below.

17. I hoped to _____ feelings of confidence and enthusiasm in my son, so I tried to avoid talking to him in any way that would **inhibit** his growing self-esteem.

18. Careful labeling of chemical compounds is necessary in order to distinguish _____ compounds from **stable** ones.

19. He gave his speech with such _____ that the audience nearly forgot his past **deceitfulness**.

20. With a _____ smile, Lynn mocked the **sincerity** of her classmates who sat around the campfire confessing their deepest secrets.

21. The new program seeks to ensure that _____ children have access to the same education as their **wealthy** peers.

22. If you ever hope to overcome this bout of unproductive _____, you must find a way to inject some **vigor** into your life; I suggest taking up a sport or seeking out a new group of friends.

23. The _____ fighters wish to topple the current government and anyone **loyal** to the violent regime.

Applying Yourself:

Choose the best word to complete each of the following sentences.

24. We packed all the necessary _____: tents, warm clothing, and long-lasting food items.
    - (A) victuals
    - (B) volatility
    - (C) sloths
    - (D) candor
    - (E) insurgence

25. It's easy to give _____ applause when the product is terrible in the eyes of everyone but the performers.
    - (A) insurgent
    - (B) candid
    - (C) sardonic
    - (D) volatile
    - (E) impoverished

26. The volcano has been more _____ than usual, with minor eruptions indicating a large explosion sometime soon.
    (A) sardonic
    (B) candid
    (C) insurgent
    (D) impoverished
    (E) volatile

27. If you want someone to give you an honest opinion, you should not go to a flatterer but someone who will speak to you with _____.
    (A) victual
    (B) insurgence
    (C) sloth
    (D) candor
    (E) volatility

28. Though the country had plenty of valuable resources, it became _____ after foreign investors took control of the land.
    (A) slothful
    (B) insurgent
    (C) impoverished
    (D) fostered
    (E) volatile

29. Your _____ is obvious as you come to class thirty minutes late, do hardly any homework, and sleep while you should be paying attention.
    (A) volatility
    (B) insurgence
    (C) sloth
    (D) candor
    (E) victual

30. The veterinarians _____ the orphaned kittens until they were grown.
    (A) impoverished
    (B) fostered
    (C) occluded
    (D) censured
    (E) blighted

31. The military posted extra guards at the bridge to foil the incoming _____ intent on occupying the capital.
    (A) candor
    (B) sloths
    (C) victuals
    (D) insurgents
    (E) volatility

On Your Own:

Write one sentence using each word below to demonstrate your understanding of the word's meaning.

32. **insurgent** _____

33. **candor** _____

34. **sardonic** _____

35. **sloth** _____

36. **victuals** _____

37. **volatile** _____

38. **impoverished** _____

39. **foster** _____

C2 Advanced Vocabulary 63

First Impressions:
Using the example sentences below, write your own definition of each boldfaced word. Then write the letter of the definition from the box that best matches your definition.

A	verb: to isolate; to retire from public life; to segregate; to seclude	**C**	adjective: holding strongly to one course of action; stubborn
B	noun: everyday local language; slang	**D**	adjective: allowed only if certain terms are met

1. _____ During the highly-publicized murder trial, jurors were **sequestered** to avoid media attention.

SEQUESTER means: _____

2. _____ Though Surafel was well-versed in textbook Spanish, it took him several months to become comfortable with the **vernacular** of urban Peru.

VERNACULAR means: _____

3. _____ The **conditional** agreement would be fulfilled only if both parties contributed one quarter of the costs of production before beginning.

CONDITIONAL means: _____

4. _____ The **pertinacious** workers stayed on strike until every last one of their demands was met.

PERTINACIOUS means: _____

A	adjective: giving birth to live young (rather than laying eggs)	**C**	noun: a compilation of different writings
B	adjective: causing disease; related to disease	**D**	verb: to support; to keep up; to keep going

5. _____ The **pestilential** plague of frogs ruined the lettuce crop.

PESTILENTIAL means: _____

6. _____ The **anthology** of poems contains all my favorite pieces.

ANTHOLOGY means: _____

7. _____ We're not going to be able to **sustain** this kind of fossil fuel use for very much longer, and alternative energies must be developed.

SUSTAIN means: _____

8. _____ Although most mammals are **viviparous**, the echidna and the platypus lay eggs.

VIVIPAROUS means: _____

Divide and Conquer:
Choose the correct word to complete each of the following sentences.

9. Some amphibians are (**sequestered / viviparous**), while others lay eggs.

10. The mayor has moved to (**sustain / sequester**) hundreds of fee and fine hikes that the DC Council refused to renew.

11. The terms of the contract were (**vernacular / conditional**) and would not be finalized until the new employee passed a performance review.

12. The city had a (**pestilential / pertinacious**) air, as though merely walking down the street would give one a terrible disease.

13. Our exchange students had learned perfect textbook English, but they were unprepared for the confusing (**vernacular / anthology**) of our backwoods town.

14. We (**sequestered / sustained**) the writers in the back room to work in order to meet the deadline.

15. Christine was thrilled to find out that her poem would be included in a(n) (**viviparous / anthology**).

16. The (**pertinacious / viviparous**) captain of the Titanic maintained that his ship was impervious to icebergs, even as his crew warned him otherwise.

Hot and Cold:
Write the word from the lesson that is most nearly the *OPPOSITE* of the boldfaced word or words in each sentence below.

17. Since the jury had to be _____ during the trial to avoid being influenced by news reports, they were pleased to be able to **rejoin** society after the verdict was given.

18. Jolene's _____ attitude easily bulldozed anyone who showed signs of being **tentative** toward an opinion that was opposed to her own.

19. I knew that the dog's slobber was **benign**, but the others backed away like it was _____.

20. The troops were **unable to continue**; they could not _____ a defense against such an unrelenting assault.

21. Mammals are _____ and usually care for the young to whom they give birth, while reptiles are **oviparous** and rarely care for their young after they hatch.

22. The high school English teacher couldn't decide whether to accept the slangy _____ in which her students wrote or to encourage them to use more **formal language**.

23. I expected that my affection for the animal would be _____ and based on whether it behaved, but as soon as I saw the little pup it had my **wholehearted devotion**.

Applying Yourself:
Choose the best word to complete each of the following sentences.

24. My phone's battery can _____ a charge for over ten hours.
    (A) sequester
    (B) sustain
    (C) condition
    (D) expedite
    (E) reprehend

25. _____ reptiles are rare; most must lay and guard eggs.
    (A) Viviparous
    (B) Vernacular
    (C) Conditional
    (D) Pertinacious
    (E) Pestilential

26. Love should not be _____; you should embrace your partner through good times and bad.
    (A) sustainable
    (B) pestilential
    (C) conditional
    (D) viviparous
    (E) sequestered

27. The crew wanted to return to Spain, but the _____ Columbus maintained a western course despite seeing no land in sight.
    (A) vernacular
    (B) pestilential
    (C) viviparous
    (D) conditional
    (E) pertinacious

28. Since he had always lived in isolation, he was eager to _____ himself to the far outskirts of the town.
    (A) condition
    (B) expedite
    (C) sequester
    (D) sustain
    (E) anthologize

29. The flu epidemic was _____ and decreased the population even further.
    (A) pestilential
    (B) sustainable
    (C) pertinacious
    (D) conditional
    (E) viviparous

30. New Orleans, or "Nawlins" as it's called in the _____, still shows its French roots in the language of the area.
    (A) sustainability
    (B) vernacular
    (C) anthology
    (D) condition
    (E) pestilence

31. A complete _____ of the works of author Charles Dickens would be too heavy to lift.
    (A) anthology
    (B) vernacular
    (C) sustainability
    (D) condition
    (E) pestilence

On Your Own:
Write one sentence using each word below to demonstrate your understanding of the word's meaning.

32. **sustain** _____

33. **vernacular** _____

34. **pestilential** _____

35. **sequester** _____

36. **anthology** _____

37. **pertinacious** _____

38. **viviparous** _____

39. **conditional** _____

C2 Advanced Vocabulary 64

First Impressions:
Using the example sentences below, write your own definition of each boldfaced word. Then write the letter of the definition from the box that best matches your definition.

A	verb: to divide into sharply different extremes	**C**	verb: to enrage; to infuriate
B	verb: to fully destroy; to pull out by the roots	**D**	adjective: pale or lacking energy

1. _____ The angry hand gestures my father made were a sign of how much being snubbed by the cashier had **incensed** him.

INCENSE means: _____

2. _____ The landscaper sent an estimate for the cost to **deracinate** the unwanted shrubs cluttering the field.

DERACINATE means: _____

3. _____ Brian was amazed at how quickly politics could **polarize** otherwise sensible people into raving partisans of one issue or its stark opposite.

POLARIZE means: _____

4. _____ Roger's accident cost him a large quantity of blood and left him looking quite **pallid**.

PALLID means: _____

A	verb: to influence through flattery	**C**	noun: a violation of a law, rule, or contract
B	noun: an old friend	**D**	adjective: having unnecessary repetition without adding additional information

5. The phrase "SAT Test" is **tautological**, as SAT once stood for "Scholastic Aptitude Test."

TAUTOLOGICAL means: _____

6. _____ The student's blatant **infraction** of the school's honor code led to a week-long suspension.

INFRACTION means: _____

7. _____ The new mayor appointed many of his **cronies** to well-paid government positions to reward them for their continued support.

CRONY means: _____

8. _____ Rahul attempted to **blandish** the board members with gifts and compliments, but they were not influenced by his flattery.

BLANDISH means: _____

Divide and Conquer:

Choose the correct word to complete each of the following sentences.

9. The party is (**incensed / polarized**) into those who see the immediate need for deficit reduction and those who argue for more gradual spending cuts.

10. After an entire winter spent indoors with little sunlight or exercise, I began to look quite (**tautological / pallid**).

11. Some grammarians view the phrase "past experience" as (**tautological / blandished**), as all experience occurs in the past.

12. Roger attempted to (**polarize / blandish**) his teacher into giving him a higher grade by complimenting her teaching style.

13. Any (**crony / infraction**) of the rules will be met with swift discipline.

14. The goal of the Global Polio Eradication Initiative is to (**polarize / deracinate**) the virus responsible for polio from every country on Earth.

15. Jiyoung became (**pallid / incensed**) when her younger brother broke her flute.

16. When Jennifer was in financial trouble, several of her (**infractions / cronies**) stepped in to help her with her bills and groceries.

Hot and Cold:

Write the word from the lesson that is most nearly the *OPPOSITE* of the boldfaced word or words in each sentence below.

17. I was afraid that the bill's high stakes would _____ the public into "liberal" and "conservative" camps, but the bill had the opposite effect of **unifying** most Americans behind a single cause.

18. While the crop was totally _____ by the swarm of hungry locusts, farmers immediately planted new seeds and expected another full harvest to **sprout**.

19. During her illness, Rosemary had an off-color look that made her once **rosy** cheeks seem deathly _____.

20. The powerful businessmen surrounded himself with _____ he knew he could trust to defend him against any **enemies** he might have.

21. Marissa was _____ by insulting statements as easily as she was **calmed** afterwards.

22. I pointed out the _____ nature of her statement "The slow-moving cars moved forward at a snail's pace" and encouraged her to be more **concise** in her descriptions.

23. After being caught committing numerous _____ and paying heavy penalties, Marge decided **obedience** would be the safest (and cheapest) course of action.

24. While her close circle continued to _____ her no matter what quality of work she produced, most people in the fashion world actively **criticized** her recent styles.

Applying Yourself:

Choose the best word to complete each of the following sentences.

25. A minor _____ will earn the offending party a small fine; a major one will earn that person time in prison.
    - (A) infraction
    - (B) blandishment
    - (C) crony
    - (D) deracination
    - (E) polarization

26. Swaroop _____ Smith's confidence after beating his opponent four matches to none.
    - (A) blandished
    - (B) polarized
    - (C) incensed
    - (D) deracinated
    - (E) infracted

27. The Walla Walla River has among the most _____ of names; as "walla" is a Native American term for "river", the word-for-word translation is "river river river".
    (A) incensed
    (B) tautological
    (C) deracinated
    (D) pallid
    (E) polarized

28. I looked _____ after the sickness kept me bedridden during the summer months.
    (A) incensed
    (B) tautological
    (C) polarized
    (D) deracinated
    (E) pallid

29. At his high school reunion, George took his _____ to their old hangout to reminisce about the good times.
    (A) cronies
    (B) infractions
    (C) deracination
    (D) blandishment
    (E) tautology

30. The emissary _____ the formerly stoic king, and even elicited a smile while giving particularly thorough praise to his shoes.
    (A) polarized
    (B) incensed
    (C) deracinated
    (D) blandished
    (E) infracted

31. The parties have _____ our government to the point that younger members must toe the party line or risk alienating the leadership.
    (A) incensed
    (B) polarized
    (C) deracinated
    (D) infracted
    (E) blandished

32. The man was _____ to hear that someone had scratched his new Porsche.
    (A) pallid
    (B) blandished
    (C) polarized
    (D) deracinated
    (E) incensed

On Your Own:
Write one sentence using each word below to demonstrate your understanding of the word's meaning.

33. **pallid** _____

34. **blandish** _____

35. **polarize** _____

36. **infraction** _____

37. **tautological** _____

38. **crony** _____

39. **incense** _____

40. **deracinate** _____

C2 Advanced Vocabulary 65

First Impressions:
Using the example sentences below, write your own definition of each boldfaced word. Then write the letter of the definition from the box that best matches your definition.

A	adjective: lustful; filled with excessive desire for bodily pleasures	**C**	verb: to think up; to invent; to plan
B	adjective: first; original; basic; most important; primitive	**D**	noun: a person whose life is dedicated to the pursuit of pleasure and self-gratification

1. _____ Perhaps the two together can **devise** a scheme to get themselves out of their present predicaments.

DEVISE means: _____

2. _____ While **hedonists** tend to be optimistic and expressive, they can also be reckless and superficial.

HEDONIST means: _____

3. _____ The clearly **prurient** interest of one character towards another made the very traditional moviegoers uncomfortable.

PRURIENT means: _____

4. _____ When rushing into battle, the soldier gave a **primal** shout reminiscent of his ancestors' war cries.

PRIMAL means: _____

A	adjective: unsuccessful; unfortunate	**C**	noun: an attack from a surrounded group upon its besiegers
B	adjective: unable to read	**D**	noun: unfriendliness; hatred; aggression

5. _____ The **hapless** student couldn't seem to get an A no matter how hard he studied.

HAPLESS means: _____

6. _____ I volunteered helping to teach **illiterate** adults to read.

ILLITERATE means: _____

7. _____ The **hostility** between Israel and Palestine has both political and religious sources and has caused violence to both Israelis and Palestinians.

HOSTILITY means: _____

8. _____ The knights defending the castle staged a surprise **sortie** to harass the surrounding army.

SORTIE means: _____

Divide and Conquer:
Choose the correct word to complete each of the following sentences.

9. As I walked into the room in my little black dress, my father looked at my date with a cold eye, probing his face for any (**prurient / illiterate**) reactions.

10. My brother's (**hostile / hapless**) turtle has gotten shell rot several times, despite our efforts to prevent it.

11. Because they were often (**illiterate / hostile**), immigrants to America often could not read the documents they signed on Ellis Island.

12. Because Ariel had not meant to offend anyone, she was confused by the stranger's (**hostility / haplessness**).

13. The city launched a (**hedonist / sortie**) and attacked the surrounding troops.

14. Though there are times for refined methods, sometimes a person needs to invoke (**prurient / primal**) rage to complete the task.

15. The education department's mandate for schools to (**repress / devise**) a plan to raise standards has left some administrators scrambling to find a solution.

16. Although Frank's father meant the best when he fulfilled his son's every wish as a child, the lavish treatment caused Frank to become a seemingly incurable (**hedonist / sortie**).

Hot and Cold:
Write the word from the lesson that is most nearly the *OPPOSITE* of the boldfaced word or words in each sentence below.

17. A child's _____ instinct is to cry when it is unhappy; only later do the **learned habits** of compromise and civil language take root.

18. The declaration of **peace** brought an end to a long, bitter period of _____.

19. **Literate** adults are encouraged to help the _____ with their studies.

20. I was nervous that the presenter's _____ sense of humor might scandalize the mostly **chaste** and buttoned-up audience of clergymen.

21. With his simple robe and near-empty stomach, the **ascetic** couldn't imagine living the extravagant life of an indulgent _____.

22. Tanya, a known procrastinator, often wondered why one would bother to _____ a schedule by which one could simply **ignore** one's tasks indefinitely.

23. Rather than announcing a **retreat**, which they probably ought to have done, the small group launched a _____ against its numerous attackers.

24. Tony seemed like the **luckiest** guy in the world compared to his _____ brother Chet.

Applying Yourself:
Choose the best word to complete each of the following sentences.

25. Open _____ is the mark that even superficial diplomacy has degenerated.
    (A) hostility
    (B) illiteracy
    (C) prurience
    (D) haplessness
    (E) hedonism

26. The _____student skipped a question but didn't skip a bubble, getting all the rest of the answers wrong as a result.
    (A) hedonistic
    (B) primal
    (C) hapless
    (D) prurient
    (E) hostile

27. The Battle of the Bulge was a(n) _____ by German forces against the encroaching allied attack in France.
    (A) haplessness
    (B) illiteracy
    (C) prurience
    (D) hedonist
    (E) sortie

28. The professor suspected that Jordan had not _____ his own thesis but plagiarized it, for the originality and brilliance of the argument was very unlike Jordan's comments in class.
    (A) devised
    (B) compelled
    (C) mediated
    (D) documented
    (E) conceded

29. Caring for their young is a(n) _____ instinct for all parents.
    (A) hostile
    (B) prurient
    (C) hapless
    (D) hedonistic
    (E) primal

30. Many larger employers prohibit relationships between employees because _____ thoughts in the workplace can distract from productivity.
    (A) hapless
    (B) illiterate
    (C) hedonistic
    (D) primal
    (E) prurient

31. Vacation meant one thing: Jacob, normally a bashful accountant, would convert to a(n) _____ for a reckless and indulgent week in Mexico.
    (A) illiterate
    (B) prurience
    (C) hedonist
    (D) sortie
    (E) hostility

32. Many people in the world's poorest countries are _____ because they have never been formally educated.
    (A) hedonistic
    (B) primal
    (C) illiterate
    (D) hostile
    (E) hapless

On Your Own:
Write one sentence using each word below to demonstrate your understanding of the word's meaning.

33. **hostility** _____

34. **illiterate** _____

35. **devise** _____

36. **prurient** _____

37. **hapless** _____

38. **primal** _____

39. **sortie** _____

40. **hedonist** _____

C2 Advanced Vocabulary 66

First Impressions:
Using the example sentences below, write your own definition of each boldfaced word. Then write the letter of the definition from the box that best matches your definition.

A	adjective: liberal; wasteful; generous	**C**	verb: to drive or force back; to keep out; to cause distaste
B	noun: a refuge; a shelter; a shrine; a holy place	**D**	verb: to support or reinforce

1. _____ Mr. Green was always a bit of a mystery: no one understood how he could afford so **lavish** a lifestyle on such a small salary.

LAVISH means: _____

2. _____ A Nevada rancher and a wild horse advocacy group have proposed creating a Mustang **sanctuary** in the desert hills 160 miles north of Reno.

SANCTUARY means: _____

3. _____ The flimsy tower was **bolstered** against the heavy winds by several supportive cables.

BOLSTER means: _____

4. _____ The castle's defenders managed to **repel** the invaders after a long and fierce battle.

REPEL means: _____

A	verb: to hate	**C**	noun: indifference; lack of concern; composure
B	verb: to make predictions outside of the range of what has been measured	**D**	adjective: fluent; slick; easily suave, implying thoughtlessness, superficiality, or insincerity

5. _____ It is not reasonable to **extrapolate** so widely from such a small sample of data.

EXTRAPOLATE means: _____

6. _____ Joyce **loathed** her language arts teacher, but she loved the writing projects he gave.

LOATHE means: _____

7. _____ Apurva's **glib** response unintentionally hurt Kamal's feelings when he asked her out.

GLIB means: _____

8. _____ Though he affected an air of **nonchalance**, in reality he was quite excited about the news.

NONCHALANCE means: _____

Divide and Conquer:
Choose the correct word to complete each of the following sentences.

9. When David continued to show (**nonchalance /lavishness**) towards the classroom rules, the teacher called his parents in for a conference.

10. The author (**repelled / bolstered**) her analysis with lengthy dissections of several of Smith's poems, lending credence to her claims.

11. The two sisters could not be more dissimilar: Rebecca's charm was inviting while Hester's moodiness and fickle nature (**repelled / loathed**) the other students.

12. They called the area the Safety Zone because within its fortified blast walls lay a (**nonchalance / sanctuary**) for Americans in the war-torn area.

13. Roger's (**glib / lavish**) response did not reflect a sufficient respect for the gravity of the situation.

14. The scientist used the observations to create a model that would allow other researchers to (**extrapolate / sanctuary**) future trends.

15. Though Jeremy (**bolsters / loathes**) almost everything about the new album, he has to admit that the drummer shows talent.

16. The university threw a (**lavish / repellent**) banquet to celebrate being named as the site of the neuroscience conference.

Hot and Cold:
Write the word from the lesson that is most nearly the *OPPOSITE* of the boldfaced word or words in each sentence below.

17. While the comedian was capable of keeping up hours of humor though _____ banter, the producer of the show was a most **artless and sincere**, though awkward, woman.

18. The feeling of my mother squeezing my hand supportively was all it took to _____ my confidence against the criticism that had **damaged** it.

19. Using a serious of specialized "scare tactics," we hoped to _____ the crows and **entice** pleasant-sounding doves to our yard.

20. The heavily guarded compound was a _____ for refugees escaping the surrounding **danger zone** where marauding armies had overtaken the town.

21. Though Ivan **loved** the useful skills he possessed, he _____ the hours of practice required to develop them.

22. Frida's _____ as she seemingly **uncaringly** watched her children jump off the hill into the pond masked the real concern she felt.

23. While we cannot **analyze** the data, as they have not been sent back to the lab, we can _____ what we believe the data will tell us.

24. This _____ dinner party has left me feeling nearly sick with every gustatory delight and looking forward to an **austere** breakfast tomorrow.

Applying Yourself:
Choose the best word to complete each of the following sentences.

25. Based on historical data, the group is able to _____ the government's financial shortfall for the upcoming year.
    (A) bolster
    (B) repel
    (C) extrapolate
    (D) lavish
    (E) loathe

26. Should you want to _____ your guests, refrain from showering for a few days before the party.
    (A) repel
    (B) bolster
    (C) extrapolate
    (D) loathe
    (E) lavish

27. _____ our security at the embassy, or we could witness another breach of the perimeter by terrorists.
   (A) lavish
   (B) extrapolate
   (C) repel
   (D) bolster
   (E) loathe

28. When burning rocks started falling from the sky, the priestess advised the citizens to seek refuge in a religious _____.
   (A) sanctuary
   (B) extrapolation
   (C) repellent
   (D) loathing
   (E) lavishness

29. Due to his _____ attitude towards his homework, Adam's grades in his class started slipping.
   (A) lavishness
   (B) sanctuary
   (C) loathing
   (D) nonchalance
   (E) glibness

30. Please don't make me clean the bathroom; of all the chores, that's the one I _____ the most.
   (A) lavish
   (B) extrapolate
   (C) repel
   (D) bolster
   (E) loathe

31. Olivia's _____ suggestions at the meeting irritated her coworkers, who had all taken a significant amount of time to think of new ideas for the project.
   (A) repellent
   (B) bolstered
   (C) nonchalant
   (D) glib
   (E) lavish

32. The Palace of Versailles' _____ interior contrasted sharply with the poverty and sparseness right outside its gates.
   (A) glib
   (B) lavish
   (C) nonchalant
   (D) repellent
   (E) extrapolated

On Your Own:
Write one sentence using each word below to demonstrate your understanding of the word's meaning.

33. **lavish** _____

34. **sanctuary** _____

35. **loathe** _____

36. **repel** _____

37. **extrapolate** _____

38. **glib** _____

39. **bolster** _____

40. **nonchalance** _____

C2 Advanced Vocabulary 67

First Impressions:

Using the example sentences below, write your own definition of each boldfaced word. Then write the letter of the definition from the box that best matches your definition.

A	adjective: with a lively or high-spirited personality	C	adjective: having the same color as blood or flesh
B	adjective: dull and unimaginative; matter-of-fact; factual	D	noun: fellowship; friendliness among members of a group

1. _____ Though an innovative strategy is often more exciting, a **prosaic** approach is usually enough to get the job done.

PROSAIC means: _____

2. The set designer covered the wall with **incarnadine** paint to give it the appearance of a giant face.

INCARNADINE means: _____

3. _____ Whenever Eugene was feeling depressed, he spent a night on the town with some of his more **vivacious** friends in order to cheer himself up.

VIVACIOUS means: _____

4. _____ After two weeks on a lonely business trip, David looked forward to the **camaraderie** that he and his coworkers at the office enjoyed.

CAMARADERIE means: _____

A	noun: muscular strength	C	adjective: stubborn; hard to control or treat
B	noun: indifference; lack of interest or concern	D	noun: a fake name used as a disguise

5. _____ I signed into the hotel under an alias so that no one would be able to find me.

ALIAS means: _____

6. _____ Patel was so **obstinate** that he refused to change his socks even after a friend pointed out that they didn't match.

OBSTINATE means: _____

7. _____ Owen saw that the man had intimidating **brawn**, but his awkwardness in the ring showed that he had never learned how to apply that strength in fighting.

BRAWN means: _____

8. _____ At times, voter **apathy** is so high that only about half of eligible voters will participate in an election.

APATHY means: _____

Divide and Conquer:
Choose the correct word to complete each of the following sentences.

9. The artist represented the aftermath of the winter battle with splashes of (**incarnadine / obstinate**) paint on a dirty white background.

10. Sheer (**apathy / brawn**) is not sufficient to win a weightlifting competition; events such as the clean and jerk require great skill as well.

11. Spirit Week was going badly until our (**vivacious / obstinate**) cheerleaders electrified the room.

12. The teacher could tell that the reading material was particularly uninteresting due to her students' (**apathetic / incarnadine**) comments on the subject.

13. Good managers should be confident, not arrogant; extroverted, not aloof; and open-minded, not (**obstinate / prosaic**).

14. The members of the team attributed their success to their (**brawn / camaraderie**); had they not enjoyed each other's company so strongly, they would have had less success on the playing field.

15. Finding the debate (**prosaic / brawny**) and simplistic, I moved on to matters more interesting and well-reasoned.

16. When he is not wearing a cape, Superman uses the (**camaraderie / alias**) Clark Kent.

Hot and Cold:
Write the word from the lesson that is most nearly the *OPPOSITE* of the boldfaced word or words in each sentence below.

17. You are far from _____; you are **willing to consider** other points of view.

18. Friendly trust and _____ within the group of second graders grow into unfortunately bitter **enmity** as a result of parental disputes.

19. I couldn't believe such a _____ young girl had been born of such **dull** parents.

20. Having always been known for his own _____, Mr. Henry refused to accept any signs of **weakness** in his children.

21. The form asked for my **legal name** as well as any _____ I might have used.

22. My selfish _____ toward the refugees displaced by the war transformed into **deep concern** when I saw videos of the squalid camps in which they were kept.

23. Graham prefers dry, _____ military history with as few thrilling details as possible, while I prefer the **fantastic** world of science fiction with its many incredible ideas and descriptions.

Applying Yourself:
Choose the best word to complete each of the following sentences.

24. While we require _____ personalities to run our sales force, we need those people to know when to be more subdued, too.
    (A) obstinate
    (B) vivacious
    (C) prosaic
    (D) brawny
    (E) apathetic

25. The airborne division developed a feeling of _____ after their shared experiences in France.
    (A) apathy
    (B) obstinacy
    (C) brawn
    (D) vivacity
    (E) camaraderie

26. Mr. Houston's interactive and creative method of teaching excited her students, who were used to the _____ lectures of their other teachers.
    (A) prosaic
    (B) vivacious
    (C) brawny
    (D) apathetic
    (E) obstinate

27. John was very muscular and would always show off his _____.
    (A) camaraderie
    (B) apathy
    (C) brawn
    (D) vivacity
    (E) alias

28. Nancy would not make a good nurse because she feels _____ towards those who are in need of help.
    (A) camaraderie
    (B) vivacity
    (C) apathy
    (D) brawn
    (E) obstinacy

29. Mrs. Lorenz had yet to find a successful way to kill off the _____ weeds in her garden, for they grew back quickly after being pulled.
    (A) prosaic
    (B) vivacious
    (C) obstinate
    (D) brawny
    (E) incarnadine

30. The _____ walls faded to off-red with the amount of sunlight that had hit them.
    (A) obstinate
    (B) apathetic
    (C) brawny
    (D) incarnadine
    (E) prosaic

31. Desperate that no one should recognize her, Alicia gave a(n) _____ when someone asked for her name.
    (A) alias
    (B) camaraderie
    (C) brawn
    (D) vivacity
    (E) brawn

On Your Own:
Write one sentence using each word below to demonstrate your understanding of the word's meaning.

32. **camaraderie** _____

33. **incarnadine** _____

34. **obstinate** _____

35. **apathy** _____

36. **brawn** _____

37. **alias** _____

38. **vivacious** _____

39. **prosaic** _____

C2 Advanced Vocabulary 68

First Impressions:

Using the example sentences below, write your own definition of each boldfaced word. Then write the letter of the definition from the box that best matches your definition.

A	noun: mixed, conflicting	**C**	adjective: self-absorbed; unwilling to consider other points of view
B	adjective: extremely strong; intimidating	**D**	adjective: bossy; overbearing

1. _____ Coach Tilden means well, but sometimes his strict rules can come across as **domineering**.

DOMINEERING means: _____

2. _____ She couldn't understand her **ambivalence**; she knew she loved her brother, but at the same time she wished he were on the other side of the planet.

AMBIVALENCE means: _____

3. _____ It is likely that you will have difficulty relating to others if you maintain your **solipsistic** worldview.

SOLIPSISTIC means: _____

4. _____ The idea of traveling alone is quite **formidable**, and I'm not sure I'll be able to do it.

FORMIDABLE means: _____

A	adjective: describing a fault that is forgivable	**C**	noun: a critical comment
B	noun: a person who attempts to influence lawmakers	**D**	noun: an imperfect representation of something else

5. _____ The hologram was supposed to be a picture of Shari, but it was only a poor, unconvincing **simulacrum**.

SIMULACRUM means: _____

6. _____ My best friend has the **venial** habit of forgetting to call me back, which is annoying but not too bothersome.

VENIAL means: _____

7. _____ The politician responded to the **animadversions** on his character with surprising tact and goodwill.

ANIMADVERSION means: _____

8. _____ The telecommunications industry employs many **lobbyists** to ensure that the laws of the country will favor its business endeavors.

LOBBYIST means: _____

Divide and Conquer:
Choose the correct word to complete each of the following sentences.

9. The beverage company sent a delegation of (**lobbyists / simulacrums**) to present a proposal to Congress.

10. His (**domineering / formidable**) friend hardly let him make a decision for himself.

11. Don't bother trying to convince him; his (**venial / solipsistic**) stance repels even the most persuasive arguments.

12. The businessman would not tolerate such (**ambivalence / animadversions**) against his character.

13. Ava felt a great deal of (**ambivalence / formidability**) about finishing high school; she was nervous about heading to college, but also excited.

14. Concertgoers were astonished and delighted when the holograph projector created a (**lobbyist / simulacrum**) of the famous late actor.

15. The lovely little restaurant has the (**venial / ambivalent**) quality of being a bit too small for parties of more than eight.

16. Franco faced the (**formidable / solipsistic**) task of informing the siblings that their father had been injured.

Hot and Cold:
Write the word from the lesson that is most nearly the *OPPOSITE* of the boldfaced word or words in each sentence below.

17. The **empathetic** young man understood how others felt and couldn't understand how more _____ people managed to ignore the feelings of their peers.

18. Priests are known to be _____ individuals and see very few things as **unforgivable**.

19. Rufio, a **shy** man, was often taken advantage of by his _____ vice president.

20. My _____ toward this particular issue belies my **steadfastness** for human equality and rarely make compromises in this regard.

21. This _____ of the famous painting will never pass for the original; we need a **genuine article**.

22. During her review, Carrie felt like a target at which her managers threw every hurtful _____ they could think of, determined not to let anything remotely resembling a **compliment** sneak through.

23. Tony hoped to find a _____ opponent at the wrestling competition, but most of his competitors were **laughable**.

Applying Yourself:
Choose the best word to complete each of the following sentences.

24. Politicians pay special attention to the _____ of voters, as those on the fence often determine the outcome of an election.
    - (A) formidability
    - (B) lobbyist
    - (C) animadversion
    - (D) ambivalence
    - (E) solipsism

25. I couldn't wait to quit my job so that I would never have to work for my _____ manager again.
    - (A) domineering
    - (B) formidable
    - (C) solipsistic
    - (D) venial
    - (E) ambivalent

26. The Room, widely considered the worst movie ever made, has had to endure _____ from websites, newspapers, and social media sites.
    (A) formidability
    (B) lobbyism
    (C) solipsism
    (D) animadversion
    (E) veniality

27. Philip was a(n) _____ opponent; I hoped I would never have to face him in combat.
    (A) venial
    (B) domineering
    (C) formidable
    (D) solipsistic
    (E) ambivalent

28. The worst of her offenses was a series of _____ mistakes that had no real bearing on the company's prosperity.
    (A) venial
    (B) formidable
    (C) domineering
    (D) solipsistic
    (E) ambivalent

29. Those who criticize the banking industry point out that it spends millions of dollars each year on _____ who attempt to buy congressional votes.
    (A) simulacrums
    (B) lobbyists
    (C) animadversions
    (D) venialities
    (E) ambivalence

30. Rather than demonstrate a _____ attitude, we must be open minded to all possibilities.
    (A) formidable
    (B) solipsistic
    (C) ambivalent
    (D) venial
    (E) domineering

31. Forgive us for being critical, but Katie is a mere _____ of the wonderful and recently departed Susan.
    (A) simulacrum
    (B) veniality
    (C) ambivalence
    (D) solipsism
    (E) lobbyist

On Your Own:

Write one sentence using each word below to demonstrate your understanding of the word's meaning.

32. **formidable** _____

33. **domineering** _____

34. **lobbyist** _____

35. **animadversion** _____

36. **solipsistic** _____

37. **ambivalence** _____

38. **simulacrum** _____

39. **venial** _____

C2 Advanced Vocabulary 69

First Impressions:

Using the example sentences below, write your own definition of each boldfaced word. Then write the letter of the definition from the box that best matches your definition.

A	noun: someone who studies languages	**C**	adjective: present from birth, especially a disorder
B	verb: to displace or substitute	**D**	noun: an alphabetical list of words or topics contained in a book (such as the Bible); agreement or harmony

1. _____ I learned from my **concordance** that the word "alas" appears in 16 different verses of the Bible.

CONCORDANCE means: _____

2. _____ Though blindness acquired later in life can often be cured, many forms of **congenital** blindness have no known treatment.

CONGENITAL means: _____

3. _____ The birth of my brother made me feel **supplanted** as the favorite child.

SUPPLANTED means: _____

4. _____ The **linguist** will settle in Tanzania for 3 years to study the particular style of language spoken there.

LINGUIST means: _____

A	verb: to disagree	**C**	adjective: firmly fixed in purpose
B	adjective: able to be shaped by pressure; changeable	**D**	adjective: refined and respectable; polite

5. _____ Humphrey's manners were old-fashioned and **genteel**: he removed his hat when entering a building, held doors open, and never swore.

GENTEEL means: _____

6. _____ Franklin flattened the **malleable** metal into sheets by pounding it with a hammer.

MALLEABLE means: _____

7. _____ The citizens added their names to a petition to voice their **dissent** toward the new bill.

DISSENT means: _____

8. _____ While his fellow guards became bored and left their posts, Mercutio was **resolute** in his determination to defend his position.

RESOLUTE means: _____

Divide and Conquer:

Choose the correct word to complete each of the following sentences.

9. He used a (**concordance / resolution**) to find out how many times the word "auspicious" was used in the book.

10. He was (**dissented / supplanted**) by a younger, more efficient worker and so had to find another job.

11. As a (**dissenter / linguist**), Mr. Robert is required to learn 5 languages fluently.

12. The rules of the organization were sufficiently (**genteel / malleable**) to allow for adaptation to unexpected circumstances.

13. Some members (**dissent / supplant**), saying the Fed should set a timetable soon, even before a rate hike.

14. Despite the daunting task, Marlow was (**malleable / resolute**) in his quest.

15. Jacob's (**genteel / resolute**) manners were a surprising contrast among the rough and tough members of the motorcycle club.

16. The doctor specialized in performing difficult surgeries on newborns to treat (**genteel / congenital**) deformities.

Hot and Cold:

Write the word from the lesson that is most nearly the *OPPOSITE* of the boldfaced word or words in each sentence below.

17. The _____ between the two parties, who were usually at each other's throats, could not withstand another major **disagreement**.

18. Our visitor's **coarse manners** and off-color jokes did not sit well with our _____ grandparents, whose ideas of "breeding" and "refinery" were quite narrow indeed.

19. My opinions on war strategies, uninfluenced by any personal involvement in the matter, are much more _____ than the **rigid** views of my brother John, who has personally experienced battle and takes a strong position on the matter.

20. Though the new car _____ the old car's place in the garage, the old car **remains** my favorite.

21. Type 1 diabetes is _____, and children will often have symptoms from birth, whereas Type 2 is **acquired** due to health circumstances later in life.

22. I was _____ in my desire to get in shape but **wary** of buying a gym membership I couldn't afford.

23. We all seem to **agree** on this matter, but it would be rash to move forward before we've opened the floor to anyone who might _____ from our opinion.

Applying Yourself:

Choose the best word to complete each of the following sentences.

24. The old orange grove has been _____ by a stretch of new apartment buildings.
    (A) loathed
    (B) compelled
    (C) devised
    (D) dissented
    (E) supplanted

25. The 300 Spartans stood _____ against the attacking Persian hordes, refusing to back down.
    (A) malleable
    (B) resolute
    (C) genteel
    (D) congenital
    (E) supplanted

26. As a _____, I am trying to understand how English has developed into the language it is today.
 (A) linguist
 (B) concordance
 (C) resolution
 (D) gentility
 (E) sortie

27. The _____ of views came at a point when we were worried that the two sides would never agree.
 (A) linguist
 (B) gentility
 (C) concordance
 (D) dissent
 (E) supplanting

28. Hakeem had to retire prematurely from basketball due to the discovery of a _____ heart defect that made running dangerous.
 (A) dissenting
 (B) supplanted
 (C) malleable
 (D) resolute
 (E) congenital

29. Many yearn for the _____ days of publishing, in which those from old money would hobnob with one another over drinks and classic literature.
 (A) genteel
 (B) linguistic
 (C) concordant
 (D) supplanted
 (E) malleable

30. Justice Blackmon _____ when all other justices upheld the ruling.
 (A) supplanted
 (B) dissented
 (C) loathed
 (D) compelled
 (E) devised

31. In addition to its luster, gold is one of the most _____ metals; smiths are able to manipulate it into extremely thin strands.
 (A) linguistic
 (B) malleable
 (C) genteel
 (D) resolute
 (E) congenital

On Your Own:
Write one sentence using each word below to demonstrate your understanding of the word's meaning.

32. **linguist** _____

33. **concordance** _____

34. **malleable** _____

35. **supplant** _____

36. **congenital** _____

37. **dissent** _____

38. **resolute** _____

39. **genteel** _____

C2 Advanced Vocabulary 70

First Impressions:

Using the example sentences below, write your own definition of each boldfaced word. Then write the letter of the definition from the box that best matches your definition.

A	verb: to cause extreme distaste, dislike, or disgust; to drive back, repel	**C**	noun: success, growth, or flourishing
B	noun: harsh criticism or condemnation	**D**	adjective: wise; sound in judgment

1. _____ Although Grace wanted to watch TV, she figured it would be more **judicious** to finish her homework first.

JUDICIOUS means: _____

2. _____ The response to the album was mixed; some heaped praise upon it, while others unleashed harsh **invectives**.

INVECTIVE means: _____

3. _____ The nation entered a period of **prosperity** as unemployment numbers dropped and profits increased across the board.

PROSPERITY means: _____

4. _____ Laura was **repulsed** by the rotten cherries and the maggots that were crawling over them.

REPULSE means: _____

A	adjective: sturdy; robust or healthy; able to withstand harsh weather	**C**	verb: to trespass or take what is considered to be another's; to make an impression
B	noun: the ability to change in form; fickleness	**D**	verb: to seize (a position of power) by force

5. _____ The United States Constitution guarantees that the government will not **impinge** upon a citizen's right to speak freely, but that does not stop other citizens from doing so.

IMPINGE means: _____

6. _____ The ability to modify an outdated law is important for a strong government, but excessive **mutability** leads to instability.

MUTABILITY means: _____

7. _____ Few believe that the enemy troops will be able to **usurp** power from the government by the end of the year.

USURP means: _____

8. _____ The storm did not prevent the **hardy** warriors from storming the battlefield.

HARDY means: _____

Divide and Conquer:
Choose the correct word to complete each of the following sentences.

9. Some lawmakers worry that the new bill will (**impinge** / **repulse**) on citizens' rights in a negative way.

10. The cable must first be (**mutable** / **hardy**) enough to withstand the extreme forces.

11. Though Ariel wanted to quickly reach a decision, Sabrina thought it would be (**judicious** / **impinged**) to gather more information first.

12. Roma, who used to be infatuated with Cody, now felt (**judicious** / **repulsed**) at the very sight of him.

13. We hope the recent rains and moderate temperatures will lead to (**prosperity** / **invectives**) for your crop.

14. The airwaves filled with harsh (**invectives** / **impingements**) after the president's controversial speech.

15. One of the strengths of the United States Constitution is its (**mutability** / **prosperity**); revisions can be made as needed by passing amendments.

16. Whenever my uncle stays with our family, he tries to (**repulse** / **usurp**) power from my parents by making household decisions and disciplining my siblings and me.

Hot and Cold:
Write the word from the lesson that is most nearly the *OPPOSITE* of the boldfaced word or words in each sentence below.

17. One of the goals of education is to help **naïve and immature** thinkers to become _____ decision makers.

18. Most of the visitors to the exhibit were _____ by the grotesque statue, but some were **drawn to** the strange forms and subject matter.

19. Francisco's personality was far from **fixed** and stodgy; in fact, his _____ was legendary.

20. The _____ tree will be able to withstand the bad weather much better than these **frail** flowers, which will surely wither and die.

21. Rather than receiving the _____ I expected for my utter disregard of the rules, I received **praise** for having the audacity to do what I thought was right.

22. The king's brother tried to _____ the crown, but was forced to **surrender** when he was surrounded by the castle's guards.

23. I was worried I might _____ on your relaxing evening with my noisy cleaning, but I'm glad you say my doings **had no effect** on you.

24. After a long period of gleeful _____, I suppose it's no surprise that the company would hit a time of **financial hardship** and have to be much more careful with its assets.

Applying Yourself:
Choose the best word to complete each of the following sentences.

25. Skeptical of her friend's ignorant input on the matter, Judy sought a more _____ opinion elsewhere.
    (A) mutable
    (B) prosperous
    (C) judicious
    (D) repulsive
    (E) hardy

26. Should you wish you avoid a(n) _____ from Coach Smith, make sure to practice hard every day.
    (A) invective
    (B) repulsion
    (C) impingement
    (D) hardiness
    (E) mutability

27. While the nation has experienced decades of _____ in the form of GDP growth, not everyone has benefitted from the economic boom.
    (A) usurpation
    (B) invective
    (C) judiciousness
    (D) prosperity
    (E) mutability

28. Rather than attract followers to his position, LaVar's speech _____ them.
    (A) repulsed
    (B) mutated
    (C) usurped
    (D) impinged
    (E) prospered

29. The bear is a sturdy and tough animal, and her _____ body can withstand extreme temperatures well.
    (A) judicious
    (B) hardy
    (C) repulsed
    (D) impinged
    (E) prosperous

30. The concept _____ upon my peace of mind and gave me no peace for days.
    (A) usurped
    (B) prospered
    (C) mutated
    (D) impinged
    (E) repulsed

31. I only got up from my chair for a minute, but when I returned, it had already been _____ by the dog.
    (A) usurped
    (B) impinged
    (C) mutated
    (D) repulsed
    (E) prospered

32. Certain metals, such as gold and lead, display great _____, making them easy to form into works of art.
    (A) repulsion
    (B) invective
    (C) mutability
    (D) prosperity
    (E) hardiness

On Your Own:

Write one sentence using each word below to demonstrate your understanding of the word's meaning.

33. **judicious** _____

34. **usurp** _____

35. **repulse** _____

36. **invective** _____

37. **impinge** _____

38. **hardy** _____

39. **prosperity** _____

40. **mutability** _____

C2 Advanced Vocabulary 71

First Impressions:

Using the example sentences below, write your own definition of each boldfaced word. Then write the letter of the definition from the box that best matches your definition.

A	noun: a spoken blessing, usually given by a priest or other spiritual figure	**C**	noun: an excessive interest in one's self
B	adjective: indecently sexual	**D**	noun: a reason to be upset or complain

1. _____ The **salacious** book was banned from high schools for its sexual content.

SALACIOUS means: _____

2. _____ I've held a **grievance** against my sister ever since she ripped my prom dress before I got

   to wear it.

GRIEVANCE means: _____

3. _____ A mild selfishness in Louie's teenage years expanded into full-blown **narcissism** by

   adulthood.

NARCISSISM means: _____

4. _____ The priest delivered the **benediction** at the end of the service.

BENEDICTION means: _____

A	adjective: unruly; stubborn; unyielding	**C**	noun: a stimulus or moving force; momentum
B	adjective: serving as a model; outstanding	**D**	verb: to sparkle

5. _____ Though setbacks in their dog's obedience training left Shirley ready to give up, Edward

   thought that their poodle was far from **intractable** and could indeed be taught better behavior.

INTRACTABLE means: _____

6. _____ As the sun set over the beach, the last rays of light **scintillated** from the rippling water.

SCINTILLATE means: _____

7. _____ Somsri didn't know how her brother was able to be such an **exemplary** student;

   participating in many clubs and maintaining straight Aís seemed terribly difficult.

EXEMPLARY means: _____

8. _____ Yolanda's **impetus** to apply for the job was her need to find a workplace nearer to her

   home.

IMPETUS means: _____

Divide and Conquer:

Choose the correct word to complete each of the following sentences.

9. The poem was once considered (**salacious / intractable**) for its sexual themes, but today, it is considered a valuable piece of literature.

10. In the petition, the students listed their many (**benedictions / grievances**) against the university administration.

11. "Go with God," he told me, as a (**benediction / scintillation**).

12. Jake's (**narcissism / impetus**) compelled him to gaze admiringly into every mirror he passed.

13. Since the student possessed great motivation, he had enough of a(n) (**impetus / benediction**) to study and improve his grades.

14. The new horse proved nearly (**intractable / narcissistic**) until an expert trainer was called in.

15. Las Vegas (**scintillates / relegates**) with millions of lights, beckoning those from far away to try their luck at the tables.

16. College admissions committees often have a difficult time choosing between groups of equally (**exemplary / scintillating**) students who maintained good grades and led clubs and out-of-school activities.

Hot and Cold:

Write the word from the lesson that is most nearly the *OPPOSITE* of the boldfaced word or words in each sentence below.

17. Although the chef received a short list of _____ about the meal he'd prepared, he also received a very warm **compliment** from the lady of the house.

18. Mrs. Martin knew that the _____ her teenaged students exhibited—their rude self-interest and inability to relate meaningfully to others—would fade, in time, to a more mature **humility**.

19. The family sent the _____ teenager to see a priest, hoping his **pious and restrained** ways would help the teenager.

20. Because he had once been an _____ student, making the honor roll and dean's list three years in a row, Greg considered his less-than-stellar grades the most **shameful** aspect of his senior year.

21. The Owl King's _____ to his subjects was interrupted by a dreadful **curse** from the evil Owl-Witch.

22. I knew that without an _____ edging me forward in my job search, I'd find only **stagnancy** in my current situation.

23. The _____ old governor, whose unwillingness to compromise has slowed the legislative process for years, is being replaced by the **compliant** Pat Gray, who has promised to remain open to all discussions.

Applying Yourself:

Choose the best word to complete each of the following sentences.

24. Her _____ arrogance has become the biggest challenge in the group project since it prevents her from compromising.
    (A) salacious
    (B) intractable
    (C) exemplary
    (D) scintillating
    (E) narcissistic

25. Our _____ for action was clear: without intervention, nothing would ever get done.
    (A) narcissism
    (B) impetus
    (C) intractability
    (D) benediction
    (E) grievance

26. The slipshod work of the newly hired janitor made the store manager miss the previous, _____ one even more.
   (A) intractable
   (B) narcissistic
   (C) scintillating
   (D) salacious
   (E) exemplary

27. We have a number of _____, and if you don't do something about them, we are going to quit.
   (A) impetuses
   (B) benedictions
   (C) grievances
   (D) narcissism
   (E) intractability

28. Don't be blinded by your own _____, or you'll grow self-satisfied and stop looking for ways to improve.
   (A) impetus
   (B) scintillation
   (C) benediction
   (D) narcissism
   (E) intractability

29. I found his _____ messages inappropriate and disrespectful to my husband, so I deleted them without responding.
   (A) salacious
   (B) intractable
   (C) scintillating
   (D) narcissistic
   (E) exemplary

30. Jenny's gown, covered with rhinestones, _____ under the full moon.
   (A) adumbrated
   (B) scintillated
   (C) relegated
   (D) occluded
   (E) implemented

31. Most weddings end with a(n) _____ from the priest.
   (A) benediction
   (B) narcissism
   (C) scintillation
   (D) impetus
   (E) grievance

On Your Own:
Write one sentence using each word below to demonstrate your understanding of the word's meaning.

32. **salacious** _____

33. **exemplary** _____

34. **narcissism** _____

35. **scintillate** _____

36. **impetus** _____

37. **grievance** _____

38. **benediction** _____

39. **intractable** _____

C2 Advanced Vocabulary 72

First Impressions:

Using the example sentences below, write your own definition of each boldfaced word. Then write the letter of the definition from the box that best matches your definition.

A	adjective: speaking fluently and with ease; speaking persuasively	**C**	noun: a contradiction to what one expects would happen normally
B	noun: ecstasy; great joy; something extremely emotional	**D**	noun: the act of transferring something from one person or place to another

1. _____ When talking about poetry, Kevin goes into a **rhapsody** of excitement and passion.

RHAPSODY means: _____

2. _____ A **transfusion** of plasma from a healthy donor meant that Marnie would live to see another day.

TRANSFUSION means: _____

3. _____ The **irony** of the situation lay in the fact that I injured myself while putting on protective gear.

IRONY means: _____

4. _____ The **eloquent** speaker captivated audiences and got his points across quite clearly.

ELOQUENT means: _____

A	verb: to foreshadow or suggest in an unclear way; to indicate faintly	**C**	adjective: very wicked
B	noun: ability or talent	**D**	verb: to turn into a liquid; to melt

5. _____ One's perceived righteousness of a cause does not justify the carrying out of **nefarious** and potentially dangerous actions.

NEFARIOUS means: _____

6. _____ If you **liquefy** vegetables alongside fruit in a blender, they taste sweet and delicious.

LIQUEFY means: _____

7. _____ Students showing high **aptitude** in science will be eligible to participate in intramural competitions.

APTITUDE means: _____

8. _____ The minor disagreement between the two parties **adumbrated** larger disputes that were yet to come.

ADUMBRATE means: _____

Divide and Conquer:

Choose the correct word to complete each of the following sentences.

9. The purpose of the test is to measure students' (**aptitude / nefariousness**) and readiness for college-level scholarship.

10. The powerful sounds of Beethoven's Ninth Symphony put me into an appreciative (**rhapsody / aptitude**).

11. The sun will (**transfuse / liquefy**) crayons if they are left outside on a hot day.

12. My mother, a(n) (**nefarious / eloquent**) speaker, was always chosen to defend the school board's positions.

13. Many people predicted that the world would come to an end when this bill was passed, that there was some sort of (**adumbrated / nefarious**) government takeover in the works.

14. The flickering light of the lamp dimly (**liquefied / adumbrated**) the dark staircase.

15. Some found (**irony / transfusion**) in the fact that the man known as the "world's most honest leader" was caught stealing money from the state.

16. Because she was able to receive a blood (**aptitude / transfusion**) quickly, she is expected to recover fully from the accident.

Hot and Cold:

Write the word from the lesson that is most nearly the *OPPOSITE* of the boldfaced word or words in each sentence below.

17. If you **solidify** water, you'll get ice; if you _____ ice, you'll get water.

18. Dennis _____ that something I had said or done was the cause of his distress, but because he did not **hint at the specifics**, I couldn't defend myself.

19. Carl's _____ for poetry meant that he never bothered much with subjects for which he had disinclinations, such as math and sports.

20. I'd pictured myself as a wonderfully _____ actor, so my **tongue-tied** performance disappointed me.

21. Our _____ aunt has stolen money from each of us and ruined our credit by forging our signatures; I have lost all hope of her doing something **good** for our family.

22. After spending 5 years living, working, and going to school together, the _____ of Sharon and Francine's personalities was complete; **separation** between them was unthinkable.

23. There was no _____ in Michael's voice when he said it was the best day he'd ever had; his **sincerity** became apparent when he described how despite the day's misfortunes, he felt a deep inner peace.

24. After their toddler was kidnapped, the parents were in a state of **despair**, but after the police found their child, the parents experienced a moment of _____.

Applying Yourself:

Choose the best word to complete each of the following sentences.

25. The _____ wizard placed a curse upon the baby as soon as it was born.
    (A) nefarious
    (B) adumbrated
    (C) ironic
    (D) transfused
    (E) eloquent

26. A(n) _____ speaker, Henry had the audience mesmerized.
    (A) transfused
    (B) eloquent
    (C) nefarious
    (D) adumbrated
    (E) ironic

27. Brief glimpses through the rolling fog _____ troops on the far bank; how many there were, we could not guess.
    (A) expedited
    (B) censured
    (C) liquefied
    (D) adumbrated
    (E) transfused

28. Beethoven's music is thought to invoke a(n) _____ that causes people to cry with joy.
    (A) adumbration
    (B) aptitude
    (C) eloquence
    (D) rhapsody
    (E) transfusion

29. She showed _____ in her interview, and we knew immediately that we had found our new manager.
    (A) adumbration
    (B) irony
    (C) transfusion
    (D) eloquence
    (E) aptitude

30. The afternoon was so hot that the chocolate bar in my bag _____.
    (A) liquefied
    (B) transfused
    (C) adumbrated
    (D) shunted
    (E) rhapsodized

31. As a baby with a blood disorder, I required many _____ from the day I was born.
    (A) adumbrations
    (B) transfusions
    (C) liquefactions
    (D) ironies
    (E) rhapsodies

32. In a twist of _____, the material that he had studied so hard didn't appear on the test.
    (A) eloquence
    (B) transfusion
    (C) irony
    (D) aptitude
    (E) adumbration

On Your Own:

Write one sentence using each word below to demonstrate your understanding of the word's meaning.

33. **adumbrate** _____

34. **nefarious** _____

35. **liquefy** _____

36. **aptitude** _____

37. **irony** _____

38. **rhapsody** _____

39. **transfusion** _____

40. **eloquent** _____

C2 Advanced Vocabulary 73

First Impressions:

Using the example sentences below, write your own definition of each boldfaced word. Then write the letter of the definition from the box that best matches your definition.

A	adjective: pertinent or important; closely or significantly related	**C**	verb: to disprove through evidence
B	noun: a good or just reason; a defense; an excuse	**D**	adjective: lively or friendly; fond of lively group activities

1. _____ Soledad is not normally a **convivial** person, but she had a great time at the dinner party.

CONVIVIAL means: _____

2. _____ The judge didn't think there was enough evidence to provide **justification** for an arrest

warrant.

JUSTIFICATION means: _____

3. _____ The debater outlined three points to **rebut** her opponent's argument.

REBUT means: _____

4. _____ Keep your comments **germane** to the issue so that we don't waste time.

GERMANE means: _____

A	verb: to narrate or tell; to count over again	**C**	noun: resistance to authority or opposing force; contempt
B	verb: to surround with troubles or military forces	**D**	adjective: shared or returned between two parties

5. _____ During the messy divorce, the celebrities were **beleaguered** with photographers and

journalists seeking juicy details for their magazines.

BELEAGUER means: _____

6. _____ In **defiance** of his father's wishes for him to get a college degree, Feival decided to run

away and join the circus.

DEFIANCE means: _____

7. _____ The producers and creators **recounted** the difficult casting processes that led them to the

most talented new TV star in years, delighting in the tale.

RECOUNT means: _____

8. _____ Both business leaders were satisfied with the transaction, as the benefits were **reciprocal**.

RECIPROCAL means: _____

Divide and Conquer:

Choose the correct word to complete each of the following sentences.

9. The old group of friends enjoyed meeting once a year for a (**reciprocal / convivial**) evening of laughter and reminiscing.

10. The Fourth Amendment states that the homes of American citizens cannot be searched by officers of the law without (**reciprocity / justification**).

11. Inspector Gomez (**recounted / rebutted**) Tina's alibi with a litany of eyewitness accounts showing that Tina in fact had been at the scene of the crime.

12. The facts related to those incidents are not (**reciprocal / germane**) to this appeal and should not be brought into the courtroom.

13. Merry and Pippen (**reciprocated / recounted**) their story of the days they had spent in captivity.

14. The celebrity was (**rebutted / beleaguered**) with photographers as soon as he stepped outside his door.

15. One of best-known symbols of (**rebuttual / defiance**) is an image of a single man facing a line of tanks in Tiananmen Square.

16. Symbiotic organisms exist because of the (**recounted / reciprocal**) benefits each gives the other.

Hot and Cold:

Write the word from the lesson that is most nearly the *OPPOSITE* of the boldfaced word or words in each sentence below.

17. Enemies had _____ the port city, preventing allies from coming in to **help relieve** the famine within its walls.

18. Vern tried to find a _____ for his bad behavior, but there was **no good reason** for how he had treated his mother.

19. Normally, Greg loved this kind of large, _____ gathering full of food, drinks, laughter, and friends; today, though, he was feeling **reticent** and desired only to be alone.

20. Our curiosity was piqued, and we asked Marcia again and again to _____ the story of why she was arrested, but she was determined to **silence herself** on the matter.

21. The eager student tried to _____ his professor's claim, but he had no grounds to **prove his own point** and appeared foolish.

22. When it came to civil rights, Malcolm X advocated violent _____ in opposition to unfair treatment and viewed Martin Luther King's nonviolent protests to be a form of **acquiescence**.

23. We ask that, due to time constraints, only _____ questions be asked at the end of the presentation and that **irrelevant** queries be kept to an absolute minimum.

24. Judy hung her head and tried not to show her emotions when she learned that her feelings for Jaime, which she hoped were _____, turned out to be **one-sided**.

Applying Yourself:

Choose the best word to complete each of the following sentences.

25. When your host compliments your outfit, you are expected to give her _____ praise.
(A) recounted
(B) rebutted
(C) convivial
(D) germane
(E) reciprocal

26. The rebels showed open _____ of the king, whose strict laws oppressed his people.
(A) defiance
(B) conviviality
(C) justification
(D) reciprocity
(E) germaneness

27. The desire to protect freedom is no _____ for violating our civil liberties.
    (A) conviviality
    (B) justification
    (C) germaneness
    (D) reciprocity
    (E) defiance

28. The defense deftly _____ the prosecution's case with the introduction of a surprise eyewitness.
    (A) reciprocated
    (B) justified
    (C) rebutted
    (D) recounted
    (E) beleaguered

29. How many times will I have to _____ the terrible story before you'll all leave me alone?
    (A) defy
    (B) recount
    (C) rebut
    (D) justify
    (E) reciprocate

30. The _____ mayor elect had to cope not only with the disaster of the previous administration, but with his own scandal as well.
    (A) defiant
    (B) beleaguered
    (C) germane
    (D) reciprocal
    (E) rebutted

31. We are sure that our _____ friend Sandy can use her smile to smooth over any sticky social situation.
    (A) convivial
    (B) defiant
    (C) beleaguered
    (D) reciprocal
    (E) recounted

32. I fail to see what _____ purpose your ridiculous proposal might have for this meeting.
    (A) beleaguered
    (B) defiant
    (C) convivial
    (D) reciprocal
    (E) germane

On Your Own:
Write one sentence using each word below to demonstrate your understanding of the word's meaning.

33. **defiance** _____

34. **germane** _____

35. **beleaguer** _____

36. **convivial** _____

37. **rebut** _____

38. **recount** _____

39. **justification** _____

40. **reciprocal** _____

C2 Advanced Vocabulary 74

First Impressions:
Using the example sentences below, write your own definition of each boldfaced word. Then write the letter of the definition from the box that best matches your definition.

A	adjective: impossible to get rid of; essential	**C**	adjective: highly flattering to win others' favor; oily
B	adjective: sober and respectable	**D**	noun: outside boundary; margin

1. _____ Before asking for a raise, Ernie proved that he was **indispensable** to the company's daily operations.

INDISPENSABLE means: _____

2. _____ Marcine was not convinced by the salesman's **unctuous** flattery.

UNCTUOUS means: _____

3. _____ Mr. Utterson was a **staid** professional—honest in his dealings with his fellow men and reliable in a spot of difficulty.

STAID means: _____

4. _____ A true solution to this problem must take into account the needs of the **periphery**, not just the core members.

PERIPHERY means: _____

A	verb: to adorn or ornament; to enhance with false details	**C**	noun: a reference to something else, often a work of art
B	adjective: pitiless; cruel	**D**	adjective: sorrowful or mournful

5. _____ He has a reputation for helping Jamaica's poor with food and education, despite allegations of being a **ruthless** drug dealer.

RUTHLESS means: _____

6. _____ Caiden **embellished** his biology report by supporting his thesis with the testimonies of imaginary scientists.

EMBELLISH means: _____

7. _____ One of the characters in the book made an **allusion** to the author's favorite TV show.

ALLUSION means: _____

8. _____ Les Miserables is a musical is known for its **plaintive** melodies and tragic situations.

PLAINTIVE means: _____

Divide and Conquer:
Choose the correct word to complete each of the following sentences.

9. Your teacher will explain some of the (**embellishments / allusions**) to other literary works to give you more insight into the passage.

10. Sanjayís short story is too short; he needs to (**allude / embellish**) it with more details about his life.

11. Sheila left the (**staid / embellished**) suburbs to seek an exciting but less stable life in city.

12. This fence protects the (**periphery / embellishment**) of the federal building from intruders.

13. Baking powder is one of the (**indispensable / staid**) ingredients of pancakes; without it, the batter would fail to rise on the skillet.

14. With a greasy smile, the (**unctuous / peripheral**) visitor heaped praise upon our leader.

15. The film has a(n) (**unctuous / plaintive**) ending in which the loyal dog dies in its loving owner's arms.

16. Genghis Khan's (**embellished / ruthless**) armies exercised no mercy on their enemies.

Hot and Cold:
Write the word from the lesson that is most nearly the *OPPOSITE* of the boldfaced word or words in each sentence below.

17. Wood and nails are _____ in the building of a chair, but paint is **unnecessary**.

18. The _____ dictator, whose rule had been a time of terror and chaos for his countrymen, was replaced by his more **merciful** sister, whose first act was to free most political prisoners.

19. The _____ wails of the funeral mourners gave way to **joyous** singing as the procession demonstrated the process of loss, healing, and celebration of the deceased.

20. I saw flashes of light in my _____ that seemed to vanish as soon as I tried to look straight at them; they distracted me from the display in the **center** of my vision.

21. The artist strove to **clearly define** the basic essence of his subjects rather than _____, and thus hide, that essence.

22. While your _____ flattery rings insincere, a **harsh or abrasive** attitude toward your superiors won't get you very far, either.

23. The _____ board of directors was unimpressed by the **frivolous** young woman who had inherited the company.

Applying Yourself:
Choose the best word to complete each of the following sentences.

24. Tell Captain Smith to form a(n) _____ of troops to form a secure line against enemy incursions.
   (A) embellishment
   (B) periphery
   (C) allusion
   (D) indispensability
   (E) ruthlessness

25. The last thing that Jenna wanted to do was invite the _____ bank clerk with her to the wild party.
   (A) staid
   (B) ruthless
   (C) plaintive
   (D) unctuous
   (E) embellished

26. I would have an easier time believing you if you would not _____ your stories with so many unlikely anecdotes.
    (A) rebut
    (B) recount
    (C) defy
    (D) allude
    (E) embellish

27. I made a(n) _____ to my favorite sitcom, but Jack hadn't seen it and didn't get the reference.
    (A) indispensability
    (B) ruthlessness
    (C) periphery
    (D) allusion
    (E) embellishment

28. _____ speech rarely serves any purpose; instead, try to lift everyone's spirits in the face of tragedy.
    (A) Plaintive
    (B) Ruthless
    (C) Indispensable
    (D) Unctuous
    (E) Periphery

29. Vegetables are a(n) _____ part of a good diet.
    (A) ruthless
    (B) plaintive
    (C) indispensable
    (D) staid
    (E) unctuous

30. The _____ king told his soldiers to imprison the peasants who could not pay their taxes.
    (A) unctuous
    (B) indispensable
    (C) ruthless
    (D) staid
    (E) embellished

31. We couldn't stand the advisor's _____ ways, but so long as the king was susceptible to flattery, we could not remove her from court.
    (A) plaintive
    (B) ruthless
    (C) staid
    (D) unctuous
    (E) peripheral

On Your Own:
Write one sentence using each word below to demonstrate your understanding of the word's meaning.

32. **ruthless** _____

33. **plaintive** _____

34. **indispensable** _____

35. **allusion** _____

36. **unctuous** _____

37. **embellish** _____

38. **periphery** _____

39. **staid** _____

C2 Advanced Vocabulary 75

First Impressions:

Using the example sentences below, write your own definition of each boldfaced word. Then write the letter of the definition from the box that best matches your definition.

A	noun: the academic study of religion, especially by those who intend to enter ministry	**C**	noun: a person who pretends to know or to be capable of more than they really are
B	adjective: detestable; extremely bad	**D**	noun: a comparison using the words "like" or "as"

1. _____ One of my favorite **similes** is "Her eyes were as blue as the oceans of Bermuda."

SIMILE means: _____

2. _____ The general's war crimes were denounced as **execrable** by the international court.

EXECRABLE means: _____

3. _____ Dorothy knew she should not have listened to that **charlatan** who said he thought the Red

Brick Road would be quicker.

CHARLATAN means: _____

4. _____ Robert earned a degree in **theology** before he became a pastor at a large church.

THEOLOGY means: _____

A	adjective: not easily satisfied; greedy	**C**	verb: to contradict; to show as false; to misrepresent
B	adjective: ruling with absolute authority	**D**	adjective: immature or inexperienced

5. _____ Aidan claimed that he hadn't stolen the cookies from the cookie jar, but the trail of crumbs

in his lap **belied** his assertions.

BELIE means: _____

6. _____ It is because of man's **insatiable** curiosity that technology and science have progressed

as far as they have.

INSATIABLE means: _____

7. _____ The **autocratic** ruler would accept no criticism of his judgments.

AUTOCRATIC means: _____

8. _____ Wilson left for war as a **callow** youth but returned as a grim and experienced man.

CALLOW means: _____

Divide and Conquer:
Choose the correct word to complete each of the following sentences.

9. Rome had been a republic until Julius Caesar seized control of the government and became its (**belied / autocratic**) ruler.

10. The course in medieval (**charlatans / theology**) contrasts older views of religion with our own.

11. The goal of education is to turn (**callow / execrable**) students into mature citizens and problem solvers.

12. The (**autocrat / charlatan**) swore that the watch was solid gold, but after Michael visited a jeweler, he learned that it was only plated.

13. The song "Twinkle, Twinkle Little Star" contains several (**similes / theologies**), such as "like a diamond in the sky."

14. The criminal's actions were so (**insatiable / execrable**) that the newspaper printed them only in bold summary.

15. The recent elections (**shunt / belie**) the criticism that the revolutionary government was not democratic.

16. It was Raymond's (**insatiable / execrable**) thirst for knowledge, rather than his intellect, that impressed his professor.

Hot and Cold:
Write the word from the lesson that is most nearly the *OPPOSITE* of the boldfaced word or words in each sentence below.

17. Her scowling face _____ her nature, as Eva's generosity and compassion are **verified** by her deeds.

18. I prefer the **sage** advice of my experienced Great Aunt Helen than the _____ words of my immature friends.

19. One teacher had a(n) _____ desire to see better and better results from her students on state exams; the other was **easily pleased** by a pass rate of more than thirty percent.

20. The _____ head-of-state the people had elected, who quickly seized power from the other branches of government, was not what the newly **democratic** country had desired of its first election.

21. The orphanage, once a(n) _____ place to raise children, has transformed into a welcoming, **wonderful** environment seemingly overnight.

22. We were disappointed that Mr. Harley turned out to be a _____ who in truth had no idea how to teach a meditation class; all we needed was someone **authentic**, and that turned out to be the one thing we couldn't get.

Applying Yourself:
Choose the best word to complete each of the following sentences.

23. Those _____ high schoolers who think that college is one big party are shocked when they realize the work required.
    (A) callow
    (B) autocratic
    (C) insatiable
    (D) execrable
    (E) theological

24. The students dismissed newcomer Rob as a(n) _____ when he failed to make the basketball team after telling everyone he had gone to the state championships at his old school.
    (A) simile
    (B) charlatan
    (C) autocrat
    (D) theology
    (E) insatiability

25. If you cross our _____ regional manager even slightly, he'll see you fired.
   (A) Autocratic
   (B) Theological
   (C) Callow
   (D) Execrable
   (E) Insatiable

26. Words can hardly describe the _____ actions taken by a few that ruin everyone's time.
   (A) belied
   (B) theological
   (C) callow
   (D) insatiable
   (E) execrable

27. Songwriters have written tunes with titles containing _____ for years, including "Like a Rolling Stone".
   (A) autocrats
   (B) similes
   (C) theologies
   (D) charlatans
   (E) callowness

28. We thought that the third burrito would satisfy Nate, but after the marathon, his appetite was _____.
   (A) execrable
   (B) insatiable
   (C) autocratic
   (D) callow
   (E) belied

29. His subtle twitches and sweaty hands _____ the poker player's representation of a strong hand.
   (A) reprimanded
   (B) castigated
   (C) fluctuated
   (D) belied
   (E) marshaled

30. The school of _____ allows students to earn degrees in any of the world's major religions.
   (A) simile
   (B) charlatan
   (C) theology
   (D) callowness
   (E) insatiability

On Your Own:
Write one sentence using each word below to demonstrate your understanding of the word's meaning.

31. **simile** _____

32. **autocratic** _____

33. **charlatan** _____

34. **theology** _____

35. **belie** _____

36. **callow** _____

37. **insatiable** _____

38. **execrable** _____

C2 Advanced Vocabulary 76

First Impressions:

Using the example sentences below, write your own definition of each boldfaced word. Then write the letter of the definition from the box that best matches your definition.

A	noun: the beginning of something	C	verb: to cause to break up; to scatter
B	noun: a rebirth, especially of culture, technology, and philosophy	D	adjective: obscure; profound; hard to understand

1. _____ The Harlem **Renaissance** was a period of cultural growth and experimentation among African Americans in New York City in the 1920s and 1930s.

RENAISSANCE means: _____

2. _____ Many of Foucault's writings are so **abstruse** that most people don't read them until college, if ever.

ABSTRUSE means: _____

3. _____ The general gathered his troops around him, gave each one its assignment, and then ordered them to **disperse** to carry out their tasks.

DISPERSE means: _____

4. _____ At the **onset** of the disease, patients experience flu-like symptoms that gradually worsens.

ONSET means: _____

A	adjective: planning well for the future	C	adjective: lacking food and clothing; needy; poor; impoverished
B	adjective: artificial; clearly constructed	D	adjective: aimed at helping others

5. _____ Dr. Humphreys, a believer in **provident** living, stored extra food and water in his basement in preparation for natural disasters.

PROVIDENT means: _____

6. _____ The plot of the film was so **contrived** that even the most credulous audience members found the plot shallow and unbelievable.

CONTRIVED means: _____

7. _____ During the holiday season, Greta decided to donate all of her old clothes to **indigent** families.

INDIGENT means: _____

8. _____ Bill Gate's **humanitarian** efforts around the world have saved millions of lives.

HUMANITARIAN means: _____

Divide and Conquer:

Choose the correct word to complete each of the following sentences.

9. The students groaned as Dr. Horowitz launched into another long, (**abstruse / dispersed**) lecture on a topic they could never hope to understand.

10. As I face the (**dispersion / onset**) of adulthood, I couldn't feel more like a child.

11. The (**provident / humanitarian**) organization made offers of aid and asylum to the refugees.

12. After the PTA meeting the parents (**contrived / dispersed**) to their respective homes.

13. The advent of the personal computer was a (**humanitarian / renaissance**) for entrepreneurs, as it provided new ways for the individual to compete and innovate.

14. Every year the church held a canned goods donation drive to help feed the (**contrived / indigent**) members of the community.

15. The police officer requested a warrant to search the home, as the owner's explanation of the strange noises seemed rather (**contrived / indigent**).

16. Sweden, a (**humanitarian / provident**) nation, strives to make itself as free from the need of oil as possible.

Hot and Cold:

Write the word from the lesson that is most nearly the *OPPOSITE* of the boldfaced word or words in each sentence below.

17. My teenage years were a **dark age** during which I merely followed the crowd like a drone; during college, I experienced a personal _____ and began learning and experiencing as much as possible.

18. Her apology, coming as it did after a severe lecture from her mother, seemed _____, but the possibility of hearing truly **organic** remorse seemed remote, considering how angry she was.

19. The **wealthy** donors delivered basic supplies and clothing to the _____ refugees.

20. Hank was _____ with his money and was able to provide for not only his own family but for that of his more **reckless** brother Steve, too.

21. The _____ film appealed only to those of us willing to put in the time and effort to understand it, and not at all to those seeking a more **simple** plot line.

22. The timing of the _____ of my cold was horrible, given the recent **end** of my bronchitis.

23. The group's _____ efforts were delayed by **self-interested** politicians who cared little for increasing foreign aid.

24. The riot squad ordered the crowd to _____ because the officers feared that the protestors had **gathered** to break the law.

Applying Yourself:

Choose the best word to complete each of the following sentences.

25. He was a real _____, working with several charities.
    (A) renaissance
    (B) humanitarian
    (C) providence
    (D) dispersion
    (E) indigence

26. I asked my professor for help in interpreting "The Waste Land," a(n) _____ work that relies on complex allusions to convey meaning.
    (A) indigent
    (B) provident
    (C) abstruse
    (D) contrived
    (E) humanitarian

27. My _____ financial advisor diversified my investments and encouraged me to deposit money in my retirement fund.
    (A) dispersed
    (B) indigent
    (C) humanitarian
    (D) contrived
    (E) provident

28. I _____ them in all directions, scattering them north, south, east, and west.
    (A) dispersed
    (B) resolved
    (C) compelled
    (D) supplanted
    (E) belied

29. Though for years he had been very rich, a series of bad choices left him _____.
    (A) contrived
    (B) abstruse
    (C) indigent
    (D) humanitarian
    (E) provident

30. Life in the army has become more difficult since the _____ of the war.
    (A) onset
    (B) humanitarian
    (C) contrived
    (D) indigent
    (E) dispersed

31. During the 1920s, Harlem experienced a(n) _____ in music, especially jazz.
    (A) indigence
    (B) renaissance
    (C) providence
    (D) humanitarian
    (E) onset

32. Many think that "reality television" is a misnomer, as the situations on such programs are largely _____ by producers who want to see specific outcomes.
    (A) onset
    (B) contrived
    (C) dispersed
    (D) belied
    (E) compelled

On Your Own:

Write one sentence using each word below to demonstrate your understanding of the word's meaning.

33. **renaissance** _____

34. **indigent** _____

35. **disperse** _____

36. **provident** _____

37. **abstruse** _____

38. **onset** _____

39. **contrived** _____

40. **humanitarian** _____

C2 Advanced Vocabulary 77

First Impressions:

Using the example sentences below, write your own definition of each boldfaced word. Then write the letter of the definition from the box that best matches your definition.

A	adjective: related to properties other than number	**C**	adjective: clever; resourceful
B	adjective: not literal, but metaphorical; using a figure of speech	**D**	adjective: owned as property; treated as property

1. _____ **Proprietary** medications typically cost more than drugs formulated from public,

unpatented knowledge.

PROPRIETARY means: _____

2. _____ While most actresses were probably trying to the job the old fashioned way, Heidi found

an **ingenious** way to draw attention to herself: Twitter.

INGENIOUS means: _____

3. _____ Chemists are interested in both quantitative data, like density, and **qualitative** data, such

as state of matter or color.

QUALITATIVE means: _____

4. _____ No, you do not need to find Christa's marbles; I was trying to be **figurative** when I said

she'd lost them.

FIGURATIVE means: _____

A	noun: a dead human body	**C**	noun: a blessing; something that is asked for
B	noun: a saying or maxim, usually expressing some sort of general truth	**D**	adjective: interested in money or gain

5. _____ Louis' least favorite part of his college Anatomy class was having to watch the dissection

of a human **cadaver**.

CADAVER means: _____

6. _____ The king promised that winning the tournament would be a great **boon** to one lucky

knight.

BOON means: _____

7. _____ The book was full of general **aphorisms** and no specific truths.

APHORISM means: _____

8. _____ The **mercenary** worker left his old job immediately when he was offered one that paid a

higher hourly rate.

MERCENARY means: _____

Divide and Conquer:
Choose the correct word to complete each of the following sentences.

9. We wanted to use the company's findings for our own uses, but the information was (**proprietary / ingenious**).

10. Sally's (**mercenary / aphoristic**) dog will run to whoever offers the most snacks.

11. In addition to listing the percentage of people who enjoyed our product, the survey told us (**proprietary / qualitative**) information through the useful comments section.

12. Whether that (**figurative / mercenary**) glass is half full or half empty rests entirely on your perception.

13. My grandmother speaks in (**aphorisms / cadavers**) and proverbs she has learned over the years rather than expressing her own ideas.

14. The king promised to grant a (**boon / mercenary**) to any knight that could rid the land of the dragon.

15. The software developer found several (**ingenious / qualitative**) solutions that saved his company hundreds of thousands of dollars in labor costs.

16. Doctor Frankenstein collected parts from numerous (**cadavers / boons**) to piece together into his monster.

Hot and Cold:
Write the word from the lesson that is most nearly the *OPPOSITE* of the boldfaced word or words in each sentence below.

17. Franz was often called a(n) _____ opportunist who would sell his skills to the highest bidder and do anything to get ahead, but in his private life he was as **loyal** and generous as could be.

18. As students of literature, we were advised to look past the **literal** meanings of all discussions—what was said, by whom, and to whom—and to examine their less-obvious _____ elements.

19. The study of anatomy is not solely dependent on _____; the **living human body** is also a store of valuable data.

20. I'm less concerned with the **quantitative** aspects of war—how many tanks were issued, how many lives were lost—than with the _____ issues of what impact this tragedy has had on the world and what can now be done to begin the healing process.

21. My _____ plan means nothing if these **dense** architects aren't able to use their imaginations enough to make it come to life.

22. This sudden influx of cash has been such a delightful _____ for the family, which had been stricken by the **bane** of the working class: unemployment.

Applying Yourself:
Choose the best word to complete each of the following sentences.

23. "It's raining cats and dogs" is not a literal description, but rather a(n) _____ way of saying that it is raining heavily.
    (A) ingenious
    (B) proprietary
    (C) cadaverous
    (D) figurative
    (E) qualitative

24. Medical researchers in the 18th century had to endure the stigma against dissecting human _____.
    (A) property
    (B) cadavers
    (C) boons
    (D) martinets
    (E) anthologies

25. Your dog truly has a _____ attitude; it will show affection to anyone with a juicy bone.
    (A) qualitative
    (B) aphoristic
    (C) figurative
    (D) mercenary
    (E) proprietary

26. The developer won't tolerate the use of its _____ information without permission.
    (A) mercenary
    (B) proprietary
    (C) ingenious
    (D) cadaverous
    (E) qualitative

27. Benjamin Franklin coined hundreds of _____, including the famous "Early to bed, early to rise, makes a man healthy, wealthy and wise."
    (A) fluctuations
    (B) atonements
    (C) cadavers
    (D) boons
    (E) aphorisms

28. We feared that our broken car wouldn't make it to the concert, but our _____ friend fixed it with duct tape, a birdcage, and some string.
    (A) cadaverous
    (B) ingenious
    (C) figurative
    (D) qualitative
    (E) aphoristic

29. Make sure to provide _____ evidence to back your claims, as simply regurgitating statistics doesn't resonate with your reader.
    (A) aphoristic
    (B) ingenious
    (C) proprietary
    (D) qualitative
    (E) figurative

30. Cindy could not have been a greater _____ to our efforts; anytime we needed an odious task accomplished, she volunteered.
    (A) boon
    (B) mercenary
    (C) cadaver
    (D) concordance
    (E) insurgent

On Your Own:
Write one sentence using each word below to demonstrate your understanding of the word's meaning.

31. **cadaver** _____

32. **ingenious** _____

33. **figurative** _____

34. **qualitative** _____

35. **proprietary** _____

36. **mercenary** _____

37. **aphorism** _____

38. **boon** _____

C2 Advanced Vocabulary 78

First Impressions:

Using the example sentences below, write your own definition of each boldfaced word. Then write the letter of the definition from the box that best matches your definition.

A	noun: deceit; duplicity; wiliness; cunning	**C**	adjective: wise; cautious; careful; practical
B	noun: a feeling of enjoyment at the misfortune of others	**D**	noun: dominance of one member of a group over others because of power or influence

1. _____ Jasmine guiltily suppressed a feeling of **schadenfreude** when she saw the opposing goalie slip in the mud.

SCHADENFREUDE means: _____

2. _____ The revolutionaries threw out their leaders, releasing their country from the **hegemony** of the aristocrats.

HEGEMONY means: _____

3. _____ Many criminals have such **guile** that, even after their convictions, their families refuse to believe that they would be capable of committing a crime.

GUILE means: _____

4. _____ Though it is tempting to use credit to make purchases, it is more **prudent** to save and pay in cash.

PRUDENT means: _____

A	noun: one who holds absolute power	**C**	noun: a plan of events or tasks to accomplish
B	verb: to waste time; to move slowly	**D**	verb: to give new life or energy to someone or something

5. _____ Edward sent the **agenda** of the meeting to the participants a week in advance in order to give them time to prepare.

AGENDA means: _____

6. _____ The area was **revitalized** when the city tore down the abandoned warehouse and replaced it with a fancy shopping district.

REVITALIZE means: _____

7. _____ The nation was ruled by the whims of a single **dictator**.

DICTATOR means: _____

8. _____ We don't have much time, so don't **dawdle**!

DAWDLE means: _____

Divide and Conquer:
Choose the correct word to complete each of the following sentences.

9. The graduates didn't (**revitalize / dawdle**) when their names were read; some of them almost sprinted across the stage.

10. The (**guile / agenda**) for the day included a trip to the grocery store, an hour at the gym, and a quick stop at the bank on the way home.

11. The British (**prudence / hegemony**) at the height of the empire relied to a significant extent on the strength of the Royal Navy.

12. Scott often relies upon (**dawdling / guile**) to win boxing matches, at times pretending to be injured or tired in order to surprise his opponents.

13. (**Guile / Schadenfreude**) is one of the great cancers of our age; instead, we should empathize and try to remedy misfortune.

14. John had looked every bit his age of fifty when he was laid off, but the new job has (**dawdle / revitalized**) him.

15. People traveled from far and wide to ask the (**prudent / hegemonic**) elder to resolve their disagreements.

16. The (**prudence / dictator**) ordered the people to hold a parade in honor of his birthday.

Hot and Cold:
Write the word from the lesson that is most nearly the *OPPOSITE* of the boldfaced word or words in each sentence below.

17. The _____ of powerful men felt threatened by any situation that required them to show **submission**, or even respect, to women.

18. This cold winter weather **drains the energy** from all my daily activity; I don't think anything but the warm excitement of spring will _____ me.

19. After four _____ years spent responsibly studying, volunteering, and working, Katia was ready to spend a **reckless** summer vacation on the beaches of Rio.

20. As she grew, the child's **straightforwardness** vanished, and she became the embodiment of _____ and manipulation.

21. The lowly **peasants** who worked the fields had no choice but to follow every command the powerful and unfeeling _____ threw at them.

22. For as long as I can remember, I have seemed to _____ as much as possible in the mornings, slowly showering and dressing, until I have no choice but to **hurry** from the house to work to avoid being late.

23. I felt a strong sense of _____ when I saw my enemy trip in a mud puddle and had no **empathy** for his miserable condition.

Applying Yourself:
Choose the best word to complete each of the following sentences.

24. Bullies experience _____, marked by smug grins, when their words embarrass their victims.
    (A) schadenfreude
    (B) dictatorship
    (C) revitalization
    (D) guile
    (E) prudence

25. Other poker players are often surprised by Jimmy, for his innocent appearance hides his

    _____.
    (A) schadenfreude
    (B) guile
    (C) hegemony
    (D) prudance
    (E) dictatorship

26. I approach our meeting without a(n) _____, so feel free to wander from topic to topic at your whim.
    (A) guile
    (B) dictator
    (C) schadenfreude
    (D) agenda
    (E) hegemony

27. Would you please hurry up and not _____ any more?
    (A) dissent
    (B) supplant
    (C) concord
    (D) dawdle
    (E) revitalize

28. After carelessly choosing her classes for the semester and finding that she disliked all of her professors, Ashley decided to be more _____ with such decisions in the future.
    (A) prudent
    (B) revitalized
    (C) guileful
    (D) dawdling
    (E) hegemonic

29. Mayor Booker hopes that the new plaza will _____ the lackluster downtown area.
    (A) occlude
    (B) scintillate
    (C) concordant
    (D) revitalize
    (E) dawdle

30. Julius Caesar displayed his _____ over the senate through his control over the military.
    (A) dictator
    (B) agenda
    (C) hegemony
    (D) schadenfreude
    (E) prudence

31. Those who rule without the sanction of the people may say that they act according to the common will, but in fact, they are _____.
    (A) dictators
    (B) agendas
    (C) prudence
    (D) hegemony
    (E) schadenfreude

On Your Own:

Write one sentence using each word below to demonstrate your understanding of the word's meaning.

32. **revitalize** _____

33. **dictator** _____

34. **agenda** _____

35. **guile** _____

36. **prudent** _____

37. **dawdle** _____

38. **schadenfreude** _____

39. **hegemony** _____

C2 Advanced Vocabulary 79

First Impressions:

Using the example sentences below, write your own definition of each boldfaced word. Then write the letter of the definition from the box that best matches your definition.

A	adjective: spread throughout every part	**C**	adjective: commonplace; trite; repeated too often
B	verb: to restrict; to hold back	**D**	noun: joyous celebration or excitement

1. _____ I hope I don't **constrain** my children's futures by setting goals for them or expecting them to do something they're uncomfortable with.

CONSTRAIN means: _____

2. _____ Strong creative writing requires fresh word choices rather than **hackneyed** prose.

HACKNEYED means: _____

3. _____ The city was a scene of great **jubilation** after its team won the Super Bowl.

JUBILATION means: _____

4. _____ Though it is disliked by English teachers throughout the nation, "netspeak" has become a **pervasive** part of our culture.

PERVASIVE means: _____

A	verb: to stockpile; to accumulate for future use	**C**	noun: heat; passion; intense devotion or enthusiasm
B	adjective: giving in easily to one's desires, or to the desires of another	**D**	verb: to become weak; to lose energy or enthusiasm

5. _____ Squirrels constantly **hoard** acorns to save for later.

HOARD means: _____

6. _____ Andy's **ardor** for learning gave him a reputation as a know-it-all, but he responded by calling his detractors "know-nothings".

ARDOR means: _____

7. _____ Branden **languished** in indecisiveness for several days before he strengthened his resolve and made a clear decision.

LANGUISH means: _____

8. _____ The **indulgent** parent almost never told his children "no."

INDULGENT means: _____

Divide and Conquer:
Choose the correct word to complete each of the following sentences.

9. The researcher was pleased to find that the health-inducing compound was (**hackneyed / pervasive**) in the local food supply.

10. Matieu expressed his love for Christine with great (**jubilation / ardor**) as the soundtrack soared around them.

11. Shane is an (**constrained / indulgent**) pet owner who refuses to discipline his dogs at all.

12. Maria felt that she was wise in saving money and canned goods for potential disasters, but her friend thought that she was engaged in needless (**hoarding / indulgence**).

13. While the economy around them (**constrained / languished**), the members of the company worked even harder to find ways to grow.

14. Maya hates to feel (**constrained / indulged**) by her clothing and only wears loose-fitting garments.

15. The homecoming of the soldiers was met with much (**indulgence / jubilation**) by their friends and families.

16. Unfortunately, the attempt at innovation is still shrouded in the same old (**hackneyed / languishing**) humor.

Hot and Cold:
Write the word from the lesson that is most nearly the *OPPOSITE* of the boldfaced word or words in each sentence below.

17. Because the disease was quickly **quarantined** within the infected limb—which was removed—it did not have a chance to take a(n) _____ hold on the rest of the body.

18. A **strict** father will keep careful watch on his child's activities, while a(n) _____ one will cater to his child's every wish.

19. There was such an air of _____ in the room that Francesca's utter **despair** went unnoticed.

20. As I sat bored and _____ over the interminable summer break, I hoped that the coming school year would **invigorate** me enough to start getting things done once more.

21. While classical music evokes the greatest _____ in my father, we kids feel nothing but **uninterested** when he tries to play his favorite pieces for us.

22. The government tried to _____ businesses from forming unfair monopolies, but after the new law passed, it had to **release** companies from those limitations.

23. The professor wrote that my short story was filled with _____ phrases she'd heard a million times before and that I needed to develop my own **original** voice devoid of such common language.

24. Because Sandra's father was known to _____ everything from old newspapers to paper plates to ill-fitting clothes, Sandra herself made sure to **donate** whatever she could to charity, her friends, or the trash can.

Applying Yourself:
Choose the best word to complete each of the following sentences.

25. You are gaining weight because of your _____ attitude towards candy.
    (A) constrained
    (B) ardent
    (C) hackneyed
    (D) indulgent
    (E) pervasive

26. The ferret _____ shiny objects and noisy papers in a great pile under the bed, constantly adding to its "treasure pile".
    (A) indulged
    (B) hoarded
    (C) constrained
    (D) languished
    (E) atoned

27. The Ewoks shouted with _____ once the Death Star was destroyed and their planet safeguarded.
   (A) constraint
   (B) indulgence
   (C) jubilation
   (D) ardor
   (E) pervasiveness

28. Our group _____ in the heat of the desert, almost unwilling to put one foot in front of the other.
   (A) languished
   (B) constrained
   (C) indulged
   (D) atoned
   (E) hoarded

29. The long-horned beetle has become _____ in some North American forests, leading to mass destruction of trees.
   (A) ardent
   (B) pervasive
   (C) constrained
   (D) indulgent
   (E) languishing

30. While grading his students' essays, the professor hoped to find at least one outstanding thesis among all the _____ topics.
   (A) indulgent
   (B) pervasive
   (C) languishing
   (D) hackneyed
   (E) ardent

31. Despite everything her parents have tried, nothing seems to be able to _____ her poor behavior.
   (A) indulge
   (B) pervade
   (C) languish
   (D) hoard
   (E) constrain

32. The choir sang with _____, flooding the auditorium with the sounds of their passion and enthusiasm.
   (A) obstreperousness
   (B) pervasiveness
   (C) indulgence
   (D) constraint
   (E) ardor

On Your Own:
Write one sentence using each word below to demonstrate your understanding of the word's meaning.

33. **indulgent** _____

34. **pervasive** _____

35. **hackneyed** _____

36. **constrain** _____

37. **languish** _____

38. **ardor** _____

39. **jubilation** _____

40. **hoard** _____

C2 Advanced Vocabulary 80

First Impressions:
Using the example sentences below, write your own definition of each boldfaced word. Then write the letter of the definition from the box that best matches your definition.

A	noun: a disrepute; ill fame	**C**	verb: to start; to initiate; to install into office
B	verb: to make amends for sins or wrongdoings	**D**	noun: an agreement; unanimity; harmony; peace; a treaty

1. _____ The principal offered the student a chance to **expiate** his offence through community service.

EXPIATE means: _____

2. _____ Though the delegates were of diverse backgrounds, they were in total **concord** in their choice of candidate.

CONCORD means: _____

3. _____ Though it was difficult to be a public villain, Marshall's **notoriety** allowed him to draw attention to issues he found important.

NOTORIETY means: _____

4. _____ Roughly two million people attended the ceremony at which President Barack Obama was **inaugurated** as the country's Commander in Chief.

INAUGURATE means: _____

A	noun: one who has very poor health; one who is excessively concerned about health	**C**	noun: the study of diseases and disorders
B	noun: an inclination; a natural tendency	**D**	adjective: being at peace or at rest; inactive or motionless

5. _____ Years of poor diet and stressful living left Haemin a **valetudinarian**; she was beset by more illnesses in one year than most would face in a lifetime.

VALETUDINARIAN means: _____

6. _____ Hugh spent much of his vacation **quiescent** on the beach, without a care in the world.

QUIESCENT means: _____

7. _____ He will need to make sure that his **proclivity** for earning yellow cards for his aggressive play doesn't leave them a man short.

PROCLIVITY means: _____

8. _____ Dr. Robertson took a deep interest in **pathology** in order to find ways to prevent common illnesses.

PATHOLOGY means: _____

Divide and Conquer:
Choose the correct word to complete each of the following sentences.

9. To (**inaugurate** / **expiate**) someone ceremonially may seem frivolous to some, but to others it is a symbolic acceptance of the duties and responsibilities one will inherit.

10. The (**inauguration** / **valetudinarian**) tried to encourage sympathy for her many ailments, but her friends wished she would just live life in as carefree a way as possible.

11. Jesse James had received (**pathology** / **notoriety**) as part of the James/Younger gang, which robbed banks and trains in the late 1800s.

12. The convict (**inaugurated** / **expiated**) his crimes by serving a four-year prison sentence.

13. The two nations' (**concord** / **notoriety**) was responsible for their flourishing trade.

14. He was a talented fundraiser who had a (**proclivity** / **concord**) for spending money that didn't quite belong to him.

15. The Centers for Disease Control focuses on the (**pathology** / **concord**) of infectious diseases around the world.

16. After taking the SAT, Ramona lay (**concordant** / **quiescent**) on her bed, exhausted but satisfied in her effort.

Hot and Cold:
Write the word from the lesson that is most nearly the *OPPOSITE* of the boldfaced word or words in each sentence below.

17. The beginning of the summer _____ a time of freedom and adventure for the students and **ended** a year of strict routines.

18. Wilma's _____ as a violent woman overshadowed the fact that she was also an **acclaimed** pianist and artist, having won many awards for her talents in both pursuits.

19. Jim's _____ for math, and his enjoyment of it, was probably the result of his **disinclination** for literature at an early age; he never quite understood words as well as his peers, so he took to numbers instead.

20. The preacher said he didn't have the power to _____ us and that we should ask a higher power for forgiveness rather than be eternally **chastised** for our sins.

21. Growing up, my parents were such _____ that they'd make my sister and I wear surgical masks whenever we got head colds, making the average "unconcerned" parents seem **overly confident about their health**.

22. After 300 years of war, the nations reached a _____ that promised to end the terrible **discord** that had led to so much violence between them.

23. Though it is infinitely easier to watch over _____ children who take numerous naps or prefer watching TV to playing outside, **active** children lead healthier lifestyles and encourage their caregivers to move more, too.

Applying Yourself:
Choose the best word to complete each of the following sentences.

24. Though not all cancers are inclined toward certain body parts, melanoma seems to have a(n) _____ for spreading to the liver.
    (A) proclivity
    (B) concordance
    (C) pathology
    (D) notoriety
    (E) expiation

25. The Treaty of Paris was the _____ that ended the Revolutionary War.
    (A) concord
    (B) pathology
    (C) notoriety
    (D) quiescence
    (E) proclivity

26. When she was _____ as president, it was as if she had immediately installed a new era of equality.
    (A) expiated
    (B) inaugurated
    (C) sidestepped
    (D) marshaled
    (E) deracinated

27. The Centers for Disease Control employs epidemiologists who use _____ to prevent national epidemics.
    (A) expiation
    (B) pathology
    (C) notoriety
    (D) concord
    (E) valetudinarianism

28. Father Jennings sits in the confessional booth, waiting to listen to those wishing to _____ their sins.
    (A) inaugurate
    (B) expiate
    (C) belie
    (D) shunt
    (E) sidestep

29. If you are _____ for something, people will usually refer to you with disdain.
    (A) pathological
    (B) quiescent
    (C) valetudinarian
    (D) notorious
    (E) expiated

30. Adam's wife was a(n) _____ whose use of hand sanitizer was nearly constant.
    (A) inauguration
    (B) valetudinarian
    (C) pathology
    (D) concord
    (E) proclivity

31. The meditating priest sat _____ for such a period that we felt we should check his pulse for signs of life.
    (A) quiescent
    (B) expiated
    (C) pathological
    (D) notorious
    (E) inaugurated

On Your Own:

Write one sentence using each word below to demonstrate your understanding of the word's meaning.

32. **expiate** _____

33. **pathology** _____

34. **valetudinarian** _____

35. **concord** _____

36. **notoriety** _____

37. **quiescent** _____

38. **inaugurate** _____

39. **proclivity** _____

C2 Advanced Vocabulary 81

First Impressions:

Using the example sentences below, write your own definition of each boldfaced word. Then write the letter of the definition from the box that best matches your definition.

A	adjective: cramped or crowded	**C**	noun: the peak; the highest point of something
B	noun: an expression of praise, often on the occasion of someone's death	**D**	adjective: blessed; consecrated

1. _____ Located at the **pinnacle** of a small mountain, the inn was a popular tourist destination known for its spectacular views.

PINNACLE means: _____

2. _____ The **congested** city streets make it impossible to feel peaceful in public.

CONGESTED means: _____

3. _____ Superstitions say that witches cannot set food on **hallowed** ground, so you should be safe from them in temples.

HALLOWED means: _____

4. _____ The sister of the deceased delivered the **eulogy** at the end of the service.

EULOGY means: _____

A	noun: an invasion; a sudden assault	**C**	adjective: acting without knowledge
B	adjective: passionate; devoted to a cause or belief	**D**	adjective: experimental; unsure, uncertain, or not definite; hesitant

5. _____ The pilot was shot down during an **incursion** into enemy airspace.

INCURSION means: _____

6. _____ The project director explained that final due dates were **tentative** and open to changes.

TENTATIVE means: _____

7. _____ The **zealous** missionary stood on a wall to preach to the people of the city.

ZEALOUS means: _____

8. _____ Citizens are expected to be responsible and informed; if one is **unwitting** in the commission of a crime, one is still charged.

UNWITTING means: _____

Divide and Conquer:
Choose the correct word to complete each of the following sentences.

9. Sharpton announced that he would be attending the funeral and had been asked by the family to deliver the (**eulogy / congestion**).

10. Getting straight A's was the (**pinnacle / incursion**) of my achievements in high school.

11. Many consider their church or temple to be (**hallowed / zealous**) land, an area protected by their religious figurehead.

12. (**Eulogies / Incursions**) from the border caused troops from both countries to be placed on high alert.

13. My (**congested / tentative**) sinuses make it difficult to breathe.

14. Our practical joke will only work if our (**unwitting / hallowed**) target follows the correct clues.

15. Many people didn't vote for John for class president because they believed that his (**zealous / tentative**) nature would stop him from making firm decisions.

16. We expunged the campaign of all those who were not (**unwitting / zealous**) for the cause.

Hot and Cold:
Write the word from the lesson that is most nearly the *OPPOSITE* of the boldfaced word or words in each sentence below.

17. He thought that the project would be the _____ of his career, but it instead pushed his career to its **nadir**.

18. Greg set forth a(n) _____ schedule for his employees, knowing that he could not be **certain** that the restaurant's needs wouldn't change.

19. I became a(n) _____ accomplice to the crime, assisting the robber in ways I never would have done had I been **knowledgeable**.

20. Support for the bill was lackluster due to its **wishy-washy** wording, and it failed to gain the _____ following required to bring it to the Senate for review.

21. The _____ ground was surrounded by **secular** land owned by the state.

22. The army's aggressive _____ was followed by an equally quick **retreat**.

23. Fortunately, the _____ sidewalk led into a **sparsely populated** park.

24. It was difficult for Aunt Sandy to deliver the _____ for Grandma's funeral after she had given a very public **diatribe** against the deceased but a few days before.

Applying Yourself:
Choose the best word to complete each of the following sentences.

25. We cried tears of laughter and sadness when Angie delivered the touching _____ at Grandma's gravesite.
    (A) eulogy
    (B) pinnacle
    (C) congestion
    (D) zealousness
    (E) incursion

26. The desperate robbers made a quick _____ into the town by night, grabbed what they needed, and left as soon as possible.
    (A) pinnacle
    (B) incursion
    (C) eulogy
    (D) congestion
    (E) zealousness

27. It was strange how one twin could be so determined and the other be so _____.
    (A) eulogized
    (B) hallowed
    (C) unwitting
    (D) tentative
    (E) zealous

28. Our quest to feed the homeless has room for only the most _____ volunteers, as we will encounter many trials along the way.
    (A) hallowed
    (B) eulogized
    (C) zealous
    (D) tentative
    (E) unwitting

29. Landing on the moon is the _____ of space technology, as nothing has yet surpassed it.
    (A) eulogy
    (B) pinnacle
    (C) congestion
    (D) incursion
    (E) zeal

30. The streets are so _____ today that you'll be lucky to move a mile per hour in your car.
    (A) eulogized
    (B) hallowed
    (C) tentative
    (D) congested
    (E) zealous

31. The church is _____ ground; don't swear or blaspheme while you are within its walls.
    (A) zealous
    (B) congested
    (C) tentative
    (D) eulogized
    (E) hallowed

32. Sheila was a(n) _____ accomplice in the scandal and only learned about it months after the fact.
    (A) unwitting
    (B) congested
    (C) zealous
    (D) eulogized
    (E) tentative

On Your Own:
Write one sentence using each word below to demonstrate your understanding of the word's meaning.

33. **hallowed** _____

34. **incursion** _____

35. **pinnacle** _____

36. **unwitting** _____

37. **tentative** _____

38. **eulogy** _____

39. **congested** _____

40. **zealous** _____

C2 Advanced Vocabulary 82

First Impressions:

Using the example sentences below, write your own definition of each boldfaced word. Then write the letter of the definition from the box that best matches your definition.

A	noun: immoral behavior; excessive indulgence in sensual pleasures	**C**	noun: the act or tendency to yield, conform, or cooperate
B	adjective: having areas of different colors with sharp boundaries	**D**	noun: natural consequence

1. _____ When I give a command, I expect **compliance**, not defiance.

COMPLIANCE means: _____

2. _____ Despite notions to the contrary in popular media, most college students do not spend every weekend in drunken partying and other **debauchery**.

DEBAUCHERY means: _____

3. _____ The **repercussions** of this event will affect everyone in this area for years to come.

REPERCUSSION means: _____

4. _____ The camouflage of the modern military is distinctive for its **variegated** patches of brown and green.

VARIEGATED means: _____

A	verb: to violate a rule or contract; to gradually take over	**C**	adjective: similar in appearance, behavior, or other characteristics
B	adjective: clear; allowing light to pass freely; easily understood	**D**	adjective: stealthy; sneaky; secretive

5. _____ At a glance the penguins appeared **uniform** in appearance, but after several minutes of study Jennifer began to notice individual features that distinguished one from another.

UNIFORM means: _____

6. _____ Martin refused to **infringe** upon her neighbor's land by planting a tree that would drop leaves across the property lines.

INFRINGE means: _____

7. _____ The **furtive** look shared between her friends told Carmen that she was not included in this joke.

FURTIVE means: _____

8. _____ Kevin washed and rewashed the old window until it was restored to its former **pellucid** state.

PELLUCID means: _____

Divide and Conquer:
Choose the correct word to complete each of the following sentences.

9. Without precise sensors, it is impossible to detect slight flaws in products that are otherwise (**pellucid / uniform**) to the rest.

10. Using cheap materials will have (**debauchery / repercussions**) including the reduction of the lifespan of the bridge by as many as ten years.

11. Mark embraced his new life, in which a responsible freedom and dignity replaced a (**compliant / furtive**) life of secrets and deception.

12. The rosebushes spread and spread, at first (**complying / infringing**) on the neighbor's land and then spreading through the entire neighborhood.

13. Mrs. Hudson was ashamed that any son of hers would engage in such (**compliance / debauchery**).

14. Audit checks were built into the system to ensure (**compliance / variegation**) with the criteria.

15. The teacher's presentation turned postmodernism from an obscure, esoteric concept into a (**debauched / pellucid**) one.

16. Co-dominance between the alleles for black and white coloration can lead to a(n) (**infringed / variegated**) salt-and-pepper appearance in some samples of this moth.

Hot and Cold:
Write the word from the lesson that is most nearly the *OPPOSITE* of the boldfaced word or words in each sentence below.

17. The eastern kingdom's **defiance** toward the unwelcome new ruler meant that the crown would have to spend much time and energy forcing the region into _____.

18. We were all supposed to dress in _____ shades of blue, but Sandra came to the pageant in a **unique** aqua dress.

19. Rachel was surprised when her _____ glances at the stranger across the aisle were met with an **open and welcoming** smile.

20. There's no need to _____ on others' personal space when there's certainly enough room here to **accommodate** everyone.

21. My parents always said that my seemingly wild and free lifestyle would have serious _____, but so far there have been **no consequences** to the way I have lived my life.

22. The formerly **opaque** windows, dark with dirt, now sparkled, _____, and allowed light to fill every corner of the room.

23. The _____ leaves, shining red, green, and gold on the blanket of **monochrome** snow, made me think of a child's finger paints on a white sheet of paper.

24. This year, spent studying, working, and never playing, has been one of total **prudence**—now, I think, I am permitted to indulge in a wee bit of _____ to reward myself.

Applying Yourself:
Choose the best word to complete each of the following sentences.

25. Don't expect that your scandalous behavior will go unnoticed; everything we do has _____.
    (A) uniformity
    (B) debauchery
    (C) repercussions
    (D) furtiveness
    (E) variegation

26. Please don't _____ upon my privacy by entering my cubicle without permission.
    (A) infringe
    (B) variegate
    (C) debauch
    (D) comply
    (E) constrain

27. The best geopolitical maps use several colors in a(n) _____ pattern, so that no nation filled with one color touches another of the same color.
(A) furtive
(B) uniform
(C) compliant
(D) variegated
(E) pellucid

28. The thief glanced around the store _____ before pocketing the jewelry on display.
(A) uniformly
(B) furtively
(C) compliantly
(D) pervasively
(E) indulgently

29. Should you insert two explanatory paragraphs, your argument would finally be as _____ as you had intended.
(A) uniform
(B) compliant
(C) variegated
(D) pellucid
(E) furtive

30. _____ with the rules is mandatory; those who disobey will be removed immediately.
(A) Uniformity
(B) Variegation
(C) Debauchery
(D) Infringement
(E) Compliance

31. Stylistic choices at the art festival need not be _____; feel free to choose your own materials and subject matter.
(A) furtive
(B) uniform
(C) compliant
(D) pellucid
(E) variegated

32. The fraternity, with its huge parties that required days of cleanup and police intervention, was the model of _____.
(A) compliance
(B) debauchery
(C) variegation
(D) uniformity
(E) furtiveness

On Your Own:

Write one sentence using each word below to demonstrate your understanding of the word's meaning.

33. **furtive** _____

34. **uniform** _____

35. **repercussion** _____

36. **variegated** _____

37. **pellucid** _____

38. **debauchery** _____

39. **infringe** _____

40. **compliance** _____

C2 Advanced Vocabulary 83

First Impressions:

Using the example sentences below, write your own definition of each boldfaced word. Then write the letter of the definition from the box that best matches your definition.

A	noun: a piece of wet, marshy land; a confusing or complicated situation	**C**	adjective: spotless; flawless; absolutely clean
B	adjective: relating to a religious faction; narrow-minded; limited	**D**	noun: a scornful remark; a stinging rebuke

1. _____ The commentator's cruel words dripped with **sarcasm**.

SARCASM means: _____

2. _____ Although Rosa was naturally a slob, her career as a scientist required an **immaculate** work space.

IMMACULATE means: _____

3. _____ The supposedly broad-minded organization was quick to distance itself from the **sectarian** views of its former members.

SECTARIAN means: _____

4. _____ The guide warned us to stay on the path to avoid becoming trapped and drowning in the dangerous **morass**.

MORASS means: _____

A	noun: speech that makes the speaker sound important or boastful	**C**	adjective: showy; pretentious; trying to attract attention
B	adjective: roundabout; not straight-forward; shifty or crooked	**D**	adjective: daring; bold; inventive; insolent; unrestrained

5. _____ Erica was sent to the principal's office for her **audacious** and disrespectful use of profanity in the classroom.

AUDACIOUS means: _____

6. _____ "Conspicuous consumption" is the practice of purchasing **ostentatious** homes, clothing, and cars simply because they look impressive to other people.

OSTENTATIOUS means: _____

7. _____ Beowulf and his kinsman boast of their great deeds in speeches marked by their **grandiloquence**.

GRANDILOQUENCE means: _____

8. _____ The plan was a rather **devious** one, requiring much thought to see just how it would work out.

DEVIOUS means: _____

Divide and Conquer:
Choose the correct word to complete each of the following sentences.

9. The flashy decorations of the restaurant, from the Ionic columns to the glittering chandeliers to the false Egyptian sarcophagi, could only be described as (**sectarian / ostentatious**).

10. The congratulatory speeches given at the awards ceremony were marked with pomp and (**audacity / grandiloquence**).

11. The (**audacious / immaculate**) state of the house shocked Mrs. Burrows, since she was so used to seeing it in a disarray of children's toys and dirty dishes.

12. The universally-criticized film was subject to (**grandiloquence / sarcasm**) in the form of standing ovations when it was played on TV.

13. The explorer declared that in order to progress as a civilization we must take steps that are new or possibly even (**audacious / sectarian**).

14. The savvy investor bought a soupy (**grandiloquence / morass**) for a very low price, drained and seeded the land, and built an expensive golf course.

15. With globalization, formerly isolated (**sectarian / devious**) groups have become exposed to one another, causing much political tension.

16. The supposed "shortcut" turned out to be a (**sectarian / devious**) route that crossed four roads, two backyards, and one very confused horse's stall.

Hot and Cold:
Write the word from the lesson that is most nearly the *OPPOSITE* of the boldfaced word or words in each sentence below.

17. Jaime's stinging _____ hurt Mayra, who preferred the gentle **sincerity** of their brother, Juan.

18. The Duke's _____ made him the clear choice to be made general; troops would be more inspired by his grand speech than by the **fumbling** of the others vying for the position.

19. Tracy felt that the Yacht Club, with its _____ displays of wealth and disdain for those without money, did not fit with her own **retiring personality**.

20. Because he loved drama, Roberto preferred to concoct _____ ways to get what he wanted instead of simply asking for things in a more **straightforward** way.

21. We must be **broad-minded** in our approach in order to avoid becoming embroiled in _____ conflicts.

22. Rather than daring to make a(n) _____ claim in his thesis statement and do the work to sufficiently prove it, Daniel went the safe route and made a **timid**, easily proven assertion.

23. My mother, who demanded that our rooms be _____ at all times, would tolerate no speck of dust, misaligned picture frame, or hint of anything **dirty**.

24. The brilliant executive was able to pull the company from an apparent _____ and place it on **stable ground**.

Applying Yourself:
Choose the best word to complete each of the following sentences.

25. Her _____ toward most people contrasted with his genuine concern for humanity.
    (A) morass
    (B) sarcasm
    (C) grandiloquence
    (D) deviousness
    (E) ostentation

26. It may seem _____ to purchase billboard space in Times Square, but our show desperately needs the attention.
    (A) ostentatious
    (B) sarcastic
    (C) devious
    (D) sectarian
    (E) audacious

27. The insolent student had an _____ attitude toward the teacher, always talking back and using profanity.
    (A) sectarian
    (B) grandiloquent
    (C) ostentatious
    (D) audacious
    (E) immaculate

28. Some areas of the Middle East are plagued by _____ violence between members of the different factions of Islam.
    (A) ostentatious
    (B) sarcastic
    (C) sectarian
    (D) audacious
    (E) immaculate

29. The two roommates clashed, for while one side of the room appeared filthy, the other appeared _____.
    (A) devious
    (B) immaculate
    (C) sectarian
    (D) ostentatious
    (E) grandiloquent

30. The board hired several highly-paid lawyers to pull the company from the legal _____.
    (A) audacity
    (B) deviousness
    (C) sarcasm
    (D) morass
    (E) ostentation

31. The _____ salesman had managed to steal our parents' entire savings after persuading them to participate in a hack investment plan.
    (A) ostentatious
    (B) devious
    (C) grandiloquent
    (D) sectarian
    (E) immaculate

32. He spoke with _____ in attempt to conceal his severe lack of confidence.
    (A) sarcasm
    (B) ostentation
    (C) deviousness
    (D) grandiloquence
    (E) audacity

On Your Own:
Write one sentence using each word below to demonstrate your understanding of the word's meaning.

33. **ostentatious** _____

34. **grandiloquence** _____

35. **sarcasm** _____

36. **morass** _____

37. **devious** _____

38. **sectarian** _____

39. **immaculate** _____

40. **audacious** _____

C2 Advanced Vocabulary 84

First Impressions:

Using the example sentences below, write your own definition of each boldfaced word. Then write the letter of the definition from the box that best matches your definition.

A	verb: to raise in rank or dignity; to praise	**C**	noun: one who attacks cherished traditions
B	noun: a low-class, cowardly, despicable person	**D**	verb: to give life or liveliness to someone or something

1. _____ The members who left the group were denounced as traitors and **caitiffs**.

CAITIFF means: _____

2. _____ Wells is an easygoing **iconoclast** who laughs and smiles as he openly defies the norm.

ICONOCLAST means: _____

3. _____ He used the occasion of his portrait unveiling to **exalt** politics as an honorable profession

and politicians as hard-working, honest people.

EXALT means: _____

4. _____ In the story Pinocchio, Geppetto is able to **vivify** his favorite puppet so that it can move

and think on its own.

VIVIFY means: _____

A	adjective: continuing or lasting forever; without interruption	**C**	adjective: easily irritated; irritable; irked
B	adjective: of the best quality	**D**	adjective: tending or leaning toward; bent

5. _____ Ms. Fritz said she would be **inclined** to give him an A if he would re-write the paper.

INCLINED means: _____

6. _____ My family considers me the **superlative** example of a "good son," claiming that I have

been perfectly loyal and sweet through my boyhood and until today.

SUPERLATIVE means: _____

7. _____ I have never known Hans to be sad or angry; he is a **perpetually** happy person.

PERPETUAL means: _____

8. _____ The **testy** old cat hated to be touched, called, or looked at.

TESTY means: _____

Divide and Conquer:
Choose the correct word to complete each of the following sentences.

9. As his work is (**iconoclastic** / **superlative**), we have no choice but to offer a raise.

10. Dickens is famous for (**vivifying** / **exalting**) his characters with idiosyncrasies and distinct motivations.

11. A true (**superlative** / **iconoclast**), Jeffrey loved nothing more than pointing out that various ideas commonly accepted as facts are actually faulty.

12. My grandfather has grown (**superlative** / **testy**) in his old age, getting easily angered by my active little sister.

13. The surprising success of the little-known actor's performance quickly (**exalted** / **vivified**) him to celebrity status.

14. Richard was a mere (**iconoclast** / **caitiff**) who ran at the first sign of personal danger.

15. Margaret was naturally (**exalted** / **inclined**) to be generous, often pleasing her neighbors with gifts at unexpected times.

16. The seemingly (**testy** / **perpetual**) droning of the professor's voice made his lectures seem never-ending to students.

Hot and Cold:
Write the word from the lesson that is most nearly the *OPPOSITE* of the boldfaced word or words in each sentence below.

17. The workmanship on the rug was _____; it was amazing how much more beautiful it was than the **substandard** work done by others.

18. Your presence _____ life on this old farm, giving us all a skip in our step and a reason to be excited about the day; now that you're gone, everything seems a bit **dulled**.

19. Our use of fossil fuels is **temporary**; there simply isn't enough oil in the ground to sustain _____ use of the machinery we use today.

20. Martin Luther, a(n) _____ who rejected many common practices of the Catholic church, was severely rebuked by **traditionalists** who would have seen that no church custom go challenged.

21. I have no desire to _____ myself as some kind of hero, and I know that I'm far from perfect, but I also refuse to allow people who hardly know me to **denigrate** me as inferior.

22. His mood was impossible to predict: he would be _____ one moment and **pleasant** the next.

23. One of the walls was _____ toward the garden, while the other **leaned away** from it; the two together formed a house in the shape of a triangle.

24. The Redeemer, a vigilante who fought crime in the city, was born a lowly _____ but aspired to change his ways and become a **hero** instead.

Applying Yourself:
Choose the best word to complete each of the following sentences.

25. The rookie's enthusiasm _____ his formerly tired, jaded partner.
    (A) exalted
    (B) vivified
    (C) inclined
    (D) contended
    (E) relegated

26. The man who jumped on the grenade to save his platoon deserves to be _____ from now to the end of time.
    (A) vivified
    (B) exalted
    (C) contended
    (D) inclined
    (E) atoned

25. After several months of intensive rehearsal, the high school orchestra's previous _____ had transformed into rich musical harmony.
    (A) homily
    (B) dissonance
    (C) vestige
    (D) didacticism
    (E) chicanery

26. Although boring to read like most of its kind, this instructional manual offered useful _____ advice on how to repair the lawnmower.
    (A) dissonant
    (B) pivotal
    (C) indigenous
    (D) didactic
    (E) vestigial

27. John's occasional flashes of brilliance are just _____ of his former, consistent self.
    (A) homilies
    (B) vestiges
    (C) apocalypses
    (D) didacticisms
    (E) dissonances

28. Humanity has for decades known that collision with a large asteroid could mean a(n) _____ for the inhabitants of Earth.
    (A) apocalypse
    (B) homily
    (C) chicanery
    (D) dissonance
    (E) vestige

29. Those who are overly trusting are susceptible to confidence artists and their _____.
    (A) homilies
    (B) chicanery
    (C) apocalypse
    (D) dissonance
    (E) vestiges

30. _____ from preachers, politicians, and celebrities abounded after the disaster, in an attempt to help the townsfolk make sense of the senseless killings.
    (A) Pivots
    (B) Vestiges
    (C) Didacticisms
    (D) Homilies
    (E) Chicaneries

On Your Own:

Write one sentence using each word below to demonstrate your understanding of the word's meaning.

31. **homily** _____

32. **vestige** _____

33. **apocalypse** _____

34. **didactic** _____

35. **indigenous** _____

36. **chicanery** _____

37. **pivotal** _____

38. **dissonance** _____

C2 Advanced Vocabulary 86

First Impressions:
Using the example sentences below, write your own definition of each boldfaced word. Then write the letter of the definition from the box that best matches your definition.

A	noun: a large and unruly crowd of people	**C**	noun: a book for teaching reading; any introductory text; a substance used as a preparatory coat on a surface
B	noun: marriage	**D**	adjective: easily accomplished; superficial; lazy

1. _____ Juan wanted to learn how cars worked, so he read a **primer** on auto repair.

PRIMER means: _____

2. _____ The topic of **matrimony** makes Cliff and Mary uncomfortable; they've been together for 20 years, but never felt the need to get married.

MATRIMONY means: _____

3. _____ The **horde** of visitors cramming into the auditorium produced quite a bit of noise.

HORDE means: _____

4. _____ John shook his head and, still confused, decided that he would come up with a more **facile** way to solve the problem than the one in the book.

FACILE means: _____

A	noun: a place for religious thought; a monastery or convent	**C**	adjective: thorough; comprehensive
B	verb: to reach an agreement between two people or groups through bargaining; to weaken	**D**	noun: a rhythmic falling of words, sounds, steps, etc.; a beat

5. _____ The actor William Shatner is famous for speaking his lines in an unusual **cadence**, with frequent pauses between words.

CADENCE means: _____

6. _____ Bella spent the night cramming the countless equations she'd need to know for her **exhaustive** physics final.

EXHAUSTIVE means: _____

7. _____ All the nuns in the **cloister** were required to spend a few hours a week cleaning and beautifying the convent.

CLOISTER means: _____

8. _____ After a long debate, the teachers and school board **compromised** on a contract for the next two years.

COMPROMISE means: _____

Divide and Conquer:

Choose the correct word to complete each of the following sentences.

9. Wishing to dedicate her life to a higher purpose, Susannah decided to enter a (**cadence / cloister**) and spend her days in contemplation.

10. The official estimated that a fully (**facile / exhaustive**) analysis of the issue would require six years and fourteen million dollars.

11. It seemed that no agreement was possible, but finally, the striking workers and management (**cloistered / compromised**) on a new contract.

12. As the (**horde / cloister**) of paraders marched through the streets, onlookers clapped and cheered excitedly.

13. The (**primer / cloister**) combined phonics and illustrations in a fun story about a ghost who needed to learn how to read.

14. Clark and Judy were joined in (**matrimony / compromise**) in June of 1994 and have remained close partners ever since.

15. The lead drummer laid out the (**cadence / horde**) to which each member of the band marched.

16. Dr. Robertson's report was excessively (**facile / exhaustive**), so he was asked to dig more deeply into the issue for the next week's meeting.

Hot and Cold:

Write the word from the lesson that is most nearly the *OPPOSITE* of the boldfaced word or words in each sentence below.

17. The gentle _____ of jazz music flowing from the speakers couldn't compete with the **cacophony** of people talking, laughing, and clinking glasses.

18. The institution of _____ might have to be reexamined since half of all marriages now end in **divorce**.

19. We received an _____ account of the technical aspects of the retreat including every practical detail, but **insufficient** information about whether the attendees had fun or learned anything over the weekend.

20. While one side of the debate wished to _____ and end the fighting, the other **insisted** on its own terms and would accept no other solution.

21. I'd much rather face an angry **individual** than a great _____.

22. Mom said there was no _____ answer to the question of the meaning of life; any response she could give would be **difficult** and multi-faceted.

Applying Yourself:

Choose the best word to complete each of the following sentences.

23. I was expecting the project to be difficult to do, but it turned out to be more _____ than I'd anticipated.
    (A) exhaustive
    (B) compromising
    (C) facile
    (D) matrimonial
    (E) vestigial

24. The _____ of Christopher Smart's "A Song of David" mimics the meter of an epic, Biblical poem.
    (A) compromise
    (B) primer
    (C) cloister
    (D) horde
    (E) cadence

25. The earthquake threatened to _____ the integrity of the dam, so the mayor wisely evacuated the town.
    (A) cloister
    (B) compromise
    (C) exhaust
    (D) augment
    (E) deracinate

26. He had to scramble out of the way in order to avoid the _____ of people rushing into the store during the big sale.
    (A) horde
    (B) primer
    (C) cadence
    (D) matrimony
    (E) cloister

27. A(n) _____ review convinced us that Mr. Jennings had no hand in even the smallest aspect of the matter.
    (A) dissonant
    (B) matrimonial
    (C) facile
    (D) exhaustive
    (E) compromising

28. The _____ monks emerged only to render advice from religious visitors.
    (A) matrimony's
    (B) cloister's
    (C) primer's
    (D) horde's
    (E) compromise's

29. Many ceremonies of _____ are now purely civil; the church is no longer the exclusive performer of marriage rites.
    (A) horde
    (B) cloister
    (C) matrimony
    (D) cadence
    (E) primer

30. Before you proceed with the complicated surgery, make sure to read Dr. McConnell's _____ on the subject.
    (A) primer
    (B) cadence
    (C) horde
    (D) matrimony
    (E) compromise

On Your Own:
Write one sentence using each word below to demonstrate your understanding of the word's meaning.

31. **compromise** _____

32. **primer** _____

33. **exhaustive** _____

34. **cloister** _____

35. **facile** _____

36. **horde** _____

37. **matrimony** _____

38. **cadence** _____

C2 Advanced Vocabulary 87

First Impressions:

Using the example sentences below, write your own definition of each boldfaced word. Then write the letter of the definition from the box that best matches your definition.

A	adjective: occurring suddenly and irregularly	**C**	adjective: thorough; inclusive; covering or involving a lot
B	adjective: worldly, as opposed to spiritual; lacking interest or excitement	**D**	adjective: relating to brotherhood or fellowship among men

1. _____ Marcus spent his weekends volunteering at the library with the other men in his **fraternal** organization.

FRATERNAL means: _____

2. _____ Lerner's choice of utilizing extremely **mundane** objects, preferably old objects, is part of his strategy to assert the spiritual potential in everything.

MUNDANE means: _____

3. _____ Lilith hoped that her essay on the Civil War was sufficiently **comprehensive** to receive full credit for covering the material.

COMPREHENSIVE means: _____

4. _____ Linda's **spasmodic** attempts at being nice to us weren't enough to maintain the friendship.

SPASMODIC means: _____

A	noun: truthfulness	**C**	adjective: extremely thorough, exhaustive, or accurate; the state of applying or adhering strictly to rules or a system
B	noun: a harsh, authoritarian ruler	**D**	noun: the laboring force of a society

5. _____ Because the claim seemed so doubtful, Karen was careful to establish its **veracity** before making her decision.

VERACITY means: _____

6. _____ In order to ace his next calculus exam, Jason participated in a **rigorous** week-long study marathon.

RIGOROUS means: _____

7. _____ The revolt didn't last long, but it didn't have to; a week was all it took to overthrow the **despot** and her hellish government.

DESPOT means: _____

8. _____ The Communist Manifesto states that society is made of two classes: the bourgeoisie and the **proletariat** whose inexpensive labor is exploited.

PROLETARIAT means: _____

Divide and Conquer:

Choose the correct word to complete each of the following sentences.

9. The (**despot / fraternity**) took a cruel pleasure in stripping his citizens' freedom and property, assuming total control over his people and amassing huge tracts of land.

10. The professor stated that the (**despot / proletariat**) suffers when the government lifts labor protection laws in the interests of "competition".

11. That combination of the (**mundane / despotic**) and fantastical is what sets this particular feature apart from any film you've ever seen.

12. Only the cynical doubt the (**comprehensiveness / veracity**) of a child's word without cause.

13. The fitness trainer's (**fraternal / rigorous**) diet regime and exercise routine, which left little room for argument from her clients, were grueling but effective.

14. The men of the neighborhood gathered every year to share (**fraternal / veracious**) goodwill at a barbecue.

15. The test preparation course offered a (**despotic / comprehensive**) overview of every math topic on the exam.

16. The (**fraternal / spasmodic**) earthquakes terrified the sleeping children.

Hot and Cold:

Write the word from the lesson that is most nearly the *OPPOSITE* of the boldfaced word or words in each sentence below.

17. The **benevolent** queen refused to pass power to her daughter, who she feared would grow up to be a ruthless _____.

18. After the _____ fit that he'd had earlier that evening, he was happy to just rest **uninterrupted**.

19. I vouched for the _____ of the paper, knowing full well that any **falsehood** it once might have contained had been checked and fixed by a series of editors, including myself.

20. Karl Marx wrote that the strength of the economy rested on the working _____, the members of which devoted their lives to making the **bourgeoisie** rich.

21. After spending 10 **thrilling** years traveling through the least-developed parts of the world, facing a constant risk of being maimed by wild animals or falling rocks, it was a pleasure to return to the _____ world of the suburbs.

22. Dr. Chalmers had hoped his book would serve as a _____ overview of the history of psychology, but it turned out to pay only **limited** attention to the field of cognitive behavioral therapy.

23. During the school year, the children are subjected to a _____ schedule of school, tutoring, athletics, and music lessons to make up for the **lax**, unproductive summer.

Applying Yourself:

Choose the best word to complete each of the following sentences.

24. We, the members of the _____, refuse to be pushed around by the more powerful members of society.
    (A) rigor
    (B) proletariat
    (C) veracity
    (D) despot
    (E) fraternity

25. With a _____ jerk of his hand, RJ dropped the lamp.
    (A) comprehensive
    (B) spasmodic
    (C) rigorous
    (D) fraternal
    (E) mundane

26. It was hard for us to find any _____ behind his words, for he had a history of dishonesty.
    (A) veracity
    (B) rigor
    (C) despot
    (D) proletariat
    (E) comprehensiveness

27. After exploring the fantastic world of wizardry in the Harry Potter book series, Sarah was loathe to return to her _____ world of chores and homework.
    (A) spasmodic
    (B) mundane
    (C) comprehensive
    (D) fraternal
    (E) despotic

28. I suggest you read the product's _____ manual so that you can know every bit of information about it.
    (A) rigorous
    (B) veracious
    (C) despotic
    (D) comprehensive
    (E) mundane

29. I felt an everlasting _____ bond with my unit after we withstood the enemy's assault for over a week.
    (A) fraternal
    (B) comprehensive
    (C) rigorous
    (D) mundane
    (E) despotic

30. Each special agent must endure _____ testing before he or she is approved for dangerous duty.
    (A) despotic
    (B) comprehensive
    (C) fraternal
    (D) despotic
    (E) rigorous

31. The real-life Dracula was a _____ in present-day Romania who savagely murdered those who displeased him.
    (A) rigor
    (B) fraternity
    (C) veracity
    (D) despot
    (E) proletariat

On Your Own:

Write one sentence using each word below to demonstrate your understanding of the word's meaning.

32. **comprehensive** _____

33. **rigorous** _____

34. **spasmodic** _____

35. **veracity** _____

36. **despot** _____

37. **mundane** _____

38. **fraternal** _____

39. **proletariat** _____

C2 Advanced Vocabulary 88

First Impressions:
Using the example sentences below, write your own definition of each boldfaced word. Then write the letter of the definition from the box that best matches your definition.

A	adjective: prone to seizing what is desired by force	**C**	adjective: fluent; glib; talkative
B	verb: to wait patiently [usually to "bide one's time"]	**D**	adjective: unable to be doubted; unquestionable

1. _____ Though the Vikings had a complex culture, they are depicted in today's media as **rapacious** pirates who survived by raiding and pillaging coastal villages.

RAPACIOUS means: _____

2. _____ The security camera footage was **indubitable** evidence against the murderer, so it was no surprise when she was convicted.

INDUBITABLE means: _____

3. _____ I'm **biding** my time until I can ask for a raise at work.

BIDE means: _____

4. _____ Mikhail was so **voluble** that in some months he spent almost as much on his phone bill as on his groceries.

VOLUBLE means: _____

A	noun: a lack of proper respect	**C**	adjective: unfriendly; hostile; harmful; detrimental
B	adjective: generally accepted; supposed	**D**	verb: to openly state

5. _____ To throw a shoe at the President is a display of great **irreverence**, especially in countries that consider feet to be the dirtiest parts of the body.

IRREVERENCE means: _____

6. _____ Conspiracy theorists believe that the real causes of certain historical events are far more sinister than the **putative** explanations suggest.

PUTATIVE means: _____

7. _____ Thomas Henry Huxley became known as "Darwin's Bulldog" because of the passion with which he **avowed** his support of the theory of evolution.

AVOW means: _____

8. _____ Several citizens believe that the War on Iraq has had an **inimical** effect on the American economy, forcing the country to take out huge foreign loans.

INIMICAL means: _____

Divide and Conquer:

Choose the correct word to complete each of the following sentences.

9. Though William Shakespeare is the (**putative / voluble**) author of many classic plays, some have suggested that Francis Bacon or Christopher Marlowe was the actual writer.

10. It is not yet clear whether the overall effects of the medicine are beneficial or (**voluble / inimical**).

11. The teacher frowned at the (**irreverence / avowal**) of a few members of the audience at the graduation ceremony.

12. The airline has been (**biding / voluble**) in its demand for a third runway at Heathrow, at times even turning to news reporters to get its message to the public.

13. Chloe is (**biding / avowing**) her time until she feels comfortable asking Richard on a date.

14. For years, it was considered (**indubitable / irreverent**) that the world was flat, but this was later shown to be incorrect.

15. It is difficult to trust Alexander because his actions often are not consistent with his (**avowed / inimical**) beliefs.

16. The gang of (**voluble / rapacious**) pirates sailed up and down the coast, raiding each port and carrying off countless valuables.

Hot and Cold:

Write the word from the lesson that is most nearly the *OPPOSITE* of the boldfaced word or words in each sentence below.

17. Either the younger sister was **not talkative** or the older sister was simply too _____ to allow any competition.

18. The old dog took a(n) _____ attitude toward strangers, barking and growling at anyone she didn't already know, but was friendly and loving as ever to her family.

19. The _____ cause of the illness was the consumption of spoiled milk, but the **unrecognized** cause is that poverty had driven her to partake of unsafe foods.

20. His reputation as an honest lawyer meant that his integrity was _____ in the community; his partner's integrity, however, had always been **questionable**.

21. The comedian's _____ and willingness to mock any of the important figures in the room amazed the host, who had hoped for more **gravitas** from his guests.

22. Aesop's fable tells of the hare who **acts in haste** only to be undone by the tortoise who _____ his time.

23. Father _____ that he had never taken a sick day in his life and **denied** ever having left work early, too.

24. Young children are often _____, interested more in taking whatever they want by any means necessary, and only grow **generous** with age.

Applying Yourself:

Choose the best word to complete each of the following sentences.

25. I can be patient; I will _____ my time until the situation improves.
    (A) avow
    (B) bide
    (C) cloister
    (D) languish
    (E) hoard

26. With her many years of experience fighting breast cancer, she was a(n) _____, active spokesperson for the cause.
    (A) inimical
    (B) voluble
    (C) putative
    (D) irreverent
    (E) rapacious

27. I _____ that my wife is the most deserving, loving person on Earth.
    (A) bide
    (B) avow
    (C) deviate
    (D) meander
    (E) facilitate

28. We are not _____ to the concept, but we aren't exactly in love with it, either.
    (A) avowed
    (B) indubitable
    (C) voluble
    (D) inimical
    (E) putative

29. Skeptical scientists routinely question _____ information.
    (A) irreverent
    (B) voluble
    (C) putative
    (D) indubitable
    (E) inimical

30. Sadly, the evidence proved that the storm damage was too severe and the fact that we had to rebuild was _____.
    (A) indubitable
    (B) inimical
    (C) irreverent
    (D) putative
    (E) rapacious

31. The boy's _____ towards the churchgoers' religion showed when he chatted away during the sermon.
    (A) irreverence
    (B) volubility
    (C) rapaciousness
    (D) biding
    (E) avowal

32. Genghis Khan and his _____ Mongol hordes conquered much of Asia, one nation at a time.
    (A) putative
    (B) rapacious
    (C) voluble
    (D) irreverent
    (E) avowed

On Your Own:
Write one sentence using each word below to demonstrate your understanding of the word's meaning.

33. **inimical** _____

34. **indubitable** _____

35. **bide** _____

36. **avow** _____

37. **rapacious** _____

38. **putative** _____

39. **voluble** _____

40. **irreverence** _____

C2 Advanced Vocabulary 89

First Impressions:
Using the example sentences below, write your own definition of each boldfaced word. Then write the letter of the definition from the box that best matches your definition.

A	verb: to help bring about; to make less difficult	**C**	noun: a false statement
B	adjective: untidy or dirty	**D**	noun: the placement of two items together for comparison

1. _____ Two weeks of wear without washing left Micah's sweater looking rather **frowzy**.

FROWZY means: _____

2. _____ The new program will also support networks to **facilitate** collaboration between

researchers.

FACILITATE means: _____

3. _____ Though some of the explanations seem reasonable, others are bald-faced **fabrications**.

FABRICATION means: _____

4. _____ Sergei Eisenstein developed and refined montage, the technique of **juxtaposing** images

in film in order to create new effects from their collision.

JUXTAPOSITION means: _____

A	verb: to harm someone's reputation	**C**	noun: opposition to success
B	adjective: dried out	**D**	noun: honesty; care about moral correctness

5. _____ The doctor felt that the **adversity** that he faced and overcame in his youth taught him the

lessons that led to his eventual success.

ADVERSITY means: _____

6. _____ The band members' throats were parched after they practiced in the hot, dry sun for two

hours.

PARCHED means: _____

7. _____ Matieu's **probity** led him to be promoted to positions of greater and greater trust and

responsibility.

PROBITY means: _____

8. _____ The newspaper made no false statements about Schulz and did not **defame** him.

DEFAME means: _____

Divide and Conquer:
Choose the correct word to complete each of the following sentences.

9. Psychologist Martin Seligman believes that optimism is a measurable quality that largely determines whether one will continue striving in the face of (**facilitation / adversity**).

10. The larger challenge will be working with existing programs to (**facilitate / defame**) more far-reaching access for young people.

11. My throat was (**fabricated / parched**) after hiking on a hot day, and I eagerly downed the tall glass of ice water.

12. The phrase "there is no bad press" suggests that attempts to (**defame / juxtapose**) a person will only make that person more prominent.

13. After lying under Mark's bed for two weeks, the sweater looked extremely (**frowzy / parched**).

14. Squiggy's (**fabrication / probity**) occasionally got him into trouble, as sometimes people are not ready to accept straightforward honesty.

15. The (**defamation / juxtaposition**) in the ad of a starving child and a wealthy politician sent a striking and startling message.

16. The assumption underlying the lie detector test is that small physical changes indicate that a speaker is engaging in (**adversity / fabrication**).

Hot and Cold:
Write the word from the lesson that is most nearly the *OPPOSITE* of the boldfaced word or words in each sentence below.

17. The old woman, who had spent most of her life lying in the sun or in tanning beds, looked _____ even when she was totally **soaked**.

18. While the mob boss tried to convey himself with a sense of _____ while in the public eye, all were aware of the **untrustworthiness** of his private doings.

19. Having a "study buddy" can _____ learning if you work well in groups, but if you're prone to chatting and getting off-topic, having others around may only **hinder** your progress.

20. He was known for being _____ in his appearance, but Mark was actually very **tidy** when it came to the maintenance of his house.

21. We have faced every manner of _____ in trying to set up a school in the rural area, but hopefully we'll have more **ease** now that we have all the proper permits.

22. Among the many _____ the group told to try and cover its tracks, one **truth** remained: They had not intended for their scheme to go as far as it did.

23. Though the critic had once _____ her as a cheater and a thief of other authors' material, he now **lauded** her as one of the great writers of her generation.

24. The _____ of my receipt of a love letter and the overdue water bill highlighted the highs and lows of my life and indicated that there was no **separation** in the experience of good and bad.

Applying Yourself:
Choose the best word to complete each of the following sentences.

25. President Clinton _____ the negotiations by inviting both of the parties to the serene Camp David to resolve their differences.
    (A) parched
    (B) facilitated
    (C) defamed
    (D) fabricated
    (E) augmented

26. Upon the _____ of the two applications, we realized that Jeff's was the far more impressive.
    (A) defamation
    (B) facilitation
    (C) juxtaposition
    (D) adversity
    (E) probity

27. Jurists aspire to the highest _____, as they are the stewards of moral behavior in a society.
    (A) adversity
    (B) probity
    (C) defamation
    (D) juxtaposition
    (E) frowziness

28. The prosecution uncovered several _____ in the defendant's statements, which led to a conviction on all counts.
    (A) compromises
    (B) adversities
    (C) facilitations
    (D) defamations
    (E) fabrications

29. When Michael Jordan suffered a knee injury, it was the greatest _____ he had faced in his brief career.
    (A) probity
    (B) fabrication
    (C) juxtaposition
    (D) facilitation
    (E) adversity

30. One should never _____ the memory of someone who has died; rather, every effort should be made to hold him or her in high esteem.
    (A) parch
    (B) defame
    (C) facilitate
    (D) juxtapose
    (E) fabricate

31. Global warming will cause radically different effects for various parts of the globe, from newly _____ landscapes to rising water levels.
    (A) juxtaposed
    (B) fabricated
    (C) defamed
    (D) frowzy
    (E) parched

32. Max arrived at the door _____ after a day of playing outside, so we sent him straight to the bathtub.
    (A) frowzy
    (B) defamed
    (C) parched
    (D) fabricated
    (E) juxtaposed

On Your Own:
Write one sentence using each word below to demonstrate your understanding of the word's meaning.

33. **fabrication** _____

34. **defame** _____

35. **probity** _____

36. **facilitate** _____

37. **juxtaposition** _____

38. **frowzy** _____

39. **adversity** _____

40. **parched** _____

C2 Advanced Vocabulary 90

First Impressions:

Using the example sentences below, write your own definition of each boldfaced word. Then write the letter of the definition from the box that best matches your definition.

A	noun: a transformation from one thing into another	C	adjective: pretentious; ridiculously exaggerated; impressive
B	adjective: pleasant and agreeable	D	adjective: shabby or poor; ineffectively stale

1. _____ Tanya went through a **metamorphosis** from an outgoing, happy girl into a shell of her former self.

METAMORPHOSIS means: _____

2. _____ The **congenial** host showed the guests to the most comfortable room and offered them a selection of snacks and beverages.

CONGENIAL means: _____

3. _____ To truly become a high-achiever requires vision so bold as to appear **grandiose**.

GRANDIOSE means: _____

4. _____ After six years of constant use, Kayla's beloved blanket was becoming **threadbare**.

THREADBARE means: _____

A	noun: a historical record of events	C	adjective: related to children or childhood; immature
B	verb: to destroy completely	D	verb: to applaud; to announce with great celebration

5. _____ Consumers **acclaimed** the latest version of the phone, saying that its usefulness exceeded their wildest expectations.

ACCLAIM means: _____

6. _____ Mrs. Montoya hoped that as Kenny aged he would move beyond his **puerile** fascination with video games and take a more mature approach to his studies.

PUERILE means: _____

7. _____ Had the fire department not quickly built a wall of sandbags, the rising flood waters would have **obliterated** the home.

OBLITERATED means: _____

8. _____ Ken Burns' documentary "The Civil War" is a compelling **chronicle** of the lives of Americans during that difficult era.

CHRONICLE means: _____

Divide and Conquer:
Choose the correct word to complete each of the following sentences.

9. Mommy laughed at her son's (**grandiose / obliterated**) descriptions of what he would do if he were the King of the United States.

10. The caterpillar went through (**metamorphosis / congeniality**) and transformed into a butterfly.

11. The new film was (**obliterated / acclaimed**) by critics and moviegoers alike, and it is expected to become a classic.

12. One account was kept secret and never made the history books; the other became a (**metamorphosis / chronicle**) that was read for years to come.

13. Siwon decided to buy a new pair of jeans; his old pair was quickly becoming ragged and (**threadbare / acclaimed**).

14. "Shock and Awe" is a military tactic based upon overwhelming the opponent with a sudden display of superior force to (**obliterate / acclaim**) them.

15. Harold was a (**grandiose / congenial**) host who always did his best to make guests in his home feel comfortable and welcome.

16. Should you wish to continue your (**acclaimed / puerile**) practical jokes during this somber time, I'll have no choice but to ask you to leave.

Hot and Cold:
Write the word from the lesson that is most nearly the *OPPOSITE* of the boldfaced word or words in each sentence below.

17. Rather than _____ the fungus, the chemical acted as a fertilizer that helped to **facilitate** mold.

18. While the beginning chapters of the story were **developed**, the ending was disappointingly _____.

19. The weather will determine whether the flower undergoes a _____ or remains in **stasis**.

20. Known for his _____ humor, the comedian does not appeal to more **mature** audiences looking to laugh at something besides crude jokes.

21. Not even our one constantly **hostile** aunt could take away from the _____ tone of the family gathering; we were all happy to be together.

22. While the book has been _____ by liberals as a manifesto of proper political process, conservatives **criticize** it as a biased piece of party propaganda.

23. My _____ ideas about what the business could be make my partner, more **meek** in his ambitions, laugh.

Applying Yourself:
Choose the best word to complete each of the following sentences.

24. I could not imagine a person being more _____; her manners are beyond perfect and her speech is soothing.
    (A) obliterated
    (B) grandiose
    (C) puerile
    (D) congenial
    (E) threadbare

25. The tadpole's _____ into a frog amazed us all.
    (A) grandiosity
    (B) obliteration
    (C) chronicle
    (D) acclaim
    (E) metamorphosis

26. The New York Times _____ the new show as having the freshest screenplay on all of Broadway.
    (A) acclaimed
    (B) metamorphosized
    (C) obliterated
    (D) deviated
    (E) assented

27. _____ plans often muddle situations in which more simple and elegant solutions would do.
    (A) Grandiose
    (B) Congenial
    (C) Acclaimed
    (D) Threadbare
    (E) Puerile

28. The _____ of the war highlights the army's movements between 1862 and 1864.
    (A) grandiosity
    (B) audacity
    (C) metamorphosis
    (D) chronicle
    (E) obliteration

29. _____ attitudes abounded at the meeting; people cried, threw staplers, and yelled when they didn't get their way.
    (A) Obliterated
    (B) Threadbare
    (C) Grandiose
    (D) Congenial
    (E) Puerile

30. Their brand new drapes, barely touched, did not match their old, _____ carpet.
    (A) grandiose
    (B) threadbare
    (C) chronicled
    (D) congenial
    (E) acclaimed

31. We destroyed our rivals at the homecoming game, and we _____ them in the semi-finals as well.
    (A) acclaimed
    (B) obliterated
    (C) shunted
    (D) castigated
    (E) lauded

On Your Own:

Write one sentence using each word below to demonstrate your understanding of the word's meaning.

32. **metamorphosis** _____

33. **grandiose** _____

34. **obliterate** _____

35. **chronicle** _____

36. **puerile** _____

37. **threadbare** _____

38. **acclaim** _____

39. **congenial** _____

27. That particular version of the software is _____ to errors and, therefore, prone to freeze up.
    (A) contended
    (B) relegated
    (C) vivified
    (D) inclined
    (E) exalted

28. It is of _____ importance that candidates turn in their applications before the deadline.
    (A) perpetual
    (B) testy
    (C) superlative
    (D) iconoclastic
    (E) exalted

29. The rebelling _____ stood in front of the temple every week and shouted dissenting statements against the religion.
    (A) iconoclast
    (B) vivification
    (C) caitiff
    (D) exaltation
    (E) inclination

30. The _____ motion machine is the Holy Grail of Newtonian physics, but it is impossible because of frictional forces.
    (A) inclined
    (B) exalted
    (C) perpetual
    (D) superlative
    (E) testy

31. We were set to sacrifice our lives for our country if necessary, but the _____ in the other platoon chose to save themselves instead of performing their duty.
    (A) iconoclasts
    (B) superlatives
    (C) caitiffs
    (D) manifestos
    (E) charlatans

32. My old box turtle has grown _____ in his later years and will bite your fingers if you bother him.
    (A) perpetual
    (B) superlative
    (C) exalted
    (D) testy
    (E) inclined

On Your Own:
Write one sentence using each word below to demonstrate your understanding of the word's meaning.

33. **vivify** _____

34. **perpetual** _____

35. **testy** _____

36. **caitiff** _____

37. **superlative** _____

38. **iconoclast** _____

39. **exalt** _____

40. **inclined** _____

C2 Advanced Vocabulary 85

First Impressions:

Using the example sentences below, write your own definition of each boldfaced word. Then write the letter of the definition from the box that best matches your definition.

A	noun: a sermon or moral lesson	**C**	adjective: instructional; preachy or pedantic
B	adjective: native to a certain habitat; local	**D**	noun: deception intended to take advantage of others

1. _____ The **indigenous** population is known for resenting contact by new arrivals and refuses to take on modern luxuries.

INDIGENOUS means: _____

2. _____ Through his **chicanery**, the con artist was able to convince gullible victims to give him their life savings.

CHICANERY means: _____

3. _____ We don't need yet another **didactic** film telling us what to do and who we ought to be.

DIDACTIC means: _____

4. _____ The chaplain delivered a brief **homily** on the importance of caring for the less fortunate.

HOMILY means: _____

A	noun: a small part that remains from a larger whole	**C**	noun: worldwide destruction or disaster, especially when predicted by prophecy
B	adjective: crucial; key; vital	**D**	noun: an inharmonious or harsh sound; cacophony; a disagreement

5. _____ This **pivotal** program will be one of the largest trials of immunotherapy treatments for stomach cancer ever conducted.

PIVOTAL means: _____

6. _____ The violinist's untuned violin created an unpleasant **dissonance** when he played it.

DISSONANCE means: _____

7. _____ The preacher on the street corner warned passers-by to repent before they faced the **apocalypse** of an angry god.

APOCALYPSE means: _____

8. _____ After so many years, the last **vestige** of the old farmhouse was the crumbling stone chimney rising from the grass.

VESTIGE means: _____

Divide and Conquer:
Choose the correct word to complete each of the following sentences.

9. The only (**vestige** / **homily**) of the ghost town's prosperity was the hotel's sign that read "No Vacancy".

10. The movie's (**pivotal** / **vestigial**) moment occurs when the protagonist realizes that her sister had been deceiving her all along.

11. The pastor opened the meeting with a brief (**vestige** / **homily**) on the importance of charity.

12. The purpose of the work is (**pivotal** / **didactic**), so the author focuses on details relevant to learning the skill.

13. A truly skilled musician can create meaningful sounds with both harmony and (**dissonance** / **chicanery**).

14. After the boys tricked several other students out of money they were punished for their (**apocalypse** / **chicanery**).

15. Those flowers are (**indigenous** / **dissonant**) to California and can't be found anywhere else in the world.

16. The possibility of nuclear (**apocalypse** / **homily**) was a daily worry for those who lived through the Cold War.

Hot and Cold:
Write the word from the lesson that is most nearly the *OPPOSITE* of the boldfaced word or words in each sentence below.

17. As we stepped into the club, the _____ of car horns, traffic, and helicopters gave way to the **harmony** of orchestral chamber music.

18. In my culture, which tends to utilize extreme subtlety and at times even _____, we aren't used to such **straightforwardness**.

19. The _____ plants were destroyed by kudzu, an **invasive** vine that smothers all other flora.

20. I perceived this moment as _____ to our relationship, assuming it would determine whether or not we'd get married, but Sandra considered the event **unimportant**.

21. These videos are intended to be informative and teach salespeople how to handle rude customers, but the terrible acting and lack of interesting information within them makes them more **mind-numbing** than _____.

22. The appendix may be a _____ of the body's system to handle early man's diet, but the large intestine is a **core part** of our digestive tract.

Applying Yourself:
Choose the best word to complete each of the following sentences.

23. Having a statistically valid control group during an experiment is _____ to arriving at a worthwhile conclusion.
    (A) vestigial
    (B) indigenous
    (C) didactic
    (D) pivotal
    (E) dissonant

24. We came here from another country to see the region's _____ animals.
    (A) vestigial
    (B) indigenous
    (C) dissonant
    (D) didactic
    (E) pivotal

C2 Advanced Vocabulary 91

First Impressions:
Using the example sentences below, write your own definition of each boldfaced word. Then write the letter of the definition from the box that best matches your definition.

A	noun: a catastrophe; a major failure	**C**	noun: skillful sleight of hand or trickery
B	adjective: not genuine, authentic, or true; counterfeit	**D**	adjective: invigorating and refreshing

1. _____ Through **legerdemain**, the magician made the coin seem to vanish and reappear in the child's pocket.

LEGERDEMAIN means: _____

2. _____ Jane tried to pass off her bag as an expensive designer brand, but the label was **spurious**.

SPURIOUS means: _____

3. _____ While many people find seesaws to be **exhilarating** and exciting, some find them scary and sickening.

EXHILARATING means: _____

4. _____ The minor problem turned into a major **debacle** when each party misunderstood the other.

DEBACLE means: _____

A	adjective: cautious and prudent	**C**	noun: someone who shuns society; a hermit
B	verb: to put into effect; to carry out	**D**	adjective: easily and rapidly changing in shape or function; versatile

5. _____ During times of change, the bold often find opportunities that the more **circumspect** miss.

CIRCUMSPECT means: _____

6. _____ He is confident Washington has the players to **execute** the scheme effectively.

EXECUTE means: _____

7. _____ I've been called rude and cold, but never been accused of being an outright **misanthrope**.

MISANTHROPE means: _____

8. _____ The **protean** actor played a cruel and heartless tyrant as believably as a kindly preacher.

PROTEAN means: _____

Divide and Conquer:

Choose the correct word to complete each of the following sentences.

9. To (**exhilarate** / **execute**) their business plans, students had to secure their own loans and negotiate with local restaurants and shops to obtain the product to sell.

10. A (**circumspect** / **protean**) company can adjust its product line to meet the needs of a changing market.

11. It was too bad that what should have been a beautiful party turned into a stressful (**debacle** / **execution**).

12. The financial planner stressed the importance of being (**circumspect** / **misanthropic**) before launching into any risky investments.

13. The members of the Polar Bear Club found a quick swim in icy water to be a(n) (**circumspect** / **exhilarating**) way to start the morning.

14. It takes a talented specialist to distinguish a genuine artifact from one that is (**exhilarating** / **spurious**).

15. Far from a (**debacle** / **misanthrope**), Kittiboon spent several hours every weekend volunteering at public service events.

16. The magician entertained the audience with masterful feats of (**circumspection** / **legerdemain**).

Hot and Cold:

Write the word from the lesson that is most nearly the *OPPOSITE* of the boldfaced word or words in each sentence below.

17. The president was pleased to be able to _____ his vision for the country's health care system, since for years he had been **prevented** from doing so by Congress.

18. The document that seemed at first _____ turned out to be **genuine**.

19. The con man's carefully executed _____ would not have been possible if he were touched by even a hint of **clumsiness**.

20. It's amazing how a board game can turn a _____ of a party, during which no one in the room will speak to one another, into a happy **success**.

21. Jim's work as a **philanthrope** in war-torn countries ended up turning him into a _____ who hated mankind for committing such terrible acts.

22. As an artist, Gene's style is as _____ as a flame; he has never maintained a **steady** method of producing art for longer than a year.

23. I find a life among my friends and family much more _____ and enjoyable than the **boring** planning of dissatisfying vacations.

24. Trying to be _____ about the job offer, Craig asked to come in and tour the office before he could feel **enthusiastic** about accepting.

Applying Yourself:

Choose the best word to complete each of the following sentences.

25. The party was a(n) _____; only one other person even showed up.
    (A) misanthrope
    (B) exhilaration
    (C) debacle
    (D) legerdemain
    (E) circumspection

26. The politician's _____ statements were quickly debunked when independent watchdog groups invoked contradictory evidence.
    (A) spurious
    (B) exhilarating
    (C) misanthropic
    (D) protean
    (E) circumspect

27. Although we had bought the materials necessary to build a tree house, we never _____ the project and instead let the lumber lay idle in the tool shed.
    (A) pivoted
    (B) executed
    (C) exalted
    (D) revered
    (E) absolved

28. _____ cells can be used in a number of bodily functions, depending on the need.
    (A) Executed
    (B) Circumspect
    (C) Protean
    (D) Spurious
    (E) Exhilarating

29. The brilliant general Sun Tzu maintained that a commander should be _____ in battle, waiting for the fight to come to him.
    (A) exhilarating
    (B) circumspect
    (C) spurious
    (D) protean
    (E) executed

30. John is a(n) _____, sitting alone in his house and warning everyone else to stay away.
    (A) circumspection
    (B) legerdemain
    (C) execution
    (D) debacle
    (E) misanthrope

31. Magicians rely on _____ to maintain their illusions and keep their audiences enthralled.
    (A) circumspection
    (B) executions
    (C) misanthropes
    (D) legerdemain
    (E) debacles

32. Some people feel _____ after having a caffeine-laden cup of coffee.
    (A) circumspect
    (B) executed
    (C) exhilarated
    (D) legerdemain
    (E) spurious

On Your Own:
Write one sentence using each word below to demonstrate your understanding of the word's meaning.

33. **spurious** _____

34. **legerdemain** _____

35. **execute** _____

36. **circumspect** _____

37. **exhilarating** _____

38. **debacle** _____

39. **protean** _____

40. **misanthrope** _____

C2 Advanced Vocabulary 92

First Impressions:

Using the example sentences below, write your own definition of each boldfaced word. Then write the letter of the definition from the box that best matches your definition.

A	adjective: unclear or doubtful in meaning; open to many different interpretations	**C**	verb: to lower in rank or dignity; to bring into contempt
B	adjective: related to the processes of thinking	**D**	adjective: unlikely; unbelievable

1. _____ Testimony that is **implausible** in light of the background evidence can greatly weaken the credibility of the witness.

IMPLAUSIBLE means: _____

2. _____ Dr. Young was upset to see an important historical monument **degraded** by littering and graffiti.

DEGRADE means: _____

3. _____ The **ambiguous** instructions were impossible to understand, so Dustin threw them away and tried to solve the problem for himself.

AMBIGUOUS means: _____

4. _____ Experiments in learning and decision-making in chimpanzees can reveal a great deal about the **cognitive** development of human beings.

COGNITIVE means: _____

A	adjective: novel; unparalleled; original	**C**	noun: a song or hymn for the dead
B	noun: an increase by a specific amount	**D**	noun: enmity; the state of being against someone or something else

5. _____ The contract specified that the engineer's pay would increase in $1 per-hour **increments** over the course of several years.

INCREMENT means: _____

6. _____ The singer's **unprecedented** performing style garnered praise from fans who were tired of seeing copies of older musical icons.

UNPRECEDENTED means: _____

7. _____ As the organist played a **requiem**, the mourners paid their last respect to the deceased.

REQUIEM means: _____

8. _____ Glenda's **antagonism** made her lose many friends, who were tired of feeling defensive around her.

ANTAGONISM means: _____

Divide and Conquer:

Choose the correct word to complete each of the following sentences.

9. Jean stood up for herself, refusing to let the unkind words of the bully (**degrade** / **antagonize**) her.

10. For only a small (**increment** / **ambiguity**) in your monthly bill you will gain access to the premium channels, including the sports network!

11. The (**requiem** / **ambiguity**) for Paul echoed through the church as we listened in silence, reflecting on our fallen friend.

12. Before Roger Bannister's record-breaking feat in 1954, many thought it entirely (**implausible** / **unprecedented**) that a human being would ever run a mile in less than four minutes.

13. Many argue that those styles that people label as (**antagonistic** / **unprecedented**) in fashion are simply updated versions of old trends.

14. The (**ambiguity** / **antagonism**) between the brothers increased with time, and soon they had gone twenty years without speaking.

15. The fortune-teller's predictions were so (**ambiguous** / **antagonistic**) that the customer felt he had learned nothing definite about what would happen to him.

16. (**Cognitive** / **Ambiguous**) psychologists study the ways in which the human mind takes in information, operates upon it, and uses it to make decisions.

Hot and Cold:

Write the word from the lesson that is most nearly the *OPPOSITE* of the boldfaced word or words in each sentence below.

17. The **friendship** between the two actors withstood the _____ the media tried to produce by comparing them.

18. Renee hoped her vague answer had been _____ enough to put off making a final decision, but to me the answer was **clear**: She didn't want to go to prom with me.

19. Our profits have grown by steady _____ of 1 percent and have shown no **fluctuations** for nearly 3 years now.

20. While it's _____ that we'll have a colony on Mars by 2050, it's very **reasonable** to expect that we'll have learned much about "the Red Planet" by then.

21. The _____ piece of performance art, which shocked everyone with its unfamiliarity, stood out among the rows of more **traditional** pieces.

22. Never settle for a partner who _____ you in public or in private; instead, seek someone who **dignifies** you at all times and helps you put your best foot forward.

Applying Yourself:

Choose the best word to complete each of the following sentences.

23. No one could explain the _____ between the two of them; they had just always hated each other.
    (A) implausibility
    (B) degradation
    (C) antagonism
    (D) increment
    (E) ambiguity

24. Due to the _____ of the proposed plan's success, the council voted that a new, less improbable solution be found.
    (A) requiem
    (B) implausibility
    (C) increment
    (D) antagonism
    (E) ambiguity

25. We sang a(n) _____ for our brothers who had died in the war.
    (A) sarcasm
    (B) implausibility
    (C) increment
    (D) ambiguity
    (E) requiem

26. Chess, unlike checkers, requires the _____ agility of a practiced mind.
    (A) implausible
    (B) degraded
    (C) incremental
    (D) cognitive
    (E) ambiguous

27. Tension in the theater rose in _____ as the play careened toward the climax.
    (A) increments
    (B) requiems
    (C) degradations
    (D) antagonisms
    (E) ambiguity

28. The recent oil spill has been without previous instance, and its long-term effects look to be _____ as well.
    (A) degraded
    (B) cognitive
    (C) ambiguous
    (D) unprecedented
    (E) antagonistic

29. Janet refused to let her boss _____ her with his unduly cruel words any longer and quit on the spot.
    (A) antagonize
    (B) degrade
    (C) belie
    (D) occlude
    (E) sequester

30. She wondered how she could be sure of the answer when the supporting evidence was so _____.
    (A) implausible
    (B) cognitive
    (C) antagonistic
    (D) ambiguous
    (E) unprecedented

On Your Own:

Write one sentence using each word below to demonstrate your understanding of the word's meaning.

31. **implausible** _____

32. **requiem** _____

33. **cognitive** _____

34. **degrade** _____

35. **increment** _____

36. **antagonism** _____

37. **unprecedented** _____

38. **ambiguous** _____

C2 Advanced Vocabulary 93

First Impressions:

Using the example sentences below, write your own definition of each boldfaced word. Then write the letter of the definition from the box that best matches your definition.

A	adjective: intentional; headstrong; determined to get one's way	**C**	noun: a gathering of people, especially for worship
B	adjective: unresistingly or humbly willing to obey or give in	**D**	adjective: basic; primary; essential

1. _____ The **congregation** collected donations to repair the storm's damage to the church building.

CONGREGATION means: _____

2. _____ She announced her own disagreement with one of the most **fundamental** aspects of her husband's policy, causing many to question her loyalty.

FUNDAMENTAL means: _____

3. _____ The **willful** child refused to take a nap even after he was offered a toy as a reward.

WILLFUL means: _____

4. _____ It is unlikely that someone so **submissive** will ever take charge of the project.

SUBMISSIVE means: _____

A	noun: partnership in an illegal or immoral act	**C**	adjective: uninteresting; dull; ordinary; happening frequently
B	verb: to forcefully eject	**D**	noun: deep wisdom and sound judgment

5. _____ Pilgrims travelled from far and wide to ask questions of the guru and benefit from the **sagacity** he had gained during years of study and contemplation.

SAGACITY means: _____

6. _____ With several items of incriminating evidence the prosecution proved the **complicity** of the defendant in the embezzlement case.

COMPLICITY means: _____

7. _____ The bailiff was asked to **oust** the unruly witness from the courtroom.

OUST means: _____

8. _____ Bored with her **quotidian** life, Margaret decided to go on a wild vacation.

QUOTIDIAN means: _____

Divide and Conquer:
Choose the correct word to complete each of the following sentences.

9. The (**willful** / **quotidian**) days blended together into a great blur of boredom.

10. The legal battle is part of a (**fundamental** / **ousted**) dispute between Internet and media companies over copyright that cuts to the very core of the issue.

11. Even if the argument turns against you, don't become (**willful** / **submissive**); just move on to the next topic.

12. The judge was unwilling to overlook her (**congregation** / **complicity**) in the crime, and so she was charged with a fine.

13. We questioned the (**willfulness** / **sagacity**) of the plan of selling the state's prison to a contractor for short-term profit.

14. After being disciplined, he exhibited (**sagacious** / **submissive**) behavior in an attempt to show that he knew he wasn't in charge.

15. Security (**ousted** / **submitted**) me from the meeting as soon as I suggested that our CEO had committed fraud.

16. The (**submission** / **congregation**) gathered in the sanctuary for the weekly service.

Hot and Cold:
Write the word from the lesson that is most nearly the *OPPOSITE* of the boldfaced word or words in each sentence below.

17. Because he tended toward a more _____ approach to conflict resolution, Randy allowed his **dominant** older brother to exert his will in most cases.

18. This kind of complex problem requires some _____ and plenty of thought, not just whatever **foolishness** comes into your mind first.

19. This **unusual** series of events is certainly not _____ by any standards.

20. Of the two brothers, one was _____ and difficult to manage, while the other was more **passive** and much easier to control.

21. Audience participation is a _____ part of the show, and I won't be able to perform without it, but whether or not the audience members I call on perform well is **inessential**.

22. You may not have kidnapped Sandra, but your claimed **innocence** in her disappearance when 12 witnesses place you at the scene points to your _____.

23. After the former president of the board was _____ by the majority who disliked him, a newer leader with a higher approval rating was **instated**.

Applying Yourself:
Choose the best word to complete each of the following sentences.

24. The student's discovery of his talent in the performing arts has transformed him from a meek nobody into a(n) _____ actor.
    (A) willful
    (B) submissive
    (C) fundamental
    (D) quotidian
    (E) sagacious

25. After the scandal, the people chose to _____ the disgraced politician in the next election.
    (A) acclaim
    (B) oust
    (C) submit
    (D) congregate
    (E) deviate

26. Jeffrey's demeanor immediately changed from gregarious to _____ whenever a stronger personality entered the room.
    (A) ousted
    (B) sage
    (C) submissive
    (D) quotidian
    (E) willful

27. Were I to cover for your crime, I would be engaging in _____ and could be charged.
    (A) sagacity
    (B) complicity
    (C) submission
    (D) willfulness
    (E) congregation

28. Going to work is a(n) _____ activity that people have to do every week day, all year.
    (A) ousted
    (B) willful
    (C) fundamental
    (D) quotidian
    (E) sage

29. John Locke argued that humans should have three _____ rights: life, liberty, and the pursuit of property.
    (A) congregated
    (B) submissive
    (C) willful
    (D) quotidian
    (E) fundamental

30. Maya had no doubt that her _____ would vote to donate some of the church's money to victims of the disaster.
    (A) grandiosity
    (B) complicity
    (C) fundament
    (D) congregation
    (E) sagacity

31. We would do well to rely upon the _____ of our forefathers in these times of crisis.
    (A) willfulness
    (B) submissiveness
    (C) willfulness
    (D) sagacity
    (E) congregation

On Your Own:
Write one sentence using each word below to demonstrate your understanding of the word's meaning.

32. **oust** _____

33. **willful** _____

34. **complicity** _____

35. **submissive** _____

36. **fundamental** _____

37. **congregation** _____

38. **sagacity** _____

39. **quotidian** _____

C2 Advanced Vocabulary 94

First Impressions:

Using the example sentences below, write your own definition of each boldfaced word. Then write the letter of the definition from the box that best matches your definition.

A	verb: to spend; to use up	**C**	noun: someone who enjoys luxuries of life, such as food
B	noun: generous giving of gifts	**D**	adjective: seemingly indifferent to, or unaffected by, pleasure or pain; indifferent

1. _____ Many sought the **largess** of the Godfather on the day of his daughter's wedding, as they knew that by tradition he would not refuse any request made on this day.

LARGESS means: _____

2. _____ My father **expended** all his resources sending me to an expensive private school.

EXPEND means: _____

3. _____ A **bon vivant** of the first order, Nelson refused to eat anywhere but at the fanciest, most expensive restaurants.

BON VIVANT means: _____

4. _____ John's **stoic** nature made him emotionally unresponsive to any sort of event.

STOIC means: _____

A	verb: to absolve (someone) from blame or fault; to release someone from an obligation	**C**	noun: a tendency to behave a certain way
B	adjective: overly theatrical or melodramatic in character or style	**D**	adjective: oppressively constant; harsh or inflexible

5. _____ The child's **histrionic** wails did not impress his mother, who knew that her son was only crying in order to get a new toy.

HISTRIONIC means: _____

6. _____ Tina has a **propensity** for lying, so Gene had learned to take her claims as fiction rather than fact.

PROPENSITY means: _____

7. _____ The townspeople gathered together to build a wall of sand bags, hoping to slow the **relentless** onslaught of the flood waters.

RELENTLESS means: _____

8. _____ Franklin's confession **exonerated** me from the crime.

EXONERATE means: _____

Divide and Conquer:
Choose the correct word to complete each of the following sentences.

9. My mother has the (**propensity / stoicism**) to see only the good in her children and never the bad.

10. Richard, a true (**bon vivant / exoneration**), held huge dinner parties full of rare delicacies several times each year.

11. The little boy who cried wolf fooled everyone so many times with his (**histrionics / propensity**) that when there was genuine reason to fear, no one believed him.

12. Though he had injuries ranging from a sprained hand to a gash on his forehead, the (**relentless / exoneration**) running back continued to power forward for yards.

13. Our family (**exonerated / expended**) all its collective energy during an exhausting week of painting the house and preparing it for sale.

14. His (**histrionic / stoic**) reactions to any emotional or painful event gave him a reputation for being unfeeling.

15. Olivia was (**exonerated / expended**) of any wrong-doing in the matter, as she was in the Netherlands at the time of the accident.

16. The (**largess / stoicism**) of the business tycoon ranged from the donation of necessary foodstuffs to the founding of entire universities.

Hot and Cold:
Write the word from the lesson that is most nearly the *OPPOSITE* of the boldfaced word or words in each sentence below.

17. The criminal was _____ during his second trial but **convicted** in his first.

18. The child's short attention span meant he had a _____ for straying away from the task at hand and a **disinclination** for finishing his homework on his first attempt.

19. After 3 months of living as an **ascetic** in the mountains with little more than a stone cabin to cover my head and berries to sustain me, I took up the life of a _____ in the city and enjoyed every luxury I could afford.

20. The blank, _____ face Fernando wore masked the deeply **sensitive** person within; he was much more affected by what people said and did than he ever let on.

21. Under its original CEO, the corporation was known for its _____ with its employees, distributing large Christmas bonuses; these days, however, upper management is in a terrible rut of **miserliness** and the pocket strings are tighter than ever.

22. Alongside the king's _____ taxing of the lower classes was his occasionally **merciful** distribution of bread and vital goods.

23. Try to **save** as much money as possible rather than _____ it on pointless items.

24. Leonard found that the best way to handle his boyfriend's _____ mood swings was to take a totally **stoic** approach and refuse to take part in the emotional display.

Applying Yourself:
Choose the best word to complete each of the following sentences.

25. Sheila, a socialite extraordinaire, attracted _____ from across the city to sample the delicacies at her dinner party.
    (A) histrionics
    (B) propensities
    (C) stoicism
    (D) bon vivants
    (E) largess

26. The new evidence _____ him; it proved he could not have possibly committed the crime.
    (A) expended
    (B) exonerated
    (C) assented
    (D) acclaimed
    (E) deviated

27. The student had a(n) _____ for art; she could effortlessly produce amazing pencil drawings.
    - (A) propensity
    - (B) largess
    - (C) stoicism
    - (D) exoneration
    - (E) bon vivant

28. _____ defensive pressure over the course of the entire game caused the other team to lose its nerve by the final buzzer.
    - (A) Relentless
    - (B) Histrionic
    - (C) Exonerated
    - (D) Stoic
    - (E) Puerile

29. I don't think we should _____ our resources on this process; it doesn't seem that helpful.
    - (A) exonerate
    - (B) assent
    - (C) acclaim
    - (D) deviate
    - (E) expend

30. By your _____ outburst, I take it that you are begging for sympathy.
    - (A) stoic
    - (B) histrionic
    - (C) relentless
    - (D) exonerated
    - (E) expended

31. Larry hoped that his _____ would encourage Lisa to come back to him, but material gifts weren't important to her.
    - (A) largess
    - (B) stoicism
    - (C) relentlessness
    - (D) propensity
    - (E) exoneration

32. The _____ expression that Henry had on his face while watching the World War II documentary made it look like he was not affected by what he saw.
    - (A) stoic
    - (B) histrionic
    - (C) exonerated
    - (D) expended
    - (E) scintillating

On Your Own:

Write one sentence using each word below to demonstrate your understanding of the word's meaning.

33. **bon vivant** _____

34. **largess** _____

35. **stoic** _____

36. **expend** _____

37. **relentless** _____

38. **propensity** _____

39. **histrionic** _____

40. **exonerate** _____

C2 Advanced Vocabulary 95

First Impressions:

Using the example sentences below, write your own definition of each boldfaced word. Then write the letter of the definition from the box that best matches your definition.

A	noun: a system of belief that motivates a person or group	**C**	verb: to censor a piece of writing by removing offensive portions
B	adjective: complete; necessary for completeness	**D**	adjective: unable to be hurt; invincible

1. _____ Capitalism and socialism are two economic **ideologies** that have impacted the course of history for the last century.

IDEOLOGIES means: _____

2. _____ The film was considered unfit for publication until it was heavily **bowdlerized** by the censors.

BOWDLERIZE means: _____

3. _____ Supposedly, the new type of plane is **invulnerable** to missiles and is excellent for use in combat.

INVULNERABLE means: _____

4. _____ Many teenagers consider the Internet to be an **integral** part of their lives, despite the thousands of generations that did without it.

INTEGRAL means: _____

A	noun: a mark of something disgraceful	**C**	verb: to claim without a right or justification
B	verb: to be thankful for; to increase in value; to be fully conscious of; to hold in high regard	**D**	adjective: obscure; known only by a few

5. _____ While some value the idea of universal healthcare, others feel that it requires the government to **arrogate** the right to make decisions usually reserved for individuals.

ARROGATE means: _____

6. _____ Timothy was a regular winner on trivia night because of his deep knowledge of even the most **arcane** subjects.

ARCANE means: _____

7. _____ Shop owners once held a **stigma** against the Irish immigrants to the US, refusing to do business with them.

STIGMA means: _____

8. _____ Only now that I have children of my own can I **appreciate** all that my parents have done for me.

APPRECIATE means: _____

Divide and Conquer:
Choose the correct word to complete each of the following sentences.

9. The course dealt with defining and outlining the major (**ideologies** / **stigmas**) that have driven history, including religions, political systems, and social structures.

10. Many feel that a (**arcane** / **bowdlerized**) edition of Orwell's 1984 embodies the acts of censorship warned against in the novel.

11. Miguel spent his Saturday nights in the deep archives of the library, immersing himself in (**invulnerable** / **arcane**) lore.

12. I felt that my peers held a(n) (**arrogation** / **stigma**) against me for studying so hard.

13. Micah's hope was that the value of his home would (**stigmatize** / **appreciate**) as the economy improved.

14. Iron Man is (**invulnerable** / **integral**) to attack by bullets due to his heavy armor.

15. The fear of the chairman was that a few committee members were (**arrogating** / **bowdlerizing**) to themselves responsibilities usually fulfilled by other individuals.

16. The citizens rallied to save the aging civic center, which they felt had served as an (**stigmatized** / **integral**) part of the community for decades.

Hot and Cold:
Write the word from the lesson that is most nearly the *OPPOSITE* of the boldfaced word or words in each sentence below.

17. The tablet, written in a(n) _____ language, will have to be translated into the **common** language by one of the few academics who can actually read it.

18. I am only concerned with the advancements that will be _____ to our success; anything **peripheral** is of no interest to me.

19. Though the rebels _____ the royal land that they technically had no claim to, they made up for their crime by **donating** the land to struggling farmers.

20. Greg thought he was _____ to illness, but he soon found he was **susceptible** to throat infections.

21. The new student feared that coming from out-of-state would be a _____ against her in her new classmates' eyes, but it turned out that her unique past was a **credit** to her.

22. The value of the stock has _____ significantly over the years, meaning we were wise to have bought more shares of this company and to have sold the shares that are now **depreciating**.

Applying Yourself:
Choose the best word to complete each of the following sentences.

23. I _____ your need to have your own space, but we have too many people on the floor for each person to get his or her own office.
    (A) execute
    (B) arrogate
    (C) appreciate
    (D) stigmatize
    (E) bowdlerize

24. The history of the ancient empire is a(n) _____ subject studied only by the most dedicated scholars.
    (A) arcane
    (B) integral
    (C) arrogated
    (D) stigmatized
    (E) invulnerable

25. The current American government is a clash of two _____, one advocating limited government and the other advocating large government.
    (A) integrations
    (B) appreciations
    (C) arrogations
    (D) stigmas
    (E) ideologies

26. There is definitely a _____ against those who physically bully the disabled, for who could respect someone so cruel?
    (A) ideology
    (B) appreciation
    (C) arrogation
    (D) stigma
    (E) invulnerability

27. The workers' contract stipulated that they would receive a cut of the profits, but management _____ those funds in a brazen power play.
    (A) appreciated
    (B) arrogated
    (C) stigmatized
    (D) bowdlerized
    (E) executed

28. The Titanic was supposed to be _____, but it sank anyway.
    (A) integral
    (B) appreciated
    (C) ideological
    (D) invulnerable
    (E) arcane

29. While many consider the movie's original script hilarious, the _____ version removed the colorful humor that gives the story its charm.
    (A) integral
    (B) bowdlerized
    (C) arrogated
    (D) arcane
    (E) stigmatized

30. Precise timing is _____ to the tumbling routine's success; if we're even a split-second off, everyone will crash to the ground.
    (A) appreciated
    (B) ideological
    (C) arcane
    (D) bowdlerized
    (E) integral

On Your Own:
Write one sentence using each word below to demonstrate your understanding of the word's meaning.

31. **integral** _____

32. **appreciate** _____

33. **arrogate** _____

34. **ideology** _____

35. **arcane** _____

36. **invulnerable** _____

37. **stigma** _____

38. **bowdlerize** _____

C2 Advanced Vocabulary 96

First Impressions:

Using the example sentences below, write your own definition of each boldfaced word. Then write the letter of the definition from the box that best matches your definition.

A	adjective: stingy; miserly; cheap	**C**	noun: a false statement intended to hurt another's reputation
B	noun: a cause of ruin, destruction, or death	**D**	adjective: commonplace; overused

1. _____ College would be the **bane** of Anahi's life: if the lack of sleep didn't kill her, then her boring classes would.

BANE means: _____

2. _____ While Samson felt that the speech was fresh and original, Miguel found many of its ideas rather **trite**.

TRITE means: _____

3. _____ I've grown **parsimonious** since I lost my job and have had to count every penny I spend.

PARSIMONIOUS means: _____

4. _____ Such **calumny** is reprehensible; even if you disagree with your opponent, there is no excuse for spreading lies about her.

CALUMNY means: _____

A	verb: to weaken or spoil	**C**	noun: one who wanders from place to place
B	adjective: traveling regularly from place to place	**D**	noun: the mood or atmosphere of a place

5. _____ The dim lights and modern music contributed greatly to the hip **ambience** of the restaurant.

AMBIENCE means: _____

6. _____ The people are **nomads**, travelling from city to city selling medicines.

NOMAD means: _____

7. _____ The emotional impact of the film's scene was **vitiated** by the loudly talking couple in the front row.

VITIATE means: _____

8. _____ Kyle spent his youth as an **itinerant** musician before settling down from his wanderings to take up an office job.

ITINERANT means: _____

Divide and Conquer:

Choose the correct word to complete each of the following sentences.

9. Though hundreds of theories have been put forward to explain the fall of the Roman empire, no one can name the (**bane / ambience**) of the great civilization with any certainty.

10. The (**parsimonious / itinerant**) young man refused to spend more than a few dollars on his entire family for holiday gifts.

11. The case, which granted corporations the right to contribute vast amounts of money to political campaigns, (**vitiated / defamed**) years of campaign finance reform.

12. I've always dreamed of living the life of a (**parsimony / nomad**) and visiting every country in the world.

13. The (**trite / itinerant**) musician played shows in 38 states in one year.

14. The senator was unwilling to tolerate (**bane / calumny**) and so countered each false accusation with several recriminations.

15. The head speechwriter will dismiss all (**trite / itinerant**) ideas, so be as creative as you can be.

16. The (**nomad / ambience**) of the library is far more conducive to studying than that of the noisy coffeehouse.

Hot and Cold:

Write the word from the lesson that is most nearly the *OPPOSITE* of the boldfaced word or words in each sentence below.

17. _____ by a prolonged flu, Margaret was unable to attend a single meeting, write a single document, or **assist** in any way until her condition improved.

18. False as it may be, a bit of _____ from an otherwise reputable source is enough to ruin the reputation of any aspiring director, regardless of the **accolades** she has received up to that point.

19. I have always been _____, spending no longer than a year in any one place, and have never understood how anyone could be content to be **stationary**.

20. Able to provide years of clean energy or level cities to the ground, nuclear power can be civilization's _____ or its **salvation**.

21. While the _____ enjoyed his life of movement, he sometimes wondered what it would have been like to be a **person with a permanent home**.

22. The _____ business man suddenly shocked everyone by presenting them with a **lavish** feast with generous portions.

23. It may sound _____, but the phrase "You mean the world to me" can express a variety of meaningful and **unique** emotions.

Applying Yourself:

Choose the best word to complete each of the following sentences.

24. The restaurant enhanced its romantic _____ by lowering the lights and playing light Spanish guitar music over the speakers.
    - (A) bane
    - (B) ambience
    - (C) vitiation
    - (D) parsimony
    - (E) calumny

25. Sam was a(n) _____, never staying in one place for long.
    - (A) vitiation
    - (B) bane
    - (C) ambience
    - (D) calumny
    - (E) nomad

26. The _____ life of a nature photographer is not for everyone, as it makes having a family life almost impossible.
    (A) itinerant
    (B) parsimonious
    (C) vitiated
    (D) trite
    (E) nomadic

27. During the meeting, it became apparent that Tom had not researched the project subject very well, for while the other members had thought of original solutions to the problem, Tom offered only _____ ideas.
    (A) nomadic
    (B) ambient
    (C) parsimonious
    (D) trite
    (E) vitiated

28. I couldn't believe how my sterling reputation fell apart so quickly based on the _____ of a dodgy witness.
    (A) nomads
    (B) ambience
    (C) bane
    (D) vitiation
    (E) calumny

29. In his time, Galileo was considered to be the _____ of religion because of his teachings on the composition of the solar system.
    (A) triteness
    (B) ambience
    (C) calumny
    (D) bane
    (E) vitiation

30. Ebenezer Scrooge was a(n) _____ banker who never bought fancy things or gave to charity.
    (A) ambient
    (B) trite
    (C) itinerant
    (D) nomadic
    (E) parsimonious

On Your Own:
Write one sentence using each word below to demonstrate your understanding of the word's meaning.

31. **calumny** _____

32. **ambience** _____

33. **trite** _____

34. **nomad** _____

35. **itinerant** _____

36. **bane** _____

37. **vitiate** _____

38. **parsimonious** _____

C2 Advanced Vocabulary 97

First Impressions:

Using the example sentences below, write your own definition of each boldfaced word. Then write the letter of the definition from the box that best matches your definition.

A	adjective: courteous, gracious, or friendly; heartfelt	**C**	noun: a system in which wealth, goods, and businesses are controlled by individuals instead of a government
B	adjective: obstinately stubborn; determined to resist authority	**D**	verb: to babble

1. _____ One debater argued that **capitalism** promotes selfishness, but the other stated that when citizens are the owners of property they are actually more likely to cooperate with each other.

CAPITALISM means: _____

2. _____ Bridgett was so **recalcitrant** in her ways that a stack of scientific papers three inches tall wouldn't change her mind.

RECALCITRANT means: _____

3. _____ Michaela was pleased with the **cordial** welcome she received on her first day at her new job.

CORDIAL means: _____

4. _____ I won't **prattle** on about how making your coffee at home is the key to getting rich, but I will say that it serves a money-saving purpose.

PRATTLE means: _____

A	verb: to make worse	**C**	verb: to recognize or point out differences between things or people
B	adjective: polite; chivalrous; brave	**D**	adjective: extremely demanding

5. _____ The new health reform law might **exacerbate** emergency room overcrowding, according to health care facility experts.

EXACERBATE means: _____

6. _____ The company's stated policy is to **discriminate** only based on merit, not on gender or ethnicity.

DISCRIMINATE means: _____

7. _____ The officer demanded fifty push-ups in an **exacting** voice, and the new recruit didn't dare disobey.

EXACTING means: _____

8. _____ The **gallant** young boy ran after me to return a $50 bill that had dropped out of my pocket.

GALLANT means: _____

Divide and Conquer:

Choose the correct word to complete each of the following sentences.

9. Joan of Arc was a (**gallant** / **discriminating**) figure known for her bravery and sacrifice.

10. During the Cold War, the (**capitalist** / **gallant**) United States competed technologically, economically, and ideologically against the communist Soviet Union.

11. Mrs. Landingham, a (**gallant** / **cordial**) hostess, courteously took her guests' jackets at the door.

12. Unhealthful eating not only adds extra pounds, but may also (**exact** / **exacerbate**) existing health problems.

13. Could we kindly have an end to candidates who lie, get caught by the press, and then (**prattle** / **discriminate**) on about their integrity?

14. A skilled conductor can (**prattle** / **discriminate**) a single flat note from a correctly tuned one in the midst of an entire symphony.

15. The associate, convinced of her own brilliance, remained (**exacting** / **recalcitrant**) as her superiors refuted her argument.

16. The performances of acrobats are extremely (**gallant** / **exacting**), requiring incredible strength, stamina, and precision.

Hot and Cold:

Write the word from the lesson that is most nearly the *OPPOSITE* of the boldfaced word or words in each sentence below.

17. Having received such a _____ welcome upon his first visit to the restaurant, Frank was shocked to have been snubbed with a **rude** gesture upon his next trip.

18. Priya asked her brother to stop his _____ and instead **speak clearly** about serious matters.

19. In the early 1990s, many Eastern European countries switched from a form of government called **communism** to that of _____ and had to transfer control of property and resources from governments to people.

20. We were rewarded for a year of _____ training with a **relaxing**, free vacation on the beaches of Hawaii.

21. Sir James, a _____ knight, defeated the **cowardly** warlock Merdinir.

22. I found it difficult to _____ between artists of the period since their styles were so similar and tended to **conglomerate** them into one great mass labeled "The Modernists".

23. Between the twins, the differences were clear: Tony, always _____, refused to do anything his mother asked, while Tito, ever **obedient**, couldn't be persuaded to break the rules.

24. Because politicians had _____ the recession by cutting public spending, it was difficult for their successors to **improve** the situation quickly.

Applying Yourself:

Choose the best word to complete each of the following sentences.

25. Most economists adopt a balanced version of _____, in which government oversight regulates excesses of the free market.
    (A) cordiality
    (B) capitalism
    (C) exacerbation
    (D) recalcitrance
    (E) prattling

26. His brother's impromptu visit _____the bad mood he was in, instead of making him feel better.
    (A) exalted
    (B) circumvented
    (C) exacerbated
    (D) prattled
    (E) exacted

27. As Robert grew into his teens, his once docile nature transformed into a more _____ one, and he often found himself in detention.
    (A) recalcitrant
    (B) capitalistic
    (C) discriminating
    (D) exacerbated
    (E) gallant

28. The teenager _____ on in response to her mother's speech.
    (A) discriminated
    (B) exacted
    (C) circumvented
    (D) prattled
    (E) exalted

29. When the students first met their teacher, they assumed her coursework would be easy due to her informal manners, but they soon realized that her tests were _____ and her grading system was harsh.
    (A) cordial
    (B) exacting
    (C) capitalistic
    (D) discriminating
    (E) exacerbated

30. Although they made a _____ attempt to retake the lead, they ultimately lost to the opposing team.
    (A) recalcitrant
    (B) gallant
    (C) exacerbated
    (D) exacting
    (E) cordial

31. She extended _____ greetings to the delegates of the other countries, hoping to make them feel welcome.
    (A) gallant
    (B) exacting
    (C) recalcitrant
    (D) discriminating
    (E) cordial

32. Knowledgeable critics will _____ between a genuine Da Vinci and a cheap imitation.
    (A) exact
    (B) discriminate
    (C) prattle
    (D) exacerbate
    (E) exalt

On Your Own:
Write one sentence using each word below to demonstrate your understanding of the word's meaning.

33. **gallant** _____

34. **exacting** _____

35. **cordial** _____

36. **exacerbate** _____

37. **recalcitrant** _____

38. **discriminate** _____

39. **capitalism** _____

40. **prattle** _____

C2 Advanced Vocabulary 98

First Impressions:
Using the example sentences below, write your own definition of each boldfaced word. Then write the letter of the definition from the box that best matches your definition.

A	noun: excited activity or movement	**C**	noun: use of force or intimidation to get someone to behave or act in a desired way
B	verb: to lessen; to fade	**D**	adjective: having a tendency to drink, especially alcohol

1. _____ The moon will continue to **wane** until it is a crescent.

WANE means: _____

2. _____ The case was thrown out of the court after it was discovered that the defendant had confessed under **coercion**.

COERCION means: _____

3. _____ Alcoholics Anonymous has helped members to overcome their **bibulous** tendencies since its founding in 1935.

BIBULOUS means: _____

4. _____ The **bustle** of the city made it impossible for Ricardo to sleep.

BUSTLE means: _____

A	adjective: rising again, or tending to rise again; reviving	**C**	verb: to act out without using words
B	adjective: difficult to change because of habit or custom	**D**	adjective: related to a cow or ox

5. _____ In rare instances, **bovine** illnesses such as cowpox or hoof and mouth disease can mutate and affect humans.

BOVINE means: _____

6. _____ The **resurgent** basketball team scored 20 points in a row to turn a sure defeat into a narrow victory.

RESURGENT means: _____

7. _____ Gesturing toward the door, I **pantomimed** that I was ready to leave.

PANTOMIME means: _____

8. _____ Because Thomas is an **inveterate** braggart, it is unlikely that he will change his ways any time soon.

INVETERATE means: _____

Divide and Conquer:
Choose the correct word to complete each of the following sentences.

9. Because I didn't know sign language, I used (**pantomime** / **coercion**) to communicate with Marlene.

10. As the movie dragged on, her initial interest in it began to (**wane** / **resurge**).

11. Mitchell's mother worried that his (**inveterate** / **bibulous**) habits would lead him to trouble with his health or the law.

12. She (**bustled** / **waned**) up the stairs, eager to share her good news.

13. Asked for the secret of his success, the aged athlete said that he had always been a(n) (**coerced** / **inveterate**) competitor.

14. Professor Lamberski accused students who failed to follow current events of wallowing in (**bovine** / **coercion**) ignorance.

15. After Congress passed an amendment that allowed African-Americans to vote, some southerners used (**waning** / **coercion**) to prevent them from going to the voting booths.

16. The (**inveterate** / **resurgent**) Falcons have overcome a winless opening day to win five straight games.

Hot and Cold:
Write the word from the lesson that is most nearly the *OPPOSITE* of the boldfaced word or words in each sentence below.

17. We were all surprised Uncle John was so _____ when the rest of the family was totally **abstemious** and never touched even a drop of alcohol.

18. People tend to respond much better to being **gently convinced** using facts and reason than to _____, which makes them feel attacked and threatened.

19. While adults appear to be _____ creatures, impossible to reprogram, children in their early lives are quite **customizable** and easy to imbue with certain habits or to be prevented from forming others.

20. The popularity of heavily padded jackets has _____, and skinny jeans have **grown** in popularity instead.

21. The game restricted him from **speaking**, so he had to tell the whole story in _____.

22. As the crowd _____ through the train station, Muriel **drifted** among them like an untethered balloon.

23. While old-fashioned financial conservatism is _____ in the area—teens seem to be adopting the ideals of their grandparents rather than those of their parents—social conservatism is **declining** as the youth shifts toward progressive social policies.

Applying Yourself:
Choose the best word to complete each of the following sentences.

24. Since I had laryngitis that day, I had to _____ instructions about how to feed the cat to the neighbor.
    (A) exact
    (B) resurge
    (C) pantomime
    (D) bustle
    (E) coerce

25. Our family would love for our _____ grandma to use email, but she refuses to learn how to use a computer.
    (A) inveterate
    (B) resurgent
    (C) bovine
    (D) bibulous
    (E) waning

26. Governments have increasingly used _____ to extract information from their own citizens, raising objections from human rights organizations.
    (A) bustling
    (B) coercion
    (C) resurgence
    (D) pantomimes
    (E) waning

27. The worldwide _____ population has exploded since the demand for steak has increased in the developing world.
    (A) resurgent
    (B) inveterate
    (C) bovine
    (D) coerced
    (E) bibulous

28. The _____ revelers gathered at the bar during the raucous fraternity party.
    (A) resurgent
    (B) bovine
    (C) inveterate
    (D) coerced
    (E) bibulous

29. The economic recession has many worried of lasting effects, but I think that the economy will show its _____ quality by bouncing back soon enough.
    (A) bovine
    (B) resurgent
    (C) bustling
    (D) bibulous
    (E) inveterate

30. Justin's aunt _____ around the kitchen, seemingly trying to do everything at once.
    (A) bustled
    (B) waned
    (C) resurged
    (D) pantomimed
    (E) prattled

31. The power of the sun _____ as sunset approached.
    (A) waned
    (B) bustled
    (C) pantomimed
    (D) prattled
    (E) resurged

On Your Own:
Write one sentence using each word below to demonstrate your understanding of the word's meaning.

32. **pantomime** _____

33. **resurgent** _____

34. **bovine** _____

35. **bustle** _____

36. **bibulous** _____

37. **inveterate** _____

38. **coercion** _____

39. **wane** _____

C2 Advanced Vocabulary 99

First Impressions:

Using the example sentences below, write your own definition of each boldfaced word. Then write the letter of the definition from the box that best matches your definition.

A	noun: combination of multiple items to create a single new item	**C**	adjective: lacking energy; gloomy
B	adjective: true to life; intense in color; producing clear images	**D**	noun: excessive desire, especially for wealth

1. _____ The novel is **vivid** in its description of both the beauty and the filth of Elizabethan England so that the reader feels as if he or she is seeing what the protagonist sees.

VIVID means: _____

2. _____ Such was Susan's **cupidity** that she swore that she would let no obstacle stand in the way of her becoming a billionaire.

CUPIDITY means: _____

3. _____ The book is a **synthesis** of ideas from many sources, combining a variety of information into a single useable source.

SYNTHESIS means: _____

4. _____ When Carlotta found out that her novel had been rejected for publication for the fifth time, she spent the rest of the day in a **saturnine** mood.

SATURNINE means: _____

A	verb: to prevent from happening; to make impossible	**C**	adjective: immoral; dirty or filthy
B	adjective: changeable frequently; variable	**D**	noun: bitterness; hatred

5. _____ The public was shocked when news of the politician's **sordid** love affair reached them.

SORDID means: _____

6. _____ Liz's moods were somewhat **fickle**; one minute she would be giggling in childlike glee, and the next minute she would be sulking angrily.

FICKLE means: _____

7. _____ Though he wanted to be a fighter pilot, his color-blindness **precluded** his acceptance into the Air Force.

PRECLUDE means: _____

8. _____ The feud between the Hatfields and the McCoys was marked by decades of **rancor** and ill-will.

RANCOR means: _____

Divide and Conquer:
Choose the correct word to complete each of the following sentences.

9. The (**fickleness / synthesis**) of the puzzle pieces revealed a picture of a waterfall.

10. It is best to forgive and forget so that minor annoyance does not fester and become (**rancor / fickleness**) toward your friends and family.

11. I'm afraid your actions (**synthesize / preclude**) any constructive discussion.

12. I've never seen the equal of today's rainbow; the conditions produced such (**vivid / fickle**) colors as may never be seen again.

13. Albert was so (**saturnine / fickle**) that he changed his major five times before graduating from college.

14. Rather than feeling (**saturnine / precluded**) at the prospect of a six-hour study session, the students were filled with energy and enthusiasm.

15. The villain's (**cupidity / rancor**) ultimately led to his demise when his refusal to let go of the golden statue caused him to fall from the helicopter.

16. The (**vivid / sordid**) account of the scandal served as fodder for the tabloids for months. I'll have no choice but to ask you to leave.

Hot and Cold:
Write the word from the lesson that is most nearly the *OPPOSITE* of the boldfaced word or words in each sentence below.

17. The bright sun in the middle of the painting was made all the more _____ by its setting of **dull**, murky waters and a brown horizon.

18. After months of feeling as **happy** and vivacious as can be, a sudden _____ mood overtook me and threatened to send me into a state of depression the likes of which I'd never experienced.

19. Having been impressed by Beth's **compassion**, I was surprised to hear such _____ in her voice.

20. Joining the swim team may _____ you from getting an after-school job, but it will **facilitate** increased fitness and the odds of your getting an athletic scholarship.

21. The family's _____ came to a head when they realized they were more than $200,000 in debt and had to learn some **humility** if they were ever going to climb out.

22. My intentions for the future are _____, and I can never stick to the same plan for longer than a few weeks, but I believe that, in time, my desires will become more **constant**.

23. The details of this _____ affair of corruption and deceit will surely ruin the formerly **pristine** reputation of the respected senator.

24. The _____ of music from composers from different nations will do much to reduce the apparent **separation** of people by nation.

Applying Yourself:
Choose the best word to complete each of the following sentences.

25. Should we hope to have a lasting peace between Israel and Palestine, we must first eliminate the _____ that exists between the two nations.
    (A) rancor
    (B) vividness
    (C) cupidity
    (D) fickleness
    (E) synthesis

26. The painter's hallmark is the contrast of _____ colors in surrounding darkness.
    (A) vivid
    (B) sordid
    (C) saturnine
    (D) fickle
    (E) synthesized

27. Although he now led a moral life, his _____ past reminded him of the person he once was.
    (A) precluded
    (B) fickle
    (C) sordid
    (D) synthesized
    (E) vivid

28. Remember that though the fans can be occasionally _____, they tend to have at least one team they constantly favor above all others.
    (A) sordid
    (B) vivid
    (C) fickle
    (D) precluded
    (E) rancorous

29. Lottery winners must guard their fortunes against the _____ of relatives looking to gain a piece of the pie for themselves.
    (A) fickleness
    (B) cupidity
    (C) sordidness
    (D) vividness
    (E) preclusion

30. A _____ pall descended upon the funeral, indicative of the sad occasion.
    (A) vivid
    (B) saturnine
    (C) rancorous
    (D) fickle
    (E) precluded

31. Steel is not an element; rather it is the _____ of iron ore, coal, and alloys.
    (A) grandiose
    (B) vividness
    (C) fickleness
    (D) preclusion
    (E) synthesis

32. A prior engagement will _____ me from attending your party.
    (A) preclude
    (B) obliterate
    (C) laud
    (D) vivify
    (E) synthesize

On Your Own:
Write one sentence using each word below to demonstrate your understanding of the word's meaning.

33. **vivid** _____

34. **sordid** _____

35. **saturnine** _____

36. **cupidity** _____

37. **rancor** _____

38. **fickle** _____

39. **preclude** _____

40. **synthesis** _____

C2 Advanced Vocabulary 100

First Impressions:

Using the example sentences below, write your own definition of each boldfaced word. Then write the letter of the definition from the box that best matches your definition.

A	verb: to become clear; to harden into a clear shape	**C**	noun: a sign of future events or circumstances
B	adjective: impatient; stubborn	**D**	noun: a curse or insult

1. _____ The king's soothsayer warned that the eclipse was a **portent** of a deadly war that was yet to come.

PORTENT means: _____

2. _____ After standing in line under the hot sun for two hours, the fans became **restive** and eager to get inside the air-conditioned theater.

RESTIVE means: _____

3. _____ The details of the situation **crystallized** slowly as we asked more and more questions.

CRYSTALLIZED means: _____

4. _____ On his deathbed, the warlord declared a **malediction** upon the households of his enemies.

MALEDICTION means: _____

A	adjective: concerned only with the self	**C**	adjective: desiring greater power or influence
B	verb: to defame; to destroy confidence in; to disbelieve	**D**	adjective: excessively or elaborately decorated

5. _____ The crown was covered with **ornate** scrollwork and finely-cut stones.

ORNATE means: _____

6. _____ The **ambitious** knight planned to overthrow the king.

AMBITIOUS means: _____

7. _____ The political candidates each tried to **discredit** the policies of their opponents to make themselves look better.

DISCREDIT means: _____

8. _____ Phillip is incredibly **egocentric**; he complains loudly if at any point he is not the center of attention.

EGOCENTRIC means: _____

Divide and Conquer:

Choose the correct word to complete each of the following sentences.

9. Even the most patient traveler becomes (**egocentric** / **restive**) when faced with a five-hour delay.

10. Though my first impression was mixed, my feelings for him (**crystallized** / **discredited**) after he helped bring my sick mother to the hospital.

11. The scientist felt that the fact that the Earth's temperature has risen so quickly is an alarming (**ambition** / **portent**) of global warming in the twenty-first century.

12. Her habitual dishonesty (**crystallized** / **discredited**) anything she had to say.

13. It was surprising to find a person who typically is so (**egocentric** / **crystallized**) taking a strong interest in the lives of those around him.

14. Baroque architecture is so full of (**egocentric** / **ornate**) decoration that it often looks cluttered.

15. Brittany is (**egocentric** / **ambitious**): one day she would like to become the greatest ballerina in the world.

16. Upon his death, Mercutio utters the (**ambition** / **malediction**), "A plague o' both your houses!"

Hot and Cold:

Write the word from the lesson that is most nearly the *OPPOSITE* of the boldfaced word or words in each sentence below.

17. The painting was _____ as a fake, but the skill required to produce it **validated** the talent of the imposter, regardless.

18. When the syrup began to _____, I microwaved it to help it **soften** again.

19. The good fairies countered the evil witch's _____ with a **blessing** that would serve to protect the child from harm.

20. The manager was **content** with his position and lacked the _____ to try to move up in the company.

21. It isn't my intention to be _____, though I can see that my actions primarily serve myself and are far from **altruistic**.

22. The crowd appeared to become _____ and eager for action, but the speaker remained **placid**, calmly smiling as he spoke, and discussed the most reasonable plan for the people to take.

23. The house was **plain and spare**, without a single speck of _____ decorations on its entire surface.

Applying Yourself:

Choose the best word to complete each of the following sentences.

24. The banking crisis of 2007 caused economists to _____ the role of large financial institutions in our country.
    (A) exact
    (B) resurge
    (C) discredit
    (D) crystallize
    (E) coerce

25. Cheryl was disappointed when her _____ date spent an inordinate amount of time admiring himself in the mirror.
    (A) discredited
    (B) ornate
    (C) ambitious
    (D) restive
    (E) egocentric

26. The ancient Mayans took the comet's appearance as a _____ of the end of the world.
    (A) resurgence
    (B) malediction
    (C) resurgence
    (D) portent
    (E) crystallization

27. The _____ politician would do whatever he had to do in order to become president.
    (A) restive
    (B) ambitious
    (C) egocentric
    (D) discredited
    (E) ornate

28. Ever since the witch doctor uttered a(n) _____ against me for having stepped on his lawn, I've had difficulty sleeping.
    (A) malediction
    (B) ambition
    (C) egocentricity
    (D) ornament
    (E) portent

29. As the situation began to _____, we realized that we were better off than we had thought.
    (A) discredit
    (B) resurge
    (C) exact
    (D) crystallize
    (E) coerce

30. Although a(n) _____ person attacks life with gusto, he cannot truly find tranquility without learning to relax and compromise.
    (A) discredited
    (B) ornate
    (C) ambitious
    (D) egocentric
    (E) restive

31. The old apartment screamed "old money," and its _____ decorations clashed with our modern sensibilities.
    (A) ornate
    (B) restive
    (C) ambitious
    (D) discredited
    (E) egocentric

On Your Own:
Write one sentence using each word below to demonstrate your understanding of the word's meaning.

32. **malediction** _____

33. **ornate** _____

34. **crystallize** _____

35. **discredit** _____

36. **portent** _____

37. **egocentric** _____

38. **ambitious** _____

39. **restive** _____

C2 Advanced Vocabulary 101

First Impressions:

Using the example sentences below, write your own definition of each boldfaced word. Then write the letter of the definition from the box that best matches your definition.

A	noun: words spoken as part of a magical ritual	**C**	verb: to tighten; to squeeze uncomfortably
B	verb: to sue in a courtroom	**D**	adjective: evil; hateful towards another

1. _____ The snake wrapped around his neck tightly, **constricting** his airway.

CONSTRICT means: _____

2. _____ The wizard waved his hands over the cauldron and recited an **incantation**.

INCANTATION means: _____

3. _____ Jim preferred the film's complex characters to the typical altruistic hero and **malevolent** villain.

MALEVOLENT means: _____

4. _____ The angry neighbor threatened to **litigate**, but Angelo assured her that there was no need to involve a judge in their dispute.

LITIGATE means: _____

A	verb: to criticize or condemn harshly	**C**	adjective: wordy
B	noun: a traitor who aids an invading enemy	**D**	noun: a swamp; a problem that is difficult to escape

5. _____ It was reported that the privacy policy is a whopping 5830 words long, even more **verbose** than the Constitution of the United States.

VERBOSE means: _____

6. _____ When Jacob helped the unpopular new manager, the other employees labeled him a **quisling**.

QUISLING means: _____

7. _____ The coach loudly **excoriated** the quarterback after the blunder in the third quarter.

EXCORIATED means: _____

8. _____ The heavy rains turned the dusty road into an impassible **quagmire**.

QUAGMIRE means: _____

Divide and Conquer:

Choose the correct word to complete each of the following sentences.

9. As she cast her (**verbose / malevolent**) gaze upon me, I could feel my sudden burst of bravado shrinking to nothing.

10. During the test Richard muttered the words of the memory aid under his breath as if they were a(n) (**quagmire / incantation**).

11. The man threatened to (**excoriate / litigate**) when the neighbor refused to pay for the damage to his car, but the neighbor assured him that there was no need to involve the courts.

12. The emperor, terrified of (**litigations / quislings**) supportive of the approaching hordes, started executing his own people out of paranoia.

13. Geraldine felt (**quagmired / constricted**) by the villagers' notions of what was proper behavior.

14. The Big Dig was Boston's attempt to solve the inefficient road system, but the project soon turned into a (n) (**quisling / quagmire**) that consumed billions of dollars.

15. The coach (**excoriated / constricted**) the members of the defensive line for their lazy performance at the big game.

16. Once granted the right to debate an issue, especially (**verbose / constricted**) senators can drone for hours.

Hot and Cold:

Write the word from the lesson that is most nearly the *OPPOSITE* of the boldfaced word or words in each sentence below.

17. It only takes one _____ to traitorously cause the demise of countless **loyalists** fighting for their cause.

18. Fran felt _____ by her father's displeasure, even though he hadn't intended his reaction to be taken so harshly, and sought the **praise** she was after elsewhere.

19. I know the book is a classic, but at over 500 pages, I find it much too _____; I prefer more **terse** works that pack plenty of meaning into fewer words.

20. After the **cakewalk** that was last year, the troubles and tribulations of this year make me feel like I'm stuck in a _____.

21. The fairy queen had two daughters: one a **benevolent** sorceress and the other a _____ witch.

22. Thomas cast off the shoes that _____ his feet and **freed** them from those tight leather prisons.

Applying Yourself:

Choose the best word to complete each of the following sentences.

23. The villain hatched a(n) _____ plan to destroy the life of the hero.
    (A) litigated
    (B) excoriated
    (C) verbose
    (D) malevolent
    (E) constricting

24. The witches intoned their _____ to provide Macbeth with visions of the future.
    (A) quagmires
    (B) quislings
    (C) incantation
    (D) verbosity
    (E) litigation

25. Benedict Arnold was forever branded a(n) _____ for his assistance to the invading British force.
    (A) excoriation
    (B) incantation
    (C) constriction
    (D) quagmire
    (E) quisling

26. Rather than _____ those under you for making errors, take a more tactful and positive approach to helping them improve.
    (A) quagmire
    (B) excoriate
    (C) litigate
    (D) constrict
    (E) quagmire

27. The computer company has a policy of _____ against any who would threaten their intellectual property, incurring expensive legal fees.
    (A) incanting
    (B) litigating
    (C) constricting
    (D) excoriating
    (E) eulogizing

28. The seemingly minor procedural amendment turned out to be a(n) _____ that paralyzed the budgetary process in subsequent years.
    (A) incantation
    (B) quisling
    (C) malevolence
    (D) quagmire
    (E) litigation

29. The _____ speech that he delivered to his class seemed too long to most of his classmates.
    (A) litigated
    (B) constricted
    (C) excoriated
    (D) malevolent
    (E) verbose

30. His throat _____ because of his allergy, and he had trouble breathing.
    (A) constricted
    (B) incanted
    (C) excoriated
    (D) litigated
    (E) hallowed

On Your Own:
Write one sentence using each word below to demonstrate your understanding of the word's meaning.

31. **incantation** _____

32. **quisling** _____

33. **quagmire** _____

34. **excoriate** _____

35. **verbose** _____

36. **constrict** _____

37. **malevolent** _____

38. **litigate** _____

C2 Advanced Vocabulary 102

First Impressions:
Using the example sentences below, write your own definition of each boldfaced word. Then write the letter of the definition from the box that best matches your definition.

A	adjective: paying careful attention	**C**	adjective: convincing; decisive; serving to end something
B	verb: to think deeply over a problem	**D**	adjective: aggressive or warlike; related to the military

1. _____ The **observant** dog always knew when its master was preparing to go out for a walk.

OBSERVANT means: _____

2. _____ With a **conclusive** nod, Castor ended the conversation.

CONCLUSIVE means: _____

3. _____ Karate, Judo, and Tae Kwon Do are **martial** arts that have become increasingly popular in western countries.

MARTIAL means: _____

4. _____ When faced with a particularly difficult case, Sherlock Holmes would sit quietly with his pipe and **ruminate** until he found the solution.

RUMINATE means: _____

A	noun: the perfect example of a characteristic or type	**C**	adjective: bankrupt; unable to repay one's debts
B	adjective: clever; astute	**D**	adjective: of doubtful authenticitiy

5. _____ The party made a **shrewd** choice in choosing a candidate that would appeal to diehards in their own party and moderates in the other.

SHREWD means: _____

6. _____ Urban legends are modern myths that are quite popular, if **apocryphal**.

APOCRYPHAL means: _____

7. _____ The company filed for bankruptcy when it became financially **insolvent**.

INSOLVENT means: _____

8. _____ Some consider George Washington the **epitome** of American patriotism and ethics.

EPITOME means: _____

Divide and Conquer:

Choose the correct word to complete each of the following sentences.

9. Marvin was the (**shrewdness / epitome**) of good behavior, never breaking any rules.

10. If you are (**observant / apocryphal**), you will have little difficulty recognizing when your friends are upset.

11. Most stories that begin, "A friend of my cousin's roommate said that..." are probably (**apocryphal / insolvent**).

12. After two years of poor sales, the struggling business was nearly (**observant / insolvent**).

13. The (**martial / shrewd**) student identifies the most important points and focuses her studies appropriately.

14. Horseback archery once saw application as a(n) (**martial / epitome**) art but today is largely an amusement.

15. The Thinker is a famous statue in which a sitting man (**concludes / ruminates**) on profound subjects.

16. Though some think that the evolution of organisms has been firmly established, others feel that the evidence is not (**conclusive / insolvent**).

Hot and Cold:

Write the word from the lesson that is most nearly the *OPPOSITE* of the boldfaced word or words in each sentence below.

17. The security guard was fired for not being _____, especially since he had been **oblivious** when the thief stole the precious painting.

18. While I was _____ in matters of business, economics, and management after my years of schooling, I was still **foolish** in my personal life and tended to accidentally insult my friends and family.

19. Fearful of wasting time and energy _____ over a problem I could fix, I decided to stop worrying about it and **forget** the whole situation.

20. The former colonel's _____ attitude toward running the school surprised the teachers and students who were accustomed to a more **timid** approach to school management.

21. While the data appear _____, it is actually quite easy to interpret differently and might be more **ambiguous** than previously believed.

22. Chloe was the _____ of rebellious and the **antithesis** of what her parents expected a "good daughter" would be like.

23. One of the challenges of investigative journalism lies in distinguishing _____ rumors from those with a grain of **truth**.

24. Though the business is currently _____, the owner hopes to make the business **profitable** within the next two years.

Applying Yourself:

Choose the best word to complete each of the following sentences.

25. If you were more _____, you would have noticed that your train has already left.
    - (A) apocryphal
    - (B) martial
    - (C) conclusive
    - (D) observant
    - (E) shrewd

26. At one time, she was completely capable of paying all debts; now she is totally _____.
    - (A) pinnacle
    - (B) apocryphal
    - (C) martial
    - (D) insolvent
    - (E) shrewd

27. When the revolutionaries laid siege to the city, the authorities declared _____ law and stationed soldiers on every street corner.
    (A) martial
    (B) observant
    (C) conclusive
    (D) shrewd
    (E) insolvent

28. Jessica handled the negotiation of the merger with _____ determination; in the end, she increased the purchasing price by three dollars per share.
    (A) observant
    (B) apocryphal
    (C) martial
    (D) insolvent
    (E) shrewd

29. The Thinker is a statue of a man, chin in hand, who is presumably _____ on the mysteries of existence.
    (A) epitomizing
    (B) belying
    (C) congesting
    (D) ruminating
    (E) eulogizing

30. The Battle of Yorktown proved to be the _____ battle of the Revolutionary War after Cornwallis surrendered.
    (A) observant
    (B) conclusive
    (C) shrewd
    (D) insolvent
    (E) martial

31. Devin only hoped that he would be able to present evidence to stop the _____ rumors.
    (A) shrewd
    (B) apocryphal
    (C) insolvent
    (D) martial
    (E) observant

32. He was the _____ of a good general; his troops loved him, and he won every battle.
    (A) observation
    (B) epitome
    (C) insolvency
    (D) shrewdness
    (E) rumination

On Your Own:
Write one sentence using each word below to demonstrate your understanding of the word's meaning.

33. **observant** _____

34. **epitome** _____

35. **apocryphal** _____

36. **martial** _____

37. **conclusive** _____

38. **insolvent** _____

39. **shrewd** _____

40. **ruminate** _____

C2 Advanced Vocabulary 103

First Impressions:
Using the example sentences below, write your own definition of each boldfaced word. Then write the letter of the definition from the box that best matches your definition.

A	verb: to restrict; to slow down; to prevent from functioning well	**C**	noun: a similarity; a comparison
B	noun: the developmental peak of something; the highest point	**D**	adjective: talkative

1. _____ The **garrulous** young boy was often in trouble at school for talking too much.

GARRULOUS means: _____

2. _____ Drinking alcohol can **impair** your judgment and your ability to drive well.

IMPAIR means: _____

3. _____ By way of **analogy**, we could say that a county is to a state as a continent is to a country.

ANALOGY means: _____

4. _____ The **acme** of the use of VCRs happened in the late 90s, when they were widely popular; they were soon replaced by DVD players.

ACME means: _____

A	verb: to very strongly dislike	**C**	verb: to support or prop up; to encourage
B	adjective: tending to spend a lot of time sitting	**D**	verb: to discuss or worry more than is necessary

5. _____ When Thad couldn't think of any facts or literary references to **buttress** his essay's thesis, he decided to change his thesis to something that he could support.

BUTTRESS means: _____

6. _____ More than seventy percent of Americans are completely **sedentary**, so this latest move is designed to make exercise more accessible and fun.

SEDENTARY means: _____

7. _____ Preston didn't just dislike broccoli; he absolutely **abhorred** it and could not be convinced to eat it.

ABHOR means: _____

8. _____ Rather than **belabor** this minor point, let's move on to more important matters.

BELABOR means: _____

Divide and Conquer:
Choose the correct word to complete each of the following sentences.

9. Andrew received a well-deserved raise for bringing the company to its professional (**analogy** / **acme**).

10. Alice found it difficult to create any sort of (**acme** / **analogy**) between a raven and a writing desk.

11. The heavy, unsteady walls of the cathedral were (**buttressed** / **belabored**) on every side by huge stone pillars.

12. Micah decided not to (**buttress** / **belabor**) the point of whether or not to capitalize the word "Internet".

13. There is nothing a pacifist (**buttresses** / **abhors**) more than the terrible bloodshed and cruelty of war.

14. (**Garrulous** / **Belabored**) Cindy makes it easy for the rest of us to just sit back, relax, and listen.

15. The powerful medicine cured the disease but temporarily (**impaired** / **belabored**) my cat's ability to walk straight.

16. The old dog was (**sedentary** / **garrulous**) for so long that we had to jostle it to make sure it was still breathing.

Hot and Cold:
Write the word from the lesson that is most nearly the *OPPOSITE* of the boldfaced word or words in each sentence below.

17. Because we have **ignored** the issue until now, I am _____ the point so that we are all totally assured of how important it is.

18. Romana felt _____ by her adoptive parents in a way she hadn't experienced from the biological parents, who had **abandoned** her.

19. Tad's walking has been _____ ever since his injury, but doctors say they might have a new way to **fix** the damage to his leg.

20. The **quiet** young man had a harder time making friends than his more _____ peers.

21. The newly independent country was still in the **beginning stages** of establishing an economy, and its industries wouldn't reach their _____ for many years.

22. Is it possible to draw an _____ between World War I and the American Civil War, or are the **dissimilarities** too great?

23. I wouldn't say I _____ going to the opera; I just always find myself a little bored and would prefer to do something I **like** a bit more.

24. Your post-surgery recovery will require that you spend as much time _____, in bed or sitting down, as possible; trying to maintain your old **active** lifestyle would lead you to tear your stitches immediately.

Applying Yourself:
Choose the best word to complete each of the following sentences.

25. At the _____ of his powers, the author wrote his greatest novel.
    - (A) impairment
    - (B) abhorrence
    - (C) acme
    - (D) buttress
    - (E) analogy

26. Although he had only worked at the company for eight months, Liam was able to _____ his argument for a promotion with evidence of the work he had completed.
    - (A) buttress
    - (B) abhor
    - (C) impair
    - (D) loathe
    - (E) belabor

27. Grammarians tend to _____ the liberal use of slang.
    (A) buttress
    (B) impair
    (C) abhor
    (D) belabor
    (E) loathe

28. Don't _____ the explanation; a simple synopsis will do.
    (A) loathe
    (B) abhor
    (C) impair
    (D) belabor
    (E) buttress

29. Most people lead very _____ lives even though their doctors recommend activity and exercise.
    (A) abhorrent
    (B) sedentary
    (C) belabored
    (D) garrulous
    (E) impaired

30. He was a(n) _____ young man; it was very hard to get him to stop talking.
    (A) impaired
    (B) sedentary
    (C) garrulous
    (D) abhorrent
    (E) belabored

31. My vision was _____ in the dark room.
    (A) abhorrent
    (B) impaired
    (C) buttressed
    (D) compelled
    (E) belabored

32. He pressed the _____ further, comparing the shared aspects between his favorite pet and his best friend.
    (A) acme
    (B) analogy
    (C) buttress
    (D) impairment
    (E) garrulousness

On Your Own:
Write one sentence using each word below to demonstrate your understanding of the word's meaning.

33. **abhor** _____

34. **analogy** _____

35. **belabor** _____

36. **garrulous** _____

37. **sedentary** _____

38. **impair** _____

39. **buttress** _____

40. **acme** _____

C2 Advanced Vocabulary 104

First Impressions:

Using the example sentences below, write your own definition of each boldfaced word. Then write the letter of the definition from the box that best matches your definition.

A	noun: physical beauty	**C**	adjective: harsh, strict, or plain
B	noun: an authoritative statement; a common saying	**D**	noun: scarcity; lack

1. _____ Such was the **pulchritude** of Helen of Troy that many battles were fought because of her beauty.

PULCHRITUDE means: _____

2. _____ The children of the school feared the swift punishments of the **austere** headmaster.

AUSTERE means: _____

3. _____ The school is cutting music programs due to a **paucity** of available funds.

PAUCITY means: _____

4. _____ The judge's **dictum** required Lorraine to pay her landlord $500 plus the cost of repairing the broken window.

DICTUM means: _____

A	adjective: filled to the brim or to the point of being stuffed	**C**	adjective: not staying the same; incompatible
B	verb: to cut deeply; to tear	**D**	verb: to assault; to attack

5. _____ Since his directions were **inconsistent**, we were unable how to go about completing Mr. Johnson's project.

INCONSISTENT means: _____

6. _____ Greg needed stitches after a knife **lacerated** his forearm.

LACERATE means: _____

7. _____ My brother **assailed** the bully who had been calling me names all year.

ASSAILED means: _____

8. _____ After the long, productive harvest was over, the storehouses were **replete** with grain.

REPLETE means: _____

Divide and Conquer:
Choose the correct word to complete each of the following sentences.

9. When the teacher issued a (**dictum /
pulchritude**), the students knew that they must
follow it or face the consequences.

10. The prosecution for the case tried to prove that
the company's own records were (**replete /
assailed**) with evidence of safety violations.

11. Rhonda is (**inconsistent / austere**) in her
feelings; one day she loves Ray and the next
she hates him.

12. Though (**paucity / pulchritude**) might attract
suitors, intelligence and humor will keep them
interested.

13. After the encounter with the huge dog, Trey left
with severe (**dicta / lacerations**) on his back.

14. The pirates (**lacerated / assailed**) the enemy
ship.

15. We were unable to expand our business this
year due to a (**pulchritude / paucity**) of
available funds.

16. Some critics praised the simplicity of the artist's
"Field of Snow" series, but others found the
paintings to be too (**replete / austere**).

Hot and Cold:
Write the word from the lesson that is most nearly the *OPPOSITE* of the boldfaced word or words in each
sentence below.

17. These overstuffed and underappreciated
classrooms are _____ with every
educational technology known to science but
absent of a single eager student willing to fully
utilize it.

18. The tourist was shocked by the _____
of the most basic resources in the developing
country, as opposed to the **abundance** from
which she came.

19. My difficulty in seeing objectively means that I
can never be certain of my own _____;
even when I am healthy and looking well, I feel
my own **hideousness**.

20. The _____ quarters inside the prison
included only a hard cardboard mattress and a
small window; there wasn't a single **luxurious**
amenity, not even toilet paper.

21. The hospital specializes in **healing** those who
have been _____.

22. Doctors carefully **stitched** the knee that had
been _____ in a bicycling accident.

23. The president's _____ stance on that
particular issue makes me wonder what else he
isn't **constant** about.

24. Renna's therapist suggested that issuing **gentle
suggestions** instead of harsh _____
to her children might encourage them to do
their chores more often.

Applying Yourself:
Choose the best word to complete each of the following sentences.

25. It seems as though the facts are _____ with
your story; are you sure you're being truthful?
   (A) lacerated
   (B) replete
   (C) pulchritudinous
   (D) inconsistent
   (E) austere

26. Leann's _____ may please the eyes, but her
genuine sweetness appeals to your sincerest
heart.
   (A) paucity
   (B) pulchritude
   (C) austerity
   (D) laceration
   (E) assailing

27. Mom unpacked the bulging suitcase, which was _____ with snorkels, wetsuits, and other gear for our dive.
    (A) austere
    (B) inconsistent
    (C) assailed
    (D) replete
    (E) lacerated

28. My thumb bled wildly, _____ by the loose nail.
    (A) scintillated
    (B) occluded
    (C) observed
    (D) assailed
    (E) lacerated

29. The religious school's teachers were a group of cheerful nuns, not the _____ ladies of Dickensian lore.
    (A) lacerated
    (B) austere
    (C) replete
    (D) inconsistent
    (E) pulchritudinous

30. After growing up with a(n) _____ of resources, they promised themselves that one day they would have an abundance to share with others.
    (A) austerity
    (B) paucity
    (C) inconsistency
    (D) laceration
    (E) assault

31. _____ from the executive committee abounded when our team fell behind on the project.
    (A) Inconsistency
    (B) Pulchritude
    (C) Austerity
    (D) Dicta
    (E) Paucity

32. If we _____ the enemy base with enough forces, we should be able to capture it.
    (A) scintillate
    (B) occlude
    (C) assail
    (D) lacerate
    (E) observe

On Your Own:
Write one sentence using each word below to demonstrate your understanding of the word's meaning.

33. **assail** _____

34. **lacerate** _____

35. **replete** _____

36. **dictum** _____

37. **pulchritude** _____

38. **inconsistent** _____

39. **austere** _____

40. **paucity** _____

C2 Advanced Vocabulary 105

First Impressions:

Using the example sentences below, write your own definition of each boldfaced word. Then write the letter of the definition from the box that best matches your definition.

A	adjective: charming; likeable	C	adjective: excessively sentimental; foolishly emotional
B	adjective: subject to spur-of-the-moment whims or decisions	D	adjective: sleepy or causing sleep

1. _____ The queen's generosity is one of her most **endearing** traits and has made her most popular with the public.

ENDEARING means: _____

2. _____ A heavy lunch and an unusually dull lecture left Brian quite **somnolent** during his trigonometry class.

SOMNOLENT means: _____

3. _____ Gigi's **capricious** physics teacher offered a different date for the exam every time he was asked.

CAPRICIOUS means: _____

4. _____ While Katherine enjoyed watching romantic dramas, Robin found the emotional reactions of the characters to be too **maudlin**.

MAUDLIN means: _____

A	noun: the raising of a person to the rank of a god	C	noun: isolation; solitude
B	noun: an award; an award ceremony	D	verb: to pay [someone] for services performed

5. _____ I don't babysit for the Johnsons anymore, since they have failed to **remunerate** me for my work in the past.

REMUNERATE means: _____

6. _____ They also offer luxury and private bungalows to ensure **seclusion**.

SECLUSION means: _____

7. _____ She received many **accolades** for her impressive performance at the race and was exhausted from attending ceremony after ceremony celebrating her victory.

ACCOLADE means: _____

8. _____ "The **Apotheosis** of George Washington" is a painting on the ceiling of the capitol building that shows Washington on a cloud surrounded by the goddesses of victory and liberty.

APOTHEOSIS means: _____

Divide and Conquer:
Choose the correct word to complete each of the following sentences.

9. In a (**maudlin / capricious**) display, the child sat in the middle of the candy aisle and cried until her mother agreed to buy a candy bar.

10. Those suffering from insomnia should read a (**secluded / somnolent**) book in bed, such as The Wonderful World of Tax Code.

11. For their help in moving his furniture the neighbor (**remunerated / secluded**) the teenagers with pizza.

12. The little boy's (**endearing / maudlin**) smile pleased everyone around him.

13. Because of Stephanie's (**endearing / capricious**) spending habits, she never knew how much money her bank account might contain.

14. This prestigious (**accolade / capriciousness**) from the League of Progressive Businesses is a wonderful testament to our positive corporate values.

15. The senator's sudden rise in popularity has been called a political (**somnolence / apotheosis**).

16. Our family shuns cities in favor of the peaceful (**seclusion / remuneration**) of the country.

Hot and Cold:
Write the word from the lesson that is most nearly the *OPPOSITE* of the boldfaced word or words in each sentence below.

17. When thieves **steal** others' credit cards, banks often _____ lost funds.

18. While you won't receive any **punishment** for breaking this particular rule, don't expect _____ from me or any of the other teachers for your "daring".

19. Clyde knew that public opinion was fickle and that while he now enjoyed the _____ it blessed him with, referring to him with such monikers as "savior" and "holy man" could just as easily subject him to **demonization**.

20. The smiling old man said that in order to be truly _____, one must have periods of complete **predictability**.

21. The _____ soap opera, whose characters seemed to break down into tears or experience extremely heartfelt reunions every episode, had no effect on the **stoic** Robert.

22. The _____ I often feel while stuck alone in my car on an empty highway melts away when I step into my home and see my loved ones enjoying the **camaraderie** of a family dinner.

23. Jessica's _____ personality made up for the **repellant** remarks she had made earlier.

24. Lying in bed for too long makes me feel _____ even if I'm ready to get up for the day, while jumping up and immediately getting into the shower makes me feel **energized**.

Applying Yourself:
Choose the best word to complete each of the following sentences.

25. The restaurant was forced to financially _____ all the people who had gotten food poisoning the previous night.
    (A) assail
    (B) eulogize
    (C) seclude
    (D) endear
    (E) remunerate

26. The actor received the award after his death, but it wasn't just a(n) _____ sympathy gesture; he deserved the honor.
    (A) maudlin
    (B) somnolent
    (C) capricious
    (D) endearing
    (E) secluded

27. The Nobel Prize is one of the most prestigious _____ a person can earn.
    (A) apotheoses
    (B) endearments
    (C) seclusions
    (D) accolades
    (E) remunerations

28. The fanaticism shown in cults frequently includes the _____ of its leader so that future generations will worship that person.
    (A) somnolence
    (B) accolade
    (C) apotheosis
    (D) remuneration
    (E) endearment

29. Mr. Vance, tired of the small talk at the housewarming party, sought _____ in his private office.
    (A) somnolence
    (B) apotheosis
    (C) endearment
    (D) seclusion
    (E) remuneration

30. After Lincoln's concise Gettysburg Address, Edward Everett's two-hour speech rendered the audience _____.
    (A) somnolent
    (B) maudlin
    (C) capricious
    (D) endeared
    (E) remunerated

31. Jon's _____ behavior added welcome variety to my predictable nine-to-six work life.
    (A) endearing
    (B) capricious
    (C) secluded
    (D) somnolent
    (E) remunerated

32. I found his use of old-fashioned slang _____; it reminded me of my grandfather.
    (A) remunerated
    (B) endearing
    (C) secluded
    (D) capricious
    (E) maudlin

On Your Own:

Write one sentence using each word below to demonstrate your understanding of the word's meaning.

33. **somnolent** _____

34. **maudlin** _____

35. **accolade** _____

36. **capricious** _____

37. **apotheosis** _____

38. **endearing** _____

39. **seclusion** _____

40. **remunerate** _____

C2 Advanced Vocabulary 110

First Impressions:

Using the example sentences below, write your own definition of each boldfaced word. Then write the letter of the definition from the box that best matches your definition.

A	adjective: flowing smoothly or beautifully	**C**	verb: to mislead or give a false impression
B	noun: great size or important; of or relating to something seriously bad	**D**	noun: impoliteness; something rude or against protocol

1. _____ Rachel **deluded** her teacher into thinking that her computer had crashed, when in reality she had not finished the assignment.

DELUDE means: _____

2. _____ The applicant's **impropriety** in addressing the interviewer meant that he wouldn't be getting the job.

IMPROPRIETY means: _____

3. _____ The singer's **mellifluous** voice rolled smoothly and luxuriously over every syllable.

MELLIFLUOUS means: _____

4. _____ The **enormity** of this project cannot be overestimated; it can be said quite reasonably that it is the most important work that we have ever undertaken.

ENORMITY means: _____

A	verb: to make use of, sometimes unjustly; to manipulate	**C**	adjective: charming, peaceful, and simple
B	verb: to spend or use extravagantly or wastefully; to scatter	**D**	adjective: hard to understand; known only to the chosen few

5. _____ Although the younger generations seem to have little trouble adapting to new technologies, the older generations sometimes find their new computers to be somewhat **esoteric** and difficult to operate.

ESOTERIC means: _____

6. _____ Politicians have bad reputations and are known to **exploit** others to achieve their own goals.

EXPLOIT means: _____

7. _____ The **idyllic** scene of the painting depicted a rustic cottage next to a field of fluffy sheep.

IDYLLIC means: _____

8. _____ Instead of saving the money from her summer job for college, Bridget **squandered** it on video games and delivery pizza.

SQUANDER means: _____

Divide and Conquer:

Choose the correct word to complete each of the following sentences.

9. Due to the (**impropriety / enormity**) of the crimes, the suspect was given the highest sentence available.

10. The subject matter was so (**esoteric / deluded**) that it was said that only three people in the world understood it fully.

11. The etiquette book lists things one ought to do to avoid (**enormity / impropriety**).

12. The song presented an (**exploited / idyllic**) vision, calling to mind petals falling from a tree into the slowly flowing waters of a brook.

13. Mr. Cato was unsuccessful in his attempt to (**delude / exploit**) the bouncer, and so he was not able to enter the club.

14. When the snows of winter began to fall, the grasshopper regretted that he had (**deluded / squandered**) the hours of summer by playing instead of gathering food.

15. The song's style was interesting and mixed, combining (**mellifluous / deluded**) vocals with harsh distorted guitar.

16. The senator worked hard to introduce legislation to give a voice to members of the population who had traditionally been (**exploited / deluded**) by those in power.

Hot and Cold:

Write the word from the lesson that is most nearly the *OPPOSITE* of the boldfaced word or words in each sentence below.

17. The **jagged** rhythms in the experimental piece surprised and repulsed those accustomed to more soothing, _____ music.

18. We were so convinced of our own **insignificance** that we couldn't fathom the _____ of the impact our small demonstration would have on international politics.

19. Madame Dervish never acted with _____, but always with the utmost **appropriateness**.

20. The once _____ fields of flowers, grazing sheep, and gentle sunshine have been transformed into a chaotic **cityscape** rife with crime.

21. "I've never understood," said Sam to his sister, "why you seem to _____ your money on every silly thing that pops into your head, while I find it fairly easy to **manage** my cash."

22. You may feel that your teachers _____ you into believing you could make a career out of writing, but I think they have **rightly guided** you to pursue your passion.

23. Though the text was rather _____ and only studied by scholars, the principle it contained, that of the importance of human dignity, was **universally understood**.

24. While settlers often _____ local resources to the detriment of the area, they also **supplemented** the local economy by buying large quantities of locally-produced goods.

Applying Yourself:

Choose the best word to complete each of the following sentences.

25. The chemistry professor's lectures were so _____ that the students formed study groups and met twice a week to make them easier to understand.
    (A) idyllic
    (B) deluded
    (C) squandered
    (D) mellifluous
    (E) esoteric

26. Don't _____ what you've learned at your internship; instead, use it to get a job in your chosen field.
    (A) exploit
    (B) squander
    (C) delude
    (D) hallow
    (E) buttress

27. To avoid _____ when visiting another country, be sure you know the local customs.
    (A) idylls
    (B) impropriety
    (C) delusion
    (D) enormity
    (E) zealousness

28. When Mrs. Chloe made him the group leader of the final project, Thomas used his power to _____ and take advantage of his peers so that he could do little work and take much of the credit.
    (A) exploit
    (B) squander
    (C) delude
    (D) hallow
    (E) buttress

29. Should your motivation waver during the college application process, consider the _____ of the consequences should you fail to get accepted.
    (A) eulogy
    (B) enormity
    (C) exploitation
    (D) impropriety
    (E) squandering

30. The mixture of milk and sugar poured _____ from the pitcher into the bowl, making a light tinkling sound.
    (A) idyllically
    (B) mellifluously
    (C) tentatively
    (D) esoterically
    (E) zealously

31. It is easy for politicians who offer impossibly easy solutions to complicated problems to _____ the public.
    (A) buttress
    (B) hallow
    (C) squander
    (D) exploit
    (E) delude

32. Rather than reside in the chaotic city, the Smiths decided to live a(n) _____ life in the countryside.
    (A) mellifluous
    (B) idyllic
    (C) exploited
    (D) squandered
    (E) esoteric

On Your Own:
Write one sentence using each word below to demonstrate your understanding of the word's meaning.

33. **enormity** _____

34. **mellifluous** _____

35. **delude** _____

36. **exploit** _____

37. **idyllic** _____

38. **impropriety** _____

39. **squander** _____

40. **esoteric** _____

C2 Advanced Vocabulary 106

First Impressions:
Using the example sentences below, write your own definition of each boldfaced word. Then write the letter of the definition from the box that best matches your definition.

A	noun: social or cultural surroundings	**C**	noun: sudden insight; the power to know without reasoning
B	noun: obscurity; forgetfulness	**D**	adjective: highly energetic; excited

1. _____ The intellectual **milieu** of life in and around a university offers nearly as much intellectual stimulation as the actual class work.

MILIEU means: _____

2. _____ "Trust in your own **intuition** and gut instincts," she says, "and they will never let you down."

INTUITION means: _____

3. _____ This author is an unsung hero whose name has long been lost to **oblivion**.

OBLIVION means: _____

4. _____ The **ebullient** crowd shouted out each number as they counted down to the new year.

EBULLIENT means: _____

A	adjective: momentary; temporary; staying for a short time	**C**	adjective: glowing; [an emotion or quality] emerging out of a person or thing
B	adjective: dull; lacking life	**D**	adjective: outspoken; frank

5. _____ It was surprising that the mayor was so quiet on the issue when he is generally quite **forthright** with his opinions.

FORTHRIGHT means: _____

6. _____ With the skillful application of a few choice spices, the chef transformed the **vapid** dish into a culinary delight.

VAPID means: _____

7. _____ He had a **radiant** inner glow.

RADIENT means: _____

8. _____ Many pleasures are **transient**, but true happiness lasts a lifetime.

TRANSIENT means: _____

Divide and Conquer:
Choose the correct word to complete each of the following sentences.

9. One of the reasons that no one reviews the terms of service is that the text is so (**vapid / transient**) as to render even the most alert reader bored.

10. The former child television star's career has now faded into (**oblivion / milieu**).

11. The (**vapid / ebullient**) performers excited the crowd with their lively and cheerful antics.

12. He ran in a fascinating (**intuition / milieu**) of artists, egotistical athletes, and book critics.

13. Though it is a curse that our joys are (**vapid / transient**), it is a blessing that our pains are, too.

14. The detective depended as much upon sheer (**intuition / milieu**) as on logical deduction.

15. Ricardo wished that his mother would be more (**intuitive / forthright**); because she tried so hard to soften her criticism, he never seemed to understand what she was saying.

16. The groom's eyes opened in delight as he saw his (**radiant / oblivious**) bride at the wedding.

Hot and Cold:
Write the word from the lesson that is most nearly the *OPPOSITE* of the boldfaced word or words in each sentence below.

17. _____ jewels are much more expensive than **dull** ones.

18. The _____ camp counselor refused to be disappointed by his seemingly **depressed** campers.

19. Within the specific _____ of my private boarding school attended by the daughters of the richest and most powerful citizens of the country, I have acquired a taste for luxury that I might not have developed if I were in a foreign **environment**.

20. I wish it were **permanent** so we could always enjoy it, but the aurora borealis has a(n) _____ nature, which is what makes it so very special.

21. Greta tired of the _____ television shows she saw, all of which lacked depth and meaning, and sought a more **intense** way to occupy her time.

22. These great deeds will be remembered in **eternity** and never be lost to _____.

23. The senator strove to be _____ with his constituency in order to avoid a reputation for **dishonest** dealings.

24. My mother seemed to know people's feelings and motivations on sudden _____; it would take me weeks to come to the same conclusions using **reason**.

Applying Yourself:
Choose the best word to complete each of the following sentences.

25. Sadly, their romantic relationship was _____, as he was taking a train to the western front the next afternoon.
    (A) ebullient
    (B) transient
    (C) vapid
    (D) forthright
    (E) radiant

26. Although many praised his uncanny skills of reason, Sherlock Holmes also had a(n) _____ about crime scenes.
    (A) radiance
    (B) forthrightness
    (C) milieu
    (D) intuition
    (E) transience

27. Earth is warmed by the _____ light and heat emitted by the sun.
    (A) forthright
    (B) ebullient
    (C) vapid
    (D) radiant
    (E) transient

28. My triumph left me in a(n) _____ mood, and I almost danced all the way home.
    (A) oblivious
    (B) forthright
    (C) ebullient
    (D) transient
    (E) vapid

29. The climbers were unfamiliar with the Himalayan _____ and were terrified of committing a faux pas before their new hosts.
    (A) intuition
    (B) radiance
    (C) forthrightness
    (D) milieu
    (E) transience

30. The forgetfulness of sleep is nothing compared to the _____ of death.
    (A) intuition
    (B) forthrightness
    (C) oblivion
    (D) transience
    (E) ebullience

31. With all of the aspiring screenwriters attending schools that teach them formulaic methods, it is a wonder that every movie produced isn't totally _____.
    (A) forthright
    (B) vapid
    (C) intuitive
    (D) ebullient
    (E) transient

32. His _____ response to her question showed a lack of sensitivity and subtlety.
    (A) forthright
    (B) ebullient
    (C) transient
    (D) vapid
    (E) intuitive

On Your Own:
Write one sentence using each word below to demonstrate your understanding of the word's meaning.

33. **milieu** _____

34. **forthright** _____

35. **oblivion** _____

36. **radiant** _____

37. **intuition** _____

38. **ebullient** _____

39. **vapid** _____

40. **transient** _____

C2 Advanced Vocabulary 107

First Impressions:
Using the example sentences below, write your own definition of each boldfaced word. Then write the letter of the definition from the box that best matches your definition.

A	adjective: lusting; full of desire	**C**	adjective: extremely clean
B	noun: a large organization of many committees, agencies, and bureaus	**D**	adjective: naturally associated with another thing

1. _____ **Concomitant** with the construction of the new sports stadium was an increase in traffic on game nights.

CONCOMITANT means: _____

2. _____ The **pristine** hills hadn't been touched by humans in thousands of years.

PRISTINE means: _____

3. _____ The preacher encouraged the young man to give up his **concupiscent** ways and to embrace a lifestyle that would lead to a happy marriage to one person.

CONCUPISCENT means: _____

4. _____ The politician promised to trim the **bureaucracy** in Washington by eliminating excessive programs and agencies.

BUREAUCRACY means: _____

A	adjective: harsh and shrill; disorderly and boisterous	**C**	adjective: perfectly clear
B	noun: double-dealing; hypocrisy	**D**	adjective: extremely ugly; repulsive

5. _____ The **grotesque** statuette, featuring the face of a hideous demon, seemed to come alive in the flickering candlelight.

GROTESQUE means: _____

6. _____ Through the **limpid** waters of the pool, ornamental fish could be seen swimming among the aquatic plants.

LIMPID means: _____

7. _____ The police officer arrived to investigate complaints of a **raucous** party.

RAUCOUS means: _____

8. _____ The politician's **duplicity** became apparent after he was elected and failed to follow through on any of his campaign promises.

DUPLICITY means: _____

Divide and Conquer:
Choose the correct word to complete each of the following sentences.

9. When the scandal was uncovered the entire committee was shocked to discover that one of its members had engaged in such (**duplicity** / **concomitance**).

10. The (**grotesque** / **bureaucratic**) film left me feeling nauseated.

11. Suelgi had difficulties with his finances because he was unable to tame his (**concomitance** / **concupiscent**) for new electronic gadgets.

12. Years of experience taught Jacob that a temporary increase in his waist size was (**raucous** / **concomitant**) with his consumption of many tasty holiday treats.

13. The (**limpid** / **bureaucratic**) tone of the cello rang out across the auditorium, deep and true.

14. There will be a series of (**grotesque** / **raucous**) cheers throughout the game as pockets of home fans erupt when Peterson crosses the goal line.

15. The (**raucous** / **pristine**) room seemed as though it belonged in a magazine instead of a busy house.

16. Herschel enjoyed the freewheeling energy of the startup company, which was free of the stultifying (**concomitance** / **bureaucracy**) of a large corporation.

Hot and Cold:
Write the word from the lesson that is most nearly the *OPPOSITE* of the boldfaced word or words in each sentence below.

17. With its flashing colors, loud bands, and exciting parades, the celebration of Mardi Gras is a _____ display of sensory delights compared to the much more **orderly** observance of Lent.

18. After the bombing, the _____ landscape was nothing like its prior, **beautiful** state.

19. Even if you feel that those around you are misleading you and acting with _____, remember the value of **honesty** and never sacrifice yours in response.

20. In an uncontrollably _____ mood, Pat called every number in his phone to try to set up a meeting, only to find out that everyone he called was **turned off** by him.

21. After being treated with a chemical cleaner, the aquarium went from a **murky** swamp to a _____ and bright home for fish.

22. While it appears **ruined**, the car will soon be back in _____ shape.

23. The building of this housing tract has led to a _____ degradation of the local environment; it isn't **unrelated** that the air quality seems poorer now that there are fewer trees around.

Applying Yourself:
Choose the best word to complete each of the following sentences.

24. Several scenes in the book were _____; I could barely read them, I was so disgusted.
    - (A) raucous
    - (B) bureaucratic
    - (C) pristine
    - (D) grotesque
    - (E) limpid

25. Macy didn't enjoy babysitting because she usually found the children to be _____ and demanding—a far cry from the calm atmosphere of her own home.
    - (A) raucous
    - (B) bureaucratic
    - (C) pristine
    - (D) duplicitous
    - (E) limpid

26. Cancun's water is _____, so we were able to see the fish 30 feet below the surface.
    (A) grotesque
    (B) limpid
    (C) bureaucratic
    (D) concomitant
    (E) concupiscent

27. Instead of indulging in _____ thoughts of the opposite sex, try to maintain your focus on the simple pleasures of studying physics.
    (A) concupiscent
    (B) pristine
    (C) grotesque
    (D) limpid
    (E) raucous

28. Increased corporate welfare, in the form of tax incentives, is _____ with an increased financial burden on the individual.
    (A) duplicitous
    (B) concupiscent
    (C) concomitant
    (D) limpid
    (E) raucous

29. The _____ of the executive branch has assumed more and more responsibilities over the years, including homeland security, housing, and social security.
    (A) concupiscence
    (B) bureaucracy
    (C) duplicity
    (D) grotesqueness
    (E) raucousness

30. The lake they hiked to was _____; it had never been touched by human hands or garbage.
    (A) raucous
    (B) pristine
    (C) limpid
    (D) duplicitous
    (E) concupiscent

31. Petr's _____ became apparent only when we realized that he had supported our rival for the throne all along.
    (A) bureaucracy
    (B) concupiscence
    (C) raucousness
    (D) limpidness
    (E) duplicity

On Your Own:
Write one sentence using each word below to demonstrate your understanding of the word's meaning.

32. **bureaucracy** _____

33. **concupiscent** _____

34. **pristine** _____

35. **duplicity** _____

36. **concomitant** _____

37. **grotesque** _____

38. **limpid** _____

39. **raucous** _____

C2 Advanced Vocabulary 108

First Impressions:

Using the example sentences below, write your own definition of each boldfaced word. Then write the letter of the definition from the box that best matches your definition.

A	adjective: doubtful; questionable	**C**	noun: active strength
B	adjective: unreasonable	**D**	noun: excessive boldness; confidence

1. _____ Feeling that the rate at which gas prices increased was **inordinate**, Mr. Lee decided to buy a more fuel-efficient vehicle.

INORDINATE means: _____

2. _____ The renowned swordsman was so surprised that the farmer had the **temerity** to face him in a duel that he spared his life.

TEMERITY means: _____

3. _____ We worked with great **vigor** to complete the project on time.

VIGOR means: _____

4. _____ Campbell's behavior was inexcusable because he was using public resources for morally **dubious** private purposes.

DUBIOUS means: _____

A	adjective: not fitting; absurd	**C**	adjective: explicit, not ambiguous, direct
B	adjective: vague or cloud-like	**D**	noun: a resident of a place

5. During her presentation, Alexis felt somewhat **incongruous** standing in front of the class instead of sitting as a member of it.

INCONGRUOUS means: _____

6. _____ Though the concept of entropy is actually relatively simple, it can seem quite **nebulous** to people exposed to it for the first time.

NEBULOUS means: _____

7. _____ The senator's response on the question of introducing new taxes was a **categorical** denial: there would not be a single increase.

CATEGORICAL means: _____

8. _____ The **denizens** of the city were highly pleased when the city planners announced a reduction in property taxes.

DENIZEN means: _____

Divide and Conquer:
Choose the correct word to complete each of the following sentences.

9. A policeman was called to investigate the (**inordinate** / **vigorous**) amount of noise from the neighbors' party.

10. A writer to the newspaper criticized the study, saying that the evidence was shaky and the conclusions (**inordinate** / **dubious**) at best.

11. Everett's (**vigor** / **temerity**) was a source of frustration and worry for his parents as they taught him to drive.

12. The task at hand is not easy, and will require (**dubiousness** / **vigor**) over the coming weeks to complete.

13. He approached the building with (**categorical** / **nebulous**) intent: would he confront his duplicitous girlfriend, or would he pretend that everything was normal?

14. (**Denizens** / **Invigorations**) of the building are advised to let their faucets drip overnight in order to reduce the risk of frozen pipes.

15. Harold's stylish tuxedo looked highly (**incongruous** / **nebulous**) in the cheap bar.

16. Immanuel Kant's (**categorical** / **incongruous**) imperative states that in every situation one should act according to what he or she would will to be a universal law.

Hot and Cold:
Write the word from the lesson that is most nearly the *OPPOSITE* of the boldfaced word or words in each sentence below.

17. The tiny shoes seemed _____ on the giant man to whom they belonged, but given that his size was due to muscle mass and not a large skeleton, it was quite **fitting** that he should have average, or even small, feet.

18. The puppy's _____ was unusual for his breed, which was known for its **cowardliness**; while his siblings shied away from danger, Sparky faced it head-on.

19. The _____ of this particular town are tired of foreigners and have ceased welcoming **outsiders** at all.

20. My editor said my source seemed _____, but I assured him that the contact was very **trustworthy** and had never lied to me in the past.

21. The workers seemed to load an _____ amount of food into the kitchen, but the quantity seemed more **reasonable** when we learned that it was the busiest dining day of the year.

22. Among these many _____ and difficult-to-pinpoint possibilities, we need one **definite** plan for how we intend to raise the needed funds.

23. Curing my old constant **lethargy**, my new running routine has given me the _____ to approach nearly any new task with energy and excitement.

24. I had hoped that Dad would give me a _____ answer about whether I could go to the party so that I could either begin making plans or not, but his response was **ambiguous** and left me uncertain of how to act.

Applying Yourself:
Choose the best word to complete each of the following sentences.

25. The port is home to thugs, thieves, and other unsavory _____.
    (A) eulogy
    (B) denizens
    (C) dubiousness
    (D) temerity
    (E) vigor

26. James Joyce employs language that, while _____, becomes clear when the reader connects the words and the books' themes.
    (A) nebulous
    (B) incongruous
    (C) dubious
    (D) categorical
    (E) inordinate

27. Getting anything through this deadlocked government requires a(n) _____ amount of effort that I'm unwilling to give.
    (A) vigorous
    (B) incongruous
    (C) nebulous
    (D) inordinate
    (E) categorical

28. Derrick insisted on _____ restrictions on spending to get our family out of debt.
    (A) dubious
    (B) categorical
    (C) nebulous
    (D) incongruous
    (E) congested

29. Random guesses are totally _____ with the rigorous approach of science.
    (A) dubious
    (B) vigorous
    (C) incongruous
    (D) categorical
    (E) nebulous

30. The children were being very active and their energy reminded Grandpa of his own youthful _____.
    (A) incongruity
    (B) temerity
    (C) vigor
    (D) dubiousness
    (E) denizen

31. That Thomas was telling the truth about the accident was _____, for he had a questionable sense of morals to being with.
    (A) incongruous
    (B) categorical
    (C) dubious
    (D) inordinate
    (E) nebulous

32. Some would describe Captain Jack's actions as the result of undue _____, but I would say that boldness is what makes him the best captain in the fleet.
    (A) dubiousness
    (B) nebulousness
    (C) vigor
    (D) temerity
    (E) incongruity

On Your Own:
Write one sentence using each word below to demonstrate your understanding of the word's meaning.

33. **incongruous** _____

34. **temerity** _____

35. **vigor** _____

36. **dubious** _____

37. **inordinate** _____

38. **nebulous** _____

39. **categorical** _____

40. **denizen** _____

C2 Advanced Vocabulary 109

First Impressions:
Using the example sentences below, write your own definition of each boldfaced word. Then write the letter of the definition from the box that best matches your definition.

A	noun: the process of examining one's own internal thoughts and emotions	C	verb: to make invalid; to void; to abolish
B	verb: to reduce the resources of; to run out of	D	adjective: able to be done; worth doing; able to survive

1. _____ Due to public opposition, the Eighteenth Amendment to the United States Constitution was **nullified** with the ratification of the Twenty-first Amendment.

NULLIFY means: _____

2. _____ Once you **deplete** glycogen stores in your muscles, your body begins running on compounds called "ketones" instead.

DEPLETE means: _____

3. _____ The study of religion requires not only personal **introspection**, but also the study of outside texts.

INTROSPECTION means: _____

4. _____ The plan to blast all of the city's garbage into outer space was creative but not **viable** because it would cost far too much money.

VIABLE means: _____

A	verb: to specifically deny; to state the opposite	C	verb: to nourish; to educate; to foster
B	adjective: related to a father	D	noun: a person of no importance; nonexistence

5. It's nice to see someone with real talent on television, rather than vacuous celebrity **nonentities**.

NONENTITY means: _____

6. _____ It is important to properly **nurture** infants during the first few years of their lives, as this period of growth will have a lasting impact on the following decades.

NURTURE means: _____

7. _____ The politician, who was known for frequently changing his opinion, **contradicted** his past positions several times during the debate.

CONTRADICT means: _____

8. _____ The teacher had a concern for his students that was almost **paternal**; he felt the same pain at their setbacks and joy at their successes that a father would.

PATERNAL means: _____

Divide and Conquer:
Choose the correct word to complete each of the following sentences.

9. The goal of therapy is to help patients with their own (**introspection / nullification**) so that they can understand themselves better.

10. My (**viable / paternal**) grandfather was always a jokester, and he passed along that trait to my father.

11. The environmental activists launched a campaign to get local authorities actively (**nullifying / nurturing**) and encouraging community wind power.

12. The debater pointed out that recent evidence (**contradicted / nurtured**) his opponent's point.

13. For the plan to be (**nullified / viable**), it must have a greater potential for profit than for loss.

14. He quickly went from being a (**nonentity / viability**) to being one of the most famous actors in film.

15. When Phillip learned that his checkbook had been stolen, he quickly called his bank to have his checks (**nurtured / nullified**).

16. I (**introspect / deplete**) my savings account during my costly trip around the world.

Hot and Cold:
Write the word from the lesson that is most nearly the *OPPOSITE* of the boldfaced word or words in each sentence below.

17. Through hard work and good timing, he rose from his position as a _____ to a **power broker**.

18. Craig spent so much time on _____ that none could accuse him of **thoughtlessness**.

19. After ten years, my driver's license was _____; I had to retake the test to have my new license **validated**.

20. Branden was pleased to discover that the facts that once had seemed to _____ his point in fact **confirmed** it.

21. It may seem **impractical**, but moving each penguin by hand from one glacier to the next seems to be the most _____ way of helping them find new fishing grounds.

22. Anne hoped that leaving her children to their own devices would _____ a sense of independence within them, but instead they felt that their mother had **neglected** them.

23. Development has _____ the topsoil, so the city is making an effort to **replenished** the shores to the necessary heights.

Applying Yourself:
Choose the best word to complete each of the following sentences.

24. My _____ grandfather, Francois, raised my father to be an independent, carefree spirit.
    (A) depleted
    (B) paternal
    (C) viable
    (D) introspective
    (E) contradictory

25. I spent a great deal of my time in quiet _____, trying to understand myself.
    (A) introspection
    (B) nullification
    (C) depletion
    (D) nurturing
    (E) viability

26. The defense _____ my testimony with the argument of its expert witness, making me out to be a liar.
    (A) nullified
    (B) contradicted
    (C) nurtured
    (D) assailed
    (E) abraded

27. These _____ are of no relevance to the project, so let's leave them out of the equation.
    (A) contradictions
    (B) nonentities
    (C) nebulae
    (D) martinets
    (E) anthologies

28. Animal shelters often _____ young animals whose mothers have died until those animals are ready to be released into the wild.
    (A) preclude
    (B) contradict
    (C) nurture
    (D) nullify
    (E) deplete

29. Our reserves of oil were vastly _____ after weeks of constant use of the machinery.
    (A) nullified
    (B) depleted
    (C) nurtured
    (D) contradicted
    (E) introspected

30. Although Yun's plan to widen the highway is _____, we won't be able to begin until after winter.
    (A) nullified
    (B) contradictory
    (C) viable
    (D) depleted
    (E) paternal

31. You can claim that my opinion is contradicted by the facts, but it is likely that the facts _____ your opinion, too.
    (A) assail
    (B) nurture
    (C) introspect
    (D) nullify
    (E) deplete

On Your Own:

Write one sentence using each word below to demonstrate your understanding of the word's meaning.

32. **nullify** _____

33. **deplete** _____

34. **introspection** _____

35. **nonentity** _____

36. **nurture** _____

37. **paternal** _____

38. **viable** _____

39. **contradict** _____

C2 Advanced Vocabulary 111

First Impressions:

Using the example sentences below, write your own definition of each boldfaced word. Then write the letter of the definition from the box that best matches your definition.

A	noun: a trite remark; a commonplace statement	**C**	verb: to cause someone to feel isolated or hostile
B	adjective: easily understood; clear; intelligible	**D**	verb: to find a way around (usually an obstacle); to overcome, typically in a sneaky way

1. _____ The teacher noticed that Rebekah seemed to have been **alienated** from the rest of the class, so he created more opportunities for her to participate.

ALIENATE means: _____

2. _____ Tom couldn't really talk clearly in the mornings, but once he was more awake, he became much more **lucid**.

LUCID means: _____

3. _____ He was looking for insightful advice, but he received only general **platitudes**.

PLATITUDE means: _____

4. _____ The spy **circumvented** the security system by crawling through the air ducts.

CIRCUMVENT means: _____

A	adjective: marked by kindness or consideration	**C**	adjective: boring; draining of enthusiasm
B	adjective: willing to make allowances; intending to appease	**D**	adjective: the most noticeable or important

5. _____ The plain white room had a **stultifying** effect on the children's creativity.

STULTIFYING means: _____

6. _____ Activists advocated for the **humane** treatment of all animals and an end to animal cruelty.

HUMANE means: _____

7. _____ The musician studied for hours every day until he became the **preeminent** cellist of his time.

PREEMINENT means: _____

8. _____ Every child received a small **conciliatory** certificate for playing in the game so that none would feel like a loser.

CONCILIATORY means: _____

Divide and Conquer:
Choose the correct word to complete each of the following sentences.

9. Parenting is both challenging and rewarding, as the old (**platitude / preeminence**) says.

10. The older politician's inept attempts to appear more "hip" to the young voters only further (**conciliated / alienated**) him from the public.

11. Standard bearers stood bravely, (**preeminent / conciliatory**) on the battlefield, knowing that they could be seen easily by the enemy.

12. The spy inserted a chip into the camera to (**circumvent / alienate**) the building's security system.

13. The signs of the protestors declared their lack of support for animal testing that they felt was not conducted in a (**humane / circumvented**) manner.

14. Claire felt the environment at home, with her strict parents, to be quite (**stultifying / preeminent**).

15. Compared to his previous two novels, which were highly confusing, Albert's latest work is refreshingly (**alienating / lucid**).

16. In his relaxed, (**stultifying / conciliatory**) tone, he tried to mediate the dispute.

Hot and Cold:
Write the word from the lesson that is most nearly the *OPPOSITE* of the boldfaced word or words in each sentence below.

17. Some citizens tried to _____ the law prohibiting alcohol by smuggling it in from Canada, but others strictly **adhered** to prohibition.

18. Though I'm now a **minor, unimportant** research scientist in my field, I hope to become a _____ scholar within the next fifteen years.

19. Though most politicians' speeches contain countless meaningless _____ we've all heard time and time again, Senator Truitt's seem to be composed of mostly **original** statements.

20. When Sheila saw that one group of our coworkers was doing its best to _____ me by refusing to invite me to lunch, she stepped in and made sure to **include** me in her own lunchtime plans.

21. There are moments when my thoughts are as _____ and straightforward as the ABC's, but there are times when all the ideas swirling through my head are totally **unintelligible**.

22. Witnessing the **cruel** acts committed against the inhabitants of the refugee camp, I was desperate to find any evidence of _____ treatment.

23. Despite his _____ appearance, he was actually a **vibrant** worker.

24. The boy's **stubborn** father refused to amend or allow leeway within any of his strict rules; mother, a more _____ parent, tended to see wiggle room wherever she could.

Applying Yourself:
Choose the best word to complete each of the following sentences.

25. The company _____ the laws meant to curb pollution by using a loophole in the regulations.
    (A) stultified
    (B) circumvented
    (C) alienated
    (D) conciliated
    (E) impaired

26. As a compassionate man, Mr. Ziegler was very _____ towards those less unfortunate than himself.
    (A) conciliatory
    (B) preeminent
    (C) alienated
    (D) humane
    (E) platitudinous

27. Instead of getting along peacefully with the other students, Charles remained _____ throughout the year.
    (A) alienated
    (B) conciliatory
    (C) lucid
    (D) humane
    (E) preeminent

28. Our class feared that the introduction to quantum mechanics would be too difficult to understand, but the professor's speech made the topic quite _____.
    (A) preeminent
    (B) stultifying
    (C) platitudinous
    (D) lucid
    (E) humane

29. The scandal had a _____ effect on company morale.
    (A) conciliatory
    (B) stultifying
    (C) preeminent
    (D) lucid
    (E) humane

30. T.S. Eliot strove to be the _____ poet of the modernist movement, and he was rewarded for his efforts with the Nobel Prize.
    (A) stultifying
    (B) conciliatory
    (C) preeminent
    (D) humane
    (E) lucid

31. While the other speakers offered insightful statements on the matter, Mr. Bennet's speech was full of _____.
    (A) platitudes
    (B) conciliations
    (C) stultification
    (D) preeminence
    (E) circumvention

32. Neville Chamberlain's _____ behavior toward Hitler allowed Germany to exercise power over a large swath of Europe without struggle.
    (A) conciliatory
    (B) circumvented
    (C) platitudinous
    (D) lucid
    (E) preeminent

On Your Own:
Write one sentence using each word below to demonstrate your understanding of the word's meaning.

33. **conciliatory** _____

34. **stultifying** _____

35. **preeminent** _____

36. **alienate** _____

37. **circumvent** _____

38. **lucid** _____

39. **humane** _____

40. **platitude** _____

C2 Advanced Vocabulary 112

First Impressions:

Using the example sentences below, write your own definition of each boldfaced word. Then write the letter of the definition from the box that best matches your definition.

A	verb: to deliver something somewhere in order to get rid of it	C	adjective: useful; intended to be used instead of enjoyed
B	verb: to make something continue	D	verb: to increase or add to something

1. _____ Trudy worked against those who would **perpetuate** negative stereotypes.

PERPETUATE means: _____

2. _____ The curriculum of the military boarding school was highly **utilitarian**; courses focused on

practical skills related to military tactics and engineering rather than the arts or humanities.

UTILITARIAN means: _____

3. _____ The police force **consigned** the disgraced officer to a solitary post in the middle of

nowhere.

CONSIGN means: _____

4. _____ I have been working to **augment** our sales effort so that we can achieve record profits.

AUGMENT means: _____

A	adjective: not material; not able to be perceived by touch; vague; elusive	C	adjective: modest; shy
B	adjective: very small	D	adjective: made of many varied parts

5. _____ She was never brash or boastful and usually had a **retiring** disposition.

RETIRING means: _____

6. _____ I tried to punch it, but my fist just went right through the ghost's **intangible** body.

INTANGIBLE means: _____

7. _____ There's a **minute** chance that we'll land a human on Mars in my lifetime, but I haven't

stopped hoping.

MINUTE means: _____

8. _____ The **multifarious** duties of the new assistant ranged from checking email and filling out

spreadsheets to walking the dog and taking the executive's son to his piano lessons.

MULTIFARIOUS means: _____

Divide and Conquer:
Choose the correct word to complete each of the following sentences.

9. He was a shy, (**utilitarian** / **retiring**) boy who needed encouragement to speak his mind.

10. After costing the company thousands of dollars, I was (**consigned** / **perpetuated**) to a tiny office in the middle of the desert.

11. Those who wish to survive in these harsh environs should adopt a (**utilitarian** / **minute**) viewpoint, in which each plant is evaluated according to its nutritional value.

12. If resort operators (**augment** / **consign**) rates too much and too quickly, they could hurt visitation.

13. He disliked learning about theoretical science and philosophy due to both fields' (**multifarious** / **intangible**) arguments.

14. The professor was knowledgeable in (**multifarious** / **minute**) topics, but this variety did not prevent him from studying in depth.

15. Don hoped to (**perpetuate** / **consign**) his good mood by having his favorite dessert.

16. The queen demanded that every (**augmented** / **minute**) detail must be perfect for the king's birthday party.

Hot and Cold:
Write the word from the lesson that is most nearly the *OPPOSITE* of the boldfaced word or words in each sentence below.

17. The population here is quite _____, consisting of people from all over the world, which encourages a much greater diversity of food and clothing choices than a **homogeneous** population would.

18. When I **ordered** the aging game machine, the sellers were thrilled to _____ it to me.

19. Hank wanted the cottage to have a(n) _____ feel so that nothing went inside that didn't have a direct purpose; his wife, who favored a more **decorative** feel, felt unwelcome in the cold space.

20. I began the night as a _____ newcomer, undesirous of drawing attention to myself, but became more and more **bold** and willing to meet people as time went on.

21. There was a _____ possibility that we would win the contest, but Paul's excitement made the odds seem **significant**.

22. "Suffering" and "war" are _____ concepts that reflect very material realities; you may not be **able to touch** the concept of "suffering," but you can see with your eyes and feel with your hands a home blown apart by a bomb.

23. Getting a full night's sleep _____ my mental clarity, while staying up all night tends to **deplete** my ability to concentrate.

24. Knowing that human lives are **temporary**, he tried to _____ his legacy by doing a stunt nobody could top.

Applying Yourself:
Choose the best word to complete each of the following sentences.

25. Reggie's parents _____ him to cleaning the basement, not wanting him around on the first floor of the house.
    - (A) augmented
    - (B) consigned
    - (C) perpetuated
    - (D) inscribed
    - (E) assailed

26. The _____ farmer never bragged of his flourishing crops, but instead, humbly used his money on the bare necessities and gave the rest to charity.
    - (A) perpetuated
    - (B) utilitarian
    - (C) augmented
    - (D) minute
    - (E) retiring

27. He became a vegetarian to enjoy the corporeal benefit of a healthy body and for the _____ benefit of having a clean conscience.
    (A) perpetuated
    (B) minute
    (C) intangible
    (D) multifarious
    (E) retiring

28. Our trek will be difficult, so be _____ rather than sentimental when choosing what you take.
    (A) multifarious
    (B) utilitarian
    (C) retiring
    (D) intangible
    (E) minute

29. We were only able to read a broad outline, so we don't understand all the _____ details of the situation yet.
    (A) minute
    (B) intangible
    (C) utilitarian
    (D) retiring
    (E) multifarious

30. People _____ rumors by retelling stories to others long after the events have happened.
    (A) consign
    (B) perpetuate
    (C) augment
    (D) assail
    (E) inscribe

31. A classroom cannot function on the teacher's work alone; a(n) _____ organization of administrators, parents, and specialists works together to make this happen.
    (A) intangible
    (B) minute
    (C) augmented
    (D) multifarious
    (E) perpetuated

32. Dr. Jones _____ the course with materials written by his research partner.
    (A) perpetuated
    (B) augmented
    (C) inscribed
    (D) consigned
    (E) assail

On Your Own:
Write one sentence using each word below to demonstrate your understanding of the word's meaning.

33. **perpetuate** _____

34. **minute** _____

35. **augment** _____

36. **intangible** _____

37. **utilitarian** _____

38. **consign** _____

39. **retiring** _____

40. **multifarious** _____

C2 Advanced Vocabulary 113

First Impressions:

Using the example sentences below, write your own definition of each boldfaced word. Then write the letter of the definition from the box that best matches your definition.

A	noun: oppression; a cruel government	**C**	adjective: conspicuously wicked; blatant; obvious; outrageous
B	noun: one who believes that events are governed by fate	**D**	verb: to leave one's native area to live in another

1. _____ Living under the **tyranny** of such an absolute government meant few civil rights for citizens.

TYRANNY means: _____

2. _____ Thampaly **emigrated** from Laos to escape the dangerous climate of the civil war.

EMIGRATE means: _____

3. _____ A dyed-in-the-wool **fatalist**, Josephine spent hours every week reading her star charts to learn what the future had in store for her.

FATALIST means: _____

4. _____ The accountant's acceptance of a bribe was a **flagrant** violation of the company's ethical standards.

FLAGRANT means: _____

A	adjective: dark; vague; unclear	**C**	noun: self-important behavior; arrogance
B	verb: to reprove severely; to rebuke	**D**	verb: to drive or force onward

5. _____ The mother **reprimanded** her son for teasing the young girl.

REPRIMAND means: _____

6. _____ Sun's **pomposity** amazed everyone when she demanded that she be allowed to cut to the front of the long line.

POMPOSITY means: _____

7. _____ It's now a luxury for a reporter to write a story about an **obscure** but important topic; most periodicals favor popular, flashy subjects.

OBSCURE means: _____

8. _____ After putting it off for as long as he could, his motherís threats finally **impelled** Jacob to clean his room.

IMPEL means: _____

Divide and Conquer:
Choose the correct word to complete each of the following sentences.

9. The author, who had escaped the (**tyranny / emigration**) of his homeland's government, became famous for his writing's explicit details of the horrors that he had witnessed.

10. Marjorie had a (**fatalistic / flagrant**) outlook, but her brother always felt that the future is uncertain and changeable.

11. The new principal carried himself with such (**pomposity / flagrance**) that the teachers mockingly referred to him as "his majesty."

12. The sociologist was engaged in creating an exhaustive list of the reasons citizens (**emigrate / reprimand**) from their countries, ranging from wars to economic factors.

13. After the thirty-minute lecture from his principal, Joshua knew that his mother would (**impel / reprimand**) him even more harshly.

14. The broadcaster's knowledge of baseball was so deep that he could always be counted on to recall (**flagrant / obscure**) bits of trivia.

15. As the girls' soccer coach, it was Mr. Brownís duty to (**reprimand / impel**) the players to reach higher levels of athleticism and skill.

16. The basketball player was ejected from the game for repeated (**flagrant / fatalistic**) violations of the rules.

Hot and Cold:
Write the word from the lesson that is most nearly the *OPPOSITE* of the boldfaced word or words in each sentence below.

17. Donna, a **believer in free will**, was certain that everyone was responsible for his or her own actions and was less forgiving than Marcia, a _____ who supposed that one's life was out of one's control.

18. Given the _____ of the last dictator, it was surprising that the rebels who implemented the new government didn't allow for more **liberalism** within it.

19. After the war, the Porcek family _____ from its homeland and arrived at a new country where thousands of other refugees were **immigrating**.

20. The _____ of the grand celebration embarrassed the king, who was known for his **humility** and unwillingness to display his importance or wealth.

21. Rather than _____ me for every little thing I do wrong, why not **praise** me occasionally for the things I do right?

22. If you were going to break every one of my rules, you might at least have been **subtle** about it, as this _____ display of defiance is humiliating to me.

23. Some parents must _____ their children to study using force or persuasion; Mr. Tyle has to **curb** his daughter's study habits for fear of her overworking herself.

Applying Yourself:
Choose the best word to complete each of the following sentences.

24. After several cars crashed on Applecross Boulevard due to its poor lighting, the city installed new lamps to light the once _____ street signs.
    (A) reprimanded
    (B) flagrant
    (C) fatalistic
    (D) tyrannical
    (E) obscure

25. Judge Mehta _____ the prosecuting attorney for his misbehavior.
    (A) bowdlerized
    (B) emigrated
    (C) reprimanded
    (D) impelled
    (E) obscured

26. I cannot bear _____, so we must fight those who would take away our rights in the name of order.
    (A) emigration
    (B) pomposity
    (C) fatalism
    (D) tyranny
    (E) flagrance

27. Burdened by sadness and dread, we felt _____ to tell Susan of her diagnosis.
    (A) bowdlerized
    (B) obscured
    (C) emigrated
    (D) impelled
    (E) reprimanded

28. My family _____ from Somalia to Canada in hopes of finding a better life.
    (A) impelled
    (B) emigrated
    (C) bowdlerized
    (D) obscured
    (E) reprimanded

29. We grew weary of Jed's _____ as he droned on about his many achievements as counsel at a small law firm.
    (A) obscurity
    (B) pomposity
    (C) tyranny
    (D) emigration
    (E) flagrance

30. The referees called a(n) _____ foul on Blake when he threw the opposing center to the floor.
    (A) obscure
    (B) tyrannical
    (C) pompous
    (D) flagrant
    (E) fatalistic

31. The _____ who lived by the river looked at the heavens when the floods came, expecting God to deliver him from harm.
    (A) obscurity
    (B) emigration
    (C) tyranny
    (D) fatalist
    (E) flagrance

On Your Own:
Write one sentence using each word below to demonstrate your understanding of the word's meaning.

32. **obscure** _____

33. **tyranny** _____

34. **pomposity** _____

35. **emigrate** _____

36. **impel** _____

37. **fatalist** _____

38. **flagrant** _____

39. **reprimand** _____

C2 Advanced Vocabulary 114

First Impressions:
Using the example sentences below, write your own definition of each boldfaced word. Then write the letter of the definition from the box that best matches your definition.

A	verb: to start a fire; to inspire	**C**	verb: to make someone or something seem less important; disparage
B	adjective: weak or lacking substance	**D**	noun: the ability to impress, inspire, and lead others

1. _____ Why would any self-respecting person deliberately **belittle** someone to the point of such despair?

BELITTLE means: _____

2. _____ Samantha may have been lacking in **charisma**, but due to her keen business sense she was promoted to leadership positions anyway.

CHARISMA means: _____

3. _____ The plans were cancelled after the calculations revealed that the chance of success was **tenuous** at best.

TENUOUS means: _____

4. _____ The friction caused a spark, which **kindled** the pile of twigs and dry leaves.

KINDLE means: _____

A	noun: a violation of that which is sacred	**C**	verb: to lecture in a long, moralizing way
B	adjective: faithless and treacherous	**D**	noun: naturally formed layer; level or division

5. _____ The geologist explained how each **stratum** of the rock reflected a different period of time, with earlier ages on the top and older ages on the bottom.

STRATUM means: _____

6. _____ How could you expect anyone to trust you after your **perfidious** behavior?

PERFIDIOUS means: _____

7. _____ The invaders burned the villagers' chapel, overturned their altar, and committed many other acts of **sacrilege**.

SACRILEGE means: _____

8. _____ Juliet rolled her eyes as her father **harangued** her once more for her failure to arrive at the dinner table on time.

HARANGUE means: _____

Divide and Conquer:

Choose the correct word to complete each of the following sentences.

9. Fair-weather friends are those who become (**sacrilegious / perfidious**) whenever the path becomes difficult.

10. Mr. Roberts (**harangued / belittled**) his son for forty minutes about the importance of calling home before changing his plans.

11. Those who post comments that ridicule or (**belittle / harangue**) others will be warned and then blocked from making further comments.

12. Timothy's career ambitions were (**belittled / kindled**) one day after a firefighter came to his classroom on career day to give a presentation.

13. The geologists examined the (**sacrilege / strata**) in the sedimentary rock to determine the frequency of earthquakes.

14. I told my students that their project had only a (**kindled / tenuous**) link to the principles of physics.

15. Mr. Daniels possessed extraordinary (**charisma / sacrilege**) that masked any flaws in his leadership ability.

16. Members of the native tribe wouldn't help the team infiltrate the tomb, as such an action would be (**sacrilege / stratum**).

Hot and Cold:

Write the word from the lesson that is most nearly the *OPPOSITE* of the boldfaced word or words in each sentence below.

17. Greta, a devout woman, atoned for the many _____ in her early life before she had joined the church with many **acts of devotion**.

18. I didn't want to _____ Michael's achievements, but I was careful not to **praise** him too much because I knew he had exaggerated his involvement in the successful merger.

19. The _____ alliance between the typically hostile nations would shatter like glass if either tried to take a **strong** stance against the concerns of the other.

20. I'll never understand how Curtis has such _____ that he can make friends and allies wherever he goes, yet despite my best efforts, I seem to have some kind of social **repellent** attached to me.

21. Tired of being _____ by my parents, I decided to clean my room so that they'd have no choice but to **leave me alone**.

22. Though his association with a dozen convicted spies made Agent Johns seem like a(n) _____ traitor, the truth was that he was a faithful man whose only crime was being imperceptive about those around him.

23. Camping in the woods, surrounded by the sounds and smells of nature, _____ my sense of appreciation for the world, while living in the grey, crowded city **quashed** it.

Applying Yourself:

Choose the best word to complete each of the following sentences.

24. The new manager _____ the department members for over two hours about the requirement to put real pride into their work.
    (A) kindled
    (B) harangued
    (C) belittled
    (D) obscured
    (E) emigrated

25. Old baseball fans think that comparing modern players to the heroes of yesteryear is a _____ against "the greats".
    (A) charisma
    (B) stratum
    (C) sacrilege
    (D) perfidy
    (E) haranguing

26. The _____ in the soil revealed evidence of a civilization that had been rebuilt time and time again.
    (A) haranguing
    (B) perfidy
    (C) sacrilege
    (D) charisma
    (E) stratum

27. Simpson's _____ grasp of the situation forced us to add a consultant to our staff to fill the gap.
    (A) belittled
    (B) kindled
    (C) tenuous
    (D) charismatic
    (E) perfidious

28. Try not to _____ their new design, even though you don't like the unenlightened compliments they are receiving.
    (A) belittle
    (B) harangue
    (C) kindle
    (D) obscure
    (E) reprimand

29. We cannot allow dodgy behavior to gain traction in our workforce; such actions lead to a _____ atmosphere in which every worker must fend for him or herself.
    (A) belittling
    (B) charismatic
    (C) tenuous
    (D) perfidious
    (E) sacrilegious

30. As team captain, Mag always _____ their hopes of winning and inspired them to finish the game by giving it their best.
    (A) obscured
    (B) kindled
    (C) belittled
    (D) harangued
    (E) reprimanded

31. _____, particularly the ability to inspire others to act, is necessary to attract followers to your cause.
    (A) Haranguing
    (B) Sacrilege
    (C) Perfidy
    (D) Charisma
    (E) Stratum

On Your Own:

Write one sentence using each word below to demonstrate your understanding of the word's meaning.

32. **sacrilege** _____

33. **kindle** _____

34. **tenuous** _____

35. **harangue** _____

36. **charisma** _____

37. **perfidious** _____

38. **stratum** _____

39. **belittle** _____

C2 Advanced Vocabulary 115

First Impressions:

Using the example sentences below, write your own definition of each boldfaced word. Then write the letter of the definition from the box that best matches your definition.

A	noun: a wise old saying that teaches a lesson	**C**	adjective: large in scope but unrealistic; marked by profound imagination and foresight
B	verb: to avoid, dodge, or narrowly escape	**D**	verb: to confuse or complicate in order to conceal

1. _____ Some citizens feel that bills **obfuscate** the political process by hiding several small laws in a bundle with more impactful legislation.

OBFUSCATE means: _____

2. _____ Mr. Daniels reined in his **visionary** imaginings in order to find a new but practical solution to the problem.

VISIONARY means: _____

3. _____ I was able to **avert** punishment by blaming the cat for knocking over the vase.

AVERT means: _____

4. _____ Mrs. Rey keeps the following **proverb** engraved above her door: Do unto others as you would have them do unto you.

PROVERB means: _____

A	verb: to annoy by repeated attacks; to torment	**C**	adjective: believing that no knowledge is certain, especially philosophical or religious knowledge
B	noun: someone who is an expert on a particular thing	**D**	verb: to provide evidence in support of a claim

5. _____ The witness' statement **corroborated** the suspect's report, and she was released from prison.

CORROBORATE means: _____

6. _____ Lizl believed strongly in a higher power, but to her dying day remained **agnostic** about what that power might be.

AGNOSTIC means: _____

7. _____ Because I love museums, I have become a **connoisseur** of certain types of art.

CONNOISSEUR means: _____

8. _____ He claimed he was **harassed** and threatened by local policemen.

HARASS means: _____

Divide and Conquer:
Choose the correct word to complete each of the following sentences.

9. I am proud to say that the claims in my paper are (**corroborated / averted**) by expert opinion.

10. Nancy (**harassed / averted**) a social crisis by inviting everyone in her class to her birthday party instead of leaving out a jealous few.

11. Laura enjoyed reading the (**visionary / corroborated**) works of early science-fiction authors.

12. Kasparov (**obfuscated / harassed**) his intended attack by concealing his queen in the back row until it was ready to strike.

13. Kelli complained loudly that her younger sister refused to stop (**corroborating / harassing**) her.

14. An old (**obfuscation / proverb**) states that "The sourest fruits make the tastiest juice."

15. My uncle Joe is a (**proverb / connoisseur**) of baseball statistics and can tell you the batting average of any player.

16. The mathematician described himself as a devout (**corroboration / agnostic**), willing to consider any point of view but accepting it only on the basis of its evidence.

Hot and Cold:
Write the word from the lesson that is most nearly the *OPPOSITE* of the boldfaced word or words in each sentence below.

17. The seagulls seemed determined to _____ me with obnoxious noises and pecking, despite my best effort to **soothe** them.

18. He thought that what he was saying was a _____, but, in actuality, it was a **cliché**.

19. Known as he was for his **dull and everyday thinking**, Jacob surprised everyone with his _____ insight.

20. Governments were trying to _____ an energy crisis, but power companies were **aiding** the oncoming disaster.

21. I take a(n) _____ view toward spirituality in that I claim that nothing can be known for sure, but my mother, a devout Catholic, is much more **certain about her beliefs**.

22. It was impossible to _____ Miley's story, but quite easy for it to be **disproved**.

23. I am a **beginner** at painting, but my teacher is a true _____ who can paint in any style imaginable.

24. Officials may try to _____ the truth with fancy-sounding language, but this short pamphlet should **illuminate** the meaning of most of the legislation.

Applying Yourself:
Choose the best word to complete each of the following sentences.

25. Scientists must maintain a(n) _____ mindset bent toward even the most accepted theories, such as gravity.
    - (A) corroborated
    - (B) obfuscated
    - (C) agnostic
    - (D) averted
    - (E) visionary

26. As the asteroid headed towards the planet, world leaders tried desperately to _____ disaster.
    - (A) avert
    - (B) harass
    - (C) corroborate
    - (D) obfuscate
    - (E) consign

27. He is a(n) _____ of fine wines; he can tell one type from another based on taste alone.
    (A) proverb
    (B) visionary
    (C) aversion
    (D) connoisseur
    (E) obfuscation

28. If no one else can _____ your statement, we are going to suspect that you are lying.
    (A) augment
    (B) avert
    (C) corroborate
    (D) obfuscate
    (E) harass

29. Jason looked paranoid while walking through the vacant hallway, worried that the bullies might _____ him yet again.
    (A) avert
    (B) harass
    (C) corroborate
    (D) obfuscate
    (E) perpetuate

30. Leonardo da Vinci was a(n) _____ whose sketches include plans for a rudimentary helicopter.
    (A) proverb
    (B) connoisseur
    (C) visionary
    (D) aversion
    (E) agnostic

31. The spy's role is to _____ his true intentions while undercover.
    (A) harass
    (B) avert
    (C) obfuscate
    (D) corroborate
    (E) perpetuate

32. Religious figures are known to use many _____ to explain moral lesson succinctly.
    (A) agnostics
    (B) obfuscations
    (C) connoisseurs
    (D) proverbs
    (E) visionaries

On Your Own:
Write one sentence using each word below to demonstrate your understanding of the word's meaning.

33. **avert** _____

34. **harass** _____

35. **visionary** _____

36. **agnostic** _____

37. **connoisseur** _____

38. **proverb** _____

39. **corroborate** _____

40. **obfuscate** _____

C2 Advanced Vocabulary 116

First Impressions:
Using the example sentences below, write your own definition of each boldfaced word. Then write the letter of the definition from the box that best matches your definition.

A	noun: the rejection of any rational system of morality or value	**C**	adjective: acting superior to someone else; looking down on others
B	noun: a beginner	**D**	adjective: biased; having a liking for something

1. _____ Samantha prefers vanilla, but Siwon is **partial** to chocolate.

PARTIAL means: _____

2. _____ The young **novice** had only begun learning the trade of blacksmithing a few months ago.

NOVICE means: _____

3. _____ I assured my mother that my investigation of my beliefs and moral code would not result in a descent into **nihilism**.

NIHILISM means: _____

4. _____ My tutor is rather **condescending**, insulting me whenever I don't understand the material.

CONDESCENDING means: _____

A	verb: to involve as a necessary consequence	**C**	noun: lack of calm or peace; anxiety or uneasiness
B	verb: to avoid or do without	**D**	noun: what is left over from something else; remains

5. _____ The **residue** of pollen from Mom's many bouquets makes me sneeze all day.

RESIDUE means: _____

6. _____ As an experiment in simple living, Henry David Thoreau **eschewed** many of the comforts of city life while he lived in a small rustic cabin for two years.

ESCHEW means: _____

7. _____ The CEO's comments caused great **disquiet** among the company's investors, who were suddenly wondering if the company would survive another year.

DISQUIET means: _____

8. _____ The job **entails** a variety of types of work, including cleaning, bookkeeping, and customer service.

ENTAIL means: _____

Divide and Conquer:

Choose the correct word to complete each of the following sentences.

9. The plan (**entails / eschews**) improving relations between the two countries.

10. Though (**partial / disquieted**) in a variety of ways, my cousin exhibits the most bias toward people who are taller than she.

11. No matter how much I cleaned, I couldn't remove an oily (**residue / novice**) from the kitchen floor.

12. My (**condescending / novice**) brother treats me like a child even though I'm only 10 months younger than he.

13. The older apprentices teased the (**novice / condescension**) for his lack of expertise regarding the matter.

14. Richard decided to (**eschew / entail**) a flu shot and, predictably, came down with chills and a sore throat early in the winter.

15. Maxine's (**disquiet / nihilism**) deepened as the beam of the flashlight slowly faded.

16. His (**condescension / nihilism**) shows when the subject of redemption for the afterlife comes up; he simply does not see the point.

Hot and Cold:

Write the word from the lesson that is most nearly the *OPPOSITE* of the boldfaced word or words in each sentence below.

17. I'm no **expert** in grammar, and I can hardly answer high-level questions, but after taking four courses on the subject I'm hardly a _____ either.

18. The project will _____ hiring one more employee to split the burden of work but **will not require** either of you to work overtime.

19. The party had an air of _____ about it, as though a huge fight were going to break out any minute; the hostess, accordingly, couldn't catch a moment of **peace** as she ran about trying to remedy the situation.

20. My older sister is **sympathetic** to my difficulties and never takes a _____ tone toward me when I ask for help with my homework.

21. Early settlers of America were _____ to Native American cuisine, adopting many local foods, but were **biased** against the religious practices of those same people.

22. Lina had long _____ family life, preferring to go at it alone, but she began to **embrace** the close company of others in her old age.

Applying Yourself:

Choose the best word to complete each of the following sentences.

23. We could tell by the awkward unpracticedness of his golf swing that he was a(n) _____.
    (A) residue
    (B) novice
    (C) condescending man
    (D) disquieted person
    (E) eschewed athlete

24. Johnson _____ the traditional way of doing things in favor of a more dynamic plan.
    (A) belittled
    (B) condescended
    (C) disquieted
    (D) eschewed
    (E) entailed

25. I was offended by his _____ tone, as I didn't think that he was in any way better than I was.
    (A) novice
    (B) condescending
    (C) nihilistic
    (D) eschewed
    (E) partial

26. Our bankruptcy _____ our selling our house.
    (A) entailed
    (B) condescended
    (C) belittled
    (D) disquieted
    (E) eschewed

27. Macbeth, Shakespeare's anti-hero, saw life as a meaningless pursuit, and is one of the prime examples of _____ in literature.
    (A) novice
    (B) condescension
    (C) residue
    (D) nihilism
    (E) disquieting

28. Despite their vigorous cleaning, there was still a(n) _____ of dirt left on their faces after their showers.
    (A) belittling
    (B) novice
    (C) residue
    (D) nihilism
    (E) entailment

29. The _____ in the hallways after the students died in the plane crash caused the principal to make psychological counseling available.
    (A) nihilism
    (B) partiality
    (C) disquiet
    (D) residue
    (E) novice

30. Please don't serve apple pie at Thanksgiving; most of us are _____ to pumpkin.
    (A) nihilistic
    (B) partial
    (C) condescending
    (D) novice
    (E) disquieted

On Your Own:

Write one sentence using each word below to demonstrate your understanding of the word's meaning.

31. **nihilism** _____

32. **eschew** _____

33. **entail** _____

34. **condescending** _____

35. **partial** _____

36. **novice** _____

37. **disquiet** _____

38. **residue** _____

C2 Advanced Vocabulary 117

First Impressions:
Using the example sentences below, write your own definition of each boldfaced word. Then write the letter of the definition from the box that best matches your definition.

A	verb: to expand by stretching	C	adjective: repentant for wrongdoing
B	verb: to respect; to value; to judge	D	noun: a person who is high in social class

1. _____ We find it impossible to **esteem** any right or law that does not help to produce peace in the region.

ESTEEM means: _____

2. _____ The **patricians** of the city were seen every year at the exclusive Founders' Day charity ball.

PATRICIAN means: _____

3. _____ The water **distended** the balloon and eventually caused it to burst.

DISTEND means: _____

4. _____ Kevin offered to repair the broken fence himself to show that he was truly **penitent** for his mistake.

PENITENT means: _____

A	adjective: dark or obscure	C	noun: incitement of rebellion or discontent
B	noun: a person who is distrustful of human motives	D	noun: a wicked, immoral person; an unprincipled man

5. _____ Murali was unwilling to enter the **tenebrous** attic unless his father let him use the large flashlight.

TENEBROUS means: _____

6. _____ In order to preserve his position of power, the dictator regularly purged any party members suspected of **sedition**.

SEDITION means: _____

7. _____ As Oscar Wilde said, "A cynic is a man who knows the price of everything but the value of nothing."

CYNIC means: _____

8. _____ The prison's revolutionary program was successful in preparing even the worst **reprobates** to reenter society.

REPROBATE means: _____

Divide and Conquer:
Choose the correct word to complete each of the following sentences.

9. The black trees formed a (**penitent / tenebrous**) barrier to other side of the field.

10. Shay's Rebellion was a form of (**sedition / reprobate**) against the new American government.

11. Call me a (**cynic / patrician**), but I think that our two new leaders' houses suggest that they've been taking bribes.

12. After he landed the important contract, Ricardo received the (**patrician / esteem**) of his coworkers.

13. After realizing his error, Josh appeared (**penitent / cynical**) before the principal.

14. Each item of clothing added to the suitcase caused its walls to (**esteem / distend**) until it seemed ready to explode.

15. (**Seditions / Patricians**) including business leaders, heirs, and socialites attended the gala in droves.

16. Marcus stepped off the train expecting his old, safe hometown, but he was surprised to see rough streets filled with (**reprobates / patricians**).

Hot and Cold:
Write the word from the lesson that is most nearly the *OPPOSITE* of the boldfaced word or words in each sentence below.

17. The huge meal _____ my belly, and I had to wait hours before it would **shrink** again.

18. While the _____ controlled most of the land and the vast majority of the nation's wealth, the **plebeians** were the ones who worked the land.

19. I _____ Claude as an honest and respectable man, but I **despise** his ill-tempered and sometimes cruel wife.

20. Though he was accused of being a careless _____ and a danger to the community, Huckleberry Finn was actually a **decent fellow** who cared very much for his friends.

21. The **idealist** in Joanna wanted to believe the man was being honest in telling her he needed cash to repair his car, but the _____ in her suspected he was looking for a handout to feed an alcohol or drug addiction.

22. If you can find your way through the windowless, _____ hallway, shrouded in shadows, you'll find a door concealing a **bright**, cheerful room perfect for reading or merely passing the time.

23. One of the accused robbers, as he cried upon the stand, seemed truly _____ for his crimes; the other, explaining that he simply needed the money, was **unrepentant** for breaking into the home.

24. The _____ in the underground magazine was meant to encourage discontent and contrast the strict **institutionalism** in the mainstream newspapers.

Applying Yourself:
Choose the best word to complete each of the following sentences.

25. Only the _____ man can gain mercy for the jury by begging for its forgiveness.
    - (A) distended
    - (B) penitent
    - (C) seditious
    - (D) tenebrous
    - (E) cynical

26. Drinking excessive amounts of water can _____ the stomach, leaving the drinker feeling bloated.
    - (A) distend
    - (B) esteem
    - (C) delude
    - (D) entail
    - (E) buttress

27. Stephanie, a thorough _____, didn't trust her roommate's sudden friendliness and suspected that she had been the one that broke Stephanie's new laptop.
    (A) penitence
    (B) patrician
    (C) reprobate
    (D) cynic
    (E) esteem

28. The bar was filled with _____ willing to do any unsavory act for money.
    (A) reprobates
    (B) penitents
    (C) patricians
    (D) esteem
    (E) cynics

29. Kathy found that John _____ her less when it was revealed that she had lied during the campaign.
    (A) deluded
    (B) distended
    (C) buttressed
    (D) entailed
    (E) esteemed

30. After the violent populist uprising, the French Revolution gave way to the Directory, in which five _____ dictated the way in which government would be run.
    (A) reprobates
    (B) penitents
    (C) patricians
    (D) cynics
    (E) idylls

31. Napoleon quelled acts of _____ with "a whiff of grapeshot", thereby restoring order to the area.
    (A) patrician
    (B) reprobate
    (C) cynicism
    (D) esteem
    (E) sedition

32. We're entering a(n) _____ stage of our project, one which none of us can shed any light upon.
    (A) seditious
    (B) tenebrous
    (C) cynical
    (D) esteemed
    (E) penitent

On Your Own:
Write one sentence using each word below to demonstrate your understanding of the word's meaning.

33. **penitent** _____

34. **patrician** _____

35. **distend** _____

36. **reprobate** _____

37. **sedition** _____

38. **tenebrous** _____

39. **esteem** _____

40. **cynic** _____

C2 Advanced Vocabulary 118

First Impressions:

Using the example sentences below, write your own definition of each boldfaced word. Then write the letter of the definition from the box that best matches your definition.

A	noun: rebellion against a civil authority or government	**C**	noun: an expression of feelings; the act of pouring forth or out
B	verb: to make a false claim; to pretend to do something	**D**	noun: a shaking or a quivering movement

1. _____ The leaders of the American Revolution knew that, if they went forward with their **insurrection** and were caught by the British, they would surely be hung.

INSURRECTION means: _____

2. _____ The magazine **purports** that the financial crisis was caused by overspending at restaurants, but that claim seems false.

PURPORT means: _____

3. _____ **Effusions** of thanks flowed forth from Sreyas after he received the unexpected but needed help.

EFFUSION means: _____

4. _____ The **tremor** made Lucia run to a doorframe, afraid it was the beginning of yet another earthquake.

TREMOR means: _____

A	noun: the appearance of being true or real	**C**	adjective: reliant on begging to survive
B	noun: combativeness; a disposition to fight	**D**	adjective: diligent and unceasing

5. _____ Rebecca was **assiduous** in her efforts to learn the material and was rewarded with high marks.

ASSIDUOUS means: _____

6. _____ Members of **mendicant** orders live simple lives devoid of worldly possessions, having taken vows of poverty to spend all of their energy in service to God or the poor.

MENDICANT means: _____

7. _____ The photograph had been altered, but the changes were made with such **verisimilitude** that only a few experts could tell what had been done.

VERISIMILITUDE means: _____

8. _____ No one doubted that Swapnil would become a famous boxer; his **pugnacity** was obvious even in grade school.

PUGNACITY means: _____

Divide and Conquer:

Choose the correct word to complete each of the following sentences.

9. I was overcome with (**tremors / insurrections**) as I remembered the terrifying event.

10. The authors crafted their paper which such (**verisimilitude / assiduousness**) that some scientists were actually convinced that cold fusion was real.

11. When Li joined the (**mendicant / tremor**) order of monks, he gave up all of his possessions except his clothing, his glasses, and his begging bowl.

12. After McCloud pulled the woman out of the path of the speeding automobile she expressed her gratitude with a(n) (**effusion / mendicant**) of thanks.

13. The successful (**insurrection / verisimilitude**) resulted in the toppling of the newly formed military government.

14. Marigold was (**effusive / assiduous**) in her studies, and, for her dedication, she was rewarded with high marks.

15. Sometimes, there is only a fine line between assertiveness and (**pugnacity / mendicant**).

16. The professor (**purports / effuses**) to know every major political figure we discuss.

Hot and Cold:

Write the word from the lesson that is most nearly the *OPPOSITE* of the boldfaced word or words in each sentence below.

17. For a long time we enjoyed **stillness**, but suddenly the _____ came back and everyone fell over again.

18. I couldn't help that my feelings for James tumbled out in a(n) _____ every now and then; some things are too strong to be subject to **tacitness**.

19. **Careless** and disorganized during my first semester, I managed to fail almost every class and have since adopted much more _____ and productive study habits.

20. The **wealthy** company chose to devote 20% of its income to _____ individuals, families, and other beggars.

21. Though the novel's use of actual wartime footage gave it some _____, the overwrought dialogue evidenced its **inauthentic** quality.

22. The man who had _____ to be the heir to the king was proven to have been an imposter; no one has **rightfully claimed** the throne.

23. I was astonished to witness such _____ in one whom I had always respected for his **cool-headedness**.

Applying Yourself:

Choose the best word to complete each of the following sentences.

24. Drita's _____ of sorrow at the death of her only daughter rang through the somber church.
    (A) verisimilitude
    (B) insurrection
    (C) mendicant
    (D) effusion
    (E) pugnacity

25. San Francisco's population is a study of contrasts: on one hand is the wealthy, and on the other, is a(n) _____ population on the streets, hats in hand.
    (A) assiduous
    (B) effusive
    (C) pugnacious
    (D) mendicant
    (E) purported

26. There hasn't been a big earthquake here for years, but there have been many minor _____.
    (A) insurrections
    (B) verisimilitudes
    (C) effusions
    (D) tremors
    (E) mendicants

27. Our counterfeited $20 bill shows _____, enough to fool all but the most sophisticated experts.
    (A) insurrection
    (B) effusion
    (C) verisimilitude
    (D) pugnacity
    (E) assiduity

28. His _____ constantly got him in trouble; he never looked for a way to compromise peacefully.
    (A) pugnacity
    (B) effusion
    (C) verisimilitude
    (D) insurrection
    (E) pugnacity

29. Our government could not expect democracy to have taken hold so quickly after the _____ had toppled the tyrant.
    (A) mendicant
    (B) verisimilitude
    (C) effusion
    (D) insurrection
    (E) tremor

30. Because of the importance of the contract, I will devote _____ effort to its development until the signing on Monday morning.
    (A) effusive
    (B) assiduous
    (C) mendicant
    (D) purported
    (E) pugnacious

31. The man was _____ to be from the bank, but he was really a secret agent working for the government.
    (A) pugnacious
    (B) purported
    (C) assiduous
    (D) effused
    (E) insurrected

On Your Own:
Write one sentence using each word below to demonstrate your understanding of the word's meaning.

32. **purport** _____

33. **tremor** _____

34. **effusion** _____

35. **verisimilitude** _____

36. **insurrection** _____

37. **mendicant** _____

38. **assiduous** _____

39. **pugnacity** _____

C2 Advanced Vocabulary 119

First Impressions:

Using the example sentences below, write your own definition of each boldfaced word. Then write the letter of the definition from the box that best matches your definition.

A	adjective: dark; not transparent	**C**	noun: a critical or hurtful remark
B	noun: a male leader, especially one that is advanced in age	**D**	adjective: weak; fragile

1. _____ During election season, the candidates cast **aspersions** against each other's characters in heated political advertisements.

ASPERSION means: _____

2. _____ Though he was too advanced in age to participate in the hunt, the **patriarch** of the tribe was a source of valuable wisdom to the younger members.

PATRIARCH means: _____

3. _____ Although chemotherapy is a reliable treatment for cancer, its side-effects can render cancer patients extremely **frail**.

FRAIL means: _____

4. _____ The **opaque** envelope revealed none of the letter's secrets.

OPAQUE means: _____

A	adjective: concerned with following specific rules exactly, especially without considering alternatives	**C**	verb: to threaten someone in order to intimidate them into doing something
B	adjective: inconsistent; lacking order, plans, or purpose	**D**	adjective: pretending to feel or have virtues one does not

5. _____ I understand being told when I've done something wrong, but you needn't **browbeat** me with it.

BROWBEAT means: _____

6. _____ In times of change, a **doctrinaire** attitude may prevent one from finding a new solution.

DOCTRINAIRE means: _____

7. _____ Kyle studied in a **desultory** manner, working his way through courses ranging from chemistry to painting to computer programming and saving the decision of a specific focus for later years.

DESULTORY means: _____

8. _____ Landon thought it was **hypocritical** for Diego to go partying after all that talk about the importance of tomorrow's big test.

HYPOCRITICAL means: _____

Divide and Conquer:
Choose the correct word to complete each of the following sentences.

9. The heavy loss of blood from the accident left April in a(n) (**opaque / frail**) state for several days.

10. Despite his slight drop in energy, Grandfather remained the (**patriarch / frailty**) of our family, and we followed his direction unquestioningly.

11. Bridgette completed her chores in a (**desultory / patriarchal**) fashion, sulkily wishing to be elsewhere doing something more interesting.

12. The malicious newspaper editorial was filled with many cruel (**patriarchs / aspersions**).

13. The new bill is so (**frail / opaque**) that even experienced legal and political scholars have struggled with it.

14. My friends (**impelled / browbeat**) me into going out with them, although I really wanted to stay home.

15. An experienced leader recognizes the value of tradition but avoids the temptation of a (**doctrinaire / hypocritical**) approach.

16. The students found it (**opaque / hypocritical**) for the teacher to lecture about the importance of completing homework on time but repeatedly put off grading quizzes.

Hot and Cold:
Write the word from the lesson that is most nearly the *OPPOSITE* of the boldfaced word or words in each sentence below.

17. I maintained a **strong** opposition to the recommendation of bed rest, knowing that lying around for months would make me as _____ as a little lamb.

18. Lynn found the attendees at the downtown church _____ and resented them for pretending to be good while acting sinfully; she much preferred the **genuine** women and men at the church across town.

19. For the church windows, the designers alternated each pane between **clear** glass to let in plenty of light and _____ glass to obscure the view from outside.

20. My parents' _____ interest in my studies has meant that I've been the party most **concerned** about my own progress.

21. If you want your children to be happy, **encourage** them to explore their ideas; don't _____ them with your own.

22. The old doctor's _____ unwillingness to bend the rules in any situation made him less popular than the more **liberal** chief of medicine.

23. Jimmy's teacher wrote a report card full of _____ against the boy, accusing him of being lazy and cruel, and included not a single piece of **praise**.

Applying Yourself:
Choose the best word to complete each of the following sentences.

24. Sarah thought her sister, Mariah, was being _____ when she chastised Sarah for spending too much money, for Mariah had maxed out their parents' credit card just a few weeks earlier.
    (A) hypocritical
    (B) opaque
    (C) desultory
    (D) frail
    (E) browbeaten

25. The glass shower doors, which were once crystal clear, had become _____ due to years of residue build-up.
    (A) hypocritical
    (B) frail
    (C) opaque
    (D) eulogized
    (E) squandered

26. The _____ old man could barely walk up the stairs, requiring assistance from his grandchildren.
    (A) browbeaten
    (B) doctrinaire
    (C) opaque
    (D) frail
    (E) desultory

27. The general organized what had been, prior to her arrival, a(n) _____ system.
    (A) browbeaten
    (B) frail
    (C) desultory
    (D) doctrinaire
    (E) opaque

28. Interpreting the law in a(n) _____ rather than a flexible way can lead to gross injustice.
    (A) frail
    (B) doctrinaire
    (C) desultory
    (D) hypocritical
    (E) browbeaten

29. The school bully _____ Reed into doing whatever the bully wanted.
    (A) eulogized
    (B) browbeat
    (C) precluded
    (D) deluded
    (E) squandered

30. Our respectable _____ has the wisdom and experience to render his decision in a fair way.
    (A) opacity
    (B) hypocrite
    (C) doctrinaire
    (D) aspersion
    (E) patriarch

31. During the breakup, each person's _____ were intended to cut the other to the core.
    (A) doctrinaires
    (B) frailties
    (C) hypocrites
    (D) aspersions
    (E) patriarchs

On Your Own:
Write one sentence using each word below to demonstrate your understanding of the word's meaning.

32. **browbeat** _____

33. **doctrinaire** _____

34. **hypocritical** _____

35. **patriarch** _____

36. **opaque** _____

37. **desultory** _____

38. **frail** _____

39. **aspersion** _____

C2 Advanced Vocabulary 120

First Impressions:

Using the example sentences below, write your own definition of each boldfaced word. Then write the letter of the definition from the box that best matches your definition.

A	noun: the point at which two things come together	**C**	noun: an irresistible urge to do something
B	noun: a general feeling of lack of wellness	**D**	adjective: fat; large and round, usually describing a person

1. _____ When the feelings of **malaise** first hit Jaewon, he began to get more rest in order to stave off stronger symptoms.

MALAISE means: _____

2. _____ Her **rotund** belly suggested that she was about to give birth at any moment.

ROTUND means: _____

3. _____ Our ideas met in a **confluence** of joint creativity.

CONFLUENCE means: _____

4. _____ After brushing my teeth, I feel the **compulsion** to wash my hands even though I know they aren't dirty.

COMPULSION means: _____

A	verb: to waver; to fluctuate	**C**	adjective: held back in action or speech
B	adjective: actual; the opposite of metaphorical; interpreting words at their most basic meaning	**D**	adjective: oval in shape; unclear or cryptic

5. _____ The **elliptical** orbit of the earth around the sun is partly responsible for the seasons: the earth's closeness to the sun has a direct effect on surface temperatures.

ELLIPTICAL means: _____

6. _____ I was surprised to see my friend, who is typically quite talkative, so unusually **restrained** in speech.

RESTRAINED means: _____

7. _____ We were instructed to list not only the words' **literal** definitions, but also what the words made us think of.

LITERAL means: _____

8. _____ His tendency to **vacillate** on decisions caused others to label him a flip-flopper.

VACILLATE means: _____

Divide and Conquer:
Choose the correct word to complete each of the following sentences.

9. Frank's parents (**bide** / **vacillate**) over the decision of whether to send their son to soccer camp, uncertain whether it would be fun or a terrible burden for him.

10. Jeremy was not sure whether his (**malaise** / **confluence**) was the first sign of an illness or simply the result of a lack of sleep.

11. It was surprising to see my friend, who typically is extremely vocal, so (**restrained** / **literal**) in her speech.

12. In a courtroom, it's very important to be (**compulsive** / **literal**) and not take any liberties with the truth.

13. Despite common belief, the earth's shape is not quite a sphere; the cross section is slightly (**elliptical** / **vacillated**).

14. The (**confluence** / **malaise**) of the rivers was a popular vacation spot.

15. Looking at the pie cooling on the windowsill, I felt a strong (**malaise** / **compulsion**) to eat it.

16. Her cat is getting so (**rotund** / **compulsive**) that the vet advised it be put on a diet.

Hot and Cold:
Write the word from the lesson that is most nearly the *OPPOSITE* of the boldfaced word or words in each sentence below.

17. I am waiting for this dreadful _____ to pass before taking on any activities of exertion; I haven't been in full **health** in weeks.

18. In **figurative** language, you might use one phrase to represent something else; in _____ language, you mean exactly what you say.

19. The _____ of our ideas into one masterful plan marked our **divergence** from mediocrity into greatness.

20. Apple-shaped people are _____ in their mid-sections, but they have relatively **slender** legs.

21. Because they were _____ and decorous people, the Wilsons' **wild** children were an unexpected result of their union.

22. Whenever Frank had a scab, he was incapable of **ignoring** it and felt a _____ to pick it.

23. These instructions are so _____ that I doubt we'll be able to follow them unless they are rewritten to be more **clear**.

24. After _____ for months between which wedding dress to choose, it was time for me to **decide**.

Applying Yourself:
Choose the best word to complete each of the following sentences.

25. The _____ man was so large that he was too wide to fit through the doors of his house.
    (A) compulsive
    (B) literal
    (C) elliptical
    (D) rotund
    (E) restrained

26. I have a _____ for cleanliness; I dust my room at least once a day.
    (A) confluence
    (B) vacillation
    (C) malaise
    (D) compulsion
    (E) restraint

27. The _____ of the two rivers is an important place for ships to meet.
    (A) compulsion
    (B) confluence
    (C) restraint
    (D) malaise
    (E) vacillation

28. A _____ overcame Yuri upon returning from space, so he checked into the hospital to see what the problem was.
    (A) restraint
    (B) malaise
    (C) vacillation
    (D) compulsion
    (E) confluence

29. The _____ prophesy has mystified scholars for centuries.
    (A) rotund
    (B) literal
    (C) compulsive
    (D) elliptical
    (E) confluent

30. It was so hot that the old exaggeration that "you could cook an egg on the sidewalk" became _____.
    (A) literal
    (B) restrained
    (C) elliptical
    (D) vacillated
    (E) rotund

31. He remained constant in his choice of favorite dessert but _____ between favorite sports teams from year to year.
    (A) restrained
    (B) revered
    (C) vacillated
    (D) bided
    (E) avowed

32. The director, typically outlandish in his presentation, decided on a more _____ approach in his most recent film.
    (A) restrained
    (B) compulsive
    (C) confluent
    (D) vacillated
    (E) elliptical

On Your Own:
Write one sentence using each word below to demonstrate your understanding of the word's meaning.

33. **restrained** _____

34. **elliptical** _____

35. **malaise** _____

36. **literal** _____

37. **vacillate** _____

38. **rotund** _____

39. **compulsion** _____

40. **confluence** _____

C2 Advanced Vocabulary 121

First Impressions:
Using the example sentences below, write your own definition of each boldfaced word. Then write the letter of the definition from the box that best matches your definition.

A	noun: one who is a new member of a group	**C**	verb: to give up a claim, right, or position of power
B	noun: a great commotion and confusion	**D**	noun: excessive amount

1. _____ Heart disease and obesity caused by chronic overeating show that a **surfeit** of nutritious food can be nearly as hazardous as a lack.

SURFEIT means: _____

2. _____ The revolution left the country in **turmoil** for weeks before the new government took power.

TURMOIL means: _____

3. _____ After more than 20 years as the CEO of Microsoft, Bill Gates **abdicated** his position in order to concentrate on running his charitable foundation.

ABDICATE means: _____

4. _____ The veteran monks welcomed the **neophytes** and helped them to become accustomed to their new lives.

NEOPHYTE means: _____

A	noun: seriousness; gravity	**C**	adjective: related to shepherds or peaceful rural life
B	adjective: not constant; happening at random intervals	**D**	adjective: capricious; fanciful

5. _____ After the hustle and bustle of decades as a public official, Nancy retired to a **bucolic** existence on her family's Wyoming ranch.

BUCOLIC means: _____

6. _____ The **solemnity** of my father's voice made me realize how upset he was with my mistake.

SOLEMNITY means: _____

7. _____ I'm usually happy, but I feel **intermittent** sadness, too.

INTERMITTENT means: _____

8. _____ The stern and serious Lizzie was a stark contrast to her playful and **whimsical** husband Frank.

WHIMSICAL means: _____

Divide and Conquer:

Choose the correct word to complete each of the following sentences.

9. The (**whimsical / neophyte**) contractor had just learned the basics of floor installation, so we ended up with an odd mix of wood and linoleum.

10. The jurors returned to the courtroom, and the (**neophyte / solemnity**) of their expressions indicated a guilty verdict.

11. The painter showed (**solemn / bucolic**) scenes in edgy, modern ways; one work shows a farmer in a spiked leather jacket relaxing against a haystack.

12. The (**abdicated / intermittent**) pain I feel is nothing compared to the constant pain I had before surgery.

13. After 40 years as the nation's ruler, the king (**obviated / abdicated**) his throne in order to live in scholarly seclusion.

14. I lost Shelly in the (**neophyte / turmoil**) of the packed club's power outage.

15. Charlotte's (**bucolic / whimsical**) personality was a breath of fresh air among all of the other stuffy students.

16. Unemployment meant that Charles had a (**neophyte / surfeit**) of idle time on his hands.

Hot and Cold:

Write the word from the lesson that is most nearly the *OPPOSITE* of the boldfaced word or words in each sentence below.

17. The two sides of my family could not have experienced more different upbringings: My mother's _____ childhood involved milking cows, raising sheep, and building barns, while my father's **metropolitan** one involved living in a high-rise apartment in the middle of a bustling city.

18. I felt a(n) _____ panic that I'd lost my passport, so I'd made **constant** checks for it.

19. The sitcom's characters included a **sober and steady** lawyer and a _____ artist forced to share a small apartment.

20. The farmer was thrilled with the crop _____ that would mean there would be no **lack** of food to last through the winter.

21. After the queen _____ the throne, leaving a void of power, anyone was free to **claim authority** and instate him or herself as the monarch.

22. The room, heavy with the _____ of the sad occasion, was injected with **levity** when the child asked why everyone looked like their favorite toy was lost.

23. The **veterans** of the club took the _____ under their wings.

24. Tania's head spun with inner _____ about the jury's decision, unsure whether they were making the right decision, but her face maintained a countenance of **peace** as she read the verdict out loud: Not guilty.

Applying Yourself:

Choose the best word to complete each of the following sentences.

25. Rather than accept the responsibilities of ruling, Edward _____ the English throne.
    (A) abdicated
    (B) excoriated
    (C) absolved
    (D) obscured
    (E) scintillated

26. A(n) _____ fell over the students as they contemplated the seriousness of Mrs. Johnson's condition.
    (A) solemnity
    (B) turmoil
    (C) abdication
    (D) surfeit
    (E) whimsicality

27. _____ in World War II were greeted cautiously by veteran units, because the veterans knew that newcomers didn't possess the experience necessary to survive.
   (A) Grievances
   (B) Benedictions
   (C) Neophytes
   (D) Sanctions
   (E) Abdications

28. The highway from Brisbane gave way to a country road with _____ scenes of sheep and quaint cottages.
   (A) abdicated
   (B) bucolic
   (C) whimsical
   (D) intermittent
   (E) solemn

29. I wouldn't expect a tragedy such as Hamlet to have any _____ moments, but I had to smile when Rosencrantz and Guildenstern spoke.
   (A) bucolic
   (B) intermittent
   (C) solemn
   (D) whimsical
   (E) abdicated

30. A civil war had thrown the once-peaceful country into a frenzied state of _____.
   (A) solemnity
   (B) whimsicality
   (C) surfeit
   (D) turmoil
   (E) abdication

31. The alarm went off _____, making me suspect that the clock was broken.
   (A) intermittently
   (B) whimsically
   (C) solemnly
   (D) bucolically
   (E) narcissistically

32. Jesse feels that her large, close family leaves her with a(n) _____ of emotional riches.
   (A) neophyte
   (B) whimsicality
   (C) solemnity
   (D) surfeit
   (E) turmoil

On Your Own:
Write one sentence using each word below to demonstrate your understanding of the word's meaning.

33. **turmoil** _____

34. **abdicate** _____

35. **neophyte** _____

36. **whimsical** _____

37. **solemnity** _____

38. **intermittent** _____

39. **bucolic** _____

40. **surfeit** _____

C2 Advanced Vocabulary 122

First Impressions:
Using the example sentences below, write your own definition of each boldfaced word. Then write the letter of the definition from the box that best matches your definition.

A	adjective: lacking energy or interest	**C**	adjective: devout; religious
B	noun: secret plotting and schemes	**D**	noun: any nourishing food

1. _____ Through careful **machinations**, the pair bribed, backstabbed, and plotted its way to the top of the criminal organization.

MACHINATION means: _____

2. _____ During summer vacation, Jezebel spent many **languid** hours lounging by the pool with a magazine.

LANGUID means: _____

3. _____ The hungry survivors of the disaster were offered **pabulum** in the cafeteria of the university.

PABULUM means: _____

4. _____ The Puritans were particularly **pious** individuals who attended church regularly and believed their faith to be the most important aspect of their lives.

PIOUS means: _____

A	adjective: arrogant and superior	**C**	verb: to express great joy and excitement
B	verb: to forbid or do away with by official order	**D**	adjective: capricious; changing; fickle

5. _____ Rick's family **exulted** when he won the spelling bee.

EXULT means: _____

6. _____ Due to the **mercurial** weather patterns of the area, a clear morning sky could be filled with storm clouds by early afternoon.

MERCURIAL means: _____

7. _____ The laws of Prohibition were **abrogated** by the Twenty-First Amendment because they were unpopular with the public at large.

ABROGATE means: _____

8. _____ Mitchell's **haughty** attitude frustrated his coworkers, who found his boasting excessive and unwarranted.

HAUGHTY means: _____

Divide and Conquer:
Choose the correct word to complete each of the following sentences.

9. While not the most glamorous fare, the freeze-dried (**exultation** / **pabulum**) provided all the nutrients we needed.

10. In a popular decision, the city (**abrogated** / **exulted**) the act that had raised taxes to an unprecedented rate and returned to its prior taxation policy.

11. After running the marathon, Isabel was happy to relax on her couch in a(n) (**languid** / **abrogated**) haze for the evening.

12. A (**mercurial** / **pious**) decision-making style can be helpful to people working in creative fields, but business leaders must be more reliable and predictable to succeed.

13. Through years of careful (**machination** / **haughtiness**), the villain rose to a position of power.

14. Kathy, who was not religious, often clashed with her (**languid** / **pious**) parents, who regularly attended church and urged their daughter to go as well.

15. The (**languid** / **haughty**) celebrity refused to even look at the crowd of adoring fans.

16. The athlete (**exulted** / **machinated**) in his success after he achieved first place in the state competition.

Hot and Cold:
Write the word from the lesson that is most nearly the *OPPOSITE* of the boldfaced word or words in each sentence below.

17. My family's _____ to try and get me to date Jaime bother me in their secretiveness; I would respond much better to **openness**.

18. The more _____ members of the congregation insisted that no **irreverent** action be committed within the church walls.

19. The most **attentive** students sit in the front of the room, taking notes and asking questions, while the more _____ ones tend to stay in the back, napping or chatting.

20. Frieda's _____ air made her a terrible associate to bring to meetings with new clients, who always preferred someone more **humble** and less arrogant.

21. While most of the employees _____ at the news of getting raises, Maria **frowned** knowing that the increase in her pay would likely precede an increase in hours.

22. The earlier decrees _____ interracial marriage were stricken down as archaic and nearly barbarian, and new laws banning marriage restrictions were **sanctioned**.

23. While my opinions on certain political topics are _____ and dependent on the latest evidence I've seen, or even what's happening in my personal life, my general conservative leaning is **steadfast** and hasn't changed over many years.

Applying Yourself:
Choose the best word to complete each of the following sentences.

24. A(n) _____ attitude from an incoming boss will earn that person enmity among the underlings in the company, as they resent any hint of arrogance.
    (A) exulted
    (B) mercurial
    (C) pious
    (D) haughty
    (E) supplanted

25. The _____ fans would lambast their star in one moment and praise her the next.
    (A) machinating
    (B) mercurial
    (C) haughty
    (D) mercurial
    (E) languid

26. Rather than engage in a potentially disastrous military conflict, we should quietly employ _____ to render the leadership of our enemy ineffective.
    (A) piety
    (B) exultation
    (C) haughtiness
    (D) machinations
    (E) abrogation

27. Military rations contain dried fruit, vegetables, and a variety of other healthful _____.
    (A) abrogation
    (B) haughtiness
    (C) exultation
    (D) pabulum
    (E) languidness

28. When a city's team wins the Stanley Cup, players from that side are able to tour with it, allowing regular fans to _____ in the victory.
    (A) dissent
    (B) supplant
    (C) machinate
    (D) exult
    (E) abrogate

29. Sheila gave up a _____ life in order to follow the rules of man rather than those of God.
    (A) exulted
    (B) pious
    (C) mercurial
    (D) haughty
    (E) languid

30. King Henry _____ the practice of Catholicism by his subjects after he had founded the Anglican church.
    (A) supplanted
    (B) dissented
    (C) abrogated
    (D) machinated
    (E) exulted

31. Our _____ roommate elected to sleep in and watch cartoons rather than join us on the hike.
    (A) machinating
    (B) mercurial
    (C) pious
    (D) haughty
    (E) languid

On Your Own:
Write one sentence using each word below to demonstrate your understanding of the word's meaning.

32. **exult** _____

33. **mercurial** _____

34. **pious** _____

35. **machination** _____

36. **haughty** _____

37. **pabulum** _____

38. **abrogate** _____

39. **languid** _____

C2 Advanced Vocabulary 123

First Impressions:

Using the example sentences below, write your own definition of each boldfaced word. Then write the letter of the definition from the box that best matches your definition.

A	verb: to give birth to or create, especially something unpleasant	**C**	noun: animal life
B	noun: an unethical or immoral act by a public official	**D**	noun: seriousness; avoidance of excess, especially of alcohol

1. _____ The performance of such an act by any member of society cannot be tolerated, and its perpetration by an elected leader is a **malfeasance** of the worst kind.

MALFEASANCE means: _____

2. _____ After rabbits were introduced to Australia their population exploded, as the local **fauna** contained none of the rabbit's natural predators.

FAUNA means: _____

3. _____ Kevin's college career was marked by **sobriety**; on Friday nights, he could be found at his desk while his roommate was out partying.

SOBRIETY means: _____

4. _____ The unpopular new regulations **spawned** unruly protests and even riots all over the city.

SPAWN means: _____

A	adjective: fearful; cautious due to fear	**C**	adjective: exuberant; bubbly and excited
B	verb: to work together to achieve a common goal	**D**	adjective: unmoved; lacking concern

5. _____ Tess's **effervescent** attitude was contagious, and soon I found myself jumping up and down alongside her.

EFFERVESCENT means: _____

6. _____ Having expected their teacher to be excited by the surprise, the students were puzzled by her **indifferent** response.

INDIFFERENT means: _____

7. _____ Timothy bragged about his bravery, but he was clearly **timorous** when he saw the neighbor's large dog.

TIMOROUS means: _____

8. _____ We cannot hope to succeed unless all of the parties involved **collaborate** to find a solution.

COLLABORATE means: _____

Divide and Conquer:
Choose the correct word to complete each of the following sentences.

9. The (**fauna / indifference**) of the island include several large reptiles and birds but surprisingly few mammals.

10. The president was impeached in disgrace for his (**collaboration / malfeasance**).

11. Dissolved carbon dioxide is responsible for the (**effervescence / fauna**) of champagne, soda, and other beverages.

12. Globalization has (**spawned / collaborated**) an age in which multinational corporations can play one country against another in an attempt to secure benefits.

13. In an effort to encourage (**sobriety / malfeasance**), the senior class hosted a free party after prom with adult chaperones.

14. Nikhil was largely (**indifferent / effervescent**) to the holiday, perfectly willing to allow others their fun but personally not interested in participating.

15. The mountain is treacherous, so the (**sober / timorous**) tend to survive, while the arrogant do not.

16. The software developer specialized in tools that would enable workers in different areas to (**spawn / collaborate**) on projects as if they were in the same room.

Hot and Cold:
Write the word from the lesson that is most nearly the *OPPOSITE* of the boldfaced word or words in each sentence below.

17. Few members of the opposing political parties wanted to _____ to produce results; most were interested in the bad-spirited **bickering** they had been engaging in for years.

18. That first visit to a casino _____ a terrible love for gambling in me that no reason or sense could **kill**.

19. It was refreshing to see such _____ children after enduring the **uninteresting** board meeting.

20. Though the government appeared _____ toward the suffering of its citizens, it was more a lack of resources than a lack of **concern** that kept federal aid from the people.

21. After years of _____ avoiding alcohol and any other mood-altering substances, my father fell back into his old **indulgence** and bought a bottle of vodka.

22. Geraldine's **brazen** attitude toward new situations makes her brother's _____ approach seem almost cowardly.

23. Years of **ethical action** could not excuse the governor's major _____, which cost him both his reputation and his title.

Applying Yourself:
Choose the best word to complete each of the following sentences.

24. The amount of bubbles in the _____ brew fascinated the scientists.
    (A) timorous
    (B) indifferent
    (C) sober
    (D) effervescent
    (E) collaborated

25. Mrs. Lundburgh's kids are as repulsive as she is, and I hear she will _____ another before the year's end.
    (A) define
    (B) censure
    (C) spawn
    (D) collaborate
    (E) effervesce

26. The flora of the grounds consists largely of rose bushes; the _____ is more diverse, with deer, raccoons, hawks, and wild turkeys.
    (A) fauna
    (B) collaboration
    (C) malfeasance
    (D) effervescence
    (E) sobriety

27. The children were _____ toward the clowns at the birthday party and ignored the antics of the costumed comedians.
    (A) collaborative
    (B) timorous
    (C) effervescent
    (D) sober
    (E) indifferent

28. Those with _____ children should avoid the amusement park entirely, for an endless river of tears would be the result.
    (A) collaborative
    (B) timorous
    (C) effervescent
    (D) sober
    (E) indifferent

29. Once bitter rivals, the two scientists finally _____ on a project and won the Nobel Prize.
    (A) defined
    (B) expedient
    (C) collaborated
    (D) spawned
    (E) censured

30. Becoming the best athlete one can be demands _____ and clean, simple living.
    (A) fauna
    (B) timorousness
    (C) effervescence
    (D) sobriety
    (E) indifference

31. The constituents grew weary of their candidate's _____ and decided to replace her with a more upstanding person.
    (A) collaborations
    (B) malfeasances
    (C) fauna
    (D) effervescence
    (E) sobriety

On Your Own:

Write one sentence using each word below to demonstrate your understanding of the word's meaning.

32. **collaborate** _____

33. **fauna** _____

34. **malfeasance** _____

35. **spawn** _____

36. **timorous** _____

37. **effervescent** _____

38. **sobriety** _____

39. **indifferent** _____

C2 Advanced Vocabulary 124

First Impressions:
Using the example sentences below, write your own definition of each boldfaced word. Then write the letter of the definition from the box that best matches your definition.

A	noun: a large, dangerous whirlpool	**C**	noun: the release of emotional tension through action
B	adjective: able to be understood without logic or evidence	**D**	adjective: friendly; without serious disagreement

1. _____ Kenneth was delighted by his **amicable** new coworkers, who by the end of his first workday had already invited him to two parties and a basketball game.

AMICABLE means: _____

2. _____ After a stressful day at work Devon enjoyed the **catharsis** of swinging a golf club as hard as he could at the driving range.

CATHARSIS means: _____

3. _____ The ship steered well clear of the dangerous **maelstrom** that had claimed so many other vessels.

MAELSTROM means: _____

4. _____ Ingrid had an **intuitive** sense of grammar, but she had trouble expressing this understanding in words to other people.

INTUITIVE means: _____

A	adjective: related to the intellect rather than emotion	**C**	adjective: yearning; thoughtful and longing
B	verb: to scold or condemn	**D**	noun: chaos; the state of being without government or control

5. _____ The teacher **vituperated** the student for his failure to complete three homework assignments in a row.

VITUPERATE means: _____

6. _____ Chess is considered by some to be the most **cerebral** of games; in fact, the grand masters of chess are among the greatest intellectuals of their nations.

CEREBRAL means: _____

7. _____ Some people favor strong governments, while some favor total **anarchy**.

ANARCHY means: _____

8. _____ Henry looked through his old photograph albums with a **wistful** look on his face.

WISTFUL means: _____

Divide and Conquer:
Choose the correct word to complete each of the following sentences.

9. Without a teacher, the kindergarten classroom was reduced to (**catharsis** / **anarchy**) as the children ran and screamed.

10. The ability of Sherlock Holmes to solve crimes with his incredible deductive skills makes him one of the most (**cerebral** / **anarchistic**) figures in fiction.

11. I was worried that the debate would degenerate into a heated argument, but the discussion remained quite (**amicable** / **cerebral**).

12. After my first year of working 80-hour weeks, I grew (**wistful** / **cathartic**) for the relatively carefree days of college.

13. The instruction manual of the product is largely unnecessary, as the operation of the product is highly (**amicable** / **intuitive**).

14. The sailors directed their course around the terrible (**vituperation** / **maelstrom**) that had pulled many vessels to their doom.

15. After a stressful day of studying Neil enjoyed the (**amicability** / **catharsis**) of lifting heavy barbells.

16. Although it might seem correct to (**vituperate** / **permeate**) new workers for their slow pace, a more encouraging tact produces better results.

Hot and Cold:
Write the word from the lesson that is most nearly the *OPPOSITE* of the boldfaced word or words in each sentence below.

17. Denise cast a _____ glance at her ex-boyfriend, Todd, remembering the good times they had shared, but Todd's **unfeeling** return stare threw cold water on her thoughtful mood.

18. Finally being able to cry was a tremendous _____ for June, who had been **stoic** for too long.

19. The entire school was harshly _____ by some news sources for allowing teen mothers to bring their children to class, but most people in the community **praised** the school's inclusive attitude.

20. I have no **logical** explanation for why I decided to stay home from work that day, but my _____ feeling was that something bad would happen at my workplace—and it did.

21. For me, music is less of a _____ concern than an **emotional** one—I don't mind if I don't play technically correctly, but I do mind if I don't feel in my heart what I play with my hands.

22. It's time the **hostile** feelings between the two former friends were resolved; it's be nice if you could at least be _____, even if you don't want to be best friends.

23. The sergeant favored **order** and strict rules, fearing that any sign of weakness on his part would lead to _____ in the platoon.

Applying Yourself:
Choose the best word to complete each of the following sentences.

24. In the science fiction story, a(n) _____ sucks ships into a magical underground lake beneath the sea.
    (A) catharsis
    (B) anarchy
    (C) amicability
    (D) vituperation
    (E) maelstrom

25. Words of _____ rarely serve the reader; save your confessions for your diary.
    (A) wistfulness
    (B) catharsis
    (C) anarchy
    (D) vituperation
    (E) amicability

26. Don't allow the rest of your life to be only a(n) _____ remembrance of youth.
    (A) vituperated
    (B) wistful
    (C) amicable
    (D) intuitive
    (E) cathartic

27. After the government collapsed, the city quickly disintegrated into _____.
    (A) wistfulness
    (B) amicability
    (C) catharsis
    (D) vituperation
    (E) anarchy

28. Many think learning languages is _____, but it is more of a deductive process.
    (A) wistful
    (B) intuitive
    (C) amicable
    (D) cerebral
    (E) anarchic

29. It is best for a commanding officer to think of his job as a _____ exercise, as emotional responses can jeopardize the success of a mission.
    (A) wistful
    (B) cerebral
    (C) intuitive
    (D) cathartic
    (E) vituperated

30. Jonas had to listen to his parents _____ him for hours after he missed his curfew.
    (A) intuit
    (B) vituperate
    (C) desiccate
    (D) assail
    (E) belie

31. Chelsea's prickly demeanor contrasted sharply with Marie's _____ nature; indeed, Marie was generally more popular for this reason.
    (A) amicable
    (B) cerebral
    (C) vituperated
    (D) wistful
    (E) anarchic

On Your Own:

Write one sentence using each word below to demonstrate your understanding of the word's meaning.

32. **wistful** _____

33. **maelstrom** _____

34. **amicable** _____

35. **anarchy** _____

36. **intuitive** _____

37. **catharsis** _____

38. **cerebral** _____

39. **vituperate** _____

C2 Advanced Vocabulary 125

First Impressions:

Using the example sentences below, write your own definition of each boldfaced word. Then write the letter of the definition from the box that best matches your definition.

A	adjective: high-pitched and grating; difficult to listen to	**C**	adjective: clever; cunning; noticing small details
B	noun: change; the introduction of something new	**D**	adjective: hostile; aggressive; warlike

1. _____ "If you insist on taking such a **belligerent** stance on the issue," Eliska warned, "you're

going to make several enemies."

BELLIGERENT means: _____

2. _____ The Florida outbreak might have gone unnoticed if it hadn't been for an **astute** physician

in upstate New York.

ASTUTE means: _____

3. _____ The university president stressed the importance of constant **innovation** to stay

competitive in a changing world.

INNOVATION means: _____

4. _____ My brother emits a **shrill** scream when he wants to watch Power Rangers, indicating that

he's more than a little obsessed with the show.

SHRILL means: _____

A	noun: a small system which contains in miniature every important part of a larger system	**C**	noun: a small and often uncredited appearance in a play, movie, or TV show
B	verb: to pollute or destroy something that is sacred	**D**	noun: flattery; admiration

5. _____ The terrarium was a **microcosm** of the Florida everglades, containing a sample of thirty-

two plants and twelve animals common to the environment.

MICROCOSM means: _____

6. _____ Fortunately, even the constant **adulation** of his adoring fans hasn't gone to Craig's head.

ADULATION means: _____

7. _____ The celebrity surprised everyone by making a **cameo** in the local play.

CAMEO means: _____

8. _____ Police are in search of the individuals who **desecrated** several homes with racial slurs.

DESECRATE means: _____

Divide and Conquer:

Choose the correct word to complete each of the following sentences.

9. After he solved the problem that had been plaguing the company for months, Kevin enjoyed the (**adulation / cameo**) of his coworkers.

10. Some thought it was inappropriate for the queen to make a (**shrill / cameo**) appearance on a comedy show.

11. After Achilles defeated Hector in battle he (**innovated / desecrated**) the body by dragging it behind his chariot in front of the gates of Troy.

12. Though the area was officially a neutral zone, both armies were guilty of committing secretly (**astute / belligerent**) actions in the region.

13. Dr. Milan exhibited his (**microcosmic / astute**) business sense at a young age by building the most profitable lemonade stand in the tri-state area.

14. The bird's (**belligerent / shrill**) call keeps me up all night.

15. Several well-timed (**innovations / shrillness**) helped the company to leap ahead of its competition by bringing new ideas to the market.

16. The island in Lord of the Flies is a(n) (**innovation / microcosm**) of human society, complete with the conflict between civilized and primitive thoughts.

Hot and Cold:

Write the word from the lesson that is most nearly the *OPPOSITE* of the boldfaced word or words in each sentence below.

17. A small business, with its complex social interactions and economy, is a _____ of a city, and a global economy is a **macrocosm** of the small business.

18. Harriet's busy schedule prevented her from accepting the **lead role**, so she offered instead to make a _____.

19. The marauders _____ the holysite, and it had to be **hallowed** by church members before it could again be used for religious purposes.

20. A lack of sleep turned Wynona from a **gentle, compliant** student into a _____ nuisance in class.

21. I always feel frustrated when I'm looking for an _____, or at least interesting, response to a question, and a student finds it funny to respond with something **utterly silly**.

22. She was relieved to go to the beach and listen to the **soothing** waves after hearing her _____ boss speak all day.

23. One company encouraged _____; the other, mired in **tradition**, demanded that workers strictly follow old-fashioned methods.

24. Because she had enjoyed such enthusiastic _____ when she announced her decision to run for governor, Mayor McGuff was surprised by the **criticism** she now received as an official gubernatorial candidate.

Applying Yourself:

Choose the best word to complete each of the following sentences.

25. Pollsters pay attention to certain precincts in Ohio that are _____ of the demographics the state.
    (A) microcosms
    (B) cameos
    (C) adulations
    (D) desecrations
    (E) shrill

26. When she's angry, my mother's voice can get quite _____.
    (A) innovative
    (B) belligerent
    (C) desecrated
    (D) shrill
    (E) microcosmic

27. His _____ nature was well-suited for the physically demanding combat he often engaged in.
    (A) innovative
    (B) shrill
    (C) belligerent
    (D) desecrated
    (E) astute

28. I'm not sure if it was him, but I'm pretty sure I saw Will Ferrell make a brief _____ in that movie.
    (A) desecration
    (B) belligerence
    (C) cameo
    (D) microcosm
    (E) innovation

29. Creative teachers will seek development in their classroom demeanors as well as _____ in the overall curricula from time to time.
    (A) innovations
    (B) desecrations
    (C) belligerence
    (D) shrillness
    (E) adulation

30. The star-struck fan devolved into an _____-spouting wreck when meeting her idol for the first time.
    (A) microcosm
    (B) cameo
    (C) adulation
    (D) belligerence
    (E) innovation

31. Crazed fans often _____ with paint the tombstones next to the grave of rock legend Jim Morrison.
    (A) desecrated
    (B) adulated
    (C) innovated
    (D) censured
    (E) augmented

32. The _____ observer will see the differences between the original and the forgery.
    (A) shrill
    (B) belligerent
    (C) astute
    (D) innovative
    (E) desecrated

On Your Own:

Write one sentence using each word below to demonstrate your understanding of the word's meaning.

33. **desecrate** _____

34. **belligerent** _____

35. **astute** _____

36. **shrill** _____

37. **adulation** _____

38. **innovation** _____

39. **microcosm** _____

40. **cameo** _____

Glossary

Use this glossary to find the definitions of words and study for vocabulary quizzes.

Word	PoS	Definition	Lesson
abdicate	verb	to give up a claim, right, or position of power	121
abhor	verb	to very strongly dislike	103
abject	adjective	hopeless or pitiful	38
abjure	verb	to shun or renounce	57
abortive	adjective	undeveloped; unable to succeed	4
abrasive	adjective	grinding down; irritating in manner	2
abrogate	verb	to forbid or do away with by official order	122
absolute	adjective	complete; certain; pure; perfect; ultimate	4
absolve	verb	to release from guilt; to declare someone free from blame	6
abstract	adjective	theoretical; existing as an idea, but not in reality	39
abstruse	adjective	obscure; profound; hard to understand	76
accessible	adjective	easily approachable; obtainable	33
acclaim	verb	to applaud; to announce with great celebration	90
accolade	noun	an award; an award ceremony	105
accord	noun	harmony; agreement	37
accost	verb	to approach or confront boldly	25
acme	noun	the developmental peak of something; the highest point	103
acquiesce	verb	to assent, submit, or agree without resistance	27
acrid	adjective	sharp; harsh; having a particularly bad taste or smell	9
acrimonious	adjective	marked by strong resentment or bitterness	58
acumen	noun	good judgment; skill	7
adage	noun	a traditional saying that teaches a lesson	45
adherent	noun	supporter; follower	33
admonish	verb	to scold	46
adulation	noun	flattery; admiration	125
adumbrate	verb	to foreshadow or suggest in an unclear way; to indicate faintly	72
adversary	noun	opponent; enemy	11
adversity	noun	opposition to success	89
advocate	verb	to urge; to support	56
affable	adjective	easily approachable; friendly; pleasant	3
affectation	noun	an attempt to give a false impression	12
affinity	noun	a natural liking; a similarity	61
agenda	noun	a plan of events or tasks to accomplish	78
aggressor	noun	attacker	6
agnostic	adjective	believing that no knowledge is certain, especially philosophical or religious knowledge	115
alacrity	noun	cheerful readiness for action	43
albeit	conjunction	although	28
alias	noun	a fake name used as a disguise	67
alienate	verb	to cause someone to feel isolated or hostile	111
allocate	verb	to distribute a collected resource among several parties	26
allusion	noun	a reference to something else, often a work of art	74
altercation	noun	an argument or fight, usually in public	23
altruistic	adjective	unselfishly generous; concerned for others	31
ambience	noun	the mood or atmosphere of a place	96
ambiguous	adjective	unclear or doubtful in meaning; open to many different interpretations	92

Word	PoS	Definition	Lesson
ambitious	adjective	desiring greater power or influence	100
ambivalence	noun	uncertain or fluctuating emotions	68
amenity	noun	a special feature that adds value or comfort	20
amiable	adjective	friendly	37
amicable	adjective	friendly; without serious disagreement	124
amnesty	noun	forgiveness for wrongdoings, especially when granted by a government	46
amoral	adjective	lacking a sense of right and wrong	14
amorous	adjective	related to love, especially sexual love	32
ample	adjective	abundant; sufficient; many	51
anachronism	noun	something that is not in its correct historical time	30
analogy	noun	a similarity; a comparison	103
anarchy	noun	chaos; the state of being without government or control	124
anathema	noun	something disliked universally	44
anecdote	noun	a short account of an amusing or interesting event	48
animadversion	noun	a critical comment	68
animated	adjective	excited; moving quickly	21
animosity	noun	a feeling of strong dislike that might lead to a fight	32
anomaly	noun	something unusual or out of the ordinary	20
antagonism	noun	enmity; the state of being against someone or something else	92
antagonist	noun	an opponent or adversary	9
anthology	noun	a compilation of different writings	63
apartheid	noun	a formal system that separates people by race or other criteria	13
apathy	noun	indifference; lack of interest or concern	67
aphorism	noun	a saying or maxim, usually expressing some sort of general truth	77
aplomb	noun	composure and self-assurance	32
apocalypse	noun	worldwide destruction or disaster, especially when predicted by prophecy	85
apocryphal	adjective	untrue; false; made up	102
apotheosis	noun	the raising of a person to the rank of a god	105
appreciate	verb	to be thankful for; to increase in value; to be fully conscious of; to hold in high regard	95
approbation	noun	approval, especially from an official source	47
aptitude	noun	ability or talent	72
arcane	adjective	obscure; known only by a few	95
ardor	noun	heat; passion; intense devotion or enthusiasm	79
arid	adjective	dry; lacking in water	37
aristocrat	noun	a member of a powerful, wealthy ruling class	1
arrogate	verb	to claim without a right	95
artful	adjective	cunning or skillful	19
aspersion	noun	a critical or hurtful remark	119
assail	verb	to assault; to attack	104
assess	verb	to analyze; to test out	46
assiduous	adjective	diligent and unceasing	118
astute	adjective	clever; cunning; noticing small details	125
asylum	noun	a place of safety and protection; a hospital for the mentally ill	16
atheism	noun	the belief that no god or gods exist	52
atone	verb	to make amends for a crime or sin	52
attentive	adjective	considerate; thoughtful; paying attention; polite	44
attrition	noun	a wearing down or reduction over time	10
audacious	adjective	daring; bold; inventive; insolent; unrestrained	83
augment	verb	to increase or add to something	112
auspicious	adjective	favorable of success	50

Word	PoS	Definition	Lesson
austere	adjective	harsh, strict, or plain	104
authentic	adjective	real; genuine; reliable; not false or copied	39
authoritarian	adjective	favoring or exercising total control; not democratic	3
autocratic	adjective	ruling with absolute authority	75
avarice	noun	excessive greed for wealth	54
avert	verb	to avoid, dodge, or narrowly escape	115
avid	adjective	fervent; passionate; devoted	40
avow	verb	to openly state	88
avuncular	adjective	related to an uncle; having the qualities of an uncle	8
awry	adjective	twisted out of shape; incorrect	18
axiom	noun	a basic principle that is accepted as true without proof	35
bane	noun	a cause of ruin, destruction, or death	96
bastion	noun	someone or something strongly upholding certain beliefs or principles; a feature of a fortress	26
belabor	verb	to discuss or worry more than is necessary	103
beleaguer	verb	to surround with troubles or military forces	73
belie	verb	to contradict; to show as false; to misrepresent	75
belittle	verb	to portray as less impressive than something really is	114
belligerent	adjective	hostile; aggressive; warlike	125
bemused	adjective	puzzled; lost in thought	13
benediction	noun	a spoken blessing, usually given by a priest or other spiritual figure	71
benevolent	adjective	generous; charitable; not intended for profit	18
benign	adjective	showing gentleness or kindness; not harmful	20
biased	adjective	having a strong opinion for one side of an issue	6
bibulous	adjective	having a tendency to drink, especially alcohol	98
bide	verb	to wait patiently [usually to "bide one's time"]	88
blandish	verb	to influence through flattery	64
blight	noun	a disease; an agent that causes widespread harm	1
blockade	verb	to cut off from additional supplies, especially with ships	36
bolster	verb	to support or reinforce	66
bon vivant	noun	someone who enjoys luxuries of life, such as food	94
boon	noun	a blessing; something that is asked for	77
boorish	adjective	obnoxious and stubborn	59
bountiful	adjective	filled with plenty; abundant	4
bovine	adjective	related to a cow or ox	98
bowdlerize	verb	to censor a piece of writing by removing offensive portions	95
braggadocio	noun	empty and excessive boasting	7
brawn	noun	muscular strength	67
browbeat	verb	to threaten someone in order to intimidate them into doing something	119
brusque	adjective	sudden and blunt	10
bucolic	adjective	related to shepherds or peaceful rural life	121
bureaucracy	noun	a large organization of many committees, agencies, and bureaus	107
bustle	verb	to move quickly, excitedly, and busily	98
buttress	verb	to support or prop up; to encourage	103
cacophony	noun	a loud, unpleasant mixture of sounds	52
cadaver	noun	a dead human body	77
cadence	noun	a rhythmic falling of words, sounds, steps, etc.; a beat	86
caitiff	noun	a low-class, cowardly, despicable person	84
callow	adjective	immature or inexperienced	75
calumny	noun	a false statement intended to hurt another's reputation	96

Word	PoS	Definition	Lesson
camaraderie	noun	fellowship; friendliness among members of a group	67
cameo	noun	a small and often uncredited appearance in a play, movie, or TV show	125
candor	noun	the quality of being frank, open, and sincere	62
capitalism	noun	a system in which wealth, goods, and businesses are controlled by individuals instead of a government	97
capitulate	verb	to surrender unconditionally	59
capricious	adjective	subject to spur-of-the-moment whims or decisions	105
captious	adjective	prone to noticing small defects; difficult to please	6
cascade	noun	a waterfall; something that resembles a waterfall	59
castigate	verb	to scold	38
casualty	noun	any person that is harmed as a result of an event	59
categorical	adjective	without any exceptions	108
catharsis	noun	the release of emotional tension through action	124
catholic	adjective	universal; involving a wide range of tastes or ideas	54
cavort	verb	to dance and celebrate in an excited fashion	12
censorious	adjective	severely critical; eager to find fault	50
censure	verb	to blame, criticize, or disapprove harshly	51
cerebral	adjective	related to the intellect rather than emotion	124
certitude	noun	certainty; freedom from doubt	52
charisma	noun	the ability to impress, inspire, and lead others	114
charlatan	noun	a person who pretends to know or to be capable of more than they really are	75
chicanery	noun	deception intended to take advantage of others	85
chimera	noun	a fictional creature made from parts of different animals; an unlikely product of imagination	47
choleric	adjective	impatient; easily angered	48
chronic	adjective	constant; habitual; continuing over a long period	34
chronicle	noun	a historical record of events	90
chronological	adjective	arranged in order by time	30
circuitous	adjective	not direct	15
circumspect	adjective	cautious and prudent	91
circumvent	verb	to avoid by strategy or deception	111
clamor	noun	a loud noise	60
claustrophobia	noun	a fear of being in enclosed or narrow places	60
clemency	noun	the tendency or act of being compassionate or merciful	37
clerisy	noun	the group of members of society who are highly educated or literate	47
cliché	noun	an expression or idea that is very common or unoriginal	54
clique	noun	a small exclusive group	19
cloister	noun	a place for religious thought; a monastery or convent	86
cloying	adjective	unpleasant because of excess; excessively sweet	3
coda	noun	an additional passage added onto the end of an existing work	15
coercion	noun	use of force or intimidation to get someone to behave or act in a desired way	98
cognitive	adjective	related to the processes of thinking	92
coherent	adjective	consistent and logically connected	29
collaborate	verb	to work together to achieve a common goal	123
commemorate	verb	to honor the memory of; to serve as a memorial or reminder of	58
commensurate	adjective	having the same or proportional measures	61
compelling	adjective	overpowering; having an irresistible effect	23
compendium	noun	a brief but complete collection of a body of knowledge	51
competent	adjective	having sufficient, skill, knowledge, etc.; adequate	31
compile	verb	to assemble; to gather into one place or source; to make of materials from various sources	38

Word	PoS	Definition	Lesson
compliance	noun	the act or tendency to yield, conform, or cooperate	82
complicity	noun	partnership in an illegal or immoral act	93
comprehensive	adjective	thorough; inclusive; covering or involving a lot	87
comprise	verb	to consist of; to be made up of	12
compromise	verb	to reach an agreement between two people or groups through bargaining; to weaken	86
compulsion	noun	an irresistible urge to do something	120
concede	verb	to admit or acknowledge as true, just, or proper; to grant as a right or privilege; to yield or admit	3
conciliatory	adjective	willing to make allowances; intending to appease	111
conclusive	adjective	convincing; decisive; serving to end something	102
concomitant	adjective	naturally associated with another thing	107
concord	noun	an agreement; unanimity; harmony; peace; a treaty	80
concordance	noun	an alphabetical list of words or topics contained in a book (such as the Bible); agreement or harmony	69
concupiscent	adjective	lusting; full of desire	107
concur	verb	to agree; to cooperate; to happen at the same time	43
condescending	adjective	acting superior to someone else; looking down on others	116
conditional	adjective	allowed only if certain terms are met	63
condone	verb	to overlook; to forgive; to imply approval	5
confirm	verb	to establish truth or accuracy; to settle; to establish	49
confluence	noun	the point at which two things come together	120
confront	verb	to challenge; to oppose; to stand or meet face-to-face	16
congenial	adjective	pleasant and agreeable	90
congenital	adjective	present from birth, especially a disorder	69
congested	adjective	cramped or crowded	81
congregation	noun	a gathering of people, especially for worship	93
conjure	verb	to call forth or summon	47
connoisseur	noun	someone who is an expert on a particular thing	115
consecutive	adjective	occurring one after the other	26
consign	verb	to deliver something somewhere in order to get rid of it	112
consonant	adjective	in agreement; consistent	50
constrain	verb	to restrict; to hold back	79
constrict	verb	to tighten; to squeeze uncomfortably	101
construe	verb	to interpret or understand in a particular way	49
contagion	noun	an infection; the process of being infected	4
contend	verb	to struggle; to compete; to assert passionately	42
contentious	adjective	causing or involving argument or controversy	48
contingent	adjective	dependent on something else	52
contradict	verb	to specifically deny; to state the opposite	109
contrite	adjective	sincerely remorseful or repentant	11
contrived	adjective	artificial; clearly constructed	76
conventional	adjective	typical or customary	45
convergence	noun	the coming together of multiple items at one point	13
conviction	noun	a firmly held belief	25
convivial	adjective	lively or friendly; fond of lively group activities	73
cordial	adjective	courteous, gracious, or friendly; heartfelt	97
corollary	noun	a natural consequence; an obvious result	58
corroborate	verb	to provide evidence in support of a claim	115
corrosion	noun	destruction by chemical action, such as rust	6
covenant	noun	a sacred agreement between two or more individuals	27

Word	PoS	Definition	Lesson
covet	verb	to desire something that belongs to another	16
crass	adjective	without proper manners or standards of politeness	24
credulous	adjective	inclined to believe with little evidence	4
criterion	noun	a rule or principle for evaluating or testing something	40
crony	noun	an old friend	64
cryptic	adjective	mysterious; hidden; secret	30
crystallize	verb	to become clear; to harden into a clear shape	100
culminate	verb	to reach the final stage or highest point	41
cumbersome	adjective	burdensome; heavy and awkward	43
cupidity	noun	excessive desire, especially for wealth	99
cynic	noun	a person who is distrustful of human motives	117
dawdle	verb	to waste time; to move slowly	78
dearth	noun	a lack of something	20
debacle	noun	a catastrophe; a major failure	91
debauchery	noun	immoral behavior; excessive indulgence in sensual pleasures	82
debilitate	verb	to make weak	36
debunk	verb	to expose false claims and ideas	9
decadence	noun	a falling into an inferior condition; moral decay	1
deciduous	adjective	having leaves that fall off annually; not permanent	5
decorous	adjective	showing proper behavior or manners	10
defame	verb	to harm someone's reputation	89
deference	noun	courteous consideration of another person's wishes	49
defiance	noun	resistance to authority or opposing force; contempt	73
definitive	adjective	most reliable or complete; fully developed	51
defray	verb	to pay part of the cost of something expensive	22
degenerate	verb	to worsen; to deteriorate	39
degrade	verb	to lower in rank or dignity; to bring into contempt	92
deliberate	verb	to consider; to think over	1
delicacy	noun	an item of food that is rare but desirable	12
delineate	verb	to represent in a picture; to portray in words; to describe or outline with precision; to describe or depict in words or gestures	17
delude	verb	to mislead or give a false impression	110
demagogue	noun	a leader who gains influence through emotion instead of clear reasoning	35
demure	adjective	modest and reserved	57
denizen	noun	a resident of a place	108
depict	verb	to portray; to describe	9
deplete	verb	to reduce the resources of; to run out of	109
depravity	noun	corruption; wickedness	50
deracinate	verb	to fully destroy; to pull out by the roots	64
desecrate	verb	to pollute or destroy something that is sacred	125
desiccated	adjective	dried out; dehydrated	29
despot	noun	a harsh, authoritarian ruler	87
desultory	adjective	inconsistent or lacking order	119
devious	adjective	roundabout; not straight-forward; shifty or crooked	83
devise	verb	to think up; to invent; to plan	65
dialectical	adjective	involving a discussion between people of different points of view to arrive at a common ground	57
diaphanous	adjective	hazy and light; nearly transparent	54
dictate	verb	to say aloud for recording; to give orders	25
dictator	noun	one who holds absolute power	78

Word	PoS	Definition	Lesson
diction	noun	style of speaking or writing; word choice; enunciation	20
dictum	noun	an authoritative statement; a common saying	104
didactic	adjective	instructional; preachy or pedantic	85
digression	noun	wandering away from the subject	37
dilettante	noun	a person who studies a subject, especially art, merely for personal amusement	5
diminish	verb	to lessen; to weaken	6
discord	noun	lack of harmony; disagreement; war; a harsh noise	30
discredit	verb	to defame; to destroy confidence in; to disbelieve	100
discriminate	verb	to recognize or point out differences between things or people	97
discursive	adjective	digressing; rambling; going off the subject	22
disdain	noun	to view with scorn or contempt; to consider unworthy of notice or response	45
disinterested	adjective	unprejudiced; impartial; neutral	13
disparage	verb	to belittle	8
dispassionate	adjective	impartial or neutral	12
dispel	verb	to drive away; to scatter; to cause to vanish	31
disperse	verb	to cause to break up; to scatter	76
disputatious	adjective	argumentative; fond of arguing	42
disquiet	noun	lack of calm or peace; anxiety or uneasiness	116
dissemble	verb	to give a false appearance	41
dissent	verb	to disagree	69
dissipate	verb	to squander; to waste; to scatter	35
dissonance	noun	an inharmonious or harsh sound; cacophony; a disagreement	85
distend	verb	to expand by stretching	117
distinguish	verb	to recognize differences between items	53
docile	adjective	peaceful; able to be trained or controlled	41
doctrinaire	adjective	concerned with following specific rules exactly, especially without considering alternatives	119
document	verb	to provide written evidence; to record in detail	2
domineering	adjective	bossy; overbearing	68
dovish	adjective	innocent; peaceful	15
dubious	adjective	doubtful; questionable	108
duplicity	noun	double-dealing; hypocrisy	107
duration	noun	the length of time for which something lasts	19
ebullient	adjective	highly energetic; excited	106
eccentric	adjective	odd or unusual in behavior	55
efface	verb	to erode to the point of unrecognizability; to cause to disappear	17
effervescent	adjective	exuberant; bubbly and excited	123
effrontery	noun	disrespectful boldness	40
effulgent	adjective	shining brilliantly	50
effusion	noun	an expression of feelings too strong to be restrained	118
effusive	adjective	showing heartfelt approval	34
egalitarian	adjective	concerned with equality and fairness	17
egocentric	adjective	concerned only with the self	100
elliptical	adjective	oval in shape; unclear or cryptic	120
eloquent	adjective	speaking fluently and with ease; speaking persuasively	72
elude	verb	to avoid or escape, especially to avoid capture	41
embellish	verb	to adorn or ornament; to enhance with false details	74
emigrate	verb	to leave one area to travel to another	113
empirical	adjective	based on facts	5
endearing	adjective	charming; likeable	105

Word	PoS	Definition	Lesson
endemic	adjective	naturally occurring in a place	22
endorse	verb	to approve; to support	5
enervate	verb	to weaken; to disturb the composure of; to faze	47
enfranchise	verb	to grant the rights of citizenship, especially the right to vote	16
engender	verb	to cause; to produce; to create	48
enhance	verb	to advance; to improve	57
enigma	noun	a puzzle; a mystery	43
enmity	noun	hatred	46
enormity	noun	terribleness; great size or importance	110
entail	verb	to produce as a necessary consequence	116
enumerate	verb	to list; to mention one by one	2
epigram	noun	a short, witty saying	7
epitome	noun	the perfect example of a characteristic or type	102
epoch	noun	a long period of historical time	44
equivocal	adjective	ambiguous; intentionally misleading	53
erratic	adjective	odd; unpredictable; wandering	61
erudite	adjective	scholarly or learned, especially from books	15
eschew	verb	to avoid or do without	116
esoteric	adjective	hard to understand; known only to the chosen few	110
espouse	verb	to adopt; to support	57
esteem	verb	to respect; to value; to judge	117
estivation	noun	a period of very low activity during a warm season	22
ethereal	adjective	light; heavenly; unusually refined	25
eulogy	noun	an expression of praise, often on the occasion of someone's death	81
evince	verb	to prove or demonstrate	26
exacerbate	verb	to make worse	97
exacting	adjective	extremely demanding	97
exalt	verb	to raise in rank or dignity; to praise	84
exasperation	noun	a state of high annoyance or impatience	12
excel	verb	to do extremely well	13
excoriate	verb	to criticize or condemn harshly	101
exculpate	verb	to free from blame	60
execrable	adjective	detestable; extremely bad	75
execute	verb	to put into effect; to carry out	91
exemplary	adjective	serving as a model; outstanding	71
exhaustive	adjective	thorough; comprehensive	86
exhilarating	adjective	invigorating and refreshing	91
exhort	verb	to sincerely or passionately suggest a course of action	27
exigency	noun	urgent need or situation	60
exigent	adjective	requiring immediate attention	2
exonerate	verb	to prove not guilty of wrongdoing	94
expatriate	noun	one who gives up residence in his or her own country	32
expedient	adjective	suitable to achieve a particular end; practical; politic	51
expend	verb	to spend; to use up	94
expiate	verb	to make amends for sins or wrongdoings	80
exploit	verb	to make use of, sometimes unjustly; to manipulate	110
expunge	verb	to completely erase	44
extant	adjective	in existence; part of reality	28
extol	verb	to praise, to glorify	18
extrapolate	verb	to make predictions outside of the range of what has been measured	66

Word	PoS	Definition	Lesson
extrovert	noun	one who enjoys spending time with others	58
exult	verb	to express great joy and excitement	122
fabrication	noun	a false statement	89
facet	noun	one particular aspect of something	33
facetious	adjective	not serious; intended to be humorous	30
facile	adjective	easily accomplished; superficial; lazy	86
facilitate	verb	to help bring about; to make less difficult	89
fallacious	adjective	false; misleading	8
farcical	adjective	ridiculous; intended to amuse through an absurd situation	41
fastidious	adjective	difficult to please; excessively particular, critical, or demanding	34
fatalist	noun	one who believes that events are governed by fate	113
fatuous	adjective	foolish or silly	24
fauna	noun	animal life	123
feasible	adjective	capable of being done, affected, or accomplished; probable; suitable; practical	34
fecund	adjective	fertile or productive	14
felicity	noun	happiness; a source of happiness	40
fetid	adjective	having a poor odor	21
fickle	adjective	changeable; faithless	99
figurative	adjective	not literal, but metaphorical; using a figure of speech	77
flagrant	adjective	conspicuously wicked; blatant; obvious; outrageous	113
flinch	verb	to make a sudden movement due to shock or pain	43
flippant	adjective	lacking proper seriousness	61
flout	verb	to defy openly	17
fluctuate	verb	to waver; to change repeatedly	54
foist	verb	to force something that a person doesn't want onto him or her	3
foment	verb	to promote growth; to cause to begin	36
forgo	verb	to do without; to refrain from	45
formidable	adjective	extremely strong; intimidating	68
forthright	adjective	outspoken; frank	106
foster	verb	to rear; to encourage; to nurture	62
founder	noun	a person who establishes an organization, business, etc.	36
fractious	adjective	irritable and complaining	58
frail	adjective	weak; fragile	119
frangible	adjective	capable of being broken or damaged	38
fraternal	adjective	relating to brotherhood or fellowship among men	87
frenetic	adjective	rushing and wild with excitement	9
frivolous	adjective	lacking in seriousness; self-indulgently care-free; relatively unimportant; unnecessary	3
frowzy	adjective	untidy or dirty	89
frugal	adjective	spending very little	29
fuliginous	adjective	related to soot or smoke	27
funambulist	noun	a tightrope walker	4
fundamental	adjective	basic; primary; essential	93
fungible	adjective	not able to be distinguished from others of its kind	43
furtive	adjective	stealthy; sneaky; secretive	82
gallant	adjective	polite; chivalrous; brave	97
gamut	noun	the total range of a thing	19
garrulous	adjective	talkative	103
genteel	adjective	refined and respectable; polite	69
germane	adjective	pertinent or important; closely or significantly related	73
glacial	adjective	extremely cold; happening or moving very slowly	58

Word	PoS	Definition	Lesson
glib	adjective	fluent; slick; easily suave, implying thoughtlessness, superficiality, or insincerity	66
glutton	noun	someone who eats too much; a greedy person	60
grandiloquence	noun	speech that makes the speaker sound important or boastful	83
grandiose	adjective	pretentious; ridiculously exaggerated; impressive	90
gravity	noun	seriousness	21
gregarious	adjective	sociable	27
grievance	noun	a reason to be upset or complain	71
grotesque	adjective	extremely ugly; repulsive	107
guile	noun	deceit; duplicity; wiliness; cunning	78
hackneyed	adjective	commonplace; trite; repeated too often	79
hallowed	adjective	blessed; consecrated	81
hapless	adjective	unsuccessful; unfortunate	65
harangue	verb	to lecture in a long, moralizing way	114
harass	verb	to annoy by repeated attacks; to torment	115
hardy	adjective	sturdy; robust or healthy; able to withstand harsh weather	70
haughty	adjective	arrogant and superior	122
hedonist	noun	a person whose life is dedicated to the pursuit of pleasure and self-gratification	65
hegemony	noun	dominance of one member of a group over others because of power or influence	78
heresy	noun	an idea contrary to popular belief or accepted religion	40
histrionic	adjective	excessively dramatic; intentionally emotional	94
hoard	verb	to stockpile; to accumulate for future use	79
homily	noun	a sermon or moral lesson	85
horde	noun	a large and unruly crowd of people	86
hostility	noun	unfriendliness; hatred; aggression	65
hubris	noun	excessive pride that leads to downfall	46
humane	adjective	marked by kindness or consideration	111
humanitarian	adjective	aimed at helping others	76
husbandry	noun	care for and maintenance of crops, livestock, or a household	48
husk	noun	the dried shell or withered remains of a living thing	27
hypocritical	adjective	pretending to be virtuous; deceiving	119
iconoclast	noun	one who attacks cherished traditions	84
ideology	noun	a system of belief that motivates a person or group	95
idyllic	adjective	charming, peaceful, and simple	110
ignominy	noun	deep disgrace; shame; dishonor	42
illiterate	adjective	unable to read	65
immaculate	adjective	spotless; flawless; absolutely clean	83
immaterial	adjective	irrelevant; having nothing to do with the topic of discussion	28
impair	verb	to restrict; to slow down; to prevent from functioning well	103
impartial	adjective	not biased; fair	22
impassive	adjective	without feeling; imperturbable; stoical	10
impecunious	adjective	without money	5
impediment	noun	an obstacle; something blocking one's way	18
impel	verb	to drive or force onward	113
imperial	adjective	related to the rule of one area by an outside nation	56
impertinent	adjective	rude and disrespectful	50
impetuous	adjective	acting on instinct without much thought	59
impetus	noun	a stimulus or moving force; momentum	71
impinge	verb	to trespass or take what is considered to be another's	70
implacable	adjective	impossible to satisfy	37
implausible	adjective	unlikely; unbelievable	92

Word	PoS	Definition	Lesson
implement	verb	to put into effect; to supply with tools	8
implicit	adjective	understood, but not stated	45
impotent	adjective	lacking power or liveliness	1
impoverished	adjective	poor	62
impropriety	noun	impoliteness; something rude or against protocol	110
impudence	noun	impertinence; insolence; disrespect	51
impute	verb	to name one thing as the cause of another	32
inaugurate	verb	to start; to initiate; to install into office	80
incantation	noun	words spoken as part of a magical ritual	101
incarnadine	adjective	having the same color as blood or flesh	67
incense	verb	to enrage; to infuriate	64
inchoate	adjective	not fully developed	15
incipient	adjective	in an early stage	5
inclined	adjective	tending or leaning toward; bent	84
inclusive	adjective	tending to include everything	57
incompatible	adjective	not able to exist in harmony	3
incongruous	adjective	not fitting; absurd	108
inconsistent	adjective	not staying the same; incompatible	104
incontrovertible	adjective	indisputable; not open to question	16
incorrigible	adjective	not easily changed; uncontrollable or unruly	23
increment	noun	an increase by a specific amount	92
incursion	noun	an invasion; a sudden assault	81
indefatigable	adjective	tireless	56
indifferent	adjective	unmoved; lacking concern	123
indigenous	adjective	native to a certain habitat; local	85
indigent	adjective	lacking food and clothing; needy; poor; impoverished	76
indispensible	adjective	impossible to get rid of; essential	74
indubitable	adjective	unable to be doubted; unquestionable	88
indulgent	adjective	giving in easily to one's desires, or to the desires of another	79
inept	adjective	not skilled; incompetent	21
infamous	adjective	notoriously bad	61
infatuated	adjective	filled with unreasonable fascination	47
infraction	noun	a violation of a law, rule, or contract	64
infringe	verb	to violate a rule or contract; to gradually take over	82
ingenious	adjective	clever; resourceful	77
inherent	adjective	firmly established by nature or habit; intrinsic	17
inimical	adjective	unfriendly; hostile; harmful; detrimental	88
initiate	verb	to begin; to originate; to receive into a group	21
injunction	noun	an order of a judge requiring a change in action	7
innate	adjective	inborn, or existing since birth; inherent	29
innovation	noun	change; the introduction of something new	125
inordinate	adjective	unreasonable	108
inquisitive	adjective	curious	15
insatiable	adjective	not easily satisfied; greedy	75
insolvent	adjective	bankrupt; unable to repay one's debts	102
insomnia	noun	the inability to sleep	42
instigate	verb	to urge; to start; to provoke	4
insurgent	noun	one who rebels against an authority, often violently	62
insurrection	noun	rebellion against a civil authority or government	118
intangible	adjective	not material; not able to be perceived by touch; vague; elusive	112

Word	PoS	Definition	Lesson
integral	adjective	complete; necessary for completeness	95
integrity	noun	uprightness; wholeness; tendency to act ethically	10
intermittent	adjective	not constant; happening at random intervals	121
intractable	adjective	unruly; stubborn; unyielding	71
intransigence	noun	refusal of any compromise; stubbornness	10
intrinsic	adjective	essential; inherent; built-in; natural	30
introspection	noun	the process of examining one's own internal thoughts and emotions	109
intuition	noun	sudden insight; the power to know without reasoning	106
intuitive	adjective	able to be understood without logic or evidence	124
invective	noun	harsh criticism or condemnation	70
inveterate	adjective	difficult to change because of habit or custom	98
involuntary	adjective	done without conscious choice	33
invulnerable	adjective	unable to be hurt; invincible	95
irascible	adjective	irritable; easily angered	12
irony	noun	a contradiction to what one expects would happen normally	72
irreproachable	adjective	blameless; impeccable	11
irresolute	adjective	uncertain how to act; weak	35
irreverence	noun	a lack of proper respect	88
itinerant	adjective	traveling regularly from place to place	96
jejune	adjective	immature; lacking experience	25
jeopardize	verb	to put in danger	18
jocular	adjective	said or done in jest; joking	13
joie de vivre	noun	energy and love of life; vitality	49
jubilation	noun	joyous celebration or excitement	79
judicious	adjective	wise; sound in judgment	70
junction	noun	the place where two things meet	45
justification	noun	a good or just reason; a defense; an excuse	73
juvenile	adjective	young and immature	42
juxtaposition	noun	the placement of two items together for comparison	89
kindle	verb	to start a fire; to inspire	114
lacerate	verb	to cut deeply; to tear	104
lampoon	verb	to mock through parody	25
languid	adjective	lacking energy or interest	122
languish	verb	to become weak; to lose energy or enthusiasm	79
largess	noun	generous giving of gifts	94
laud	verb	to praise	26
lavish	adjective	liberal; wasteful; generous	66
legerdemain	noun	skillful sleight of hand or trickery	91
lethargic	adjective	drowsy; dull	53
levity	noun	a lack of seriousness; lightness	59
licentious	adjective	not restrained by morals	8
limpid	adjective	perfectly clear	107
linger	verb	to loiter or dawdle; to continue; to persist	28
linguist	noun	someone who studies languages	69
liquefy	verb	to turn into a liquid; to melt	72
literal	adjective	actual; the opposite of metaphorical; interpreting words at their most basic meaning	120
litigate	verb	to sue in a courtroom	101
loathe	verb	to hate	66
lobbyist	noun	a person who attempts to influence lawmakers	68
logomachy	noun	an argument involving great amounts of discussion	14

Word	PoS	Definition	Lesson
loquacious	adjective	talkative	55
lucid	adjective	easily understood; clear; intelligible	111
lucrative	adjective	profitable; making money	32
machination	noun	secret plotting and schemes	122
maelstrom	noun	a large, dangerous whirlpool	124
malaise	noun	a general feeling of lack of wellness	120
malapropism	noun	the humorous confusion of one word for another that is very similar in sound	4
malediction	noun	a curse or insult	100
malevolent	adjective	evil; hateful towards another	101
malfeasance	noun	an unethical or immoral act by a public official	123
malice	noun	hatred; spite	40
malleable	adjective	able to be shaped by pressure; changeable	69
mandate	noun	an order or command	44
manifesto	noun	a document stating the principles of an organization or movement	52
marshal	verb	to command; to place in order or position	54
martial	adjective	aggressive or warlike; related to the military	102
martinet	noun	a rigid disciplinarian; a strict military officer; someone who holds strictly to rules and regulation	53
materialism	noun	a preoccupation with physical comforts and things	21
matriculate	verb	to enroll in a school or university	47
matrimony	noun	marriage	86
maudlin	adjective	excessively sentimental; foolishly emotional	105
mawkish	adjective	excessively emotional	31
meander	verb	to take a winding course; to wander; to ramble	17
mediate	verb	to settle a disagreement by acting as a third party	23
mellifluous	adjective	flowing smoothly or beautifully	110
mendacious	adjective	dishonest, especially on an everyday basis	29
mendicant	adjective	reliant on begging to survive	118
mentor	noun	one who helps another, who is less experienced, to grow and learn	39
mercenary	adjective	interested in money or gain	77
mercurial	adjective	capricious; changing; fickle	122
metamorphosis	noun	a transformation from one thing into another	90
meticulous	adjective	excessively careful; painstaking; scrupulous	9
microcosm	noun	a small system which contains in miniature every important part of a larger system	125
milieu	noun	social or cultural surroundings	106
minuscule	adjective	extremely small	42
minute	adjective	very small	112
misanthrope	noun	someone who shuns society; a hermit	91
misogynist	noun	someone prejudiced against women	33
mock	verb	to ridicule; to imitate, often in derision	35
modicum	noun	a small amount	40
moil	verb	to perform difficult labor	44
momentous	adjective	very important	37
monotone	noun	the unchanging, dull sound of a voice	36
monotony	noun	sameness leading to boredom	35
morass	noun	a piece of wet, marshy land; a confusing or complicated situation	83
moribund	adjective	moving towards death or extinction	61
mortify	verb	to cause great shame or embarrassment	57
multifarious	adjective	made of many varied parts	112
mundane	adjective	worldly, as opposed to spiritual	87

Word	PoS	Definition	Lesson
mutability	noun	the ability to change in form; fickleness	70
myopia	noun	poor eyesight at long distances; lack of ability to plan for the future	36
myriad	adjective	multiple; diverse; large in number	22
nadir	noun	the lowest point	41
narcissism	noun	an excessive interest in one's self	71
nebulous	adjective	vague or cloudlike	108
nefarious	adjective	very wicked	72
neophyte	noun	one who is a new member of a group	121
nepotism	noun	the favoring of friends and relatives in business and politics	1
nihilism	noun	the rejection of any rational system of morality or value	116
nomad	noun	one who wanders from place to place	96
nonchalance	noun	indifference; lack of concern; composure	66
nonentity	noun	a person of no importance; nonexistence	109
notoriety	noun	a disrepute; ill fame	80
novelty	noun	something new; newness	40
novice	noun	a beginner	116
nullify	verb	to make invalid; to void; to abolish	109
numinous	adjective	divine and supernatural	14
nurture	verb	to nourish; to educate; to foster	109
obdurate	adjective	stubborn	37
obfuscate	verb	to confuse or complicate in order to conceal	115
objective	adjective	not influenced by emotions; fair	35
oblation	noun	a sacred offering	39
obliterate	verb	to destroy completely	90
oblivion	noun	obscurity; forgetfulness	106
obscure	adjective	dark; vague; unclear	113
observant	adjective	paying careful attention	102
obstinate	adjective	stubborn; hard to control or treat	67
obstreperous	adjective	unruly; noisy; difficult to control	52
occlude	verb	to close; to stop up; to shut something in, out, or off	51
onset	noun	the beginning of something	76
opaque	adjective	dark; not transparent	119
opportunist	noun	an individual who sacrifices principles for expediency by taking advantage of circumstances	61
opulence	noun	extreme wealth; luxuriousness; abundance	48
ornate	adjective	excessively or elaborately decorated	100
ostentatious	adjective	showy; pretentious; trying to attract attention	83
oust	verb	to forcefully eject	93
outright	adjective	utter; complete; total	25
pabulum	noun	any nourishing food	122
pacify	verb	to make peaceful	3
palaver	noun	lengthy or idle discussion	36
palliate	verb	to reduce the negative effects of something without removing the cause	27
pallid	adjective	pale or lacking energy	64
paltry	adjective	insignificant; petty; trifling	48
pantomime	verb	to act out without using words	98
parched	adjective	dried out	89
parley	noun	a conference between opposing sides, often to negotiate a truce	18
parsimonious	adjective	stingy; miserly; cheap	96
partial	adjective	biased; having a liking for something	116

Word	PoS	Definition	Lesson
partisan	adjective	one-sided; prejudiced; committed to a party	13
paternal	adjective	related to a father	109
pathology	noun	the study of diseases and disorders	80
pathos	noun	the quality of a situation or work that causes feelings of pity or compassion	34
patriarch	noun	a male leader, especially one that is advanced in age	119
patrician	noun	a person who is high in social class	117
patronize	verb	to regularly give one's business; to treat with kindness that reveals a sense of superiority	31
paucity	noun	scarcity; lack	104
peccadillo	noun	a very slight offense or sin	12
pedantic	adjective	showing off learning; bookish	49
pejorative	noun	intended to belittle or criticize	24
pellucid	adjective	clear; allowing light to pass freely; easily understood	82
penchant	noun	a strong inclination; a liking	11
penitent	adjective	repentant for wrongdoing	117
penurious	adjective	extremely poor	11
perceptive	adjective	insightful; aware; wise	1
peremptory	adjective	unwilling to accept refusal	11
perfidious	adjective	faithless and treacherous	114
perfidy	noun	treachery or faithlessness	48
periphery	noun	outside boundary; margin	74
perjury	noun	false testimony under oath	59
perpetual	adjective	continuing or lasting forever; without interruption	84
perpetuate	verb	to make something continue	112
perquisite	noun	extra payment granted above what is typical	20
perspicacity	noun	clearness of thought or foresight	24
pertinacious	adjective	holding strongly to one course of action; stubborn	63
pervasive	adjective	pervading; spread throughout every part	79
pestilential	adjective	causing disease; related to disease	63
petulant	adjective	showing sudden irritation to minor annoyances	44
philanthropist	noun	one who donates generously to charity	33
philistine	noun	an uncultured person, especially one who is hostile towards high culture	55
pinnacle	noun	the peak; the highest point of something	81
pious	adjective	devout; religious	122
pivotal	adjective	crucial; key; vital	85
plaintive	adjective	sorrowful or mournful	74
platitude	noun	a trite remark; a commonplace statement	111
plod	verb	to walk extremely slowly, with heavy steps	55
polarize	verb	to divide into sharply different extremes	64
polemic	noun	a rant; a long, angry speech about a specific topic	19
pomposity	noun	self-important behavior	113
portent	noun	a sign of future events or circumstances	100
posit	verb	to present as a basis for argument	19
pragmatic	adjective	practical, as opposed to idealistic; concerned with the practical worth or impact of something	58
prattle	verb	to babble	97
precept	noun	a basic rule of proper behavior	46
preclude	verb	to prevent from happening; to make impossible	99
precursor	noun	something that comes before and shows that another thing is approaching	23
predilection	noun	partiality; preference	33

Word	PoS	Definition	Lesson
preeminent	adjective	the most noticeable or important	111
preface	noun	an introduction, usually to a book or article	22
prepossess	verb	to impress at the first glance	20
pretentious	adjective	pompous; making unjustified claims; overambitious	45
prevail	verb	to be successful over an opponent	41
prim	adjective	extremely tidy; excessively formal and proper	14
primacy	noun	the state of being first in order, rank, or importance	14
primal	adjective	first; original; basic; most important	65
prime	verb	to prepare for a purpose; to supply with information	60
primer	noun	a book for teaching reading; any introductory text	86
pristine	adjective	extremely clean	107
probity	noun	honesty; care about moral correctness	89
problematic	adjective	doubtful; unsettled; questionable; perplexing	28
proclivity	noun	an inclination; a natural tendency	80
procrastinate	verb	to postpone; to delay or put off	57
prodigal	adjective	wasteful; reckless with money	26
prodigious	adjective	marvelous; enormous	39
profess	verb	to declare openly	8
profligate	adjective	dissipated; wasteful; wildly immoral	16
profound	adjective	deep; not superficial; complete	56
proletariat	noun	the laboring force of a society	87
proliferate	verb	to increase in number; to reproduce	42
propel	verb	to drive or move forward; to urge onward	28
propensity	noun	a tendency to do something	94
propitious	adjective	indicating good in the future; inclined to forgive	29
proportionate	adjective	corresponding to something else in amount	6
proprietary	adjective	owned as property; treated as property	77
prosaic	adjective	dull and unimaginative; matter-of-fact; factual	67
proscribe	verb	to prohibit something that is seen as harmful	43
proselytize	verb	to spread a message in order to win others to one's point of view	50
prosperity	noun	success, growth, or flourishing	70
protean	adjective	easily and rapidly changing in shape or function	91
proverb	noun	a wise old saying that teaches a lesson	115
provident	adjective	planning well for the future	76
provisional	adjective	tentative; temporary	7
provocative	adjective	arousing anger or interest; annoying	45
prudent	adjective	wise; cautious; careful; practical	78
prurient	adjective	lustful; filled with excessive desire for bodily pleasures	65
puerile	adjective	related to children or childhood; immature	90
pugnacious	adjective	aggressive, especially in a physical way	53
pugnacity	noun	combativeness; a disposition to fight	118
pulchritude	noun	physical beauty	104
pulsate	verb	to expand and contract rhythmically; to vibrate	31
punctilious	adjective	strict about rules, manners, or ethics	23
purport	verb	to make a false claim; to pretend to do something	118
putative	adjective	generally accepted; supposed	88
quagmire	noun	a swamp; a problem that is difficult to escape	101
qualitative	adjective	related to properties other than number	77
quiescent	adjective	being at peace or at rest; inactive or motionless	80
quisling	noun	a traitor who aids an invading enemy	101

Word	PoS	Definition	Lesson
quixotic	adjective	naive; impractical; unrealistic	24
quotidian	adjective	uninteresting; dull; ordinary; happening frequently	93
radiant	adjective	glowing; [of an emotion or quality] emerging out of a person or thing	106
ramble	verb	to wander aimlessly, physically or mentally	43
rampant	adjective	widespread, usually in a negative way	55
rancor	noun	bitterness; hatred	99
rapacious	adjective	prone to seizing what is desired by force	88
raucous	adjective	harsh and shrill; disorderly and boisterous	107
rebuke	verb	to scold; to express strong disapproval	24
rebut	verb	to disprove through evidence	73
recalcitrant	adjective	obstinately stubborn; determined to resist authority	97
reciprocal	adjective	shared or returned between two parties	73
recluse	noun	a hermit; a loner	7
reconciliation	noun	the creation of agreement or compatibility between two or more things	39
recondite	adjective	related to difficult or obscure subject matter	2
recount	verb	to narrate or tell; to count over again	73
recrimination	noun	an accusation in response to another's accusation	60
rectitude	noun	proper manners or conduct	56
redoubtable	adjective	strong; powerful; formidable	17
refract	verb	to bend light by passing from one medium to another	49
regal	adjective	magnificent; dignified; royal	1
relegate	verb	to banish to an inferior position; to delegate; to assign	8
relentless	adjective	not willing to stop; unstoppable	94
remunerate	verb	to pay [someone] for services performed	105
renaissance	noun	a rebirth, especially of culture, technology, and philosophy	76
renovation	noun	reconstruction in order to make something like new	61
reparation	noun	payment to compensate for wrongs or damages	34
repeal	verb	to revoke, formally withdraw from, or annul	49
repel	verb	to drive or force back; to keep out; to cause distaste	66
repercussion	noun	natural consequence	82
replete	adjective	filled to the brim or to the point of being stuffed	104
reprehensible	adjective	deserving blame	51
repress	verb	to force into submission; to force an emotion into becoming unconscious	34
reprimand	verb	to reprove severely; to rebuke	113
reproach	verb	to express disapproval to someone	47
reprobate	noun	a wicked, immoral person	117
reprove	verb	to censure; to rebuke	2
repulse	verb	to cause extreme distaste, dislike, or disgust	70
requiem	noun	a song or hymn for the dead	92
requisite	adjective	required for a purpose	5
requital	noun	an appropriate return for something	18
residue	noun	what is left over from something else; remains	116
resigned	adjective	unresisting; patiently submissive	24
resolute	adjective	firmly fixed in purpose	69
restive	adjective	impatient; stubborn	100
restrained	adjective	held back in action or speech	120
resurgent	adjective	rising again, or tending to rise again; reviving	98
retiring	adjective	modest; shy	112
reverent	adjective	respectful	46
revitalize	verb	to give new life or energy to someone or something	78

Word	PoS	Definition	Lesson
rhapsody	noun	ecstasy; great joy; something extremely emotional	72
rigorous	adjective	severe; harsh; demanding; exact	87
robust	adjective	vigorous; strong	55
rogue	noun	a dishonest cheat, trickster, or thief; a rebel	7
rotund	adjective	fat; large and round, usually describing a person	120
ruminate	verb	to think deeply over a problem	102
ruthless	adjective	pitiless; cruel	74
saccharine	adjective	sweet; excessively sentimental	9
sacrilege	noun	a violation of that which is sacred	114
sacrosanct	adjective	extremely sacred; not able to be criticized	58
sagacity	noun	deep wisdom and sound judgment	93
sage	noun	a person known for having wisdom	14
salacious	adjective	indecently sexual	71
salutary	adjective	favorable to health	9
sanctuary	noun	a refuge; a shelter; a shrine; a holy place	66
sarcasm	noun	a scornful remark; a stinging rebuke	83
sardonic	adjective	mockingly sarcastic	62
satirical	adjective	mocking	34
saturnine	adjective	lacking energy; gloomy	99
schadenfreude	noun	a feeling of enjoyment at the misfortune of others	78
scintillate	verb	to sparkle	71
scourge	noun	something that causes a large amount of suffering	28
scrupulous	adjective	conscientious; extremely thorough	41
seclusion	noun	isolation; solitude	105
sectarian	adjective	relating to a religious faction; narrow-minded; limited	83
sedentary	adjective	requiring sitting	103
sedition	noun	incitement of rebellion or discontent	117
seduce	verb	to corrupt; to lead into temptation	30
sensory	adjective	related to the senses	60
sequester	verb	to isolate; to retire from public life; to segregate; to seclude	63
shrewd	adjective	clever; astute	102
shrill	adjective	high-pitched and grating; difficult to listen to	125
shunt	verb	to push aside; to redirect	56
sidestep	verb	to avoid; to dodge	54
simile	noun	a comparison using the words "like" or "as"	75
similitude	noun	likeness or resemblance; a shared characteristic	32
simulacrum	noun	an imperfect representation of something else	68
simultaneous	adjective	happening at the same time	35
sinecure	noun	employment that yields significant rewards with little responsibility	30
skeptical	adjective	doubting; examining evidence before deciding	55
skirmish	noun	a small battle	31
slacken	verb	to slow up; to loosen	13
slander	verb	defamation; utterance of false and malicious statements	23
sloth	noun	laziness	62
sobriety	noun	seriousness; avoidance of excess, especially of alcohol	123
solemnity	noun	seriousness; gravity	121
solicitous	adjective	eager to help	16
solipsistic	adjective	self-absorbed; unwilling to consider other points of view	68
solitude	noun	the state of being alone; seclusion	56
somnolent	adjective	sleepy or causing sleep	105

Word	PoS	Definition	Lesson
soporific	adjective	causing sleep; sleepy or drowsy	6
sordid	adjective	immoral; dirty or filthy	99
sortie	noun	an attack from a surrounded group upon its besiegers	65
spasmodic	adjective	occurring suddenly and irregularly	87
spawn	verb	to give birth to or create, especially something unpleasant	123
specious	adjective	having the appearance of merit, but actually lacking it	59
spendthrift	noun	a person who spends extravagantly or wastefully	21
splurge	verb	to indulge in a luxury; to spend money unnecessarily	38
spurious	adjective	not genuine, authentic, or true; counterfeit	91
squander	verb	to spend or use extravagantly or wastefully; to scatter	110
stagnation	noun	lack of movement or change	26
staid	adjective	sober and respectable	74
staunch	adjective	firm in support of a cause or idea	11
stigma	noun	a mark of something disgraceful	95
stoic	adjective	seemingly indifferent to, or unaffected by, pleasure or pain; indifferent	94
stolid	adjective	not easily bothered; unemotional	32
stratum	noun	naturally formed layer; level or division	114
stricture	noun	an abnormal narrowing; a restriction	46
strident	adjective	having a harsh sound; having an irritating quality	2
stultifying	adjective	boring; draining of enthusiasm	111
stupendous	adjective	very impressive	11
stymie	verb	to prevent in the course of action	27
subdued	adjective	lowered in intensity or strength; not marked by any special features; quiet; controlled	39
submissive	adjective	unresistingly or humbly willing to obey or give in	93
subordinate	adjective	placed in or belonging in a lower rank or order; of less importance; subject to or under the authority of a superior	19
subversive	adjective	critical of and seeking to change existing institutions	53
suffice	verb	to be enough; to be adequate or sufficient	19
superlative	adjective	of the best quality	84
supplant	verb	to displace or substitute	69
surfeit	noun	excessive amount	121
surmise	verb	to reason without strong evidence; to guess	26
sustain	verb	to support; to keep up; to keep going	63
swindler	noun	a person who cheats others out of money or other assets; a person who obtains things by fraud or deceit	10
synchronous	adjective	happening at the same time or at the same rate	10
synthesis	noun	combination of multiple items to create a single new item	99
tactful	adjective	showing awareness and concern for the embarrassment or offense of others	29
tautological	adjective	having unnecessary repetition without adding additional information	64
tedious	adjective	long and tiresome; wordy so as to cause boredom	50
temerity	noun	excessive boldness; confidence	108
tenable	adjective	capable of being defended against attack or occupied	24
tendentious	adjective	showing a clear bias or purpose	7
tenebrous	adjective	dark or obscure	117
tentative	adjective	experimental; unsure, uncertain, or not definite; hesitant	81
tenuous	adjective	weak or lacking substance	114
tenure	noun	a state of permanent employment after a probationary period	28
testy	adjective	easily irritated; irritable; irked	84
theology	noun	the academic study of religion, especially by those who intend to enter ministry	75
threadbare	adjective	shabby or poor; ineffectively stale	90

Word	PoS	Definition	Lesson
timorous	adjective	fearful; cautious due to fear	123
torpid	adjective	slow; dull; sluggish	31
touchstone	noun	an event that has significance to many members of a group	42
tranquil	adjective	quiet, peaceful, or calm; unaffected by emotions	16
transfusion	noun	the act of infusing someone or something with something else	72
transient	adjective	momentary; temporary; staying for a short time	106
transmute	verb	to change from one shape to another	36
transparent	adjective	completely see-through; obvious	49
travail	noun	a difficult, laborious, or painful effort	15
tremor	noun	a shaking; a trembling in one's voice	118
trenchant	adjective	sharp and incisive	14
trite	adjective	commonplace; overused	96
truculent	adjective	aggressive; savage and harsh	23
turmoil	noun	a great commotion and confusion	121
turpitude	noun	lack of morals; depravity	2
tyranny	noun	oppression; a cruel government	113
ulterior	adjective	hidden; secret, especially "ulterior motives"	29
umbrage	noun	offense or annoyance	25
unconscionable	adjective	not able to be tolerated by the conscience	38
unctuous	adjective	highly flattering to win others' favor; oily	74
undue	adjective	uncalled for; unnecessary	44
uniform	adjective	similar in appearance, behavior, or other characteristics	82
unprecedented	adjective	novel; unparalleled; original	92
unremitting	adjective	never stopping or lessening	33
unwitting	adjective	acting without knowledge	81
usurp	verb	to seize (a position of power) by force	70
utilitarian	adjective	useful; intended to be used instead of enjoyed	112
utopia	noun	a perfect, harmonious society, especially an unlikely one	55
vacillate	verb	to waver; to fluctuate	120
vacuous	adjective	empty; lacking ideas or content	38
valetudinarian	noun	one who has very poor health; one who is excessively concerned about health	80
vapid	adjective	dull; lacking life	106
variegated	adjective	having areas of different colors with sharp boundaries	82
venerate	verb	to revere	17
venial	adjective	describing a fault that is forgivable	68
veracity	noun	truthfulness	87
verbose	adjective	wordy	101
verdant	adjective	green; full of growing plants	20
verisimilitude	noun	the appearance of being true or real	118
vernacular	noun	everyday local language; slang	63
vestige	noun	a small part that remains from a larger whole	85
viable	adjective	able to be done; worth doing; able to survive	109
vibrissae	noun	stiff hairs growing along the mouths of many animals that aid in sensation; whiskers	56
vicissitude	noun	change or movement in the course of development	18
victuals	noun	food and other necessary provisions	62
vigor	noun	active strength	108
visionary	adjective	large in scope but unrealistic; marked by profound imagination and foresight	115
vital	adjective	indispensable; relating to life; required for living	15
vitiate	verb	to weaken or spoil	96
vitreous	adjective	related to glass; transparent	54

Word	PoS	Definition	Lesson
vitriolic	adjective	sharp and harsh; caustic like acid	52
vituperate	verb	to scold or condemn	124
vivacious	adjective	with a lively or high-spirited personality	67
vivid	adjective	true to life; intense in color; producing clear images	99
vivify	verb	to give life or liveliness to someone or something	84
viviparous	adjective	giving birth to live young (rather than laying eggs)	63
volatile	adjective	changeable; explosive; evaporating rapidly	62
volition	noun	free will; personal choice	38
voluble	adjective	fluent; glib; talkative	88
voluminous	adjective	bulky; large	21
wane	verb	to lessen; to fade	98
whimsical	adjective	capricious; fanciful	121
willful	adjective	intentional; headstrong; determined to get one's way	93
winsome	adjective	sweet and charming	8
wistful	adjective	yearning; thoughtful and longing	124
wizened	adjective	wrinkled and shrunken, especially because of age	22
xanthic	adjective	yellow in color	53
zealous	adjective	passionate; devoted to a cause or belief	81